Frommer's™

Newfoundland & Labrador

My Newfoundland & Labrador

by Andrew Hempstead

LYING ON CANADA'S EASTERN EXTREMITY, NEWFOUNDLAND & LABRADOR is far from the thoughts of even many Canadians planning a vacation, but it seems everyone who visits falls in love—with the province's history, with its people, and with its wildness. It doesn't matter what your budget or your interests are, each day spent in Newfoundland & Labrador will be filled with new adventures and memories that will last a lifetime.

In Trinity, a short drive west from the capital, the buildings are so perfectly preserved it's impossible not to think you've walked into a historic theme park.. If you happen to be in Ferryland for the annual folk festival, be assured that the event is not about attracting tourists—the foot-stomping, beer-drinking bands on stage are there to entertain the locals. Some of my favorite places in Newfoundland are hidden from view—and that's where your own adventurous spirit comes into play. While researching this edition, I was walking across Burnt Cape on a beautiful summer's day and was struck by the fact there wasn't another human in sight. Admittedly, the cape is about as far as it is possible to drive from the capital, but still, if a destination as geologically intriguing and ruggedly scenic was anywhere else in North America, it would be overrun by visitors. This one isn't even signposted.

The enthusiastic locals at Ferryland, the unaffected history of Trinity, and the solitude of Burnt Cape are just some of the reasons this is one of my favorite places on Earth.

© Barrett & MacKay/All Canada Photos

The capital city of St. John's is the province's cultural hub, best symbolized by the museum and art gallery known as **THE ROOMS (left),** built to resemble Newfoundland's traditional "fishing rooms".

Life in St. John's revolves around the ocean, with many private homes clinging to the cliffs surrounding **ST. JOHN'S HARBOUR (above).** A brief walk along an ocean path takes you around the corner to **SIGNAL HILL,** a National Historic Site.

Just 15 minutes south of St. John's, **CAPE SPEAR (right)** is the most easterly point in North America—it's a dramatic, rugged vantage point, where various lighthouses have stood watch since 1832.

© Darwin Wiggett/All Canada Photos

First page: top, © Andrew Hempstead; bottom, © Andrew Hempstead

© Roberta Olenick/All Canada Photos

The presence of more than half-a-million Atlantic puffins **(above)** is one of the main draws to the **WITLESS BAY ECOLOGICAL RESERVE.** Located halfway down the eastern edge of the Avalon Peninsula, this nature reserve is home to more than two million other seabirds, and its waters also welcome many playful humpback whales in season.

© Ron Erwin/All Canada Photos

A delightful stop along the Avalon's "Irish Loop" is Ferryland. The main attraction is an archaeological dig (and accompanying interpretation center) that is in the process of unearthing an original 17th-century settlement. From there it's a short walk to the **LIGHTHOUSE (above),** where you can pick up a picnic basket and dine with a view of the sea.

The village of **TRINITY (right)** may be the most charming in the province (and there is much competition for this title), with dozens of perfectly preserved 19th-century buildings. Located in an impossibly picturesque cove along the Bonavista Peninsula, it's home to interesting museums and charming inns.

© Barrett & MacKay/All Canada Photos

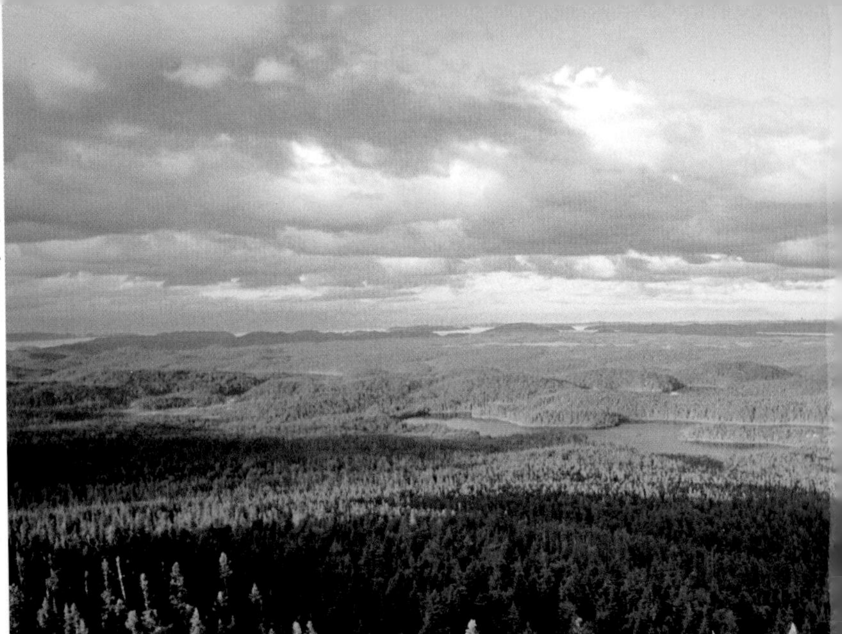

© Wayne Lynch/All Canada Photos

TERRA NOVA (above) is Newfoundland's first national park and a great place for hiking and camping amid the boreal forest. The park boasts more than 200km (125 miles) of shoreline and a number of excellent programs for families.

MOOSE (right) were only introduced to the province about 100 years ago, but there are now over 100,000 of them throughout the island. While they tend to keep out of sight, pay particular attention when driving at dusk or dawn—the 450-kg (1,000-lb.) animals are involved in close to 1,000 vehicle accidents per year, rarely in favor of the driver.

© Ron Erwin/All Canada Photos

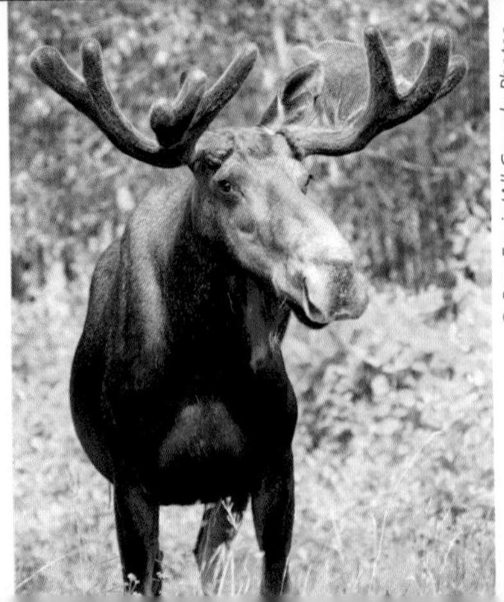

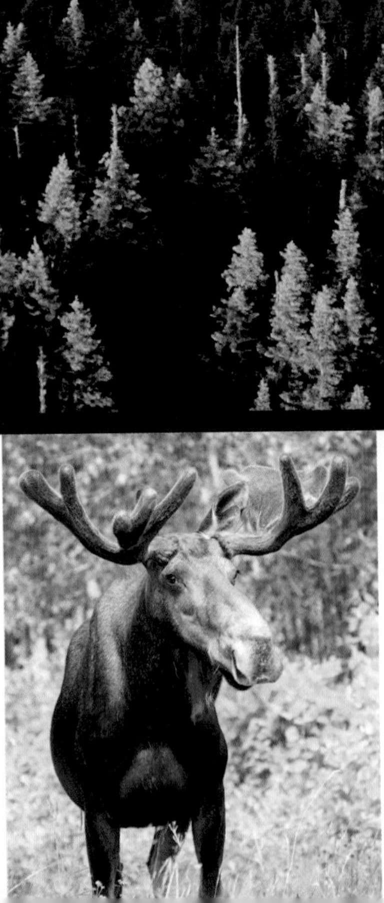

The village of **TWILLINGATE** is best known for its proximity to Iceberg Alley, the path that many majestic icebergs follow as they float southwards from Greenland and Baffin Island. Many of these icy sculptures pass these shores in spring and early summer, allowing you to move in for a good view (but not too close!). Summer is also an excellent time for viewing whales here.

© Rolf Hicker/All Canada Photos

It's for good reason that Gros Morne is considered one of the most spectacular national parks in Canada. The best way to get a sense of its grandeur is the 2½-hour boat tour through **WESTERN BROOK POND,** where you'll pass by countless waterfalls and spectacular cliffs that will simply take your breath away.

© Russ Heinl/All Canada Photos

Besides being exceptionally beautiful, Gros Morne has also earned the designation of being a UNESCO World Heritage Site. A major reason is **THE TABLELANDS (above),** where 470 million years ago the Earth's crust was pushed up until it broke through the surface here, giving you an idea of what the world would look like if the planet were turned inside out.

Vikings were the first Europeans to settle in North America, and it was far up the Northern Peninsula, at **L'ANSE AUX MEADOWS (right),** that they established a small village. It is protected as a National Historic Site, but the real fun is visiting the recreated Viking village, complete with enthusiastic re-enactors.

© Andrew Hempstead

The Labrador Straits are visited by only the most intrepid of travelers, but one of the rewards for those who come are the verdant trees and fast-flowing waters within **PINWARE RIVER PROVINCIAL PARK.** Popular with anglers, visitors can also swim and camp or watch expert kayakers negotiate the ferocious rapids.

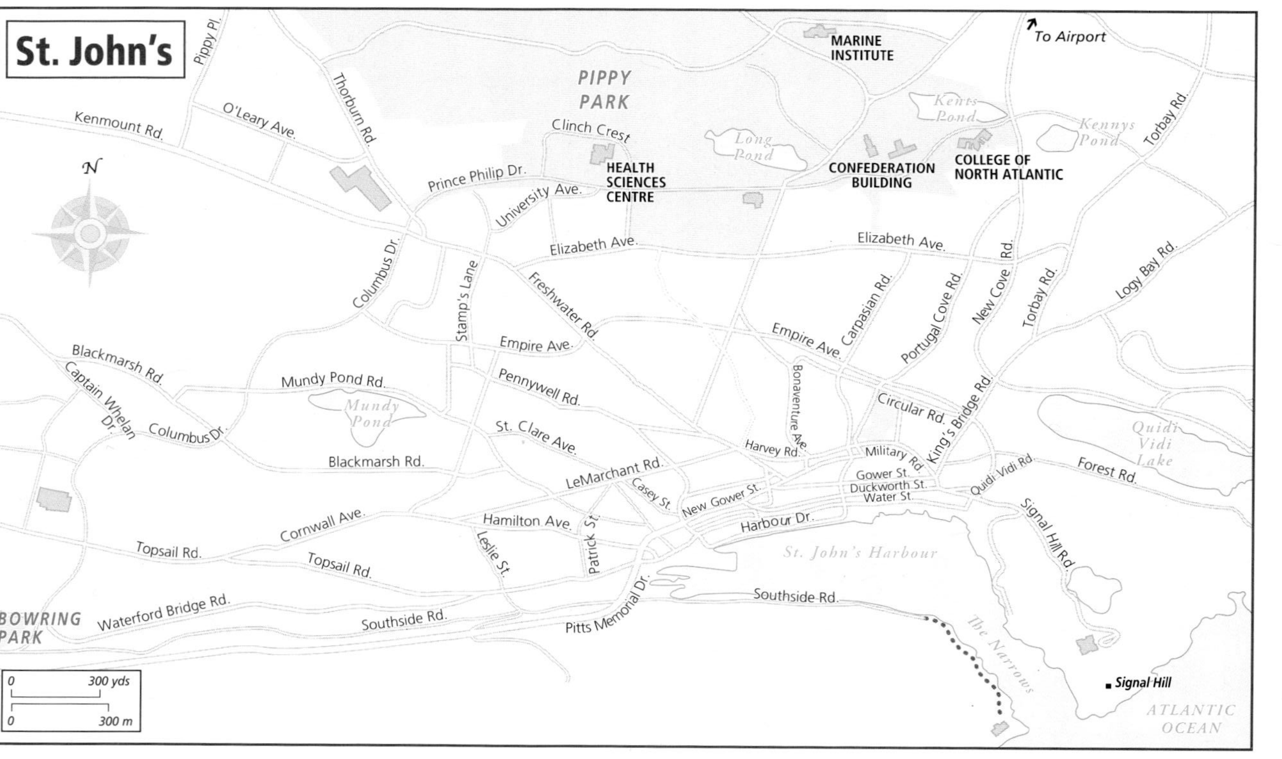
St. John's
Pippy Pl.
Kenmount Rd.
O'Leary Ave.
Thorburn Rd.
PIPPY PARK
MARINE INSTITUTE
To Airport
Torbay Rd.
Kents Pond
Kennys Pond
Long Pond
Clinch Crest
HEALTH SCIENCES CENTRE
CONFEDERATION BUILDING
COLLEGE OF NORTH ATLANTIC
N
Prince Philip Dr.
University Ave.
Elizabeth Ave.
Elizabeth Ave.
Columbus Dr.
Stamp's Lane
Freshwater Rd.
Carpasian Rd.
Portugal Cove Rd.
New Cove Rd.
Torbay Rd.
Logy Bay Rd.
Empire Ave.
Empire Ave.
Blackmarsh Rd.
Captain Whelan Dr.
Mundy Pond Rd.
Mundy Pond
Pennywell Rd.
Bonaventure Ave.
Circular Rd.
King's Bridge Rd.
Quidi Vidi Lake
Columbus Dr.
St. Clare Ave.
Harvey Rd.
Military Rd.
Blackmarsh Rd.
LeMarchant Rd.
Gower St.
Duckworth St.
Water St.
Quidi Vidi Rd.
Forest Rd.
Casey St.
New Gower St.
Signal Hill Rd.
Cornwall Ave.
Hamilton Ave.
Patrick St.
Harbour Dr.
Topsail Rd.
Topsail Rd.
Leslie St.
St. John's Harbour
Pitts Memorial Dr.
Southside Rd.
BOWRING PARK
Waterford Bridge Rd.
Southside Rd.
The Narrows
Signal Hill
ATLANTIC OCEAN
0 300 yds
0 300 m

Atlantic Canada
Torngat Mountains National Park
QUEBEC
Nain
Davis Inlet
Hopedale
Makkovik
Rigolet
ATLANTIC OCEAN
Smallwood Reservoir
LABRADOR
Esker
501
Churchill Falls
Labrador City
Wabush
500
Churchill River
389
North West River
520
Lake Melville
Happy Valley-Goose Bay
MEALY MOUNTAINS
Kenamu River
Cartwright
510
Battle Harbour
Pinware
Red Bay
U.S.
CANADA
Map area
Montreal
Ottawa
Toronto
UNITED STATES
Ferry

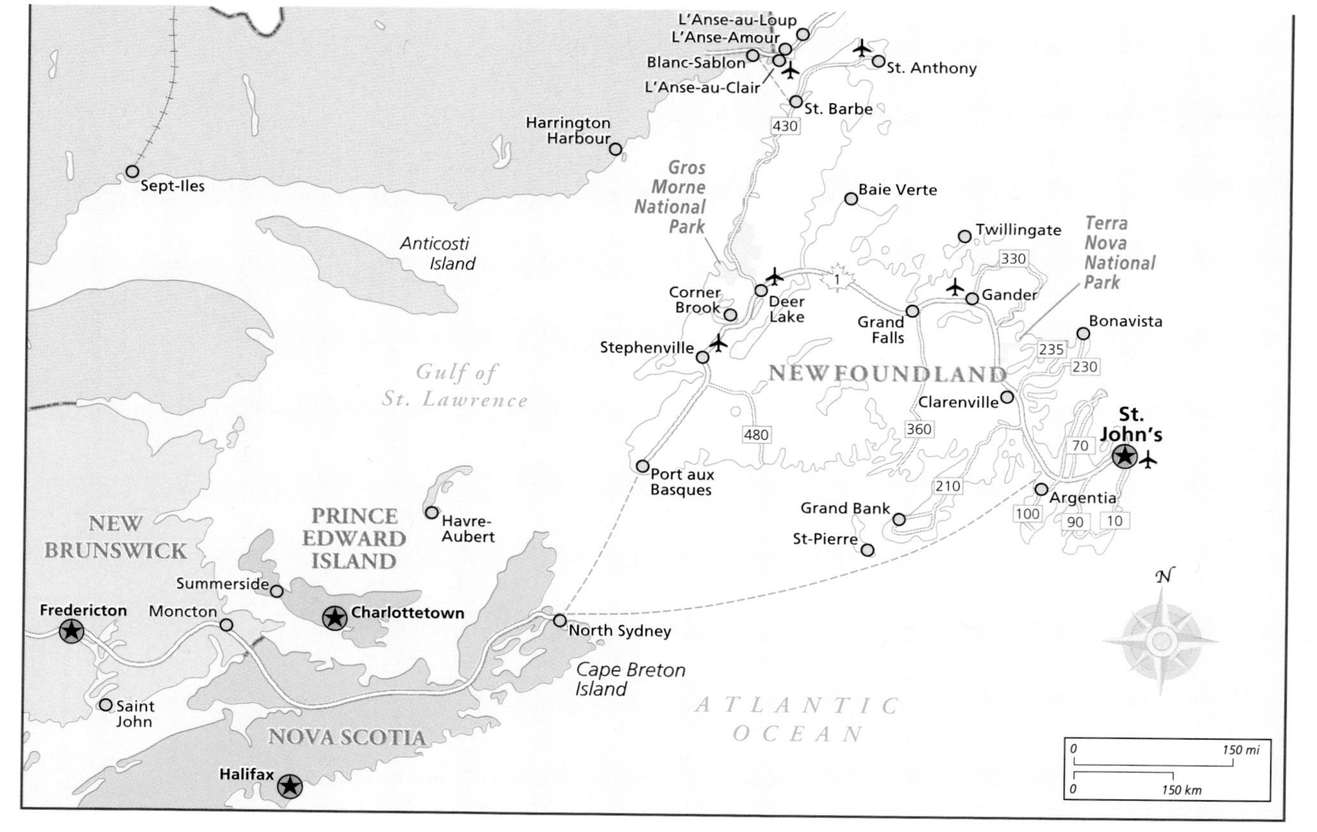
L'Anse-au-Loup
L'Anse-Amour
Blanc-Sablon
L'Anse-au-Clair
St. Anthony
St. Barbe
430
Harrington Harbour
Sept-Iles
Gros Morne National Park
Baie Verte
Twillingate
Terra Nova National Park
Anticosti Island
330
1
Corner Brook
Deer Lake
Gander
Grand Falls
Bonavista
Stephenville
235
230
Gulf of St. Lawrence
NEWFOUNDLAND
Clarenville
St. John's
480
360
70
Port aux Basques
210
Argentia
100
90
10
Grand Bank
St-Pierre
NEW BRUNSWICK
PRINCE EDWARD ISLAND
Havre-Aubert
Summerside
Fredericton
Moncton
Charlottetown
North Sydney
Cape Breton Island
ATLANTIC OCEAN
Saint John
NOVA SCOTIA
Halifax
N
0
150 mi
0
150 km

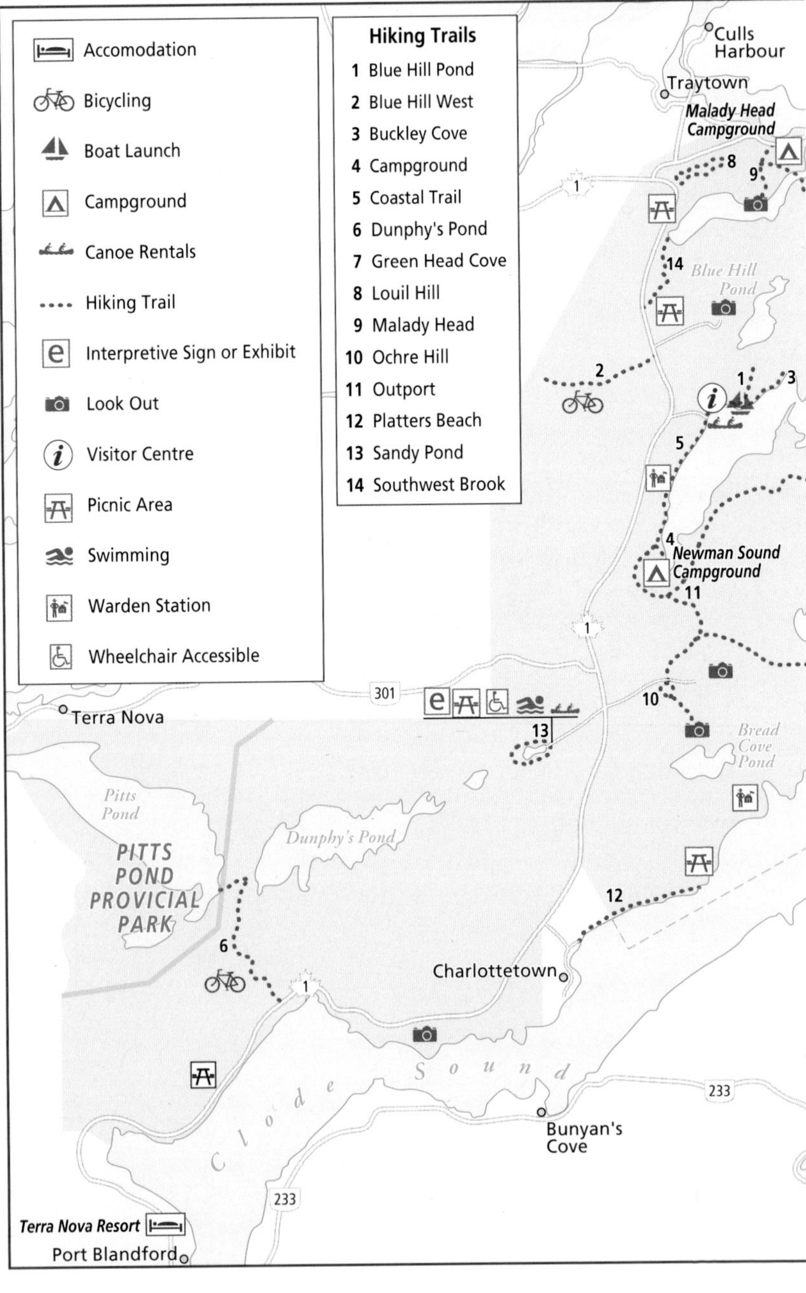
Accomodation
Bicycling
Boat Launch
Campground
Canoe Rentals
Hiking Trail
Interpretive Sign or Exhibit
Look Out
Visitor Centre
Picnic Area
Swimming
Warden Station
Wheelchair Accessible
Hiking Trails
1 Blue Hill Pond
2 Blue Hill West
3 Buckley Cove
4 Campground
5 Coastal Trail
6 Dunphy's Pond
7 Green Head Cove
8 Louil Hill
9 Malady Head
10 Ochre Hill
11 Outport
12 Platters Beach
13 Sandy Pond
14 Southwest Brook
Culls Harbour
Traytown
Malady Head Campground
Blue Hill Pond
Newman Sound Campground
Bread Cove Pond
Terra Nova
301
Pitts Pond
PITTS POND PROVICIAL PARK
Dunphy's Pond
Charlottetown
Clode Sound
233
Bunyan's Cove
Terra Nova Resort
Port Blandford

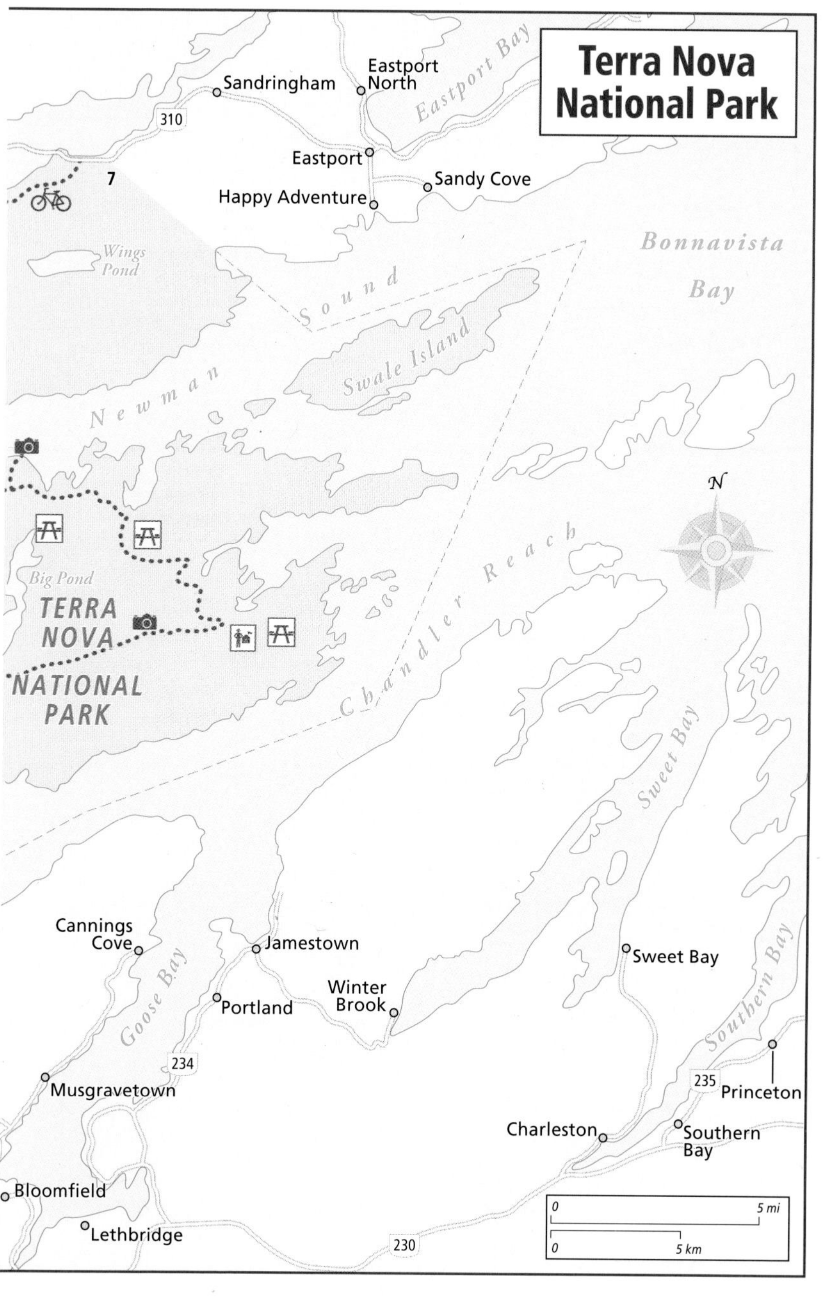

Terra Nova National Park
Sandringham
Eastport North
Eastport Bay
310
Eastport
Sandy Cove
Happy Adventure
7
Wings Pond
Bonnavista Bay
Newman Sound
Swale Island
N
Big Pond
TERRA NOVA NATIONAL PARK
Chandler Reach
Sweet Bay
Cannings Cove
Jamestown
Goose Bay
Portland
Winter Brook
Sweet Bay
Southern Bay
234
Musgravetown
235
Princeton
Charleston
Southern Bay
Bloomfield
Lethbridge
230
0
5 mi
0
5 km

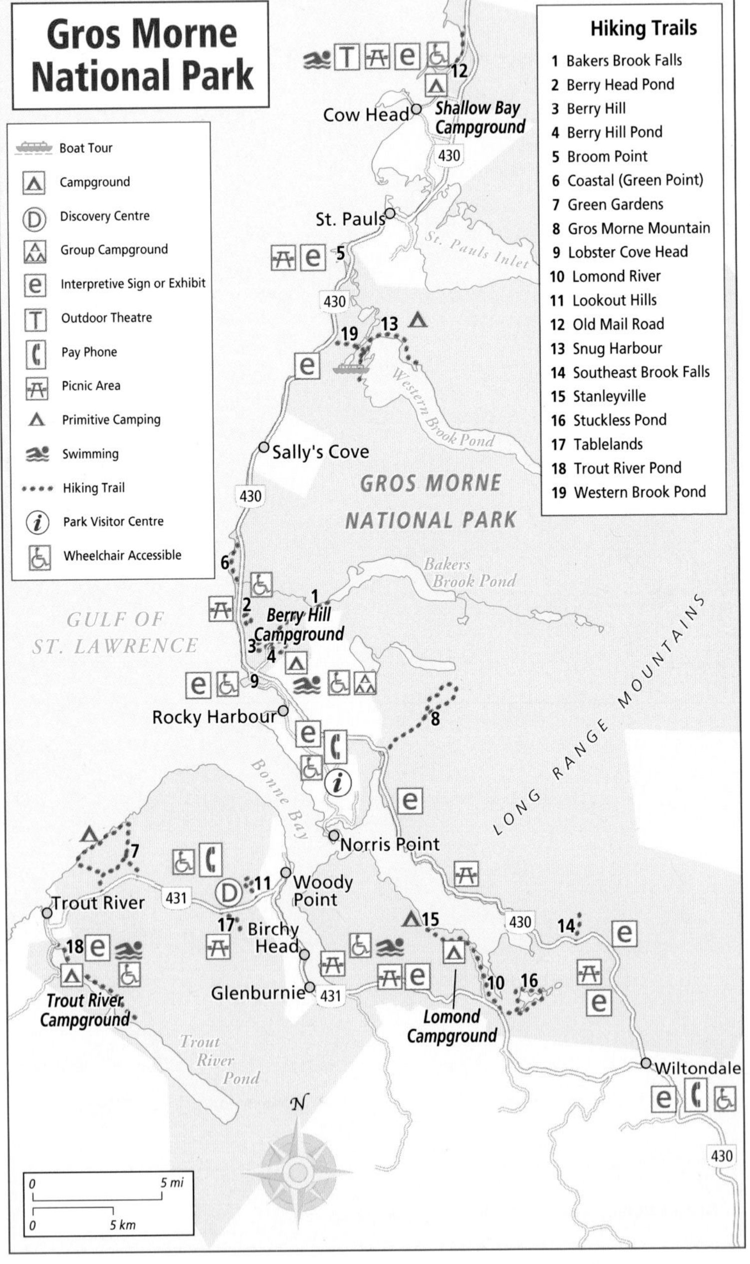

Gros Morne National Park
Boat Tour
Campground
Discovery Centre
Group Campground
Interpretive Sign or Exhibit
Outdoor Theatre
Pay Phone
Picnic Area
Primitive Camping
Swimming
Hiking Trail
Park Visitor Centre
Wheelchair Accessible
Hiking Trails
1 Bakers Brook Falls
2 Berry Head Pond
3 Berry Hill
4 Berry Hill Pond
5 Broom Point
6 Coastal (Green Point)
7 Green Gardens
8 Gros Morne Mountain
9 Lobster Cove Head
10 Lomond River
11 Lookout Hills
12 Old Mail Road
13 Snug Harbour
14 Southeast Brook Falls
15 Stanleyville
16 Stuckless Pond
17 Tablelands
18 Trout River Pond
19 Western Brook Pond
Cow Head
Shallow Bay Campground
430
St. Pauls
St. Pauls Inlet
Western Brook Pond
Sally's Cove
GROS MORNE NATIONAL PARK
Bakers Brook Pond
GULF OF ST. LAWRENCE
Berry Hill Campground
Rocky Harbour
LONG RANGE MOUNTAINS
Bonne Bay
Norris Point
Woody Point
Trout River
431
Birchy Head
Glenburnie
Trout River Campground
Trout River Pond
Lomond Campground
Wiltondale
N
0
5 mi
0
5 km

Frommer's™

Newfoundland & Labrador

4th Edition

by Andrew Hempstead

John Wiley & Sons Canada, Ltd.

Published by:

JOHN WILEY & SONS CANADA, LTD.

6045 Freemont Blvd.
Mississauga, ON
L5R 4J3

ISBN: 978-0-470-73678-4

Editor: Gene Shannon
Developmental Editor: William Travis
Editorial Manager: Alison MacLean
Project Editor: Lindsay Humphreys
Editorial Assistant: Katie Wolsley
Cartographer: Lohnes + Wright
Vice-President, Publishing Services: Karen Bryan
Production by Wiley Indianapolis Composition Services
Front cover photo: Coastal home and iceberg, Newfoundland. ©David Nunuk/All Canada Photos/AGE Fotostock, Inc.
Back cover photo: Canada, Newfoundland, Witless Bay, Razorbills. ©Patrick J. Wall/DanitaDelimont.com/Alamy Images.

For reseller information, including discounts and premium sales, please call our sales department: Tel. 416/646-7992. For press review copies, author interviews, or other publicity information, please contact our publicity department: Tel. 416/646-4582; Fax: 416/236-4448.

Wiley also publishes its books in a variety of electronic formats. Some content that appears in print may not be available in electronic formats.

Manufactured in the United States

1 2 3 4 5 RRD 14 13 12 11 10

CONTENTS

4 SUGGESTED NEWFOUNDLAND & LABRADOR ITINERARIES 62

5 ST. JOHN'S 77

6 AVALON PENINSULA 111

7 EASTERN REGION 131

8 CENTRAL REGION 158

9 WESTERN NEWFOUNDLAND 175

10 LABRADOR 207

11 FAST FACTS 228

INDEX 233

LIST OF MAPS

HOW TO CONTACT US

In researching this book, we discovered many wonderful places—hotels, restaurants, shops, and more. We're sure you'll find others. Please tell us about them, so we can share the information with your fellow travelers in upcoming editions. If you were disappointed with a recommendation, we'd love to know that, too. Please write to:

Frommer's Newfoundland & Labrador, 4th Edition
John Wiley & Sons Canada, Ltd. • 6045 Freemont Blvd. • Mississuaga, ON L5R 4J3

AN ADDITIONAL NOTE

Please be advised that travel information is subject to change at any time—and this is especially true of prices. We therefore suggest that you write or call ahead for confirmation when making your travel plans. The authors, editors, and publisher cannot be held responsible for the experiences of readers while traveling. Your safety is important to us, however, so we encourage you to stay alert and be aware of your surroundings. Keep a close eye on cameras, purses, and wallets, all favorite targets of thieves and pickpockets.

ABOUT THE AUTHOR

Andrew Hempstead is a travel writer and photographer who has traveled widely throughout Canada from his home in Banff, Alberta. His research trip for the 4th edition of this book took him throughout the province, and along the way, he found himself dancing with the locals at the Shamrock Festival in Ferryland, getting up close and personal with icebergs at Twillingate, and hiking through a snowstorm in Gros Morne National Park.

In addition to this book, Hempstead has authored guidebooks to Alberta, Atlantic Canada, British Columbia, the Canadian Rockies, Nova Scotia, and Vancouver and has co-authored guidebooks to Australia and New Zealand. His writing and photography have also appeared in many national and international publications.

FROMMER'S STAR RATINGS, ICONS & ABBREVIATIONS

Every hotel, restaurant, and attraction listing in this guide has been ranked for quality, value, service, amenities, and special features using a **star-rating system.** In country, state, and regional guides, we also rate towns and regions to help you narrow down your choices and budget your time accordingly. Hotels and restaurants are rated on a scale of zero (recommended) to three stars (exceptional). Attractions, shopping, nightlife, towns, and regions are rated according to the following scale: zero stars (recommended), one star (highly recommended), two stars (very highly recommended), and three stars (must-see).

In addition to the star-rating system, we also use **seven feature icons** that point you to the great deals, in-the-know advice, and unique experiences that separate travelers from tourists. Throughout the book, look for:

Finds	Special finds—those places only insiders know about
Fun Facts	Fun facts—details that make travelers more informed and their trips more fun
Kids	Best bets for kids, and advice for the whole family
Moments	Special moments—those experiences that memories are made of
Overrated	Places or experiences not worth your time or money
Tips	Insider tips—great ways to save time and money
Value	Great values—where to get the best deals

The following **abbreviations** are used for credit cards:

AE	American Express	**DISC**	Discover	**V**	Visa
DC	Diners Club	**MC**	MasterCard		

TRAVEL RESOURCES AT FROMMERS.COM

Frommer's travel resources don't end with this guide. Frommer's website, **www.frommers.com,** has travel information on more than 4,000 destinations. We update features regularly, giving you access to the most current trip-planning information and the best airfare, lodging, and car-rental bargains. You can also listen to podcasts, connect with other Frommers.com members through our active-reader forums, share your travel photos, read blogs from guidebook editors and fellow travelers, and much more.

1

The Best of Newfoundland & Labrador

You've done the Florida sun, the European tour, the Caribbean cruise, and the all-inclusive resort, but what you really want is something different. You want to experience something natural and untamed, to relax and rejuvenate without resorting to laziness. You want to create your own vacation memories, not reenact someone else's itinerary. You yearn for a place unlike any other, somewhere that hasn't been sanitized and packaged for official tourist consumption. Well, now you've found it: Newfoundland and Labrador, the Far East of the Western world.

Here, in Canada's youngest and most easterly province, a world of unique adventures awaits. What's around the next bend in the highway? Could it be a picturesque fishing village? A breaching humpback? A glistening iceberg? A friendly little cafe serving cod tongues? There's no script or schedule here, so you never know what you'll find when you start to explore. The key word here is "explore"—some of your most treasured memories will be found on the roads less traveled.

The rustic majesty that is Newfoundland and Labrador can be summed up in two words: "people" and "place." Both are unforgettable. The inhabitants of this isolated locale are as real as it gets. They are unpretentious, thoughtful, and witty. They'll charm you with their accents and their generous spirit. Though their lifestyle is neither opulent nor lavish, they will never hesitate to help a person in need. It comes from living in a harsh environment, where a helping hand can make the difference between survival and some other, ugly, alternative.

Newfoundland and Labrador's landscape and its animal inhabitants are equally remarkable. There are fjords and mountain vistas of stunning beauty. Places where sky meets horizon in blazing color, and where stands of spruce flow in an evergreen sea. Here, salmon launch themselves against the current and traffic slows for road-hopping rabbits. It is a place where howling winds have blown trains off their tracks and arctic air chills your backbone. As any local will tell you, this is the most blessedly cursed union of land, sea, air, and sky on creation. Come here once, and you'll have a perpetual longing to return.

Up until the last decade, Newfoundland was virtually undiscovered as a tourist destination. Even most Canadians hadn't been to "the Rock." But over the past 10 years, the province has put great effort into promoting itself throughout North America and on the global stage. Newfoundland and Labrador has revealed itself to the world as an exciting, unique, and even trendy destination.

So, be patient as you make your way throughout Newfoundland and Labrador, understanding that tourism is a new industry for the province and that services are not as abundant as they are in certain other locales. And really, isn't that why you're coming here in the first place?

Note: The following pages are designed to give you a quick overview of the best Newfoundland and Labrador has to offer. Wherever possible, I have included at least one attraction per category for every region of the province.

1 THE BEST TRAVEL EXPERIENCES

- **Walk the streets of downtown St. John's:** St. John's is one of the most interesting and visually exciting cities I've ever been to. The downtown core is relatively compact, and many of the top sights can be found within a 4-block radius of the harbor. See chapter 5.
- **Stand on top of Signal Hill:** You literally have a city at your feet when you stand at the base of Cabot Tower (walk around the tower to the other side, and you'll be gazing down at the broad expanse of the Atlantic Ocean). It's one of those must-see pilgrimages for any visitor to the capital city, and even for a good many local residents. See chapter 5, p. 99.
- **Watch the sun come up at Cape Spear:** On this, the most easterly point in North America, a spectacular sunrise, swirling surf, and picturesque lighthouse make Cape Spear the perfect location for an unforgettable marriage proposal. Find your inner romantic; see chapter 5, p. 100.
- **Dance the night away on George Street:** With the most pubs per capita in North America, the fun continues long after the sun has set in St. John's. There's something for everyone on George Street (rap, jazz, traditional, contemporary, and more). Find your favorite nighttime hot spot in "St. John's After Dark," in chapter 5.
- **Get sprayed by the Spout:** This natural geyser shoots saltwater more than 60m (197 ft.) into the air. You'll be wet, cold, and tired by the time you get there . . . and you won't even notice. You'll be too awestruck by every step along the spectacular East Coast Trail. For directions, see chapter 6, p. 129.
- **Experience an active archaeological dig at the Colony of Avalon:** Walk the oldest cobblestone street in North America and see artifacts from a 16th-century settlement. You'll learn about ancient battles for property ownership and skirmishes with marauding privateers. See chapter 6, p. 117.
- **Enjoy a bird's-eye view of Bird Rock:** After a short walk across tundra, you'll feel like you've reached the end of the world on that cliff overlooking Bird Rock at **Cape St. Mary's Ecological Reserve.** Imagine gazing into the eyes of thousands of squawking gannets nearly within arm's reach! See chapter 6, p. 122.
- **Dig into history at Bell Island:** It's just a 30-minute boat ride from Portugal Cove, but it's a giant step back in time when you explore the abandoned iron-ore mines of Bell Island. Or step back even farther, with a scuba-diving expedition to the wreckage of sunken ships that surround the island's perimeter. Find out how you can organize your own Bell Island adventure in chapter 6, p. 128.
- **Get carried away by Rising Tide:** Here's professional theater in both indoor and outdoor venues, in the heart of Newfoundland's most visually historical community, Trinity. Whether it's the comedic characters of the New Founde Lande Trinity Pageant or the haunting tragedy of a more serious dramatic production, you're sure to be impressed by the Rising Tide theater company. For details, see chapter 7, p. 138.
- **Light up your day with a trip to the Cape Bonavista Lighthouse:** This step back in time is informative, introspective, and breathtakingly beautiful. Inside, you'll be greeted by costumed interpreters and a realistic portrayal of life as it once was for the lighthouse keeper and his family. Outside, you'll be

equally enraptured by the rocky coastline and flowing seascape. See chapter 7, p. 141.

- **Chart a course for the North Atlantic Aviation Museum:** At the town of Gander, experience local aviation history, as depicted through storyboards, scale model displays, and restored aircraft. And if you've ever dreamed of becoming a pilot, you can move a step closer to that dream when you park yourself in the cockpit of a DC-38. See chapter 8, p. 163.
- **Cruise the South Coast:** Visit the most isolated communities on the island portion of the province. These gems of outport perfection are accessible only by ferry. They might not have pavement, but they're also free of traffic jams and road rage. A ferry trip along the South Coast is the best way to get up close and personal with the best (people) and worst (isolation) of rural Newfoundland. See chapter 8, p. 172.
- **Visit the province's last pocket of French settlement:** The **Port au Port Peninsula** is the only place in the province where French displaces English as the native language. *Ici, on parle Français.* Language, however, is just one part of a larger cultural dynamic. Here, you'll find a more overt Roman Catholic heritage and a genuinely French *joie de vivre*—unique in a society of primarily English and Irish descent. See chapter 9, p. 179.
- **Cruise the fjords of Gros Morne:** A tour boat excursion across **Western Brook Pond** in Gros Morne National Park will be a highlight of your trip to Newfoundland and Labrador. You pass countless waterfalls and towering peaks, and feel at peace with nature. See chapter 9, p. 193.
- **Set sail on a Viking adventure:** Take your place at the oar onboard a replica Viking *knarr* with Viking Boat Tours. It's a full-fledged Viking-style oceangoing adventure: you can even dress in traditional garb for a more authentic experience. Still, I doubt the Vikings would have approved—only good, clean fun is allowed on this ship. For information on how to book your Nordic adventure, see chapter 9, p. 206.
- **Climb the lighthouse at Point Amour:** The rewards are well worth the effort. You'll get a spectacular view (including a bird's-eye view of some of the oldest fossils found in North America) and learn quite a bit about naval history and shipwrecks. Back at ground level, you can hike the HMS *Raleigh* Trail when you're done. See chapter 10, p. 214.
- **Enjoy an outdoor lunch at Ferryland:** Lighthouse Picnics will fill a basket full of goodies—including a blanket—to make your lunch on the grassy headland of this historic community memorable. See chapter 6, p. 117.

2 THE BEST SPOTS FOR OBSERVING WILDLIFE & NATURE

- **The Fluvarium:** This interesting facility within St. John's city limits is easily accessible to those using public transport and very convenient to campers next door in Pippy Park. The Fluvarium offers a firsthand look at the underwater world of brook trout and other creatures that inhabit Newfoundland's ponds and rivers. See chapter 5, p. 102.
- **See seals in action at the Ocean Sciences Centre:** It's the unofficial star of Logy Bay, an oceanfront research facility that has an outdoor seal tank. You'll

be entertained by the comical antics of the resident seals as they splash and dive in their own private pool. If you're lucky, you may even see them interacting with Centre staff—and being rewarded for their efforts with a tasty fish. See chapter 5, p. 103.

- **Route 10, The Irish Loop:** Head south of St. John's, and you'll find a number of the province's best nature attractions within close proximity. Out at **Witless Bay Ecological Reserve,** seabirds abound, numbering more than 2.5 million, including 520,000 Atlantic puffins. The waters are also full of playful humpback whales. The whales actually heave their massive bodies out of the water and snare mouthfuls of food during their descent. The reserve is accessible by boat tour. Meanwhile, back on land, a herd of caribou can often be seen from the highway near Trepassey, and if you're really lucky, you may be able to watch the humpbacks feeding off the beach at St. Vincent's. See chapter 6, p. 112.
- **Visit with local wildlife at Salmonier Nature Park:** At this retirement/recovery home for aging and wounded animals, you'll see moose, fox, hare, lynx, and more in their natural environment (or almost natural—the holding areas are securely fenced enclosures). The Nature Park is a pleasant walk and education expedition, combined with a rare opportunity to view reclusive animals. Best of all, no admission is charged. See chapter 6, p. 120.
- **Watch salmon return to their spawning grounds at the Salmonid Interpretation Centre:** Here, you'll get both a surface and underwater view of these homeward-bound fish as they make their annual against-the-current pilgrimage. See chapter 8, p. 170.
- **White-water raft with Rafting Newfoundland:** Your exhilarating ride through breathtaking scenery just might include passing a black bear or moose. You'll see the province in a way not possible from the highway. See chapter 8, p. 170.
- **Twillingate:** This is the place to be if you're thrilled by the sight of towering icebergs and gracious whales. Icebergs float by from May through July (they seem to linger a bit longer in the bay near Twillingate than they do elsewhere around the province). Humpback whales are in abundance from June through September. See chapter 8, p. 165.
- **Northern Peninsula:** Anyone looking for a moose is bound to spot one here. This remote and rugged part of northwestern Newfoundland is home to many of the province's 130,000 big, brown, beautiful creatures. You'll often see them on or along the highway at dusk or dawn, especially during the fall. See chapter 9, p. 195.
- **Sail amid floating glacial castles with Northland Discovery Boat Tours:** You'll marvel at the cracks and colors in 10,000-year-old icebergs while traveling alongside playful dolphins, whales, and seabirds in their natural environment. To learn how you can get a taste of Northland Discovery's unique ecotourism adventure (not to mention the purest water on Earth), see chapter 9, p. 203.
- **Tablelands:** Students of geology already know that there's no better place to be than the island of Newfoundland, commonly known as the Rock. And there's no more spectacular example of the world's natural geological forces than this UNESCO World Heritage Site, where tremendous forces deep below the Earth's crust pushed upward 470 million years ago. See chapter 9, p. 192.
- **Gros Morne Adventures:** Guided sea kayaking tours through the sheltered waters of Bonne Bay give you a sea-level view of bald eagles, terns, and other wildlife. You'll be gliding through one

of the most scenic areas of the province: mountains, fjords, and glacial deposits are just a few of the features you'll encounter along your paddling adventure. See chapter 9, p. 194.

- **Pinware River Provincial Park:** Most of the Labrador Straits area is open, barren land with just a few stands of tuckamore for color. Not here. In Pinware Park, you'll find a verdant spruce carpet in a sheltered valley, as well as abundant freshwater fish and extreme kayaking conditions (for experts only!). To learn more about the park, see chapter 10, p. 216.

3 THE BEST SCENIC DRIVES

- **Cape Spear Road:** Just a 15-minute drive south of St. John's, Cape Spear is the most easterly point in North America, a National Historic Site, and site of the Cape Spear Lighthouse. If you're enjoying the drive, continue a little farther south toward the scenic fishing village of Petty Harbour. It won't take you more than an hour to drive the complete circle from St. John's to Cape Spear–Petty Harbour–Goulds–Kilbride and back to St. John's. See "Exploring St. John's" in chapter 5.
- **Middle Cove to Pouch Cove** (pronounced "pooch cove"): In the opposite direction from Cape Spear and Petty Harbour are the close-knit communities of Logy Bay–Middle Cove–Outer Cove, Torbay, Flat Rock, and Pouch Cove (follow rtes. 30 and 20). There's an interesting contrast along the drive: Nestled in between the farmland and obviously rural lifestyle are some of the most prestigious properties on the island, evidence of the growing prosperity in this part of the province. See chapter 5.
- **Irish Loop:** This loop is a 4-hour round-trip drive through the heart of Newfoundland's Irish heritage and caribou country. Along the way, you'll see beautiful coastal communities beside a panorama of rugged shore and outport loveliness. Follow Route 10 south of St. John's. If you stay on the same route (the name changes to Rte. 90 about halfway), you'll be carried back to the capital city. See "Irish Loop" in chapter 6.
- **Baccalieu Trail:** The tiny outport communities that line the shores of this finger of the Avalon Peninsula between Trinity and Conception bays are simply beautiful. Routes 80 and 70 will take you to inviting communities such as Heart's Delight, Heart's Content, and Harbour Grace. But remember to get off the highway and drive right into the villages in order to truly enjoy the beauty. See "Baccalieu Trail" in chapter 6.
- **Route 230 to Bonavista:** Beautiful in any season, this stunning stretch of highway is especially breathtaking when cloaked in early fall foliage. You'll find yourself wanting to pull over at every bend in the road so you can really appreciate the incredible views. The shining stars of the journey are the towns of Trinity and Bonavista, and the sweeping ocean panorama seen from the end of the road at Cape Bonavista. See chapter 7.
- **The foot of the Heritage Run:** If you look at the Burin Peninsula on a map, you'll notice it resembles a leg with a foot on the end. The long "leg" of the Heritage Run has some memorable moments, though for the main, it doesn't qualify as a scenic drive. But the loop journey from the ankle to the toe and back (rtes. 222, 220, and 213) is a different story. Here, you'll follow a coastal trail with an obvious maritime theme. Highlights of the trip are the lobster pots, fishing boats, and immaculate wharf facilities you'll spot along the side of the road. See chapter 7.

- **Kittiwake Coast:** It's a long drive from Gambo through the assorted towns and villages along the north coast (rtes. 320–330) before heading back to the Trans-Canada Highway at Gander, but it's so worth the effort. En route are picture-perfect picnic spots, a sandy beach (rare in this part of the world), and the community known as the "Venice of Newfoundland." See chapter 8.
- **Route 430 up the Northern Peninsula:** At Deer Lake, Route 430 spurs north along the western side of the northern peninsula. You'll pass through Gros Morne National Park, Port au Choix National Historic Site, L'Anse aux Meadows National Historic Site, and the town of St. Anthony, where you're likely to see an iceberg or two. In between all the official highlights, the road passes through some handsomely rugged and remote countryside. See chapter 9.
- **Labrador Coastal Drive:** Route 510 takes you from the ferry at Blanc Sablon, Quebec, to the captivating outport of Red Bay, Labrador. It's a paved road (one of the few in Labrador, so take advantage of it), which gives you a chance to tour the interesting communities and many historical attractions found on the Labrador Straits. Highlights include sunken Spanish galleons, a 7,500-year-old burial mound, and Atlantic Canada's tallest lighthouse. See chapter 10.

4 THE MOST PICTURESQUE VILLAGES

- **Quidi Vidi** (St. John's): Pronounced "kiddee viddee," this historical fishing village has managed to stop time in its tracks. You're not more than 5 minutes' drive from the traffic of downtown St. John's, yet Quidi Vidi has the oldest cottage in North America, horses grazing on the cliffs overlooking the peaceful lake, and timeless fishing sheds snuggling up to the granite cliffs that guard its sheltered harbor. See chapter 5, p. 100.
- **Petty Harbour** (St. John's): Just 15 minutes south of St. John's, this peaceful and quaint fishing village has been the backdrop for a number of films. With its aging fishing sheds, wooden slipways, and cliff-hugging houses tucked within a protective hillside embrace, its attraction as a movie set is readily apparent. It's amazing to find such a picturesque and well-preserved piece of traditional Newfoundland culture just minutes from the capital city. See chapter 5, p. 101.
- **Ferryland** (Avalon Peninsula): Aside from the unique lure of its ongoing archaeological dig (impressive as that is), the town of Ferryland is a strikingly attractive community. It flows down from the hills in graceful descent to sea level, layers of green grass and rocky knolls sprinkled amid stubborn settlement. On the small peninsula extending out from Ferryland Harbour is a lighthouse, its blinking eye a haunting reminder of the tragedy that can befall unwary sailors. To plan your visit to Ferryland, see chapter 6, p. 115.
- **Brigus** (Avalon Peninsula): You'll see lots of beautiful flowers and overhanging trees lining the narrow streets that lead to the harbor of this historic fishing village, and an abundance of heritage-style homes that give the place a real step-back-in-time feel. If you're looking to make the modern world go away for a while, Brigus is the perfect retreat. See chapter 6, p. 123.

Getting to Know Salvage

On the western edge of the Eastern Region, following Route 310 east of Glovertown, is one of the most picturesque (and most photographed!) fishing communities in the province. Salvage (pronounced "sal-*vage*") is a visual treat of stages, wharves, sheds, and slipways nestled in and around a granite shore. This, the never-ending ocean serenade, and houses built in the unlikeliest of places, make Salvage an unforgettable destination.

- **Dildo** (Avalon Peninsula): If the name alone isn't enough to spark your curiosity, you might be attracted by this historical fishing village's proud seafaring history. And then there's its aesthetic beauty: it was named one of Canada's prettiest towns, and you're sure to agree when looking at the wonderful view of Trinity Bay. Green space and simple wooden fences add to Dildo's rustic charm. See chapter 6, p. 125.
- **Trinity** (Eastern Region): Time seems to have stood still for this quaint fishing village that has preserved many of its 19th-century buildings. Or, if it hasn't stood still, there's certainly a concerted community effort to turn back the clock. If you climb the hill from Courthouse Road behind the Royal Bank just before sunset, you'll get one of the most beautiful views available anywhere. See chapter 7, p. 135.
- **Twillingate** (Central Region): Here is a community perfectly positioned for optimum iceberg viewing. With such impressive floating monoliths frequenting the shore every spring and early summer, you'll be forgiven if your attention wanders from the man-made beauty in and around the town. But rest assured, Twillingate is indeed a complementary composition of raw landscape and human construction. You'll find it at the northern end of Route 340. See chapter 8, p. 165.
- **François** (Central Region): At the opposite end of the compass from Twillingate is an isolated outport village, accessible only by ferry. It has neither paved road nor hotel, but that doesn't put François at a disadvantage. Majestic cliffs ring the little community, and wooden boardwalks serve as the local land highway (the real highway is the ocean). You'll have to work to find it, as it's hidden from view on a narrow strip of land at the head of a fjord. See chapter 8, p. 172.
- **Port aux Basques** (Western Newfoundland): An often underappreciated community, Port aux Basques is more than a relay station for the Newfoundland–Nova Scotia ferry. It has both traditional architectural beauty and an impressive blasted-rock harbor entrance. It takes on a romantic ambience in the twilight hours, thanks to the guide lights used to illuminate the ferry terminal. See chapter 9, p. 175.
- **Battle Harbour** (Labrador): Accessible only by boat, this one-time capital of Labrador was abandoned in the 1960s. Now restored, century-old buildings and a simple beauty create a haunting, yet memorable, destination. Escape the hustle and bustle of the modern world, whether for a day trip or overnight stay in the nostalgic Battle Harbour Inn. See chapter 10, p. 218.

5 THE BEST HIKES & WALKING TOURS

- **St. John's Haunted Hike** (St. John's): Looking for something different? Try this after-dark stroll through downtown St. John's with the Reverend Thomas Wyckham Jarvis, Esquire. He'll take you on a rather eerie walk through some of the oldest graveyards in the city and add quite a bit of theatrics along the way to keep your adrenaline pumping. See chapter 5, p. 106.
- **Signal Hill–Battery Trail** (St. John's): Not for the faint of heart! This walk starts at a pinnacle height, towering over the capital city, and follows a thigh-burning descent along a dizzying path less than 3m (9¾ ft.) from the edge of a 61m (200-ft.) drop to the Atlantic Ocean. Those brave enough to attempt it are rewarded with the most spectacular scenery in the city. See chapter 5, p. 99.
- **East Coast Trail** (Avalon Peninsula): This 220km (137-mile) route is one of North America's classic hiking trails. From St. John's, it leads south along the beautiful coastline of the Avalon Peninsula. You can see whales and seabirds close to shore, and parts of the trail are easy enough for the beginner. It's divided into sections, so you can do as much or as little as you like, tailoring your hike(s) to your time frame and fitness level. See chapter 6, p. 129.
- **British Harbour Trail** (Eastern Region): An old cart road leads to an abandoned outport village and then follows a starkly beautiful stretch of rocky coast to a second village. See chapter 7, p. 139.
- **Terra Nova National Park** (Eastern Region): Much of this park's focus is on the water, but a number of interesting hikes lace the dense mainland forest. A favorite is the **Coastal Trail,** linking the main campground and visitor center. See chapter 7, p. 149.
- **Gros Morne National Park** (Western Newfoundland): It's impossible to select one particular trail from this park as the best; they're all very different, and you can choose one that meets your own abilities or interests. If you're an experienced hiker and enjoy the challenges of a difficult climb, you'll find that the **Gros Morne Mountain Trail** offers the most spectacular rewards. See chapter 9, p. 184.
- **Port au Choix National Historic Site** (Western Newfoundland): Two connected hiking trails, each with its own attributes, crisscross this historically important site halfway up the northern peninsula. The **Phillips Garden Coastal Trail** stands out for the opportunity of watching archaeologists at work. See chapter 9, p. 197.
- **HMS *Raleigh* Trail** (Labrador): On this coastal hike at Point Amour, you can marvel at 500-million-year-old fossils, search out a shipwreck, photograph a waterfall, and pick mouthwatering berries, all without having to go too far off the beaten track. The trail begins at Atlantic Canada's tallest lighthouse. See chapter 10, p. 215.

6 THE BEST FAMILY ACTIVITIES

- **Johnson Geo Centre** (St. John's): This underground geological display is fun for the entire family. Adults will appreciate the educational interpretive program, while teenagers will be impressed by the oversize exhibits (and cool audiovisual presentation with simulated rain and volcanic eruptions).

Younger children will entertain themselves just squirting water at the exposed rock wall. See chapter 5, p. 99.

- **Fluvarium** (St. John's): This first-class interpretation facility provides visitors the opportunity to go beneath the surface to see trout and underwater species (the building boasts a glass-walled viewing area). Try to time your visit for the day's scheduled feeding. See chapter 5, p. 102.
- **Avondale Railway Station Museum** (Avalon Peninsula): For over a century, trains played a vital role in moving people and goods across Newfoundland. You can see just how important they were at the Avondale Railway Station Museum, the province's oldest railway station. There are decommissioned cars on display, and during the summer, children can go for a ride on one of the museum's small rail cars. See chapter 6, p. 125.
- **Stan Cook Sea Kayak Adventures** (Avalon Peninsula): Kayaking is fun for the young and the young-at-heart. Stan Cook's company has specially designed kayaks so children too young to paddle on their own can ride with mom or dad. And, for beginners, there's expert on-shore instruction provided prior to heading out onto the water. See chapter 6, p. 130.
- **Terra Nova Resort** (Eastern Region): This resort offers golfing, nature hikes, mini-golf, tennis, basketball, swimming, a children's program, and more. See chapter 7, p. 153.
- **Frenchman's Cove Provincial Park** (Eastern Region): This Burin Peninsula park offers a pebble beach, playground, and freshwater pond for outdoor swimming. Don't worry, the adults won't find themselves at loose ends—they can walk the fairways of a 9-hole golf course. See chapter 7, p. 148.
- **Terra Nova National Park:** Terra Nova gets high marks for its family activities. The park has an excellent interpretive program, nice campgrounds, a sandy beach for watersports and swimming, an evening interpretive program, great hands-on displays at the Visitor Centre, easy walking trails, and boat tours of Newman Sound. See chapter 7.
- **Splash-n-Putt Resort** (Eastern Region): The largest water park in the province, with a 91m-long (299-ft.) waterslide, comes complete with bumper cars, go-karts, and mini-golf. See chapter 7, p. 156.
- **Marble Mountain Resort** (Western Newfoundland): Winter fun for the entire family, the 35 named runs have something for everyone; snowboarders gravitate to the half-pipe and terrain park. For the younger set, there's certified ski and snowboard instruction and a day care, which means parents and children get to enjoy the resort on their own terms. See chapter 9, p. 182.
- **Newfoundland Insectarium** (Western Newfoundland): What kid doesn't like bugs or butterflies? Kids have a great time here, watching honeybees buzz about, stretching out their hands to catch a butterfly, getting some bug-related souvenirs to take home, and having an ice cream when they're finished. See chapter 9, p. 184.
- **Norstead** (Western Newfoundland): This reenactment village depicts the everyday life of Norsemen—and women—from A.D. 1000. Norstead's wonderful Discovery Program for kids offers a hands-on opportunity to participate in the various activities that would have been carried out in the settlement. Even the teens will be shocked out of their chronic boredom by the clanging swords and hand-to-hand combat of the mock battles. See chapter 9, p. 205.

7 THE BEST PLACES TO DISCOVER LOCAL HISTORY & CULTURE

- **The Rooms** (St. John's): Constructed to resemble "fishing rooms," where families would process their catch, this imposing complex combines the provincial museum, art gallery, and archives. Far from your typical stuffy museum, it features a distinct contemporary ambience, as the story of the province's human and natural history unfolds while you move from room to room. See chapter 5, p. 98.
- **Signal Hill** (St. John's): Just a short drive from downtown, this National Historic Site offers the best view of St. John's and the harbor. It was here that Guglielmo Marconi received the first wireless transatlantic signal, using a kite to catch the faint transmission from Poldhu, England. For the full effect, time your visit to take in the Signal Hill Military Tattoo. See chapter 5, p. 99.
- **Basilica of St. John the Baptist** (St. John's): For years the largest and most imposing structure on the St. John's skyline, the Basilica was one of the few buildings to survive the Great Fires that devastated the capital city during the early part of the 20th century. A highlight of your visit will be a viewing of the Veiled Virgin statue. See chapter 5, p. 98.
- **Quidi Vidi Battery** (St. John's): In the early battles for control of the colony of St. John's, heavy fortifications were constructed at strategic locations throughout the city. This quiet hill overlooking Quidi Vidi Harbour was one of them. Today, costumed interpreters explain the purpose of the installation and the people who resided there. See chapter 5, p. 100.
- **Colony of Avalon** (Avalon Peninsula): Make your first stop at this independently run national historic site, south of St. John's, the Interpretation Centre. From this point, it's a short stroll through the village of Ferryland to the dig site, where archaeologists are continuing to uncover remnants of the first successful planned colony in Newfoundland. See chapter 6, p. 117.
- **Hawthorne Cottage National Historic Site** (Avalon Peninsula): The former home of famous Arctic explorer Captain Bob Bartlett includes intriguing insights into the life and times of the man and his family, as well as the struggles he faced on his expeditions. See chapter 6, p. 126.
- **Dildo & Area Interpretation Centre** (Avalon Peninsula): This is a fascinating facility if you're interested in the workings of a fish hatchery and want to learn more about the way of life for Newfoundlanders of the not-so-distant past, as well as the native peoples who once inhabited the region. Plus, it comes with a replica of a giant squid that was caught in the area! See chapter 6, p. 125.

Exploring St. John's Art Galleries

Artists are acknowledged mediums for the ideas and attitudes of their cultural generations. You can see (and buy) the work of some of the most talented artists in the province through one of several St John's art galleries: Christina Parker, Emma Butler, and Lane. See chapter 5, p. 108.

- **Trinity Historical Properties** (Eastern Region): While the entire community of Trinity is a living museum, with residents embracing their past as the route to future prosperity, a few buildings are open as tourist attractions. These include the Lester-Garland Premises, Hiscock House, Trinity Museum, Court House, and Green Family Forge. See chapter 7, p. 138.
- **Ryan Premises National Historic Site** (Eastern Region): This cluster of 19th-century harborfront buildings is a restoration of the merchant premises that served as the hub of a once-thriving fishing community. The Interpretive Centre has an excellent display about changes that have affected the province's fishery. Also check out the replica in the harbor of the *Matthew,* the three-masted 15th-century vessel sailed by John Cabot to Newfoundland in 1497. See chapter 7, p. 142.
- **Burin Heritage Museum** (Eastern Region): The communities of Grand Bank and Fortune are among the closest in the world to the infamous fishing grounds of the Grand Banks. Through interpretive panels and traveling exhibits, this museum pays tribute to that heritage. See chapter 7, p. 147.
- **Barbour Living Heritage Village** (Central Region): Similar to the Ryan Premises, but on a larger scale. It's not just a restored commercial property, but a series of reconstructed buildings typical of a fishing village (ca. 1900). They're more than just historical monuments, however. These multipurpose buildings also serve as the local museum, theater, and art gallery. See chapter 8, p. 164.
- **Boyd's Cove Beothuk Interpretation Centre** (Central Region): With all the hype about John Cabot discovering Newfoundland, and even the Vikings arriving a millennium ago, it's easy to forget that there were permanent residents here long before the Europeans arrived. Boyd's Cove is one of those sites that help us remember. Although little is known about Newfoundland's now-extinct Beothuk, Boyd's Cove sheds some light on who they were and how they adapted to Newfoundland's harsh environment. See chapter 8, p. 165.
- **Dorset Soapstone Quarry** (Central Region): Even before the Beothuk, there were Dorset people living on the island of Newfoundland. Proof of their existence can be found in the province's earliest known mine, where the Dorset mined soapstone for use as bowls and cooking pots. See chapter 8, p. 171.
- **Port au Choix National Historic Site** (Western Newfoundland): What is it about Port au Choix that has made it the location of choice for five different native populations over the last 4,500 years? Archaeologists are still trying to puzzle the answer from the clues left behind from past civilizations (including the Maritime Archaics, the Groswater, and the Dorset-Paleoeskimo). See chapter 9, p. 197.
- **Grenfell Interpretation Centre** (Western Newfoundland): This is a recommended stop for anyone interested in the early medical history of northern Newfoundland and Labrador. Learn about Sir Wilfred Thomason Grenfell, the English doctor who became a local hero to the Inuit and early settlers of the region. See chapter 9, p. 202.
- **L'Anse aux Meadows National Historic Site** (Western Newfoundland): Make your first stop the visitor center, to learn about the Vikings who landed at the tip of the Northern Peninsula around A.D. 1000. Then, you'll walk among the sunken foundations of their village. Plus, there is a re-created Viking village, with reenactors on hand to demonstrate how these early settlers might have interacted with each other. See chapter 9, p. 205.

- **Red Bay National Historic Site** (Labrador): Once the whaling capital of the world, the name Red Bay came from the color of the water, which was supposedly so bright with whales' blood that it flowed red. Inside the interpretive center is a reproduction of a wooden whaling boat, surrounded by the mandible (jawbone) of a bowhead whale. The area wasn't treacherous just to whales, however; at least three Spanish galleons are known to have gone down in the waters of Red Bay. For more information, see chapter 10, p. 217.
- **Battle Harbour** (Labrador): One of my favorite places in all of Newfoundland and Labrador, this community, once the hub of Labrador, was abandoned in the 1960s; but thanks to enterprising locals, many buildings have been restored, and you can visit for a day or even stay overnight. Access is by boat in summer only. See chapter 10, page 218.

8 THE BEST FESTIVALS & SPECIAL EVENTS

- **Newfoundland & Labrador Folk Festival** (St. John's): This is an absolute must for lovers of traditional music. The 3-day event takes place in downtown St. John's during the first weekend of August and provides a good variety of music that includes folk, country, bluegrass, and Celtic. See chapter 5, p. 103.
- **Royal St. John's Regatta** (St. John's): This is the biggest event of the year for St. John's; its importance is recognized by its status as a municipal holiday. The oldest continuous sporting event in North America offers a day in early August of fixed-seat rowing races and lots of fun for the entire family at Quidi Vidi Lake. See chapter 5, p. 104.
- **George Street Festival** (St. John's): You'll enjoy the George Street Festival if you're young (or, at the very least, young-at-heart) and don't mind loud music and crowds. During the 6-day midsummer event, a 2-block stretch of the downtown street is closed off, and bars open up their doors and bring in a lineup of terrific entertainment. See chapter 5, p. 103.
- **Shamrock Festival** (Avalon Peninsula): Traditional Irish-Newfoundland music mingles with some modern material in this popular late-July event held outdoors in the community of Ferryland. Many of the province's best-known performers are from this part of the province, so the lineup is always guaranteed to impress. See chapter 6, p. 115.
- **Brigus Blueberry Festival** (Avalon Peninsula): Arrive early because there's always a crowd in Brigus for this popular mid-August event. It's an excellent venue for buying locally made products such as knitted goods, quilts, and, of course, blueberry products. See chapter 6, p. 123.
- **Summer in the Bight** (Eastern Region): Each year between June and October, the **Rising Tide Theatre** puts on a number of professional shows that give poignant life to the Newfoundland character and lifestyle. Staged at both indoor and outdoor venues, Summer in the Bight includes the renowned **New Founde Lande Trinity Pageant.** See chapter 7, p. 138.
- **The Fish, Fun & Folk Festival** (Central Region): One of the largest and longest-running folk festivals in Newfoundland, this event is held the last full weekend of July in Twillingate. If you want to have a great time with the family and gain deeper insight into what makes Newfoundlanders tick, plan to take in this event. See chapter 8, p. 168.

- **Exploits Valley Salmon Festival** (Central Region): This 5-day family event and salmon celebration is held mid-July in Grand Falls–Windsor. Take time to enjoy a performance at the highly regarded **Summer Theatre Festival.** See chapter 8, p. 170.
- **Gros Morne Theatre Festival** (Western Newfoundland): Treat yourself to a dinner-theater production of excellent regional music, comedy, and drama while in the area of Gros Morne National Park between June and September. The festival is held in the northern part of the park. Twice weekly, you'll have the chance to enjoy a theatrical performance, as well as taste some of the best pan-fried cod found anywhere. See chapter 9, p. 190.
- **Bakeapple Folk Festival** (Labrador): Time your visit to the Labrador Straits for the second weekend of August, when the cloudberry, or bakeapple berries, are ripe and the biggest summer event of the year is taking place. You'll get 4 days of fun, music, and merriment. See chapter 10, p. 216.

9 THE BEST HOTELS & RESORTS

- **Courtyard St. John's** (131 Duckworth St., St. John's; ✆ **866/727-6636** or 709/722-6636; www.marriott.com): This is the newest hotel to rise among downtown's historic core. Rooms are stylish, and the friendly and knowledgeable front-desk staffers are an unexpected bonus. See chapter 5, p. 85.
- **Murray Premises Hotel** (5 Beck's Cove, St. John's; ✆ **866/738-7773** or 709/738-7773; www.murraypremises hotel.com): You simply can't beat the attention to detail at this beautifully decorated boutique hotel, which was once a waterfront warehouse. The staff and management are top-notch, offering an exceptional standard of service to ensure your stay is enjoyable. See chapter 5, p. 86.
- **Sheraton Hotel Newfoundland** (115 Cavendish Sq., St. John's; ✆ **800/325-3535** or 709/726-4980; www.starwood hotels.com): Recently rebranded after operating as a Fairmont property for many years, this is the best-known full-service property in the province. Although it lacks an outwardly Newfoundland style—because of its size and branding—you will still find the unique island character in the personality of the caring and professional staff. See chapter 5, p. 86.
- **Bears Cove Inn** (15 Bears Cove Rd., Witless Bay; ✆ **866/634-1171** or 709/334-3909; www.bearscoveinn.com): Don't pick this lodging if a long list of amenities is important to you. But if you're looking for a place where you can see the ocean from inside your room or while sitting on your private deck overlooking the rugged coastline, this is a great choice. See chapter 6, p. 114.
- **The Wilds at Salmonier River** (Rte. 90, Salmonier Line; ✆ **866/888-9453** or 709/229-5444; www.thewilds.ca): Even Fido is welcome at this terrific family resort. The Wilds has self-contained cabins, as well as hotel-style rooms in the main building. One of the province's finest golf courses is on-site, and you're just minutes from Salmonier Nature Park. See chapter 6, p. 119.
- **Bird Island Resort** (Main Rd., St. Bride's; ✆ **709/337-2450;** www.bird islandresort.com): This resort offers fully equipped efficiency units that are ideal for traveling families. All-ages fun includes mini-golf, horseshoe pits, and a fitness center. This is the closest

accommodations to Cape St. Mary's Ecological Reserve. See chapter 6, p. 121.

- **Terra Nova Resort** (Port Blandford; ✆ **709/543-2525;** www.terranovagolf.com): This full-service family resort offers a great kids' program, an outdoor swimming pool, tennis, a challenging 27-hole golf course, and in-house dining, and it's ideally situated for day trips into Terra Nova National Park. See chapter 7, p. 153.
- **BlueWater Lodge & Retreat** (Trans-Canada Hwy. near Gander; ✆ **709/535-3003;** www.relax-at-bluewater.ca): A wonderful place to stay while touring Notre Dame Bay and other points in the Central Region, the lodge has a private, serene setting on a small lake, making it a perfect retreat for anyone really wanting to get away from it all. See chapter 8, p. 159.
- **Marble Inn Resort** (Dogwood Dr., Steady Brook; ✆ **877/497-5673** or 709/634-2237; www.marbleinn.com): It doesn't have the attitude of the official Marble Mountain Resort, and that's a good thing. I find these cabins are actually cozier and more inviting than their more expensive counterparts. The ample on-site amenities (sauna, fitness facility, canoe rentals, and playground) add even more value to the package. See chapter 9, p. 180.
- **Sugar Hill Inn** (Norris Point Rd., Norris Point; ✆ **888/299-2147** or 709/458-2147; www.sugarhillinn.nf.ca): After a long day of hiking in Gros Morne National Park, this little slice of luxury will be much appreciated. The six guest rooms are warm and inviting, and the food is top-notch. See chapter 9, p. 190.

10 THE BEST BED & BREAKFASTS, & HERITAGE INNS

- **Bluestone Inn** (34 Queen's Rd., St. John's; ✆ **877/754-9876** or 709/754-7544; www.thebluestoneinn.com): Modern chic blends effortlessly with classic architectural design for a one-of-a-kind B&B. This place has it all: splendid downtown location, an interesting history, superlative food, and spacious guest rooms. See chapter 5, p. 87.
- **Winterholme Heritage Inn** (79 Rennies Mill Rd., St. John's; ✆ **800/599-7829** or 709/739-7979; www.winterholme.com): Bring your neck brace—you'll need it from constantly staring upward at the ornately carved woodwork. If you're a real romantic, reserve one of the suites with a jetted tub and fireplace. See chapter 5, p. 89.
- **Inn by the Bay** (78 Front Rd., Dildo; ✆ **888/339-7829** or 709/582-3170; www.innbythebaydildo.com): Who can resist staying in one of "Canada's 10 Prettiest Towns"? This lovely B&B has an attentive owner and a waterfront location, and it's right in the heart of Dildo, an odd-sounding but very beautiful fishing village. See chapter 6, p. 124.
- **Artisan Inn** (High St., Trinity; ✆ **877/464-7700** or 709/464-3377; www.artisaninntrinity.com): This is a wonderful B&B in the scenic village of Trinity. The inn's Ocean Shore Apartment—with a private deck overlooking Trinity Bay—is my favorite room. See chapter 7, p. 135.
- **Fishers' Loft Inn** (Mill Rd., Port Rexton; ✆ **877/464-3240** or 709/464-3240; www.fishersloft.com): A short drive from Trinity, this remote property

with an ethereal atmosphere is perfect for anyone seeking peace, tranquillity, and fine food. See chapter 7, p. 136.

- **Elizabeth J. Cottages** (Harris St., Bonavista; ✆ **866/468-5035** or 709/468-5035; www.elizabethjcottages.com): One of the finest cottage accommodations in all of Newfoundland and Labrador—think fine cotton sheets on an oversize bed, plush bathrobes, a modern entertainment system, polished hardwood floors, and a private deck with sweeping ocean views. See chapter 7, p. 140.
- **Cape Anguille Lighthouse Inn** (Cape Anguille; ✆ **877/254-6586** or 709/634-2285; www.linkumtours.com): Experience life as a lighthouse keeper at this unique accommodation high above the Gulf of St. Lawrence. Aside from gracious hospitality and magnificent scenery, bird-watchers will love the diversity of species present in the area. See chapter 9, p. 176.
- **Quirpon Lighthouse Inn** (boat transfer from Quirpon; ✆ **877/254-6586** or 709/634-2285; www.linkumtours.com): This isolated island retreat is the perfect escape from techno-society. Amenities include hearty home-cooked meals, endless waves, iceberg views, and conversations with whales. It's just you and your thoughts for company. See chapter 9, p. 205.
- **Battle Harbour Inn** (Battle Island, Labrador; ✆ **709/921-6325** or 709/921-6216; www.battleharbour.com): Looking to step back in time? This small inn will enable you to do just that. It has wood stoves and oil lamps, and the setting is in the oldest intact salt-fish community in the province. See chapter 10, p. 219.

11 THE BEST RESTAURANTS

- **Bacalao** (65 Lemarchant Rd., St. John's; ✆ **709/579-6565**): It didn't take long for Bacalao to become one of the capital's most popular dining rooms, shortly after it opened. Order the creamy cod au gratin and you find out why. See chapter 5, p. 90.
- **Blue on Water** (319 Water St.; St. John's; ✆ **709/754-2583**): In the heart of historical downtown St. John's, this slick dining room features a bright blue-and-white interior and a kitchen that combines local game with modern cooking styles. See chapter 5, p. 91.
- **Nautical Nellies** (201 Water St., St. John's; ✆ **709/738-1120**): Great food, big portions, and reasonable prices in cozy pub surroundings—that's what you'll find at Nautical Nellies. It's both small and very popular, making it hard to get a table. See chapter 5, p. 92.
- **Colony Café** (Rte. 10, Ferryland; ✆ **709/432-3030;** www.thecolonycafe.ca): A French chef waits to tempt your taste buds with succulent seafood and rich desserts. The cafe is situated next to the Colony of Avalon archaeological dig in Ferryland. See chapter 6, p. 116.
- **Skipper's Restaurant** (42 Campbell St., Bonavista; ✆ **709/468-7982**): After touring the historical sites in Bonavista and taking in the views at Cape Bonavista, it's worth searching out this lovely waterfront restaurant if you like seafood and don't want to pay big prices. You'll find terrific chowder and, for the more adventurous, local delicacies such as fried dough smothered in molasses. See chapter 7, p. 140.
- **Bay of Islands Bistro** (13 West St., Corner Brook; ✆ **709/639-3463**): The nouvelle cuisine served here would be

just as much at home in Montreal as it is in Newfoundland's smallest city. See chapter 9, p. 181.

- **Anchor Café** (Main St., Port au Choix; ✆ **709/861-3665**): Beyond the ship-shaped entrance is a simple dining room with a wide-ranging menu of inexpensive seafood. My favorite combo is seafood chowder followed by a shrimp burger. See chapter 9, p. 195.
- **Norseman Restaurant** (Rte. 436, L'Anse aux Meadows; ✆ **877/623-2018**): Located at the extreme northern tip of the northern peninsula, this restaurant is a fantastic surprise. The waterfront setting is a delight, the food is as creative and well presented as the best restaurants in St. John's, and the service is professional. See chapter 9, p. 204.
- **Whaler's Restaurant** (Red Bay, Labrador; ✆ **709/920-2156**): Want the best fish and chips in Labrador? Then plan on trying the chalupa fish and chips at Whaler's. They're tasty, tangy, and value-priced. And the restaurant is in historic Red Bay, where you can finally find the answer to the riddle, "What is a chalupa?" See chapter 10, p. 217.

2

Newfoundland & Labrador in Depth

To really understand this unique province and the people who live here, it's important to delve into the history of the island of Newfoundland and its mainland region of Labrador, and to understand the people and the remote landscape they call home. It is the history, and sense of place, that makes Newfoundland and Labrador such a culturally unique destination.

While natural beauty is the province's greatest asset and its biggest draw for tourists, the 510,000 Newfoundlanders—known universally as "Newfies"—themselves go a long way to making the destination such a memorable place to visit. Through all the hardships endured, Newfoundlanders and Labradorians extend their hands in friendship. The Maritime provinces of New Brunswick, Nova Scotia, and Prince Edward Island have a well-deserved reputation for being gracious and welcoming, but there is still a noticeable difference between that gregarious threesome and Canada's easternmost province. Unlike the rest of the country, locals see themselves as Newfoundlanders who happen to be Canadian rather than the other way around. It must be the isolation. Newfoundland is an island, Labrador a remote northern locale; both are difficult to access. But instead of closing Newfoundlanders and Labradorians off from the world, their remoteness makes them hungry for connections beyond their borders. They greet strangers with heartfelt smiles, warm words, and genuine curiosity. Everyone is welcomed as a person with a story to tell.

1 NEWFOUNDLAND & LABRADOR TODAY

Despite experiencing difficult economic times since the collapse of the cod fishery in the early 1990s, Newfoundlanders are a proud and resourceful people, with oil and tourism keeping the economy humming along nicely.

Offshore oil developments lead the way in terms of economic growth. Currently, three fields are in operation, with a fourth, Hebron, slated to begin production in 2016.

St. John's remains an old-fashioned port city through and through, but the newfound wealth is obvious and well received by most. Less than a generation ago, thousands of young adults were fleeing the province in search of work elsewhere in Canada. Today, those finishing school are mostly choosing to remain, and many who left in the 1990s are returning, young families in tow. Unthinkable even a decade ago, today in St John's, you can sip a chai latte at a sidewalk cafe, enjoy a day spa in a converted monastery, or visit one of the world's premium museums. There are boutique hotels, Thai restaurants, and even million-dollar condominium projects. Beyond city limits of the capital, the scene is a little different. The sea of change to hit St. John's is not obvious, unemployment is high, and there is little or no reason for younger generations to remain.

Fun Facts A Cultural Time Capsule

As you travel throughout the province, you'll marvel at the distinctive dialects. Along the southern shore (in the Avalon Region), it's difficult to distinguish the brogue of the Irish-born local priest from that of the local people. Similarly, there are other places where the British accent is so strong that linguists can identify the part of England from which local ancestors emigrated. Why does it sound so pure, hundreds of years after the out-migration of these early European settlers? The answer is geography—Newfoundland's island isolation protected the original cultural identity of its settlers.

For many towns and villages across the province, tourism is the shining light for future prosperity. Postcard-perfect villages such as Trinity, which starred in the movie *The Shipping News,* have embraced tourism without changing in outward appearance. South of St. John's, fishing boats that once hauled in cod now take visitors on whale-watching trips, while along northern coastlines, it's icebergs that the visitors come to see.

FACING CHALLENGES

Despite being the oldest European settlement in North America, through the 1980s and 1990s, the province was one of the least economically developed places in Canada. But change is in the air. Since the commencement of offshore oil drilling and the development of the world's biggest nickel mine at Voisey Bay, the local economy has come ahead in leaps and bounds—so much so that economic growth in the last decade has been the highest of all Canadian provinces except Alberta.

History has taught the people of Newfoundland and Labrador a harsh lesson of exploitation. Time and again, they have seen the heartbreaking out-migration of their vast natural resources and human potential. But overall, the future for Newfoundland and Labrador looks bright. As such, for the first time in generations, a steady flow of displaced Newfoundlanders are returning to their home province and the population is remaining stable.

SOME THINGS WILL NEVER CHANGE

Through good times and bad, Newfoundlanders have never been accused of being unsociable. George Street, in downtown St. John's, is known far and wide for its concentration of pubs. Here, beer flows freely and dancing to Celtic music comes easily. The vibe for out-of-towners is welcoming. So much so that at many bars you can become an honorary Newfoundlander by participating in a "screech-in." The tongue-in-cheek ritual varies from place to place but generally requires you to recite a silly verse, drink an ounce of the hair-raising dark rum straight up, and then kiss a piece of salt cod (or, in some establishments, a stuffed puffin), upon which, you'll be presented with a certificate for a keepsake. Trapper John's, in the capital, is a well-known place to be screeched-in.

For those who prefer their liquor with a mixer, try to screech-in with a "Dark 'n' Dirty," the local name given to what most other places call a rum and cola.

MUSIC AND THEATER

Planning a celebration seems to come easily to Newfoundlanders. In simple words, they know how to party, and they certainly know how to make fabulous music. Some of the better-known acts include The Irish Descendents, Great Big Sea, The Masterless Men, and The Ennis Sisters, all known for their Celtic sound.

As well, Newfoundlanders love their live theater, and you'll find many regional festivals occurring throughout the province during summer, including in St John's, Trinity (Eastern Region), and Gros Morne National Park (Western Newfoundland). Contact **Newfoundland & Labrador Tourism** (© **800/563-6353;** www.newfoundlandlabrador.com) for current schedules and prices.

COME HOME CELEBRATIONS

Because of the province's unstable economy over the last 3 decades, many of Newfoundland's young and educated have moved away from the Rock in order to earn a good living for themselves and their families. While the province's population decreased over the last couple of decades, the outflow of people has slowed considerably and the population has stabilized.

Most of those who left the province have ended up in Ontario (because of the opportunities in commerce, science, and technology) and Alberta (for those interested in the petroleum industry, as close ties have formed between the two provinces with Newfoundland's recent involvement in offshore drilling). It is said that the population of Fort McMurray, Alberta, is now the third largest town of Newfoundlanders (after St. John's and Gander).

You may be able to take the Newfoundlander out of Newfoundland, but you can never exorcise the spirit of Newfoundland from its people. As a result, many who have left return each summer to spend time with family and friends, and to visit the place they will always call home. To commemorate this spirit, many communities throughout the province have created "Come Home Year" celebrations, filled with all sorts of food, fun, and frolic.

DICTIONARY OF NEWFOUNDLAND ENGLISH

Even though Newfoundlanders speak English, they have their own dialect that has introduced new and varied meanings for common words, and they have developed unique words of their own. These can be found in the whopping 770 pages that make up the *Dictionary of Newfoundland English,* published by the University of Toronto Press. Any visitor to the Rock will find this book extremely useful, and any student of languages will find it extremely interesting. Some examples of what you'll discover in this bulky volume include seven different meanings for the word "cat"—which include the obvious interpretation, as well as others—and some surprisingly pleasant meanings for the word "piss." The book is currently out of print, but you may find it at St. John's booksellers such as **Wordplay** (www.wordplay.com) or through the used book database **www.abebooks.com**.

Note: Not every person in every region of Newfoundland and Labrador will use words found in the *Dictionary of Newfoundland English.* Some of the recorded words and phrases are obsolete.

Native Inhabitants of Newfoundland & Labrador

Paleo-Indians (or "ancient" Indians) lived in Labrador about 9,000 years ago. Little is known about them, but based on the scant archaeological evidence, an educated guess is that they were nomadic hunters and gatherers, living along the coast in the summer and following inland caribou in the fall.

Maritime Archaic people (descendants of the Paleo-Indians) lived throughout the entire province from 3,000 to 7,500 years ago. They are the first known inhabitants of the island of Newfoundland. They were coastal dwellers, dependent on the sea (mammals, birds, and fish) for their sustenance. The Newfoundland and Labrador government has an excellent section of their website devoted to the province's earliest inhabitants, including the page **www.heritage.nf.ca/aboriginal/maritime.html** about the Maritime Archaic people.

Paleoeskimos began moving into northern Labrador about 4,000 years ago, emigrating south from Greenland. There is no evidence of direct interaction between the Paleoeskimos and Maritime Archaic people, but it seems logical that they would have met at some point since they occupied the same geographic areas at approximately the same time. Included within the Paleoeskimo tradition were the Groswater and Dorset cultures. Visit **www.heritage.nf.ca/aboriginal/palaeo.html** for a detailed analysis of the Paleoeskimos.

Innu, who have lived in Labrador and northeastern Quebec for approximately 2,000 years, are thought to be descendants of the Maritime Archaic people. Traditionally, they are nomadic hunters like the other aboriginal groups of Newfoundland and Labrador. They differ, however, in that they are an inland people who make sporadic trips to the coast. Animals, particularly caribou, play a strong role in Innu culture. To learn more about the modern Innu population, visit **www.innu.ca**.

Beothuk, the original native inhabitants of Newfoundland, are extinct. The last known Beothuk, Shanawdithit, died in 1829. It is estimated that fewer than 1,000 Beothuk lived on the island at any one time; their population was decimated by starvation, disease, and periodic skirmishes with European settlers. It's not known where they came from, or how long they lived on the island, but archaeological evidence seems to indicate they were of Algonkian

2 LOOKING BACK AT NEWFOUNDLAND & LABRADOR

Early settlement patterns of Newfoundland and Labrador followed the length of the rocky shores, providing ready access to the sea. Little has changed. Fishing has been—and for the most part, continues to be—the primary activity around which the world turns for Newfoundlanders. Even for those not directly involved in the ocean harvest, the industry and its environment are powerful social, cultural, and economic influences.

origin (similar to Mi'kmaq, Montagnais, and Naskaupi). They inhabited central and western Newfoundland. The website **www.heritage.nf.ca/aboriginal/beothuk.html** is filled with information on this almost mythical people.

Thule people were the most recent aboriginal arrivals in Labrador, crossing the Bering Strait from Asia as late as 500 to 600 years ago. They lived in small family groups and were nomadic hunters and gatherers. They were also known as whalers, hunting baleen whales using harpoons thrown from their *umiaks* (open, flat-bottomed boats) and kayaks. The Thule are the ancestors of the Inuit. For more information, visit **www.heritage.nf.ca/aboriginal/thule.html**.

Inuit (aka "Eskimo") of Nunatsiavut are traditionally nomadic hunters and gatherers known for traveling great distances in search of food and other sustenance materials. Pre–European settlement, they ranged from Cape Chidley in northern Labrador to the island of Newfoundland. The introduction of Moravian missionaries in the mid-1700s marked a change in the Inuit's traveling lifestyle, as well as the dilution of their culture through the integration of European tools and ideas. For more information, visit **www.nunatsiavut.com**.

Mi'kmaq people have lived in Newfoundland for more than 200 years, with their main settlements on the island's west coast. It's not certain where they came from, or when and why they moved here, but some anthropologists have surmised that they are of Maritimes (that is, Nova Scotian) origin and that their emigration was motivated by scarce resources. About 600 Mi'kmaq today live in Conne River, along Newfoundland's south coast. You can visit the band on the Internet at **www.mfngov.ca**.

Métis people of Labrador are striving for recognition of their native status—both from acknowledged aboriginal groups and from nonnatives. Métis are a combination of Innu or Inuit bloodlines mixed with European settlers. There are approximately 5,000 Métis living in Labrador, which makes them the largest aboriginal group in the province. You can check on their progress in the fight for the same rights as other Canadian aboriginals by visiting **www.labradormetis.ca**.

WHO DISCOVERED THE NEW FOUNDE LAND?

Newfoundland has a long and intriguing history. Evidence of a burial mound of the Maritime Archaic Indians dating back 7,500 years—the oldest discovered burial mound in the world—has been found in L'Anse Amour on the Labrador Straits. And archaeologists have determined that, as far back as 5,500 years ago, the Maritime Archaic Indians, followed by other native peoples, were living in the area of the Port au Choix on the Northern Peninsula.

It was also on this northern peninsula that Leif Eriksson and his gang of Vikings landed in A.D. 1000. Although the Vikings did not form a permanent settlement in the newfound land or officially claim what

Battle of Beaumont Hamel

Two years into World War I, the Allies planned a major offensive to break through German lines, hoping to turn the tide of war in their favor. The attack was scheduled for July 1, 1916. Miscalculating the positioning of German troops, the Allied forces ran straight into heavy bombardment from machine-gun fire. Almost 20,000 British troops died that day, but hardest hit of all was the Newfoundland Regiment. The 778 members of the Regiment were among the first wave ordered to cross no-man's-land and penetrate the German front line near the village of Beaumont Hamel. The next morning, only 68 men answered the roll call—each unanswered name a symbol of a lost generation for the fledgling colony. There is today a permanent memorial on the battlefield of Beaumont Hamel; it is a bronze statue of a caribou, the symbol of the Newfoundland Regiment.

they called Vinland, they left evidence of their community in the mounds found at L'Anse aux Meadows National Historic Site.

Next up was Giovanni Caboto, more commonly known as John Cabot, the Italian-born explorer who claimed the newfound land for England in 1497. The French and Spanish soon followed, looking for a share of the bountiful Newfoundland fisheries, and many battles ensued, with the British eventually becoming the enduring force on the Newfoundland front.

Most of the early permanent settlers to Newfoundland came from southwest England and southeast Ireland, with the majority emigrating between 1750 and 1850. And because the Newfoundland outports were so isolated and family groups kept tightly intact, contemporary Newfoundlanders continue to speak with a strong Irish accent in parts of the Avalon (particularly the Irish Loop) and a fainter British or Scottish accent in St. John's and throughout the rest of the island.

PRE-CONFEDERATION

Prior to joining Confederation and becoming part of Canada in 1949, Newfoundland was an independent British colony with its own governor and government house. Loyalty to the mother country was particularly evident during the world wars, when thousands of Newfoundland youth voluntarily sailed overseas to do what they felt was their duty in the war effort.

Until 1949, Newfoundland produced its own currency and postage stamps. Newfoundland stamps are still relatively common, so their value isn't extremely high, but they make a wonderful souvenir for any collector. Their variety is rich and colorful, and each stamp tells a fascinating story. As well, Newfoundland produced its own coinage and bank notes from 1834 to 1949, many of which are now quite valuable to collectors. The coin denominations issued were 1¢, 5¢, 10¢, 20¢, 25¢, 50¢, and $2.

CONFEDERATION

The man responsible for bringing Newfoundland—Britain's oldest colony—into Canada's Confederation was Joey Smallwood, Newfoundland's first premier. Between 1946 and 1948, Smallwood organized a number of what turned out to be very controversial and emotional debates, asking his constituents whether they were in favor of becoming a Canadian province. In 1948, the final vote was incredibly close—51% supporting and 49% opposing—which is why some Newfoundlanders still think of Smallwood as a traitor, and others see him as Newfoundland's greatest contemporary hero.

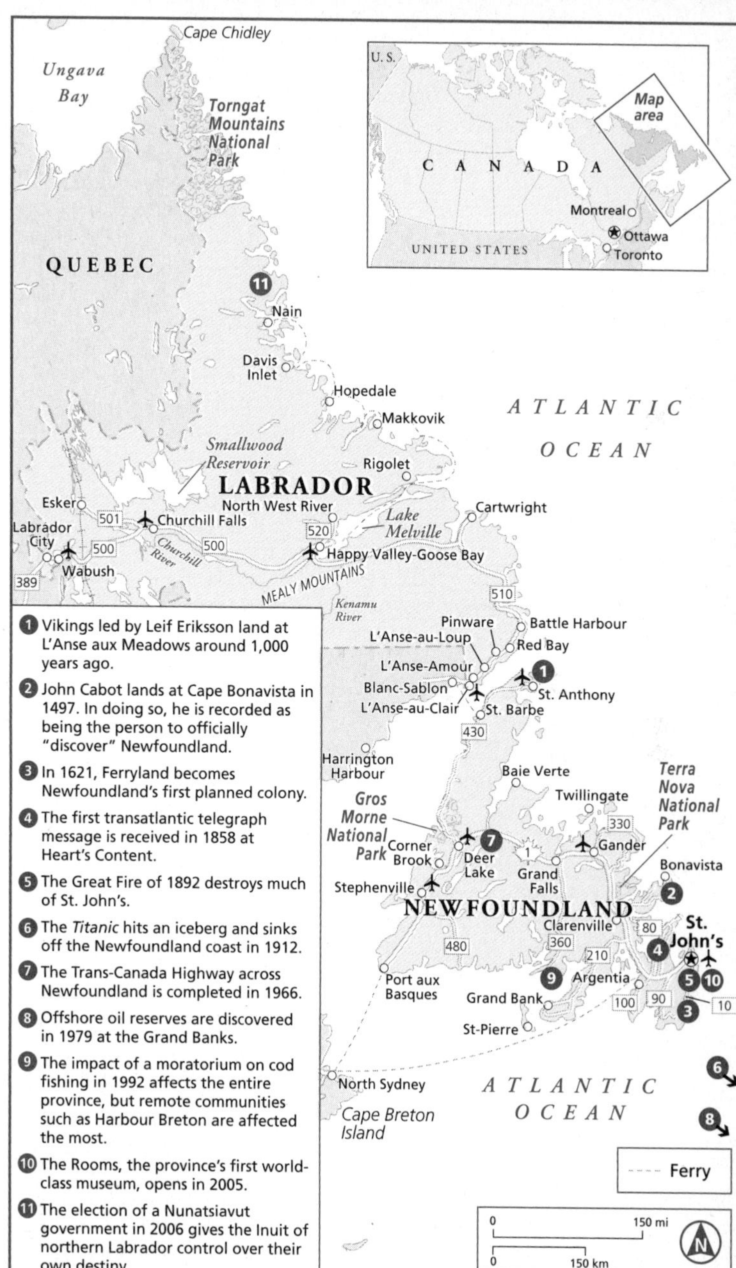
Cape Chidley
Ungava Bay
Torngat Mountains National Park
QUEBEC
Nain
Davis Inlet
Hopedale
Makkovik
Smallwood Reservoir
Rigolet
LABRADOR
Esker
North West River
Churchill Falls
Labrador City
Wabush
Churchill River
Lake Melville
Happy Valley-Goose Bay
MEALY MOUNTAINS
Cartwright
Kenamu River
Pinware
Battle Harbour
L'Anse-au-Loup
Red Bay
L'Anse-Amour
Blanc-Sablon
L'Anse-au-Clair
St. Anthony
St. Barbe
Harrington Harbour
Baie Verte
Twillingate
Gros Morne National Park
Terra Nova National Park
Corner Brook
Deer Lake
Grand Falls
Gander
Stephenville
Bonavista
NEWFOUNDLAND
Clarenville
St. John's
Port aux Basques
Argentia
Grand Bank
St-Pierre
North Sydney
Cape Breton Island
ATLANTIC OCEAN
ATLANTIC OCEAN
Ferry
0 150 mi
0 150 km
U.S.
CANADA
Map area
Montreal
Ottawa
Toronto
UNITED STATES
1 Vikings led by Leif Eriksson land at L'Anse aux Meadows around 1,000 years ago.
2 John Cabot lands at Cape Bonavista in 1497. In doing so, he is recorded as being the person to officially "discover" Newfoundland.
3 In 1621, Ferryland becomes Newfoundland's first planned colony.
4 The first transatlantic telegraph message is received in 1858 at Heart's Content.
5 The Great Fire of 1892 destroys much of St. John's.
6 The Titanic hits an iceberg and sinks off the Newfoundland coast in 1912.
7 The Trans-Canada Highway across Newfoundland is completed in 1966.
8 Offshore oil reserves are discovered in 1979 at the Grand Banks.
9 The impact of a moratorium on cod fishing in 1992 affects the entire province, but remote communities such as Harbour Breton are affected the most.
10 The Rooms, the province's first world-class museum, opens in 2005.
11 The election of a Nunatsiavut government in 2006 gives the Inuit of northern Labrador control over their own destiny.

The Little Man from Gambo

Joseph Roberts Smallwood was born in 1900 in Gambo, a central Newfoundland town of just over 2,000 residents. Although small of stature, Smallwood had a larger-than-life persona. He worked as a journalist, a farmer, and a labor organizer before striking his true vocation: politics. He was convinced that confederation with Canada was the best option for a prosperous future for Newfoundland and Labrador; his mission was to persuade enough of his fellow citizens to feel the same way. He traveled the province from one end to the other, using his impressive oratorical skill and staccato style of delivery to maximum effect. He achieved his desired goal in 1949, when Newfoundland and Labrador became the tenth province of Canada.

A particularly endearing Smallwood quirk (aside from his famous bow tie) was his habit of reiterating salient points three and four times so that they were imprinted on the minds of his listeners. He also had an incredible memory for both names and faces, often recognizing voters he had met years before and linking them to other family and friends throughout the province.

Smallwood served as premier of Newfoundland and Labrador for 22 years. His leadership was marked by an intense drive for industrialization: His government supported rubber-boot and chocolate factories, as well as an oil refinery, linerboard mills (manufacturers of the corrugated layer found in the middle of cardboard), and a hydroelectric power development at Churchill Falls. Even though many of his initiatives were fated to fail, the lack of success never diminished his dream of prosperity. Until his death in 1991, he was often affectionately referred to as the last living Father of Confederation.

LABRADOR

What is also important to understand is that most of Labrador (other than the Labrador Straits and the coastal region) has quite a different history and persona than the island of Newfoundland. Inland Labrador is a land rich in wildlife and natural resources, but its history has been spotted

DATELINE

- **1000** Leif Eriksson and his pack of Vikings land at L'Anse aux Meadows, making them the first Europeans to unofficially discover the new founde land.
- **1497** Explorer Giovanni Caboto (aka John Cabot) lands at Cape Bonavista aboard his ship, the *Matthew,* and is recorded as the man who discovered Newfoundland.
- **1583** Sir Humphrey Gilbert officially claims Newfoundland for England, making it the first overseas Crown possession.
- **1610** John Guy establishes the first British settlement in Newfoundland. It is not successful.
- **1621** Sir George Calvert (who later became Lord Baltimore) establishes the first successful planned colony, at Ferryland.
- **1651** Oliver Cromwell of England appoints a board of commissioners to govern Newfoundland.
- **1660** The French establish the colony of Placentia and build Fort Louis to defend it.
- **1763** Labrador is annexed to Newfoundland.
- **1771** The Moravians establish the community of Nain in Labrador.

with struggle about who owns these lands. Labrador first became part of Newfoundland in 1763, but control reverted to Quebec just 11 years later under the 1774 Quebec Act. In 1809, Labrador was returned to Great Britain. In a 1927 challenge to Newfoundland's ownership of Labrador by Canada on behalf of Quebec, the boundary abutting the Torngat Mountains was set to separate Labrador from the neighboring province of Quebec. When Newfoundland became a Canadian province in 1949, Labrador was included, although it wasn't until 2002 that Labrador was added to the province's official name.

In many ways, it is both physically and emotionally distant from Newfoundland, leading many in the region to argue that they should form their own provincial entity. Since the Inuit of coastal Labrador north of Happy Valley–Goose Bay gained self-governing status with the creation of Nunatsiavut in 2005, support for ceding in the rest of Labrador has waned.

WHEN COD WAS KING

No matter what tangent you go off on as you research the province's natural or sociological history, everything will always bring you back to the fishery. The abundance of fish is what undoubtedly attracted the first native inhabitants to this land of shorelines. It is also the magnet that induced European commercial interests to make an annual pilgrimage to the province's treacherous shores. The fishery is what built the province. For 300 years, cod was the most numerous and valuable of all species, with halibut, haddock, and pollock processed as a side catch. As fishing techniques improved, the catch increased. The first mega-trawlers appeared in local waters in the 1960s. Capable of hauling in up to 200 tons of cod within a single hour, they had the onboard facilities to also process and freeze the fish, and then transfer the catch to mother ships. The total catch began declining after peaking at 810,000 tons annually in 1968. It took until 1977 for the Canadian government to act by extending territorial waters from 19 to 322km (12–200 miles), thereby preventing the mostly foreign fleet from cod fishing. In an act of incredible shortsightedness, the government then encouraged Canadian companies to continue to fish using mega-trawlers, and while it was a popular short-term policy with Newfoundlanders, the end was near. Quotas were eventually established, but it was too late. By the late 1980s, fish stocks were so completely decimated that annual quotas were barely met.

By 1992, it was all over—there were no cod left to catch. The idea behind the 1992 Cod Moratorium was that if fishing were stopped completely, the fish would slowly return. What wasn't fully understood at the time was that not only were

- **1774** Control of Labrador is given to Quebec via The Quebec Act.
- **1784** Religious freedom is proclaimed, and the first Roman Catholic bishop arrives in Newfoundland.
- **1802** The Treaty of Amiens gives control of the islands of St. Pierre and Miquelon to France.
- **1809** Labrador is re-annexed to Newfoundland.
- **1813** Newfoundland's first lighthouse is built at Fort Amherst.
- **1825** The coast of Labrador is annexed to Quebec.
- **1832** Cape Spear Lighthouse is built to light the way for ships arriving at the most easterly point in North America.
- **1858** The first transatlantic telegraph message is transmitted via submarine cable from Heart's Content in Newfoundland to Ireland.
- **1866** The transatlantic telegraph cable is successfully laid.
- **1871** The Newfoundland Constabulary is formed.
- **1873** Cod fishing in Newfoundland is revolutionized with the invention of the cod trap.

continues

Petroleum Power

There are three producing oil fields on the Grand Banks, offshore from Newfoundland and Labrador: Hibernia, Terra Nova, and White Rose. Between them, the three fields produce about 145 million barrels of oil annually, with White Rose expected to expand capacity by 25 million barrels by 2009. Current output equates to about one-half of Canada's conventional light crude-oil production. And with the demand for oil increasing worldwide, interest has been renewed in a fourth Grand Banks oilfield, Hebron-Ben Nevis, as well as more remote sites such as the Orphan Basin and Labrador Shelf.

the cod gone, but the entire ecosystem had been changed forever. The effects extended well beyond the ocean. Some estimates of the resulting unemployment were as high as 60,000 people, in a provincial population of 500,000.

Today, if you order fish and chips in a local restaurant, you'll get cod. That's because a small part of the cod fishery has reopened in the Gulf of St. Lawrence. The 2009 documentary *The End of the Line,* researched by Charles Clover, is an excellent insight into the industry.

Despite the terrible economical effects of the moratorium, today the sun shines brightly (metaphorically speaking) on Canada's Far East as it turns its attentions to tourism and other newly discovered jewels of the sea to feed and clothe its people.

3 THE LAY OF THE LAND

NATURAL RESOURCES AND THE GREAT OUTDOORS

Newfoundland and Labrador is a land rich in natural resources. To commemorate this abundance, the province has designated a tree, plant, gemstone, and bird as its official representatives of nature. The provincial tree is the black spruce, which is the most common tree in the province.

Newfoundland's official floral emblem is the pitcher plant. More than 100 years ago, Queen Victoria of England chose the pitcher

- **1888** Newfoundland abandons British currency and adopts the dollar.
- **1892** The Great Fire destroys 2,000 buildings in St. John's.
- **1892** Dr. Wilfred Grenfell arrives from England to establish the Grenfell Mission.
- **1897** The first ferry service sails between North Sydney, Nova Scotia, and Port aux Basques, Newfoundland.
- **1897** Cabot Tower at Signal Hill is built.
- **1901** Sir Charles Cavendish Boyle, Governor of Newfoundland, writes the "Ode to Newfoundland."
- **1901** Marconi receives the first wireless signal from England at Signal Hill.
- **1904** France relinquishes rights to Newfoundland's "French Shore."
- **1908** William Coaker forms the Fishermen's Protective Union.
- **1912** The SS *Titanic* sinks off Cape Race after colliding with an iceberg.
- **1925** Newfoundland women get the vote by way of the Women's Suffrage Bill.
- **1927** Grenfell Mission Hospital is opened in St. Anthony, and Dr. Grenfell is knighted.

Canine Companions

Each of Newfoundland and Labrador's distinct geographic entities has its own namesake dog. The **Newfoundland dog** is a large animal with long black fur and webbed feet. Some Newfoundland dogs have a splash of white across their chest. In spite of their imposing size (weighing up to 54kg/119 lb. at 12 months), these dogs have a gentle, patient temperament that makes them ideal family pets. The history of the breed is marked by tales of strength, courage, and loyalty to their human masters. An example of their heroism can be found during the 1919 wreck of the SS *Ethie,* when the ship's Newfoundland dog jumped into the roaring sea and carried in a line, which was then secured by people on shore. The line was the lifeline by which the shipwrecked passengers were able to reach safety.

For only the second time in history, the Westminster Kennel Club awarded the 2004 Best In Show Trophy to a Newfoundland (Josh) at their 128th Annual Dog Show.

The province's other canine companion is another water-loving dog known as the **Labrador retriever.** Although they are similar to the Newfoundland in temperament, they are about half the size and have short, straight hair. As their name indicates, these dogs make excellent hunting companions.

plant to be engraved on a newly minted Newfoundland penny. In 1954, the Newfoundland Cabinet designated this fascinating plant as the official flower of the province. This unusual wine-and-green-colored flower can be found on bogs and marshes in Newfoundland and Labrador. You can see it growing on the hills surrounding Cape Spear and in Salmonier Nature Park. The plant gets its nourishment from insects that are trapped and then drowned in a pool of water at the base of its tubular leaves. If you stick your fingers into the death pod at the base of the plant, you're likely to pull out an insect or two. Don't worry: pitcher plants don't eat humans.

- **1927** Labrador becomes an official part of Newfoundland.
- **1932** Amelia Earhart takes off from Harbour Grace on her historic flight across the Atlantic.
- **1949** Newfoundland becomes a province of Canada, with Joseph Smallwood as its first premier.
- **1961** Forest fires force the evacuation of 9,000 people from 300 communities. A million acres and 35 homes are destroyed.
- **1965** The Fisheries Household Resettlement Program is introduced to encourage residents of remote outport communities to move to larger centers.
- **1965** The iron-ore mine at Wabush, Labrador, is opened.
- **1965** Newfoundland's 500,000th citizen, Bernard Joseph Hynes, is born at 2:25am on July 30 in the Twillingate Cottage Hospital.
- **1965** Come Home Year is instituted as a major tourism initiative.
- **1966** The Bell Island mine closes.
- **1966** The Newfoundland portion of the Trans-Canada Highway is completed.
- **1966** St. John's businessman Chesley Pippy donates the funds to establish Pippy Park.

continues

In summer, berries are everywhere. The most popular of the local berries is the bakeapple, internationally known as the cloudberry. The ripened berry is a cloudy orange-yellow color, and only one berry grows on each plant. Bakeapple plants grow approximately 7 to 10cm (2¾–4 in.) high—so you'll have to get down pretty low to pick them, but at least they're easy to spot because of their bright color. The berries are unique in flavor and generally ready for picking in mid-August, when you'll see many roadside stands selling basketfuls.

Another popular Newfoundland berry is the partridgeberry, internationally known as the lingonberry and a relative of the cranberry family. Each plant produces a single dark-red tart-tasting berry that usually ripens after the first frost in September. Both the bakeapple and the partridgeberry make excellent jams, spreads, and even wines that can be purchased at various shops throughout the province.

The Dark Tickle Company sells an array of local berry products from its Northern Peninsula factory outlet and online at **www.darktickle.com**. Across Labrador Straits, Pure Labrador (www.preserves.nf.ca) supplies a similar product.

ROCKS ON THE ROCK

Appropriately, Newfoundland—nicknamed the Rock—is rich in geological resources. Mistaken Point on the Avalon Peninsula has what are thought to be the world's oldest fossils, and you can find several other great places for fossil hunting throughout the province. Newfoundland's **Department of Natural Resources** (**© 709/729-2920;** www.nr.gov.nl.ca/nr) is a good resource for geology-specific maps and information.

Named the province's mineral emblem in 1975, labradorite is one of about 20 semiprecious stones found in Newfoundland and Labrador. You may spot it at a number of locations on the coast of Labrador and on the island of Newfoundland. Labradorite is an igneous, iridescent crystalline mineral (also known as Labrador feldspar) that looks like a piece of the Labrador night sky, with the colors of the aurora borealis captured inside. It's used to make lovely pieces of jewelry that you can purchase at various stores throughout the province.

WILDLIFE

Some 30 to 40 million seabirds, representing many different species, visit Newfoundland and Labrador each year. The favorite among these for most travelers is likely to be the provincial bird of Newfoundland: the Atlantic puffin, also known as the sea parrot or Baccalieu bird. Puffins are quite small compared to many other seabirds, and they're striking in appearance with their black-and-white plumage and

- **1967** Construction begins on the Churchill Falls hydroelectric generating station.
- **1969** Newfoundland introduces Medicare.
- **1969** The first ship is constructed at the Marystown shipyard.
- **1969** The Newfoundland Railway is closed.
- **1970** The Maritime Archaic Indian burial ground is discovered at Port au Choix.
- **1972** After 23 years in office, Premier Joseph Smallwood resigns.
- **1972** The Newfoundland dog is declared the province's official animal.
- **1973** The Newfoundland fishery is booming, with an estimated value of C$45 million.
- **1978** L'Anse aux Meadows is designated a UNESCO World Heritage Site.
- **1978** St. John's Day is celebrated for the first time, with parades, steak dinners, fish-splitting contests, and a street dance.
- **1979** Oil is discovered on the Grand Banks and the Hibernia well is established.
- **1979** The Matrimonial Property Act is passed, giving women financial rights in their marriage.
- **1980** The official Newfoundland flag is unveiled.

brightly colored, rounded beaks. They're exceptionally cute to watch, because their short wings seem to have difficulty supporting their chubby little bodies. Puffins need to flap their wings repeatedly to keep themselves in flight, lacking the grace or ease of flying exhibited by most birds. About 95% of all puffins in North America breed in colonies around the Newfoundland and Labrador coast.

The fertile waters of Newfoundland and Labrador are home to 22 species of whales; the more common species are the massive humpbacks and the much smaller minke whales. In fact, the waters around the province have the world's largest concentration of humpback whales. Between April and October, your chances of seeing a humpback fairly close to shore are quite good nearly anywhere in the province, with numbers peaking between June and September. The province also possesses the world's largest number of salmon rivers. The Main River near Corner Brook is the first Canadian Heritage River to be so designated in the province.

Only 14 land mammals are indigenous to the island of Newfoundland. Additional species have been introduced by humans—most notably the moose, which have taken quite nicely to the Rock and now number 130,000. Sufferers of ophidiophobia will be relieved to know that Newfoundland has no snakes.

However, certain land species are here in abundance. The province is home to one of the world's largest caribou herds, approximately 50,000 animals, at George River, Labrador. The island of Newfoundland also boasts North America's highest concentration of moose, as well as the continent's largest black bears, making the province an ideal destination for lovers of wildlife, whether you're hunting with a camera, a gun, or a fishing rod. Labrador is a great place for trophy fishing and for hunting black bear or caribou; Newfoundland offers fine moose hunting and salmon fishing. You can get a free copy of the *Hunting & Fishing Guide for Newfoundland & Labrador* through **Newfoundland & Labrador Tourism** (✆ **800/563-6353;** www.newfoundlandlabrador.com).

ICEBERGS

Thinking back to the untimely sinking of the *Titanic,* we all know that icebergs can be dangerous and even fatal if their vastness and power are not respected. Nevertheless, they are awe-inspiringly beautiful, and Newfoundland is one of the most accessible places in the world to see icebergs. Each spring, hundreds float southward from Greenland past Baffin Island and down the coast along Iceberg Alley. The largest iceberg spotted off the coast of Newfoundland was about 13km (8 miles) long, weighed more than 9 billion metric

- **1982** The offshore oil drill rig the *Ocean Ranger* sinks in a winter storm. All 84 lives aboard are lost.
- **1982** The provincial unemployment rate hits 20%.
- **1983** Construction begins on the first phase of the Trans-Labrador Highway.
- **1985** An Arrow jet crashes at Gander, killing 256 U.S. servicemen and crew.
- **1986** Legislation puts an end to the killing of seal pups.
- **1987** Gros Morne National Park becomes a UNESCO World Heritage Site.
- **1991** Former Premier Joseph R. Smallwood dies at 90 years of age.
- **1992** Ottawa enforces the Cod Moratorium in an attempt to replenish depleted cod stocks.
- **1993** Prospectors Al Chislett and Chris Verbiski discover the world's largest nickel deposit at Voisey Bay in northern Labrador.
- **1994** Recreational cod fishing is reintroduced to Newfoundland.
- **1998** The Royal Newfoundland Constabulary begins carrying firearms.
- **2001** The first oil is pumped from the Terra Nova oil field.

continues

tons, and likely took 3 years to make the journey from Greenland, where it would have calved off a gargantuan land-based glacier.

As the massive iceberg continues to float farther south into warmer waters, it weakens and begins to break apart into smaller, more manageable pieces. Bigger pieces that are comparable to the size of a large ship are called "growlers." Smaller chunks that may be the size of a car, a small house, or less are called "bergy bits." But for those of us who "come from away," it's equally exciting, whether we're fortunate enough to see a massive iceberg or just a piece of one in a lesser but still impressive form.

Newfoundlanders are respectful of icebergs. They know that one of the massive missives of compressed snow can break up or overturn at any time, taking with it a boat that has ventured too close. Seabirds seem to be able to sense when an iceberg is about to roll and will fly away just before it does its dangerous dance. Remember, only 10% of an iceberg's mass can be seen above the surface of the water, and the other 90% is submerged and cannot be seen.

When the bergs break up into growlers or bergy bits, they become more manageable and more predictable. This natural process has created some interesting opportunities for enterprising Newfoundlanders, who have begun marketing several innovative iceberg products.

Bergy bits are harvested and broken down into even smaller bits and used as ice cubes in drinks. There's something unique about iceberg ice because of its effervescence. Your drink will pop, crackle, and fizz when the air bubbles contained in the ice make contact with the liquid.

4 NEWFOUNDLAND & LABRADOR IN POPULAR CULTURE: BOOKS, FILM & MUSIC

BOOKS

Many books have been written about this colorful land, rich in history, culture, and natural resources. To make the most of your visit, I'd recommend reading at least a couple of the gems listed below.

Note: Some of these titles may be unavailable from your favorite local or Internet bookseller because of their limited distribution. If this is the case, try **Wordplay** (✆ **800/563-9100** or 709/726-9193; www.wordplay.com) for new and

- **2002** The province officially changes its name to Newfoundland and Labrador (and its postal abbreviation from NF to NL).
- **2004** Premier Danny Williams orders Canadian flags removed from provincial buildings in protest of federal policies regarding oil revenues.
- **2005** The government imposes a ban on smoking in public places, including restaurants and bars.
- **2005** The Rooms—a combined provincial museum, art gallery, and archives—opens in St John's.
- **2006** As a result of a land claim agreement with the government and the Inuit of Labrador, elections are held to form a government in Nunatsiavut.
- **2006** The federal census shows the population of Newfoundland and Labrador somewhat stable at 509,677.
- **2007** A new energy policy includes the go-ahead for a hydroelectric development on the Lower Churchill River.
- **2009** A Hebron Oil agreement is finalized between the provincial government and various companies. It is estimated that the first oil from this offshore field will be pumped in 2016.

out-of-print titles, or **Shop Downhome** (✆ **888/588-6353** or 709/722-2970; www.shopdownhome.com) for new books. Both of these outlets are located in St. John's and carry an exceptional variety of Newfoundland titles.

Of the many non-fictional accounts of Newfoundland and Labrador's history, none are more readable than *As Near to Heaven by Sea: A History of Newfoundland and Labrador,* by Kevin Major (Penguin Canada). Major does an admirable job of describing the many people and events that have contributed to the current-day personality of Newfoundland and Labrador—in under 500 pages.

Literally hundreds of books bring Newfoundland's history to life in a sympathetic and enduring form. One of the most recent is *River Thieves,* by Michael Crummey (Anchor Canada). This haunting tale, set in Newfoundland at the turn of the 19th century, depicts the uneasy relations between the Peyton family and the Beothuk Indians. Set in a similar era, *Curse of the Red Cross Ring,* by Earl B. Pilgrim (Flanker Press), is an enjoyable novel giving an insight into what it was like to be a Newfoundland fisherman in the late 19th and early 20th centuries. *Voyage of the Matthew: John Cabot and the Discovery of North America,* by Peter Firstbrook (McClelland & Stewart), is a detailed account of Cabot's history-making voyage more than 500 years ago to Bonavista, Newfoundland. *In the Hand of the Living God,* by Lilliane Bouzane (Turnstone Press), is a story about John Cabot's wife and the letters that were exchanged between her explorer husband and herself.

Much has been written about Joey Smallwood, the politician who brought Newfoundland into Confederation in 1949. One of the more readable tomes is *Smallwood: The Unlikely Revolutionary,* by Richard Gwyn (McClelland & Stewart). Better known is *The Colony of Unrequited Dreams,* by Wayne Johnston (Vintage Canada), a fantastic historical novel written by a Newfoundlander about the life and times of this Newfoundland hero and the land he so loved.

The Labradorians: Voices from the Land of Cain, by Lynne D. Fitzhugh (Breakwater Books), describes the challenges of settling the rugged untamed frontier. The book tells the story of mixed-race settlers and their battle to survive Labrador's harsh conditions. *The Danger Tree: Memory, War, and the Search for a Family's Past,* by David Macfarlane (Vintage Canada), is a memoir about a contemporary Newfoundland family and how current events have had an impact on their lives. Claire Mowat's *The Outport People* (Key Porter Books), originally published in 1983 but reprinted in 2005, tells of life in a remote fishing village, but from the perspective of an outsider. (The author is the wife of famed Canadian writer Farley Mowat.) A more recent tome, *Remarkable Stories of Newfoundland,* by Jack Fitzgerald (Creative Publishers), describes local traditions in an easy-to-read format.

Newfoundland & Labrador: Insiders' Perspectives, by James Tuck and Douglas House (Johnson Family Foundation), is a compilation of 24 short essays written by a variety of experts who call Newfoundland and Labrador home, including Dr. Tuck, an archaeologist from the Colony of Avalon. This is a great book to learn more about the province's history, politics, economics, people, culture, music, food, and natural history from people who work in the field. Plus, the book's compact size makes it ideal to bring along with you on your trip to the province.

FILM

The province of Newfoundland and Labrador stars as itself in many movies based on books. Read or watch any of the following, and you'll get a great feel for the province.

Best known is *The Shipping News,* a novel by E. Annie Proulx (Scribner), which tells the contemporary story about a troubled man coming home to his Newfoundland roots. The book was made into a movie that stars Kevin Spacey. The book *Rare Birds,* by Edward Riche (Doubleday Canada), is the humorous story about a man struggling to make a go with an unsuccessful restaurant in a Newfoundland outport. A 2002 movie based on the book and starring William Hurt was filmed in and around St. John's and nearby Petty Harbour.

Random Passage, by Bernice Morgan (Breakwater Books), is an enthralling novel about a young Irishwoman's 19th-century journey from England to Random Passage, a remote Newfoundland outport. The book was made into a 2002 CBS mini-series.

More recently, Gander played itself in the 2009 made-for-TV movie *Diverted,* which does an admirable job depicting the hospitality shown to air passengers diverted to Newfoundland on September 11, 2001.

MUSIC

The lively sounds of Celtic music can be heard throughout the province. The music was first brought across from England by Gaelic speakers over two centuries ago, but styles vary across the province, with the most traditional Irish music originating along the south shore. Here, the annual mid-summer Shamrock Festival provides a venue for visitors to soak up its captivating sounds. Traditional Celtic bands to watch for include The Irish Descendents, The Masterless Men, and Shanneyganock, who all perform throughout the province and beyond in pubs and at summer festivals. The Punters combine folk with rock and have a younger following, while Great Big Sea, a Celtic rock band, is the province's best-known export.

5 EATING & DRINKING IN NEWFOUNDLAND & LABRADOR

Traditional Newfoundland and Labrador cuisine revolves around simple cooking of locally available produce, game, and seafood—a style derived from the province's close ties with Great Britain. This unadorned style extends into most restaurants, where a full cooked breakfast may cost C$8 and a roast beef dinner will rarely set you back more than C$15.

Most seafood is deep-fried, even delicacies such as scallops. The exception is lobster (thankfully!), which is boiled and usually served with sides of melted butter, coleslaw, and a roasted potato. Fish and chips is an inexpensive favorite with the locals. You will get sizable portions of battered cod served with french-fried potatoes. Just remember that you automatically get cod when you order fish unless it's otherwise specified. A local delicacy is cod tongues, which are usually deep-fried, but request them pan-fried for the full effect. Fish and brewis is a longtime favorite that dates to the days of pre-refrigeration—the "fish" is salted cod and "brewis" is heavy, doughy bread. Wild game is common on menus along the Northern Peninsula, in Labrador, and better restaurants in St. John's. Caribou and moose come baked, braised, and in burgers, and both have a distinctively gamey taste.

The restaurant scene in St. John's is a little different from the one described above, although locals still flock to local pubs for simple meals, and to fish-and-chip shops, where everything is deep-fried.

Fun Facts **What's "Dressing"?**

Don't be surprised if you're asked if you want dressing and gravy with your fries. Just as Montrealers love their fries dipped in mayonnaise, many locals wouldn't want their fries unless they were smothered in dressing and gravy. As it relates to food, "dressing" in Newfoundland and Labrador usually means one thing: bread crumbs mixed with chopped onion, savory, and melted butter. Some people add diced celery, as well. In addition to its use as a side dish for french fries, it's also the stuffing of choice for roast turkey and chicken.

The difference in the capital is that a much wider choice of cuisines is offered, from family-style chain restaurants to traditional Thai. Best of all, a few of the better restaurants specialize in preparing local ingredients in healthy, creative ways not seen elsewhere. Prices in the city are also higher, with mains as high as C$35.

Warning: While the province boasts a smattering of fine-dining restaurants, Newfoundlanders have traditionally enjoyed simple—often deep-fried—cooking. Therefore, a local's answer to your query about favorite restaurants may lead you to a local fish-and-chip shop, as opposed to an elegant Italian eatery.

DRINKING

Newfoundlanders have a well-deserved reputation for enjoying a drink or two, whether it be among friends at a local festival or in one of the famous bars along George Street in St. John's. Popular North American beer brands are widely available, but those brewed locally by Quidi Vidi Brewing Co. are well worth trying.

You may be surprised to know that the drink most commonly associated with the province is actually from Jamaica. As early as the 1750s, salted cod was traded in Jamaica for rum, with its popularity with locals continuing to this day. It is imported in barrels, and then bottled and sold as Screech, a name which originated from the howl made by first timers downing a shot.

Easier than Screech to swallow is iceberg water, made from melted iceberg pieces. One popular brand is Canadian Iceberg Water. Just think: You're drinking water that's more than 10,000 years old! Canadian Iceberg Vodka and Canadian Iceberg Gin, both bottled in St. John's, are other interesting products made from the charcoal-filtered and triple-distilled water of iceberg growlers and bergy bits, and mixed with grain alcohol. Quidi Vidi Brewing Co. produces Iceberg Beer from local icebergs. Leave it to those fun-loving Newfoundlanders to get a buzz out of a berg!

3

Planning Your Trip to Newfoundland & Labrador

Newfoundland and Labrador is the official name for the province, which combines two very distinct regions. Newfoundland is an island, whereas Labrador is part of the mainland, adjacent to Quebec. The official abbreviation for the province is NL. A mere 3,050km (1,895 miles) from Ireland, Newfoundland is the closest point in North America to Europe. By comparison, the capital city of St. John's is double that distance from Victoria, the capital of Canada's most westerly province, British Columbia.

A visit to Canada's most easterly province takes planning, but your efforts will be amply rewarded. You'll be taken with the warmth of the people, always quick with a smile and a friendly greeting. You'll enjoy spontaneous walks off the beaten path as you go exploring for migratory birds and follow the sounds of unseen waterfalls. But first you have to get here. The information on the following pages is designed to make your travel planning as informed as possible.

For additional help in planning your trip and for more on-the-ground resources in Newfoundland and Labrador, please turn to "Fast Facts," on p. 228.

1 WHEN TO GO

WEATHER

As they say locally, "if you don't like the weather, just wait 5 minutes—it'll change." So, pack accordingly. Layered clothing and an oversize backpack or bag to carry your umbrella, rain gear, and an extra sweater are recommended.

You're apt to get the most stable weather, best whale-watching, and greatest variety of special events during July and August, but you'll also hit the highest prices and tightest availability for accommodations. Some of the most-visited places—such as St. John's and Trinity—book up well in advance during the summer, especially in St. John's during the first week of August. That's when you'll find the Royal St. John's Regatta, the Newfoundland & Labrador Folk Festival, and the George Street Festival happening simultaneously.

If you're especially keen on seeing icebergs, June is the best time to visit. You'll see a few stragglers along the northern peninsula as late as the end of July, but you're nearly guaranteed a few sightings if you visit earlier in the season.

The island of Newfoundland has a temperate marine climate, with winters offering an average norm of 0°C (32°F) and summer temperatures with an average of 16°C (61°F).

Labrador has a harsher winter climate, but its summer temperatures regularly hit upward of 25°C (77°F)—albeit for shorter periods.

The following chart provides the temperature ranges and precipitation rates for the capital city, as well as for St. Anthony on the Northern Peninsula. For current weather conditions at locations throughout

St. John's Average Temperatures (°C/°F) & Precipitation (mm/inches)

	Jan	Feb	Mar	Apr	May	June	July	Aug	Sept	Oct	Nov	Dec
Avg. High	–1/30	–2/28	1/34	5/41	11/52	16/61	20/68	20/68	16/61	11/52	6/43	1/34
Avg. Low	–9/16	–9/16	–6/21	–2/28	2/36	6/43	11/52	11/52	8/46	3/37	–1/30	–6/21
Precip.	140/ 5.5	131/ 5.2	120/ 4.7	108/ 4.3	95/ 3.7	91/ 3.6	85/ 3.3	102/ 4.0	112/ 4.4	139/ 5.5	154/ 6.1	146/ 5.7

St. Anthony's Average Temperatures (°C/°F) & Precipitation (mm/inches)

	Jan	Feb	Mar	Apr	May	June	July	Aug	Sept	Oct	Nov	Dec
Avg. High	–7/19/	–8/18	–3/26	1/34	6/43	12/54	17/63	17/63	12/54	6/43	1/34	–4/25
Avg. Low	–16/ 3.2	–16/ 3.2	–11/ 12	–5/ 23	–1/ 30	3/ 37	8/ 46	8/ 46	5/ 41	0/ 32	–5/ 23	–11/ 12
Precip.	107/ 4.2	90/ 3.5	101/ 4.0	87/ 3.4	89/ 3.5	114/ 4.5	104/ 4.1	120/ 4.7	126/ 5.0	117/ 4.6	119/ 4.7	124/ 4.9

the province, visit the **Environment Canada** website at **www.weatheroffice.gc.ca**.

HOLIDAYS

Newfoundland and Labrador respects all national statutory holidays, including New Year's Day, Good Friday, Easter Monday, Victoria Day (third Mon in May), Canada Day (July 1), Labour Day (first Mon in Sept), Thanksgiving (second Mon in Oct), Remembrance/Armistice Day (Nov 11), Christmas Day (Dec 25), and Boxing Day (Dec 26).

Holidays specific to Newfoundland and Labrador include St. Patrick's Day (Mar 17—usually just government offices and banks are closed), St. George's Day (fourth Wed in Apr), Discovery Day (fourth Tues in June), Orangeman's Day (second Sat in June), and Regatta Day (in St. John's, the first Wed in Aug, weather permitting).

Warning: Sunday shopping is not a given in Newfoundland and Labrador. You will find most shops open on Sunday afternoons in the larger centers, but many retail establishments in the smaller communities are not open at all on Sundays.

NEWFOUNDLAND & LABRADOR CALENDAR OF EVENTS

For an exhaustive list of events beyond those listed here, check http://events.frommers.com, where you'll find a searchable, up-to-the-minute roster of what's happening in cities all over the world.

FEBRUARY

Conception Bay South Winterfest, Conception Bay South, Route 60 (Avalon Peninsula). Break out of hibernation and into a sweat with free swims at the local swimming pool, free skating, and a hockey tournament. Call ✆ **709/834-6537** or visit **www.conceptionbaysouth.ca**. Mid-February.

Frosty Festival, Mount Pearl, St. John's. The community comes alive for 10 days of fun for all ages: dances, choral demonstrations, a co-ed personality pageant, dart competitions, and basketball tournaments. Call ✆ **709/727-6601** or visit **www.frostyfestival.ca**. Mid-February.

Winterlude, Grand Falls–Windsor, Route 1 (Central Region). Warm up your winter by taking part in one of these lively events. Includes a hockey tournament, figure skating competition, teen dances, snow sculpting, a bowling tournament, cross-country skiing, and more. Call ✆ **709/489-0418.** Mid-February.

Grand Bank Winter Carnival, Grand Bank, Route 220 (Eastern Region). Ten days of winter fun for all ages, including talent night, seniors' night, winter photography contest, a scavenger hunt, a torchlight parade, snow sculpturing, a snowman contest, a beard-growing competition, cross-country skiing, and traditional Newfoundland music and food. Call ✆ **709/832-2617** or visit **www.townofgrandbank.com**. Late February.

March

Newfoundland (All-Breed) Kennel Club Championship, St. John's. A panel of experts judges more than 100 dogs representing 50 different breeds, including (of course), Newfoundland dogs. Visit **www.newfoundlandkennelclub.com**. Early March.

Big Land Challenge, Happy Valley–Goose Bay. This 20km (12.4-mile) sled-dog race uses traditional sleds. Call ✆ **709/896-3489** or visit **www.biglandchallenge.com**. Second Saturday of March.

April

Smokey Mountain Annual Slush Cup, Labrador City, Route 500 (Labrador). Hosted by the local downhill ski resort, this wacky event commemorates the end of the winter season. Includes a ski run across open shallow water. Call ✆ **709/944-2129**. Mid-April.

May

Polar Bear Dip, Labrador City, Route 500 (Labrador). Are you brave enough to take the dip into the frigid waters of Northern Lake? Visit **www.labradorwest.com**. Late May.

June

National Aboriginal Day. This day is celebrated across the country, with local events held at Terra Nova National Park, North West River, Happy Valley–Goose Bay, and Nain. If sailing up the coast of Labrador is on your agenda, time your visit to coincide with this wonderful event in Nain, and you'll be able to participate in Inuit games and enjoy traditional foods. Go to **www.ainc-inac.gc.ca/nad** for a schedule of events. June 21.

July

Canada Day is commemorated across Newfoundland & Labrador, including at St. John's, Happy Valley–Goose Bay, Labrador City, Lewisporte, Port aux Basques, St. Anthony, and Stephenville, as well as at many provincial parks. Visit the Plan A Trip section of **www.newfoundlandandlabrador.com**. July 1.

Cow Head Lobster Festival, Cow Head, Route 430 (Western Newfoundland). Daily lobster suppers, an assortment of local crafts, family entertainment, local musicians, and fireworks highlight this festival.

This town also hosts the Gros Morne Theatre Festival throughout the summer, with extra shows scheduled throughout the festival.

Call ✆ **709/243-2446** or visit **www.cowheadlobsterfestival.ca.** First weekend of July.

Bird Island Puffin Festival, Elliston, Route 238 (Eastern Region). This festival features live local entertainment and one of the largest Jiggs dinners held in the province—prepared with vegetables from the town's historical root cellars. Call ✆ **709/468-7080** or see **www.puffinfestival.com**. Mid-July.

Labrador West Regatta, Wabush, Route 503 (Labrador). A smaller version of the St. John's Regatta, since 1973, this competition at Jean Lake has offered a series of Olympic-style rowing races combined with a fun day of games, food, and music. Call ✆ **709/944-7631** or visit **www.labradorwest.com**. Late July.

August

Newfoundland and Labrador Folk Festival, St. John's. The year's foremost celebration of traditional Newfoundland music, performed by some of the province's best-known musicians in downtown's Bannerman Park. Call ✆ **866/576-8508** or 709/576-8508, or visit **www.nlfolk.com**. Early August.

Big Hill Festival, Cox's Cove. The younger generation gathers for this large outdoor music concert attracting performers from throughout Canada. Call ✆ **709/688-2441** or visit **www.bighillfestival.ca**. First weekend in August.

Royal St. John's Regatta, St. John's. Join more than 40,000 spectators along the shore of Quidi Vidi Lake for North America's oldest continuous sporting event, the capital's biggest event of the year. Enjoy a full day of fixed-seat rowing competitions, in addition to games of chance, pony rides, and live music. Call ✆ **709/576-8921** or see **www.stjohnsregatta.org**. First Wednesday in August, weather permitting.

George Street Festival, St. John's. Serious partygoers will need to bank some zzz's in preparation for this event. Six days of live music, two dozen bars, a closed street, and as much liquid refreshment as your wallet allows—not to be missed! Visit **www.georgestreetfestival.com** for a complete schedule. Early August.

Bakeapple Folk Festival, Forteau, Route 510 (Labrador). A 4-day, mouth-watering celebration of the bakeapple (a wild berry found in only two places in the world: this province and Norway). In addition to irresistible desserts, this event includes folk music, knitted crafts, embroidered goods, games of chance, and children's activities. Call ✆ **709/931-2097.** Early August.

September

Festival of Colours, Corner Brook, Route 1 (Western Newfoundland). This celebration of fall's rich foliage includes craft fairs, storytelling, visual and performing arts, food fairs, dinner theater, and traditional music. Call ✆ **709/637-1584** or see **www.cornerbrook.com**. Mid-September through mid-October.

Festival of the Sea, Southern Avalon. Hosted in Ireland in odd-numbered years and in Newfoundland and Labrador in even years, this event celebrates the links between the two regions, with lots of traditional cooking and music. Call ✆ **709/227-5456** or visit **www.festivalofthesea.ca**. Third week of September.

October

St. John's International Women's Film Festival. Women filmmakers from around the world descend on St. John's for screenings, workshops, and seminars. Call ✆ **709/754-3141** or visit **www.womensfilmfestival.com**. Third week of October.

November

West Coast Craft Fair, Corner Brook, Route 1 (Western Newfoundland). The biggest and longest-running Christmas craft fair on Newfoundland's west coast has much to offer visitors, including demonstrations of crafting techniques. Call ✆ **709/753-2749** or visit **www.craftcouncil.nl.ca**. Third week of November.

Fun Facts Any Mummers Allowed In?

If you happen to be visiting the province during the Christmas season, don't be alarmed by a loud pounding on the door and the muffled cry of "Any mummers allowed in?" Mummering is a traditional working-class Christmas pastime. A group of people disguise themselves in outlandish costumes and visit various homes throughout the community, entertaining their delighted hosts with comic antics, energetic dancing, and music. The hosts join in the game by trying to guess the identity of their mysterious visitors. Mummers are often rewarded for their efforts with a drink of rum, and then they're off to the next house to continue the fun.

DECEMBER

Bay Roberts Festival of Lights, Route 70 (Avalon Peninsula). A 10-day event that kicks off with a tree-lighting ceremony and continues with community caroling, mummering (see "Any Mummers Allowed In?" above), and more. Call ✆ **709/786-2126** or visit **www.bayroberts.com/flights.htm**. Late December through early January.

New Year's Eve Celebration, St. John's. Dress warmly and prepare for an abundance of goodwill smooches from complete strangers. St. John's is the first city in North America to ring in the New Year (it's 30 min. ahead of Atlantic time). To commemorate that fact, the city hosts a terrifically popular midnight fireworks display from a barge floating in the middle of St. John's Harbour. Call ✆ **709/754-2489.** For street closure schedules, see **www.stjohns.ca**. December 31.

2 ENTRY REQUIREMENTS

ENTRY DOCUMENTS FOR U.S. CITIZENS

It is no longer possible to enter Canada and return to the U.S. by showing a government-issued photo ID (such as a driver's license) and proof of U.S. citizenship (such as a birth or naturalization certificate). The **Western Hemisphere Travel Initiative (WHTI),** which took full effect in 2009, requires all U.S. citizens returning to the U.S. from Canada to have a U.S. passport (this includes children under age 18).

In other words, if you are a U.S. citizen traveling to Canada by air, sea, or land, you must have a valid U.S. passport or a new passport card (see box below) in order to get back into the U.S.

You'll find current entry information on the website of the U.S. State Department at **www.travel.state.gov** and on the **Canada Border Services Agency** website, **www.cbsa-asfc.gc.ca**.

Permanent U.S. residents who are not U.S. citizens should carry their passport and Resident Alien Card (U.S. form I-151 or I-551). Foreign students and other noncitizen U.S. residents should carry their passport, a Temporary Resident Card (form 1688) or Employment Authorization Card

Passport Cards: The New Way to Enter Canada for U.S. Citizens

If you are traveling to and from Canada by land or sea in 2010, you can do so with the new **passport card** issued by the U.S. Department of State. The department adopted this idea in 2008 after vociferous complaints by border communities that requiring expensive passports for all visitors would harm local businesses dependent on easy cross-border access. Less expensive and more portable than the traditional passport book, the wallet-size passport card has the same validity period as a passport book: 10 years for an adult, 5 years for children 15 and younger. Adults who already have a passport book may apply for the card as a passport renewal and pay only $20. First-time applicants are charged $45 for adult cards and $35 for children.

The passport card contains a vicinity-read radio frequency identification (RFID) chip that links the card to a stored record in government databases. No personal information is written to the RFID chip itself. Note that **the passport card is valid for entry by land or sea only;** air travelers must have a valid U.S. passport. If you already have a passport, you may, of course, use that to enter Canada by land or sea. The passport card is also valid for travel to Mexico and the Caribbean. First-time applicants can apply at any one of the 9,300 Passport Acceptance Facilities across the U.S. For more information on passport cards and to locate the application office nearest you, visit www.travel.state.gov.

(1688A or 1688B), a visitor's visa, an I-94 arrival-departure record, a current I-20 copy of IAP-66 indicating student status, proof of sufficient funds for a temporary stay, and evidence of return transportation.

Visitors arriving by ferry from the U.S. must fill out International Crossing forms, which are collected before boarding.

ENTRY DOCUMENTS FOR COMMONWEALTH CITIZENS

Citizens of Great Britain, Australia, and New Zealand don't need visas to enter Canada, but they do need to show **proof of Commonwealth citizenship** (such as a **passport**), as well as evidence of funds sufficient for a temporary stay (credit cards work well here). Naturalized citizens should carry their naturalization certificates. Permanent residents of Commonwealth nations should carry their passports and resident status cards.

Foreign students and other residents should carry their passport, a Temporary Resident Card or Employment Authorization Card, a visitor's visa, an arrival-departure record, a current copy of student status, proof of sufficient funds for a temporary stay, and evidence of return transportation.

Note: With changing security regulations, it is advisable for all travelers to check with the Canadian consulate before departure to find out the latest in travel document requirements. You will also find current information on the **Canada Border Services Agency** website, **www.cbsa-asfc.gc.ca**; follow the links that appear on the Help page.

For Residents of Australia: You can pick up a passport application from your local post office or any branch of Passports Australia, but you must schedule an interview at the passport office to present your application materials. Call the **Australian Passport Information Service** at ✆ **131-232** or visit the government website at **www.passports.gov.au**.

For Residents of Ireland: You can apply for a 10-year passport at the **Passport Office,** Setanta Centre, Molesworth Street, Dublin 2 (✆ **353/1671-1633** or 890/426-888; **www.foreignaffairs.gov.ie**). Those under age 18 and over 65 must apply for a 3-year passport. You can also apply at 1A South Mall, Cork (✆ **353/21494-4700** or 890/426-900) or at most main post offices.

For Residents of New Zealand: You can pick up a passport application at any New Zealand Passports Office or download it from their website. Contact the **Passports Office** at ✆ **0800/225-050** in New Zealand or 04/474-8100, or log on to **www.passports.govt.nz**.

For Residents of the United Kingdom: To pick up an application for a standard 10-year passport (5-year passport for children under 16), visit your nearest passport office, major post office, or travel agency. You can also contact the **United Kingdom Passport Service** at ✆ **0870/521-0410** or search its website at **www.ips.gov.uk**.

CUSTOMS

You'll pass through **Canadian Customs** (✆ **800/461-9999** in Canada or 204/983-3500) upon arrival, and **U.S. Customs** (✆ **360/332-5771**), if you are traveling through the U.S., on your departure.

Arriving by air, you'll go through Customs at the airport once you clear passport control. (Even if you don't have anything to declare, Customs officials randomly select a few passengers and search their luggage.)

What You Can Bring into Canada

Your personal baggage can include the following: boats, motors, snowmobiles, camping and sports equipment, appliances, TV sets, musical instruments, personal computers, cameras, and other items of a personal or household nature. If you are bringing excess luggage, be sure to carry a detailed inventory list that includes the acquisition date, serial number, and cost or replacement value of each item. It sounds tedious, but it can speed things up at the border. Customs will help you fill out the forms that allow you to temporarily bring in your effects. This list will also be used by U.S. Customs to check off what you bring out. You will be charged Customs duties for anything left in Canada.

Tips Passport Savvy

Allow plenty of time before your trip to apply for a passport; processing normally takes 4 weeks but can take longer during busy periods (especially spring). And keep in mind that if you need a passport in a hurry, you'll pay a higher processing fee. When traveling, safeguard your passport in an inconspicuous, inaccessible place, such as a money belt, and keep a copy of the critical pages with your passport number in a separate place. If you lose your passport, visit the nearest consulate or embassy of your native country as soon as possible for a replacement.

Tips Don't Stow It—Ship It

Though pricey, it's sometimes worthwhile to travel luggage-free, particularly if you're toting sports equipment, meetings materials, or baby equipment. Specialists in door-to-door luggage delivery include **Luggage Forward** (www.luggageforward.com), **SkyCap International** (www.skycapinternational.com), and **Sports Express** (www.sportsexpress.com).

A few other things to keep in mind:

- If you're over 18, you're allowed to bring in 40 ounces of liquor and wine, or 24 12-ounce cans or bottles of beer and ale, as well as 50 cigars, 400 cigarettes, or 14 ounces of manufactured tobacco per person. Any excess is subject to duty.
- Gifts not exceeding C$60 and not containing tobacco products, alcoholic beverages, or advertising material can be brought in duty-free. Meats, plants, and vegetables are subject to inspection on entry. There are restrictions, so contact the Canadian Consulate for more details if you want to bring produce into the country, or check the Canada Border Services Agency website, www.cbsa-asfc.gc.ca.
- If you plan to bring your dog or cat, you must provide proof of rabies inoculation during the preceding 36-month period. Other types of animals need special clearance and health certification. (Many birds, for instance, require 8 weeks in quarantine.)

If you need more information concerning items you wish to bring in and out of the country, contact **Canada Border Services** (✆ **800/461-9999** in Canada or 204/983-3500; www.cbsa-asfc.gc.ca).

What You Can Take Home from Canada

For information on what you're allowed to bring home, contact one of the following agencies:

U.S. Citizens: U.S. Customs & Border Protection (CBP), 1300 Pennsylvania Ave., NW, Washington, DC 20229 (✆ **877/227-5511;** www.cbp.gov).

U.K. Citizens: Contact HM Customs & Excise at ✆ **0845/010-9000** (from outside the U.K., 020/8929-0152) or consult their website at www.hmrc.gov.uk.

Australian Citizens: Call Australian Customs Service at ✆ **1300/363-263** or log on to www.customs.gov.au.

New Zealand Citizens: New Zealand Customs, The Customhouse, 17–21 Whitmore St., Box 2218, Wellington (✆ **04/473-6099** or 0800/428-786; www.customs.govt.nz).

3 GETTING THERE & GETTING AROUND

GETTING TO NEWFOUNDLAND & LABRADOR

More than a thousand years ago, Leif Eriksson—acting on the rumored sighting of an unknown western land—stocked the Viking-era equivalent of a cargo ship with provisions, cattle, and tools. With only the most rudimentary navigational aids (a notched bearing dial, a sunstone, and the stars), Eriksson set out from Greenland. He and his crew braved the uncertain temper of the North Atlantic in an open

Destination Newfoundland and Labrador: Pre-Departure Checklist

- Are you carrying a passport?
- Do you have the address and phone number of your country's embassy or consulate with you?
- Do any lodging, restaurant, or travel reservations need to be booked in advance?
- To check in at a kiosk with an e-ticket, do you have the credit card you bought your ticket with or a frequent-flier card?
- If you purchased traveler's checks, have you recorded the check numbers and stored the documentation separately from the checks?
- Did you find out your daily ATM withdrawal limit?
- Do you have your credit card PIN? If you have a 5- or 6-digit PIN, did you obtain a 4-digit number from your bank?
- Did you stop the newspaper and mail delivery, and leave a set of keys with someone reliable?
- Did you pack your camera and an extra set of camera batteries?
- Do you have a safe, accessible place to store money?
- Did you bring your ID cards that could entitle you to discounts, such as AAA and AARP cards, student IDs, and so on?
- Did you bring emergency drug prescriptions, and extra glasses and/or contact lenses?
- Did you leave a copy of your itinerary with someone at home?

longboat for almost 3 weeks before reaching their destination. Proof of their landing can be found in L'Anse aux Meadows, on Newfoundland's northern peninsula. Fortunately for today's travelers, while the destination is just as enticing as it was for Eriksson, you no longer have to row your way across the Atlantic—unless you want to.

By Plane

Air Canada is the biggest player in Canada, offering two flight options: Air Canada's regular air service and its regional carrier Jazz. Between the two, you'll find connections from destinations around the world to St. John's, Gander, Deer Lake, and Happy Valley–Goose Bay. Call **Air Canada** at ✆ **888/247-2262** or visit them on the Web at **www.aircanada.com**.

WestJet is a low-fare airline from Western Canada that flies into St. John's from Halifax, with connections from there across the country. To compare prices, see **www.westjet.com** or call ✆ **888/937-8538.**

Provincial Airlines offers service from St. John's and Halifax to many of the smaller communities throughout Newfoundland and Labrador. For reservations, call ✆ **800/563-2800** or visit **www.provincialairlines.ca**. The customer service number is ✆ **709/576-3091.**

Air Labrador is an intraprovincial airline with connections from Montreal and St. John's to more than 20 Labrador and western Newfoundland communities. Call ✆ **800/563-3042** or 709/758-0002, or visit them online at **www.airlabrador.com**.

By Car

The vast majority of visitors arriving in Newfoundland by road do so by catching a ferry from North Sydney, Nova Scotia (see "By Boat," below), to either Port-aux-Basques, from where it's 905km (562 miles) to St. John's, or Argentia, a 90-minute drive to the capital. For information on driving within the province, see "Getting Around by Car," p. 44.

The only road access to the province is from Baie Comeau, Quebec, from where it's 570km (354 miles) of partly paved road to the Quebec/Newfoundland and Labrador border. From the border, the Trans-Labrador Highway continues eastward to Goose Bay. This is a remote, lightly traveled region of Canada, with few services and much advance planning needed for safe travel.

By Train

The island of Newfoundland isn't accessible by train, nor does it have an internal rail service. Limited rail service is available in western Labrador.

You can travel by train between Sept-Îles, Quebec, and Labrador West. The trip takes 7 hours. For information, contact **Tshiuetin Rail Transportation** at ✆ **866/962-0988** or 418/962-5530, or visit **www.tshiuetin.net**.

By Boat

Arriving by Ferry

Marine Atlantic offers service between North Sydney, Nova Scotia, and two points in Newfoundland. The shorter of the two is the 6-hour journey to Port aux Basques. Ferry service on this route operates year-round, with one-way fares of C$29 adults, C$15 children, and C$8 and up for vehicles. Extras include dorm beds (C$17) and cabins (from C$105).

If your primary destination is St. John's, you can take the approximately 14-hour sailing to Argentia, which is a 1½-hour drive from the capital city. This is a seasonal service that operates from mid-June to mid-September. One-way fares include C$81 adults, C$41 children, and C$168 and up for vehicles. A dorm bed is C$29 and cabins are C$153.

Give serious consideration to the additional cost for a cabin on the ferry, as fog and high winds can easily extend those 14 hours into 16 or 18 very long hours at sea. The more moderately priced cots are not a good choice for those who like their privacy or are even mildly claustrophobic.

Advance reservations are recommended for all sailings, and a C$25 deposit, payable through a major credit card, is required for reservations booked more than 48 hours prior to departure.

Contact **Marine Atlantic** at ✆ **800/341-7981** or 902/794-5200, or reserve online at **www.marine-atlantic.ca**.

Arriving by Private Vessel

If you're planning on sailing your own yacht to Newfoundland and Labrador, you should contact the **Canadian Coast Guard** (Search & Rescue) at **www.ccg-gcc.gc.ca**.

The volunteer **Canadian Coast Guard Auxiliary (CCGA)** offers information on boating safety and regulations you need to know while sailing Canadian waters. Visit them online at **www.ccga-gcac.com** for an online version of their *Safe Boating Guide*. The Newfoundland chapter of the CCGA can be reached by phone at ✆ **709/772-4074.**

GETTING AROUND

By Plane

Traveling by air is the best option if your time is limited. One suggestion would be to fly into St. John's, spend a few days touring the Avalon Peninsula, and then fly across to Deer Lake and pick up another rental car for exploring Gros Morne National Park.

In addition to Air Canada flights between St. John's, Gander, and Deer Lake, Provincial Airlines and Air Labrador combine to fly throughout the province, including as far north as Nain.

Air Saint Pierre (✆ **877/277-7765** or 902/873-3566; www.airsaintpierre.com) charges C$277 for a round-trip between St. John's and the islands of St. Pierre and Miquelon.

By Car

The **Trans-Canada Highway** (also known as Hwy. 1) starts in St. John's and heads west 905km (562 miles) across the province to Channel-Port-aux-Basques (about a 12-hr. drive), where you can hop the ferry to Nova Scotia. It is paved, but just two lanes wide most of the way.

You'll have the most fun—and meet the most interesting people—if you get off the Trans-Canada and take the smaller arteries into the coastal communities. ***Tip:*** You have to know ahead of time what each community offers and search out the ones that appeal to your specific interests. Otherwise, it would take months to visit them all.

Other than the Trans-Canada Highway, which has speeds of 90 or 100kmph (around 56–62 mph), the smaller regional routes have a maximum speed of 80kmph (around 50 mph), with speed limits being reduced to 50kmph (31 mph) once you enter many communities.

Warning: The island of Newfoundland is home to more than 150,000 moose. Extreme caution and reduced speeds are recommended when traveling any time between sunset and sunrise, as that's when the massive animals are most likely to be about.

Driving conditions can be severely hampered by the weather. Fog and heavy rains can happen unexpectedly, and roads are fairly narrow, leaving little room for error. Call ✆ **900/451-3300** for road conditions anywhere in the province, or ✆ **709/729-7669** for road conditions in St. John's or the Avalon Peninsula. See **www.roads.gov.nl.ca** for local road conditions, including highway webcams and moose advisories.

If you're adventuring into more remote areas, you'll find fewer gas stations (and any you encounter may not be open), so always check your tank, oil, tires, and windshield wipers before leaving a populated area.

On road trips, remember to wear your seat belt or risk facing a hefty fine. Motorcyclists are legally required to wear helmets. And the use of radar detectors is prohibited.

Renting a Car

You'll find that most of the popular rental companies have counters at the St. John's airport. If you're coming in peak season (July–Aug), be sure to book your rental as far in advance as possible.

If you're doing a cross-province trek, you'll need to find a rental company that will permit pickup in St. John's and drop-off at the Deer Lake airport. National Car Rental, which charges a drop-off fee of C$100, is the least expensive option. National is also a good company to choose if you're looking for a rental in some of the smaller communities, such as St. Anthony.

Tips Winter Driving Survival Kit

Include in the trunk of your car a scraper and brush; a shovel; booster cables; traction pads, sand, salt, or kitty litter (for traction on ice); a flashlight; flares; extra fuses, radiator hoses, and fan belts; blankets, sleeping bags, and extra winter clothing and footwear; a tow line or chain; an axe or hatchet; a supply of nonperishable food; and a first-aid kit. As an added precaution, make sure someone knows where you are traveling and when you expect to arrive at your destination.

Unlike elsewhere in Canada, where rental car companies offer unlimited mileage, you're generally looking at a rental price that includes an allowance of 200 or 300 kilometers (124–186 miles) per day, with an additional charge of C15¢ to C25¢ per additional kilometer. Deals change from time to time, so your best bet is to check the websites below.

Major companies and their contacts are **Avis** (✆ **800/879-2847;** www.avis.com), **Budget** (✆ **800/268-8900;** www.budget.com), **Hertz** (✆ **800/654-3131;** www.hertz.com), and **National** (✆ **800/227-7368;** www.nationalcar.com).

By Bus

DRL Coachlines offers scheduled bus service along the Trans-Canada Highway from St. John's west across the province. Stops include Gander, Grand Falls–Windsor, Deer Lake, Corner Brook, and Port-aux-Basques. Call ✆ **888/263-1854** or 709/263-2171 for details. You'll also find them online at **www.drlgroup.com**. DRL buses offer comfortable seats, air-conditioning, and onboard washroom facilities.

By Ferry

Provincial Ferry Services operate along 16 different routes. Some are short hops—in the case of Portugal Cove to Bell Island, an enjoyable day trip from St. John's.

For more extensive travel, there are three sailings you should be aware of. Between May and early January, daily ferry service crosses the Strait of Belle Isle from St. Barbe (Western Newfoundland) to Blanc-Sablon (Quebec), from where Route 510 winds up the southern Labrador coast. The one-way fare is C$7.50 for adults, C$6 for seniors and children, and C$23 per vehicle and driver. In Labrador, through summer, a passenger and freight ferry departs Happy Valley–Goose Bay, calling at some 20 isolated villages as far north as Nain, Labrador. The trip takes 2 days each way.

Reservations are recommended for both routes; call ✆ **866/535-2567.** You can check schedules at **www.tw.gov.nl.ca/ferryservices**.

If your destination is the French islands of St. Pierre and Miquelon, you'll need to catch the ferry from the town of Fortune on the Burin Peninsula. **St. Pierre Tours** offers walk-on passenger service only (no vehicles) to this little bit of France right off the southern coast of Newfoundland. It costs C$9 round-trip per adult. Call ✆ **800/563-2006** or 709/832-0429, or visit **www.spmtours.com** for reservations or more information.

4 MONEY & COSTS

The Value of the Canadian Dollar vs. Other Popular Currencies

C$	US$	UK£	Euro (€)	A$	NZ$
1	.95	.60	.65	1.05	1.30

Frommer's lists exact prices in the local currency. The currency conversions quoted above were correct at press time. However, rates fluctuate, so before departing consult a currency exchange website such as **www.oanda.com/convert/classic** to check up-to-the-minute rates.

It's always advisable to bring money in a variety of forms on a vacation to Canada: a mix of cash, credit cards, and traveler's checks. You should also exchange enough petty cash to cover airport incidentals, tipping, and transportation to your hotel

Tips **Go for Small Change**

When converting money into Canadian dollars, it's best to request $20 bills as the largest. Some businesses (especially corner stores and service stations) won't accept $50 or $100 denominations because of problems with counterfeiters.

before you leave home, or withdraw money upon arrival at an airport ATM.

CURRENCY

Canada uses both paper money and coins. Paper bills start at $5 and go up from there to $10, $20, $50, and $100. Coins include denominations from the penny up to the two-toned $2 toonie. The $1 coin (called the loonie) is slightly smaller and is brass-colored.

Although many places accept American dollars, it's better to arrive with Canadian currency. This is especially true if you are coming from a country other than the U.S., as Newfoundland and Labrador has no foreign currency house.

The prices of most goods in Newfoundland and Labrador are similar to those in the U.S. Canadian prices are higher for gas, liquor, and cigarettes, but you'll find prices for meals, accommodations, souvenirs, and clothing comparable to those in the U.S.

ATMS

The easiest and best way to get cash away from home is from an ATM (automated teller machine). The **Cirrus** (© **800/424-7787;** www.mastercard.com) and **PLUS** (© **800/843-7587;** www.visa.com) networks span the globe; look at the back of your bank card to see which network you're on, then call or check online for ATM locations at your destination. Be sure you know your personal identification number (PIN) and daily withdrawal limit before you depart.

Note: Remember that many banks impose a fee every time you use a card at another bank's ATM, and that fee can be up to C$5 for international transactions. In addition, the bank from which you withdraw cash may charge its own fee.

You can use your credit card to receive cash advances at ATMs. Keep in mind that credit card companies protect themselves from theft by limiting maximum withdrawals outside their home country, so call your credit card company before you leave home. And keep in mind that you'll pay interest from the moment of your withdrawal, even if you pay your monthly bills on time.

Note: Banks that are members of the **Global ATM Alliance** charge no transaction fees for cash withdrawals at other Alliance member ATMs; these include Bank of America, Scotiabank (Canada, Caribbean, and Mexico), Barclays (U.K. and parts of Africa), Deutsche Bank (Germany, Poland, Spain, and Italy), BNP Paribus (France), and Westpac (Australia and New Zealand).

CREDIT CARDS

Credit cards are another safe way to carry money. Visa and MasterCard are widely accepted across Newfoundland and Labrador. Other credit cards, such as American Express and Diners Club, are less widely accepted, especially at smaller businesses such as bed-and-breakfasts.

Credit cards provide a convenient record of all your expenses, and they generally offer relatively good exchange rates. You can also withdraw cash advances from your credit cards at banks or ATMs, provided you know your PIN. If you don't know yours, call the number on the back of your credit card and ask the bank to

Tips Small Change

When you change money, ask for some small bills or loose change. Petty cash will come in handy for tipping and public transportation. Consider keeping the change separate from your larger bills so that it's readily accessible and you'll be less of a target for theft.

send it to you. It usually takes 5 to 7 business days, though some banks will provide the number over the phone if you tell them your mother's maiden name or some other personal information.

Keep in mind that many banks assess a 1% to 3% transaction fee on *all* charges you incur abroad (whether you're using the local currency or U.S. dollars). But credit cards still may be the smart way to go when you factor in such things as exorbitant ATM fees and the higher exchange rates and service fees you'll pay with traveler's checks.

In Newfoundland and Labrador, Visa, MasterCard, and American Express are widely accepted in St. John's and across the province at major accommodations and gas stations. Outside of the capital, at places such as bed-and-breakfasts and small cafes, you should assume that credit cards aren't accepted.

TRAVELER'S CHECKS

Traveler's checks are something of an anachronism from the days before the ATM made cash accessible at any time. Given the fees you'll pay for ATM use at banks other than your own, however, you might be better off with traveler's checks if you're withdrawing money often.

The most popular traveler's checks are offered by **American Express** (✆ **800/807-6233,** or 800/221-7282 for card holders—this number accepts collect calls, offers service in several foreign languages, and exempts Amex gold and platinum cardholders from the 1% fee); **Visa** (✆ **800/732-1322**)—AAA members can obtain Visa checks for a US$9.95 fee (for checks up to US$1,500) at most AAA offices or by calling ✆ **866/339-3378;** and **MasterCard** (✆ **800/223-9920**).

Buying traveler's checks in Canadian dollars is useful if you're traveling beyond the major tourist areas and staying at locations such as bed-and-breakfasts. **American Express, Thomas Cook, Visa,** and **MasterCard** offer Canadian-dollar traveler's checks. You'll pay the rate of exchange at the time of your purchase (so it's a good idea to monitor the rate before you buy), and most companies charge a transaction fee per order (and a shipping fee if you order online).

If you do choose to carry traveler's checks, keep a record of their serial numbers separate from your checks in the event that they are stolen or lost. You'll get a refund faster if you know the numbers.

5 HEALTH

STAYING HEALTHY

Most larger communities in the province have hospitals and full medical service. Travelers who have a preexisting medical condition may wish to stay in a community offering full medical services; the more remote regions may be too far from emergency care.

Tips Dear Visa: I'm Off to Ferryland!

Some credit card companies recommend that you notify them of any impending trip abroad so that they don't become suspicious of foreign transactions and block your charges. If you don't call your credit card company in advance, you can still call the card's toll-free emergency number if a charge is refused—provided you remember to carry the phone number with you. Perhaps the most important lesson here is to carry more than one card, so you have a backup.

COMMON AILMENTS

GIARDIA Best known as "beaver fever," *Giardiasis* has been reported in Newfoundland and Labrador, with occasional boil-water advisories applying to those drinking even town water. Mostly, the concern is for those drinking water from sources such as ponds or rivers. The simplest preventive measure is to boil all water for at least 10 minutes.

Giardia is caused by an intestinal parasite that lives in freshwater. Once swallowed, its effects can be dramatic; severe diarrhea, cramps, and nausea are the most common.

WEATHER EXPOSURE Winter travel should not be undertaken lightly in Newfoundland and Labrador. Before setting out in a vehicle, check antifreeze levels and always carry a spare tire, and blankets or sleeping bags.

Dress for cold in layers, including a waterproof outer layer, and wear a warm wool cap or other headgear.

Frostbite is a major concern and sometimes deadly. Mild frostbite leaves a numbing, bruised sensation and the skin turns white. Exposed areas of skin (the nose and ears especially) are most susceptible.

Hypothermia occurs when the human body fails to produce heat as fast as it loses it. Exposure to cold weather, combined with fatigue and dampness, often leads to hypothermia. Warning signs include numbness, shivering, slurring of words, dizzy spells, and in extreme cases, unconsciousness and even death. The recommended treatment is to get the victim in a warm room, replace wet clothing with dry, and give hot liquids and sugary foods.

WHAT TO DO IF YOU GET SICK AWAY FROM HOME

If you get sick, consider asking your hotel concierge to recommend a local doctor—even his or her own. You can also try the emergency room at a local hospital. Many hospitals also have walk-in clinics for emergency cases that are not life-threatening; you may not get immediate attention, but you won't pay the high price of an emergency room visit.

If you suffer from a chronic illness, consult your doctor before your departure. For conditions such as epilepsy, diabetes, or heart problems, wear a **MedicAlert identification tag** (**✆ 888/633-4298;** www.medicalert.org), which will immediately alert doctors to your condition and give them access to your records through MedicAlert's 24-hour hot line.

Pack **prescription medications** in your carry-on luggage and carry prescription medications in their original containers, with pharmacy labels—otherwise, they won't make it through airport security. Also, carry copies of your prescriptions, in case you lose your pills or run out. Don't forget an extra pair of contact lenses or prescription glasses.

What Things Cost in Newfoundland & Labrador

The favorable exchange rate of the Canadian dollar against the U.S. dollar, the British pound, and the euro gives added value to whatever you buy. Prices in St. John's are generally a bit higher than other parts of the province. The exception is gas, which rises in price the further from the capital you are. With a limited number of rooms across the province, accommodation prices are not as seasonal as most other destinations, although it always pays to check online for packages. The prices I've listed below are approximate.

Taxi to/from St. John's airport to downtown	C$22.50
Bus fare in city	C$2.25
Cup of coffee	C$2.50
Pint of beer	C$6
Moderate hotel room	C$100–C$150
Comfortable bed and breakfast	C$70–C$100
Takeout fish and chips	C$10
Expensive 3-course dinner without wine	C$55–C$65

Carry the generic name of prescription medicines, in case a local pharmacist is unfamiliar with the brand name.

We list additional **emergency numbers** in "Fast Facts," p. 229.

6 SAFETY

Compared to other parts of the world, and even the rest of Canada, Newfoundland and Labrador is a relatively safe place to visit. Even though the level of property crime is low, take the same precautions you would elsewhere—never leave your vehicle unattended, try to avoid walking the inner city streets of St. John's after dark, and generally be aware of your surroundings.

Roads in general are well maintained, although winter driving requires extra care, and moose are a hazard year-round. (See "Moose Can be Hazardous to Your Health," p. 196).

7 SPECIALIZED TRAVEL RESOURCES

In addition to the destination-specific resources listed below, please visit Frommers.com for additional specialized travel resources.

GAY & LESBIAN TRAVELERS

The gay lifestyle is fully accepted in Newfoundland and Labrador. So much so that the province is developing a reputation as a destination for health-conscious same-sex couples. St. John's is gaining status as the San Francisco of the Eastern seaboard, with its Victorian architecture, fresh climate, hilly terrain, and the welcoming acceptance by local residents.

Avoiding "Economy Class Syndrome"

Deep vein thrombosis, or as it's known in the world of flying, "economy-class syndrome," is a blood clot that develops in a deep vein. It's a potentially deadly condition that can be caused by sitting in cramped conditions—such as an airplane cabin—for too long. During a flight (especially a long-haul flight), get up, walk around, and stretch your legs every 60 to 90 minutes to keep your blood flowing. Other preventive measures include frequent flexing of the legs while sitting, drinking lots of water, and avoiding alcohol and sleeping pills. If you have a history of deep vein thrombosis, heart disease, or another condition that puts you at high risk, some experts recommend wearing compression stockings or taking anticoagulants when you fly; always ask your physician about the best course for you. Symptoms of deep vein thrombosis include leg pain or swelling, or even shortness of breath.

Curious, Holdsworth Court, George St. (✆ **709/722-6999**) is the only dedicated gay nightclub in St. John's.

The **International Gay and Lesbian Travel Association (IGLTA; ✆ 800/448-8550** or 954/776-2626; www.iglta.org) is the trade association for the gay and lesbian travel industry and offers an online directory of gay- and lesbian-friendly travel businesses; go to their website and click on the Members link.

Many agencies offer tours and itineraries specifically for gay and lesbian travelers. **Now, Voyager** (✆ **800/255-6951** or 415/626-1169; www.nowvoyager.com) is a well-known San Francisco–based, gay-owned and -operated travel service. **Gay.com Travel** (✆ **800/929-2268** or 415/644-8044; http://travel.gay.com) provides regularly updated information about gay-owned, gay-oriented, and gay-friendly lodging, dining, sightseeing, nightlife, and shopping establishments in Canada and elsewhere.

The Canadian website **GayTraveler** (www.gaytraveler.ca) offers ideas and advice for gay travel all over the world.

The following travel guides are available at many bookstores, or you can order them from any online bookseller: ***Spartacus International Gay Guide,* 35th Edition** (Bruno Gmünder Verlag; www.spartacusworld.com/gayguide) and the ***Damron*** guides (www.damron.com), which publishes separate annual books for gay men and lesbians.

TRAVELERS WITH DISABILITIES

Most disabilities shouldn't stop anyone from traveling. There are more options and resources out there than ever before.

Newfoundland and Labrador may be a step behind some of the more populated Canadian centers in terms of providing service for persons with disabilities, but it is making progress. Part of the charm of visiting Newfoundland and Labrador is having the opportunity to stay at privately run bed-and-breakfasts, and many, if not most of them, are not accessible to people with mobility problems. Some locations may be "wheelchair friendly" and offer a room or two on the main floor, but the second- and third-floor rooms, with their beautiful winding staircases, will not be accessible.

Organizations that offer a vast range of resources and assistance to disabled travelers include **MossRehab** (✆ **800/CALL-MOSS;** www.mossresourcenet.org); the **American Foundation for the Blind**

(**AFB; ✆ 800/232-5463;** www.afb.org); and **Society for Accessible Travel & Hospitality (SATH; ✆ 212/447-7284;** www.sath.org). **AirAmbulanceCard.com** (**✆ 877/424-7633;** www.airambulance card.com) provides medical air evacuation for its members.

Access-Able Travel Source (**✆ 303/232-2979;** www.access-able.com) offers a comprehensive database on travel agents from around the world with experience in accessible travel; destination-specific access information; and links to such resources as service animals, equipment rentals, and access guides.

Many travel agencies offer customized tours and itineraries for travelers with disabilities. Among them are **Flying Wheels Travel** (**✆ 507/451-5005;** www.flying wheelstravel.com), and **Accessible Journeys** (**✆ 800/846-4537** or 610/521-0339; www.disabilitytravel.com).

Flying with Disability (www.flying-with-disability.org) is a comprehensive information source on airplane travel. **Avis Rent a Car** (**✆ 888/879-4273**) has an "Avis Access" program that offers services for customers with special travel needs. These include specially outfitted vehicles with swivel seats, spinner knobs, and hand controls; mobility scooter rentals; and accessible bus service. Be sure to reserve well in advance.

For more information specifically targeted to travelers with disabilities, the community website **www.accesstotravel.gc.ca** has destination guides and several regular columns on accessible travel. Also check out the quarterly magazine ***Emerging Horizons*** (www.emerginghorizons.com) and ***Open World*** magazine, published by SATH (see above). The Accessible Travel link at **Mobility-Advisor.com** (www. mobility-advisor.com) also offers a variety of travel resources to disabled persons.

British travelers should contact **Tourism For All** (**✆ 0845/124-9971** in UK only; www.tourismforall.org.uk) to access a wide range of travel information and resources for disabled and elderly people.

FAMILY TRAVEL

If you have enough trouble getting your kids out of the house in the morning, dragging them thousands of miles away may seem like an insurmountable challenge. But family travel can be immensely rewarding, giving you new ways of seeing the world through the eyes of children.

Vacationing with a family does require advance planning, especially to Newfoundland and Labrador, where you will spend long hours on the road and not all accommodations are suited to children, especially younger ones. An ideal scenario from St. John's is to limit your travels to the eastern half of the island, making the **Splash-n-Putt** (p. 156) your turnaround point. In the vicinity is **Terra Nova Resort** (p. 153), one of the province's most kid-friendly lodgings, and **Terra Nova National Park,** with an excellent summer activity program.

Recommended family travel websites include **Family Travel Forum** (www.family travelforum.com), a comprehensive site that offers customized trip planning; **Family Travel Network** (www.familytravel network.com), an award-winning site that offers travel features, deals, and tips; **www. travelwithyourkids.com**, a comprehensive site offering sound advice for long-distance and international travel with children; and **Family Travel Files** (www. thefamilytravelfiles.com), which offers an online magazine and a directory of off-the-beaten-path tours that includes Newfoundland and Labrador.

To locate accommodations, restaurants, and attractions that are particularly kid-friendly, refer to the Kids icon throughout this guide.

WOMEN TRAVELERS

Women traveling to Newfoundland and Labrador will find themselves welcomed throughout the province and, in smaller communities, regarded with interest and respect for wanting to explore on their own.

Check out the award-winning website **Journeywoman** (www.journeywoman.com), a "real life" women's travel-information network where you can sign up for a free e-mail newsletter and get advice on everything from etiquette and dress to safety. The travel guide ***Safety and Security for Women Who Travel*** by Sheila Swan and Peter Laufer (Travelers' Tales Guides) offers common-sense tips on safe travel.

For general travel resources for women, go to www.frommers.com/planning.

SENIOR TRAVEL

Recognizing the importance of mature travelers to the tourism industry, most establishments will reward seniors' patronage with a special discount. However, just who qualifies for a seniors' discount is determined by each provider. Some companies offer seniors' rates to anyone over 50. For others, you must be 65. If you are 50 or older, don't hesitate to ask if you are eligible for a discount—it could add up to substantial savings.

Members of **AARP** (formerly known as the American Association of Retired Persons), 601 E St. NW, Washington, DC 20049 (✆ **888/687-2277;** www.aarp.org), get discounts on hotels, airfares, and car rentals. AARP offers members a wide range of benefits, including *AARP: The Magazine* and a monthly newsletter. Anyone over 50 can join.

Many reliable agencies and organizations target the 50-plus market. **Elderhostel** (✆ **800/454-5768;** www.exploritas.org) arranges study programs for those ages 55 and older (and a spouse or companion of any age) across Newfoundland and Labrador, and around the world. Most courses last 5 to 7 days, and many include airfare, accommodations in university dormitories or modest inns, meals, and tuition.

Recommended publications offering travel resources and discounts for seniors include the quarterly magazine ***Travel 50 & Beyond*** (www.travel50andbeyond.com); ***101 Tips for Mature Travelers,*** available from Grand Circle Travel (✆ **800/221-2610** or 617/350-7500; www.gct.com); and ***Unbelievably Good Deals and Great Adventures That You Absolutely Can't Get Unless You're Over 50*** (McGraw-Hill), by Joann Rattner Heilman.

STUDENT TRAVEL

The **International Student Travel Confederation** (**ISTC;** www.istc.org) was formed in 1949 to make travel around the world more affordable for students. Check out its website for comprehensive travel services information and details on how to get an **International Student Identity Card (ISIC),** which qualifies students for substantial savings on rail passes, plane tickets, entrance fees, and more. It also provides students with basic health and life insurance, and a 24-hour helpline. The card is valid for a maximum of 18 months. You can apply for the card online or in person at **STA Travel** (✆ **800/781-4040** in North America; www.statravel.com), the biggest student travel agency in the world; check out the website to locate STA Travel offices worldwide. If you're no longer a student but are still under age 26, you can get an **International Youth Travel Card (IYTC)** from the same people, which entitles you to some discounts. **Travel CUTS** (✆ **800/592-2887;** www.travelcuts.com) offers similar services for both Canadians and U.S. residents. Irish students may prefer to turn to **USIT** (✆ **01/602-1904;** www.usit.ie), an Ireland-based specialist in student, youth, and independent travel.

Students who would like to attend lectures, seminars, concerts, and other events can contact **Brock University,** 500

Glenridge Ave., St. Catharines (✆ **905/688-5550**; www.brocku.ca) or **Niagara College** (✆ **905/641-2252**; www.niagarac.on.ca) for information on all campuses (Welland, St. Catharines, Niagara Falls, and Grimsby).

8 SUSTAINABLE TOURISM

Although Newfoundland and Labrador lags behind the rest of Canada in day-to-day green initiatives, the province's most recent energy plan incorporates concerns about climate change. Hydro-electric schemes in Labrador, which continue to be built, are a wonderful alternative to using fossil fuels, but are in place more for self-reliance than the greater good of the world. In 2009, a wind farm, the province's first, began operation on the Burin Peninsula. It has the capacity to power around 7,000 local homes. A small number of tourism-related businesses actively promote minimizing their impact on the environment. The Delta St. John's, for example, touts an "eco-green rating" but when I visited the hotel, no one seemed to know what the rating was or how it had been earned. Newfoundland has just one organic farm, on the outskirts of the capital, which sells its produce at the local farmers' market.

Transportation is the biggest source of CO_2 emissions, and with Newfoundland and Labrador being such a remote destination, it is impossible for visitors to not contribute to the problem.

Each time you take a flight or drive a car, CO_2 is released into the atmosphere. You can help neutralize this danger to our planet through "carbon offsetting"—paying someone to reduce your CO_2 emissions by the same amount you've added. Carbon offsets can be purchased in the U.S. from companies such as **Carbonfund.org** (www.carbonfund.org) and **TerraPass** (www.terrapass.org), from **Offsetters** (www.offsetters.ca) in Canada, and from **Climate Care** (www.jpmorganclimatecare.com) in the U.K.

Although one could argue that any vacation that includes an airplane flight can't be truly "green," you can go on holiday and still contribute positively to the

It's Easy Being Green

We can all help conserve fuel and energy when we travel. Here are a few simple ways you can help preserve your favorite destinations:

- Whenever possible, choose nonstop flights; they generally require less fuel than those that must stop and take off again.
- If renting a car is necessary on your vacation, ask the rental agent for the most fuel-efficient one available.
- At hotels, request that your sheets and towels not be changed daily. You'll save water and energy by not washing them as often, and you'll prolong the life of the towels, too. (Many hotels already have programs like this in place.)
- Turn off the lights and air-conditioner (or heater) when you leave your hotel room.

General Resources for Green Travel

In addition to the resources for Newfoundland and Labrador listed above, the following websites provide valuable wide-ranging information on sustainable travel. For a list of even more sustainable resources, as well as tips and explanations on how to travel greener, visit www.frommers.com/planning.

- **Responsible Travel** (www.responsibletravel.com) is a great source of sustainable travel ideas; the site is run by a spokesperson for ethical tourism in the travel industry. **Sustainable Travel International** (www.sustainable travelinternational.org) promotes ethical tourism practices and manages an extensive directory of sustainable properties and tour operators around the world.
- In the U.K., **Tourism Concern** (www.tourismconcern.org.uk) works to reduce social and environmental problems connected to tourism. The **Association of Independent Tour Operators (AITO)** (www.aito.co.uk) is a group of specialist operators leading the field in making holidays sustainable.
- In Canada, **www.greenlivingonline.com** offers extensive content on how to travel sustainably, including a travel and transport section, and profiles of the best green shops and services in Ottawa, Toronto, Vancouver, and Calgary.
- **Carbonfund.org** (www.carbonfund.org) and **TerraPass** (www.terrapass.org) provide info on "carbon offsetting," or offsetting the greenhouse gas emitted during flights.
- **Greenhotels** (www.greenhotels.com) recommends green-rated member hotels around the world that fulfill the company's stringent environmental requirements. **Environmentally Friendly Hotels** (www.environmentally friendlyhotels.com) offers more green accommodation ratings. The **Green Key Eco-Rating Program** (www.greenkeyglobal.com) audits the environmental performance of U.S. and Canadian hotels, motels, and resorts.

environment. You can offset carbon emissions from your flight in other ways. Choose forward-looking companies that embrace responsible development practices, helping preserve destinations for the future by working alongside local people. An increasing number of sustainable tourism initiatives can help you plan a family trip and leave as small a "footprint" as possible on the places you visit.

You can find eco-friendly travel tips, statistics, and touring companies and associations—listed by destination on the Ecotourism Explorer page under Your Travel Choice—at the **International Ecotourism Society** website, www.ecotourism.org. Also check out **Conservation International** (www.conservation.org), which, with *National Geographic Traveler,* annually presents **World Legacy Awards** (www.nationalgeographic.com/traveler/world legacy_winners.html) to those travel tour operators, businesses, organizations, and places that have made a significant contribution to sustainable tourism.

9 SPECIAL INTEREST TRIPS & ESCORTED GENERAL INTEREST TOURS

SPECIAL INTEREST TRIPS

Adventure Canada offers a changing schedule of expeditions aboard a small ship. Trips include high-profile tour guides (they regularly include celebrity biologists, top photographers, and distinguished chefs). You'll pay at least C$3,800 per person for a double cabin on a voyage that begins and ends in St. John's. For more information, call **Adventure Canada** at ✆ **800/363-7566** or 905/271-4000, or visit them online at www.adventurecanada.com.

ESCORTED GENERAL INTEREST TOURS

Escorted tours are structured group tours, with a group leader. The price usually includes everything from airfare to hotels, meals, tours, admission costs, and local transportation. One of the best choices of local tours is offered by **Ambassatours,** part of the Grayline tour company. Their 13-day Circle Newfoundland and Labrador tour starts and ends in Halifax, and takes advantage of both ferry services to cross the island without backtracking. The cost of C$2,780 includes hotel accommodations and all meals. The 8-day Viking Trail tour costs C$1,833 and concentrates on western Newfoundland highlights such as Gros Morne National Park and L'Anse aux Meadows, and also includes the Labrador Straits. Contact **Ambassatours** at ✆ **800/565-7173** or 902/423-6242, or visit www.ambassatours.com. **Collette Vacations** (✆ **800/340-5158;** www.collette tours.com) runs a 12-day Newfoundland and Labrador tour that begins and ends in St. John's. The cost is C$2,500.

Tour operators offering Newfoundland and Labrador packages are listed on the province's tourism website: **www.newfoundland labrador.com**.

One company, **Maxxim Vacations,** has 15 years' experience in packaging theme trips to Newfoundland and Labrador that include visiting local movie sites; taking in a Viking Trail experience; getting immersed in the traditional culture; visiting the offshore French islands; or participating in road races, golf, or skiing. Call ✆ **800/567-6666** or 709/754-6666 to request their brochure or visit www.maxxim vacations.com.

Elderhostel, the not-for-profit organization dedicated to providing learning adventures for people 55 and older, offers a good variety of inexpensively priced Newfoundland and Labrador experiences. Visit www.exploritas.org, or call ✆ **800/454-5768** to receive a copy of their catalog.

Despite the fact that escorted tours require big deposits and predetermine hotels, restaurants, and itineraries, many people derive security and peace of mind from the structure they offer. Escorted tours—whether they're navigated by bus or boat—let travelers sit back and enjoy the trip without having to drive or worry about details. They take you to the maximum number of sights in the minimum amount of time with the least amount of hassle. They're particularly convenient for people with limited mobility, and they can be a great way to make new friends.

On the downside, you'll have little opportunity for serendipitous interactions with locals. The tours can be jam-packed with activities, leaving little room for individual sightseeing, whim, or adventure—plus, they also often focus on the heavily touristed sites, so you miss out on many a lesser-known gem.

For more information on escorted general-interest tours, including questions to

Ask Before You Go

Before you invest in a package deal or an escorted tour:

- Always ask about the **cancellation policy.** Can you get your money back? Is there a deposit required?
- Ask about the **accommodations choices and prices** for each. Then, look up the hotels' reviews in a Frommer's guide and check their rates online for your specific dates of travel. Also, find out what types of rooms are offered.
- Request a complete **schedule** (escorted tours only).
- Ask about the **size** and demographics of the group (escorted tours only).
- Discuss what is included in the **price** (transportation, meals, tips, airport transfers, etc.).
- Finally, look for **hidden expenses.** Ask whether airport departure fees and taxes, for example, are included in the total cost—they rarely are.

ask before booking your trip, see www.frommers.com/planning.

PACKAGE TOURS

Package tours are simply a way to buy the airfare, accommodations, and other elements of your trip (such as car rentals, airport transfers, and sometimes even activities) at the same time and often at discounted prices.

One good source of package deals is the airlines themselves. You can book hotels and rental cars through the websites of both Canada's major airlines, **Air Canada** (www.aircanada.com) and **WestJet** (www.westjet.com), in conjunction with your flight to Newfoundland and Labrador.

Many accommodations bundle rooms with local activities. **Delta St. John's** (www.deltahotels.com; p. 85) has some excellent deals, even in midsummer. Also in the capital, check the Sheraton Newfoundland website (www.starwoodhotels.com/sheraton; p. 86). Packages offered by smaller lodgings are usually more about convenience than getting a great deal. Two standouts are **Terra Nova Resort** (www.terranovagolf.com; p. 153), which offers multi-night golf packages; and **Marble Inn,** in Western Newfoundland (www.marbleinn.com; p. 180), which bundles summer or winter activities with accommodations.

10 STAYING CONNECTED

TELEPHONES

To call Newfoundland and Labrador:

1. Dial the international access code: 00 from the U.K., Ireland, or New Zealand; or 0011 from Australia (the international access code is not required for calls within North America).
2. Dial the country code, 1.
3. Dial the Newfoundland and Labrador area code, **709,** and then the number.

Online Traveler's Toolbox

Veteran travelers usually carry some essential items to make their trips easier. Following is a selection of handy online tools to bookmark and use:

- **Airplane Seating and Food** (www.airlinemeals.net)
- **Environment Canada** (www.weatheroffice.gc.ca)
- **Mapquest** (www.mapquest.com)
- **Time and Date** (www.timeanddate.com)
- **Universal Currency Converter** (www.xe.com/ucc)
- **Visa ATM Locator** (www.visa.com); **MasterCard ATM Locator** (www.mastercard.com)
- **Newfoundland and Labrador Tourism** (www.newfoundlandlabrador.com)

To make international calls: To make international calls from Newfoundland and Labrador, first dial 011 and then the country code (U.K. 44, Ireland 353, Australia 61, New Zealand 64). Next, you dial the area code and number. For example, if you wanted to call Holiday Care in Great Britain, you would dial ✆ **011-44-845-124-9971.**

For directory assistance: Dial ✆ **411** if you're looking for a Newfoundland and Labrador phone number from within the province. Call ✆ **709/555-1212** to find a Newfoundland and Labrador number from outside the province.

For operator assistance: If you need operator assistance in making a call, dial 0.

Toll-free numbers: Numbers beginning with 866, 877, and 888 dialed within Newfoundland and Labrador are toll-free but may not be accessible from elsewhere in Canada or the United States. In general, calling a 1-800 number is toll-free within North America.

CELLPHONES

Just because your cellphone works at home doesn't mean it'll work in Newfoundland and Labrador. It's a good bet that your phone will work in St. John's and other cities such as Gander and Corner Brook, but beyond these population centers, coverage is almost nonexistent.

The three letters that define much of the world's **wireless capabilities** are GSM (Global System for Mobiles), a big, seamless network that makes for easy cross-border cellphone use throughout Europe and dozens of other countries worldwide. In the U.S., T-Mobile, AT&T Wireless, and Cingular use this quasi-universal system; in Canada, Microcell and some Rogers customers are GSM, and all Europeans and most Australians use GSM.

If your cellphone is on a GSM system and you have a world-capable multiband phone, such as many Sony Ericsson, Motorola, or Samsung models, you can make and receive calls across civilized areas around much of the globe, from Andorra to Uganda. Just call your wireless operator and ask for international roaming to be activated on your account. Unfortunately, per-minute charges can be high—usually C$1 to C$1.50 in Canada. That's why it's important to buy an unlocked world phone from the get-go. Many cellphone operators sell locked phones that restrict you from using any other removable computer memory phone chip (called a **SIM card**) than the ones they supply. Having an unlocked phone allows you to install a cheap, prepaid SIM card (found at a local retailer) in Canada. (Show your phone to the salesperson; not all phones work on all networks.) You'll get a local phone number—and much, much lower calling rates. Unlocking an already locked phone can be complicated, but it can be done; just call your cellular operator and say you'll be going abroad for several months and want to use the phone with a local provider.

Two good wireless rental companies are **InTouch Global** (✆ **800/872-7626;** www.intouchglobal.com) and **Roadpost** (✆ **888/290-1616** or 905/272-4934; www.roadpost.com, or www.roadpost.ca in Canada). Give them your itinerary, and they'll tell you what wireless products you need. InTouch will also, for free, advise you on whether your existing phone will work overseas; simply call ✆ **703/222-7161** between 9am and 4pm EST, or go to http://intouchglobal.com/travel.htm.

For trips of more than a few weeks, **buying a phone** becomes economically attractive, as Canada has a cheap, no-questions-asked prepaid phone system. Stop by **Rogers,** at 48 Kenmount Rd., St. John's (✆ **709/753-5262;** www.rogers.ca) and ask about their Pay As You Go packages; you'll pay less than C$100 for a phone and a starter calling card.

VOICE OVER INTERNET PROTOCOL (VOIP)

If you have Internet access while traveling, you might consider a broadband-based telephone service (in technical terms, **Voice over Internet Protocol,** or **VoIP**), such as Skype (www.skype.com) or Vonage (www.vonage.com), which allows you to make free international calls if you use its services from your laptop or in a cybercafe. The people you're calling must also use the service for it to work; check the sites for details.

INTERNET & E-MAIL

Travelers have any number of ways to check their e-mail and access the Internet on the road. Of course, using your own laptop—or even a PDA (personal digital assistant) or electronic organizer with a modem—gives you the most flexibility. But even if you don't have a computer, you can still access your e-mail and even your office computer from cybercafes.

Without Your Own Computer

Newfoundland and Labrador is well connected, with public libraries across the province offering free Internet access. For locations and hours, contact **Newfoundland and Labrador Public Libraries** at ✆ **709/643-0900** or visit www.nlpubliclibraries.ca. But the best resource by far is the **Community Access Program (CAP),** a government initiative that is represented in over 150 Newfoundland and Labrador communities. Usually set up in a room in a local community hall, these access centers have computers hooked up to the Internet, as well as scanners and printers. The cost of getting online is minimal or free. For locations, hours, and services, call ✆ **877/929-1829** or 709/729-1828, or visit www.nfcap.nf.ca.

With Your Own Computer

Newfoundland and Labrador has a growing number of Wi-Fi (wireless fidelity) "hotspots," from where you can get high-speed Internet connection without cable wires or a phone line. At the time of writing, St. John's International Airport, the Marine Atlantic ferries from Nova Scotia, many hotels, and some bed-and-breakfasts and cafes offer Wi-Fi service.

Many Newfoundland and Labrador accommodations have dataports for laptop modems. **Call the lodging in advance** to see what your options are. In addition, major Internet service providers (ISPs) have **local access numbers** around the world, allowing you to go online by placing a local call. Check your ISP's website, or call its toll-free number and ask how

Frommers.com: The Complete Travel Resource

Planning a trip or just returned? Head to **Frommers.com,** voted Best Travel Site by *PC Magazine.* We think you'll find our site indispensable before, during, and after your travels—with expert advice and tips; independent reviews of hotels, restaurants, attractions, and preferred shopping and nightlife venues; vacation giveaways; and an online booking tool. We publish the complete contents of over 135 travel guides in our **Destinations** section, covering over 4,000 places worldwide. Each weekday, we publish original articles that report on **Deals and News** via our free **Frommers.com Newsletters.** What's more, **Arthur Frommer** himself blogs 5 days a week, with cutting opinions about the state of travel in the modern world. We're betting you'll find our **Events** listings an invaluable resource; it's an up-to-the-minute roster of what's happening in cities everywhere—including concerts, festivals, lectures, and more. We've also added weekly **podcasts, interactive maps,** and hundreds of new images across the site. Finally, don't forget to visit our **Message Boards,** where you can join in conversations with thousands of fellow Frommer's travelers and post your trip report once you return.

you can use your current account away from home and how much it will cost.

Wherever you go, bring a **connection kit** of the right power and phone adapters, a spare phone cord, and a spare Ethernet network cable—or find out whether your accommodations supply them to guests.

11 TIPS ON ACCOMMODATIONS

St. John's has the wide range of accommodations you'd expect in a major city—the major chains, upscale heritage inns, bed-and-breakfasts, moderately priced roadside motels, and budget lodging in the local university. Outside of the capital, there are many fine accommodations, but searching them out takes some effort. Through the travel chapters of this book, I've included the very best in all price ranges and styles. In this section, I give an overview of what to expect.

HOTELS, MOTELS & RESORTS

Big hotels are limited to St. John's and other large towns such as Gander and Corner Brook. You'll find such chain properties as Holiday Inn and Best Western, as well as the upscale Fairmont and Delta, represented in St. John's.

HERITAGE INNS

You should stay in at least one heritage inn while visiting Newfoundland and Labrador. St. John's is unique for its incredible number of inns, but you will find others scattered across the province. Facilities and standards vary greatly, so it's important to know in advance not only what you're paying for, but also that the lodging has what you need to be comfortable. You can do this by reading the reviews in this book or by talking directly to the owners when making reservations.

Most of the historic lodgings in St. John's are more expensive than elsewhere in the province. The average price for one of the nicer ones is well over C$100 per night, but keep in mind you usually get a cooked breakfast.

BED & BREAKFASTS

This is the most common type of accommodations in Newfoundland and Labrador. It is also the most varied, in terms of both price and what you get for your money. The simplest are often described as "hospitality homes" (see below), while in St. John's you can pay up to C$200 for a room with its own fireplace and jetted tub. What they do have in common is that, as the name suggests, rates include breakfast, and you can expect personal service, knowledgeable hosts, and conversation with travelers from around the world.

Many people (myself included) do not especially like to share a bathroom with other travelers—or even with the owner of the home. In St. John's, you don't really have to worry about this as virtually all bed-and-breakfasts offer private bathrooms. Elsewhere in the province, accommodations with a shared bathroom become a reality. Those with mobility problems should also ask questions, as bed-and-breakfasts don't have elevators to get you up the stairs.

The best way to make reservations is directly with the bed-and-breakfast, either by phone or e-mail. My favorites are detailed in this book, or check the *Travel Guide* available from Newfoundland and Labrador Tourism for details of all the properties. You can also browse some of the better options and make reservations online through **Select Atlantic Inns** (www.selectinns.ca). **Bed and Breakfast Online** (www.bbcanada.com) doesn't take bookings, but has tools to help find bed-and-breakfasts suited to your needs and budget.

Tip: To prevent surprises, ask the following two questions before reserving a room at a bed-and-breakfast: (1) Will I be getting a private bathroom or is it shared with other guests, and (2) do you accept credit cards? ***Warning:*** Bed-and-breakfasts are not usually suited to families with young children. Of course there are exceptions, and these are noted through this guidebook.

HOSPITALITY HOMES

Hospitality homes are common in smaller communities and in coastal villages. A hospitality home brings back the simple roots of what B&Bs originally were: a basic bedroom in someone's house and breakfast for a reasonable price. In general, expect to get less (that is, usually no in-room phone or private bathroom) and pay less than you would in a commercial establishment. Properties having 3 rooms or fewer for rent are not subject to the 13% combined provincial and federal tax (HST), saving you even more. Larger homes with more than three bedrooms for rent will generally fit under the bed-and-breakfast banner and are subject to the HST tax.

CAMPGROUNDS

Campgrounds are scattered across the province. The season is short, with campgrounds usually opening sometime in June, and then closing for the season by the end of September. All campgrounds are detailed in the annual *Travel Guide.* For a free copy, contact **Newfoundland and Labrador Tourism** at ✆ **800/563-6353** or 709/729-2830, or order online at www.newfoundlandlabrador.com.

National Parks

Newfoundland and Labrador has two national parks with auto-accessible camping—Terra Nova, a few hours' drive west of St. John's, and Gros Morne, in western

Newfoundland. Both have multiple campgrounds, with at least one offering washroom facilities with hot showers. In general, campsites are private and each has its own picnic table and fire pit. Firewood is C$8 per bundle. Overnight fees range from C$18 to C$32.

To ensure a spot on the most popular weekends, contact the **Parks Canada Campground Reservation Service** (✆ **877/737-3783;** www.pccamping.ca). The cost is C$11 per reservation. For information on specific parks, click through the links at **www.pc.gc.ca**.

Provincial Parks

Fourteen provincial parks have campgrounds. They are described as **fully serviced** (showers, flush toilets, laundry facilities, powered campsites) for C$23 per night; **partially serviced** (washrooms with hot showers and flush toilets) for C$15; and **unserviced** (pit toilets, drinking water) for C$12. Bonuses at the larger facilities include convenience stores, mini-golf, bike rentals, and more. To reserve a site, use the **Provincial Parks' Reservation Service** (✆ **877/214-2267** or 514/905-3253; www.nlcamping.ca). For general park information, go to **www.env.gov.nl.ca/parks**.

4

Suggested Newfoundland & Labrador Itineraries

The first thing you need to realize is that Newfoundland and Labrador is big—very big—compared to the rest of Atlantic Canada. The island of Newfoundland alone stretches for 111,390 sq. km. (43,008 sq. miles)—it's nearly as large as the three maritime provinces of Nova Scotia, New Brunswick, and Prince Edward Island combined. Add in the vast territory of Labrador at 294,330 sq. km. (113,641 sq. miles) and the provincial total becomes a massive 405,720 sq. km. (156,649 sq. miles).

To see highlights of the entire province, you'll likely need at least 2 weeks. If you can't afford the time or resources for a lengthy visit, however, choose the first itinerary, which concentrates on the eastern portion of Newfoundland. This itinerary, like the other four, requires a rental vehicle. Driving is really the only way to get beyond St. John's, but you should read "By Car" under "Getting Around Newfoundland & Labrador" in chapter 3 for more information.

Always keep one thing in mind when planning your trip—the wonderfully slower pace of Newfoundland and Labrador is best enjoyed if you don't have to rush through it.

1 THE REGIONS IN BRIEF

ST. JOHN'S The historic capital of Newfoundland and Labrador, St. John's is a bustling, character-filled city that sprawls around a natural harbor on the island's east coast. The connection to the ocean is ever-present, from the sights, sounds, and smells of a busy port to attractions such as Signal Hill, which rises abruptly from the harbor headland. The Rooms is a modern edifice, but as the province's premier museum, it is one attraction you definitely don't want to miss. The city is also home to some of the province's best accommodations—whether you're looking for the comforts of a full-service hotel or the ambience of a historic bed-and-breakfast. The city also has a plethora of restaurants to suit all tastes.

AVALON PENINSULA When you are done visiting St. John's, adventure abounds on the surrounding Avalon Peninsula. The name is slightly deceiving, as the Avalon is actually four peninsulas, with two jutting southward and two northward.

The Irish Loop circles one of these peninsulas, passing the whale-watching hotspot of Witless Bay and the captivating village of Ferryland, which is one of North America's oldest settlements. If time is limited, or you are looking to make a day trip from St. John's, The Irish Loop should be your priority. **Cape Shore,** to the west of the Irish Loop, is home to Cape St. Mary's Ecological Reserve, protecting the oceanfront home of thousands of gannets.

Baccalieu Trail is the local name for a series of linked roads passing villages that have changed little in hundreds of years. Along the way, Newfoundland's only winery is open for tours and tastings. **Conception Bay,** which backs onto the capital, is home to Bell Island, where activities are as varied as scuba diving and touring an underground coal mine.

EASTERN REGION A couple of hour's drive west of St. John's marks the beginning of the Eastern Region, a good destination for an overnight excursion from St. John's.

Bonavista Peninsula is to the north of the Trans-Canada Highway. Here, the streets of Trinity, having changed little in generations, make this village a Bonavista highlight. Continue north to the peninsula's namesake town and you'll find a charming fishing village perched on the edge of the ocean, with history brought to life in local museums.

Burin Peninsula, angling southward for almost 200km (124 miles), is less visited than the Bonavista Peninsula. It is mostly a wild and rocky wilderness, but the rugged beauty is broken by the occasional village, such as Grand Bank, which is named for the famous offshore fishery.

Terra Nova National Park may not get as much attention as Gros Morne, but wilderness lovers will find plenty of adventures in this more accessible park. In addition to hiking and kayaking, tour boats search out whales and other wildlife, or you can stroll the forest-lined fairways of one of the province's finest golf courses.

CENTRAL REGION It's a long, seemingly uninspiring drive between Terra Nova National Park and Western Newfoundland, but those who take the time to detour from the Trans-Canada Highway will find many surprises.

Gander grew as a refueling stop for early transatlantic flights but retains its importance, as experienced on 9/11, when dozens of commercial flights were diverted and their passengers and crew enjoyed the hospitality of locals.

Kittiwake Coast is a remote stretch of oceanfront north of Gander. This region is often missed by visitors driving through to the west coast, but the detour presents delights such as Twillingate, where icebergs can be viewed from town or on a tour boat.

Grand Falls-Windsor are twin towns along the Trans-Canada Highway west of Gander and within striking distance of the west coast. **Baie Verte Peninsula** is far from the main tourist route, but for those who reach its northern tip, walking through a soapstone quarry used by the Dorset people over 1,000 years ago makes the journey worthwhile.

South Coast communities are linked to the outside world by ferry. Rarely visited by outsiders, Harbour Breton is the jumping-off point for an ocean-bound adventure like no other in Canada.

WESTERN NEWFOUNDLAND It's a long drive across the island to the west coast, so many visitors start their journey here—by catching the ferry to Port-aux-Basques or flying into Deer Lake. While Gros Morne, the region's main draw, is centrally located, it's 720km (447 miles) from one end of the peninsula to the other, so plenty of time is needed for thorough exploration. **Deer Lake** is the major gateway to Western Newfoundland for travelers arriving by air.

Gros Morne National Park is protected as a UNESCO World Heritage Site for its unique geology. For visitors, boat tours on a magnificent fjord, abundant wildlife, and challenging hiking make this one of the province's major attractions.

Northern Peninsula highlights include Port au Choix National Historic Site, which has been inhabited by humans for 4,500 years, and L'Anse aux Meadows, the landing place for Vikings over 1,000 years ago.

0
150 mi
0
150 km
N
Ferry
Labrador Sea
ATLANTIC
OCEAN
Ungava
Bay
Cape Chidley
Torngat
Mountains
National Park
QUEBEC
Nain
Davis
Inlet
Hopedale
Makkovik
Rigolet
Smallwood
Reservoir
LABRADOR
North West River
Esker

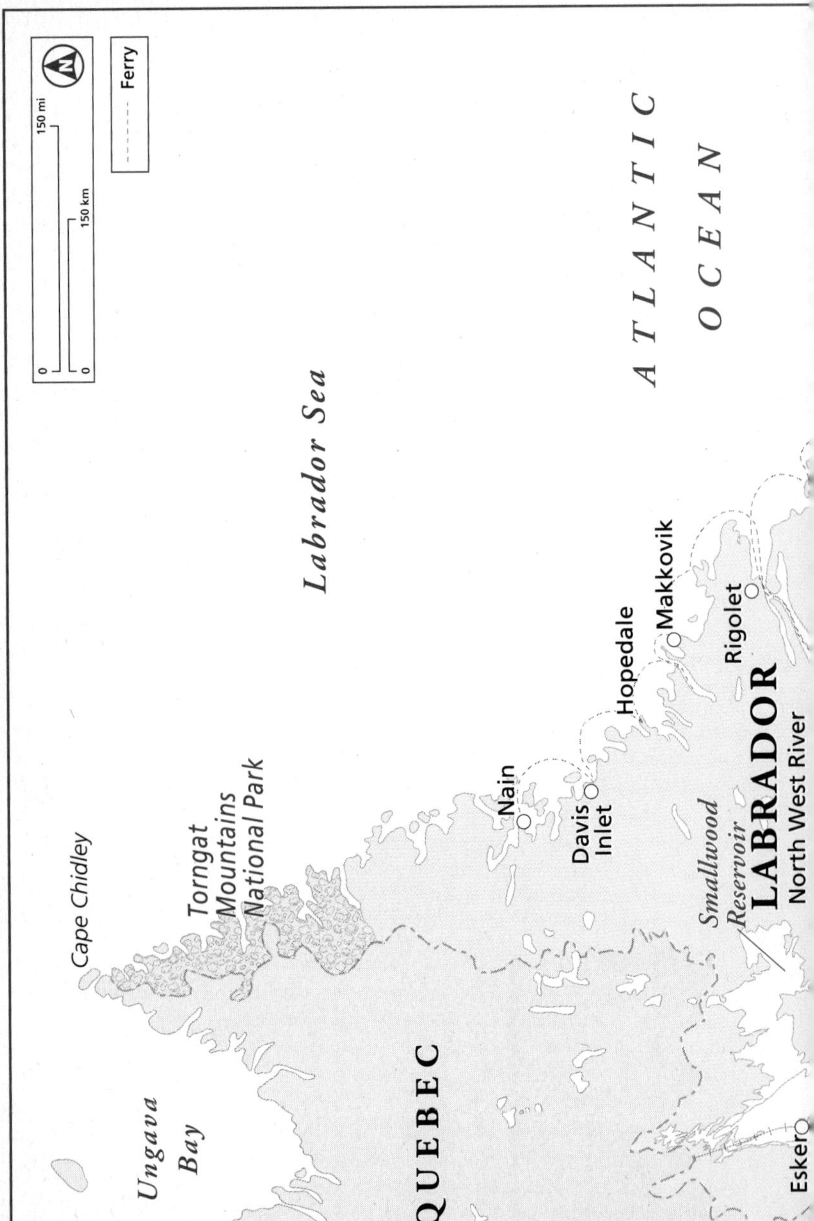

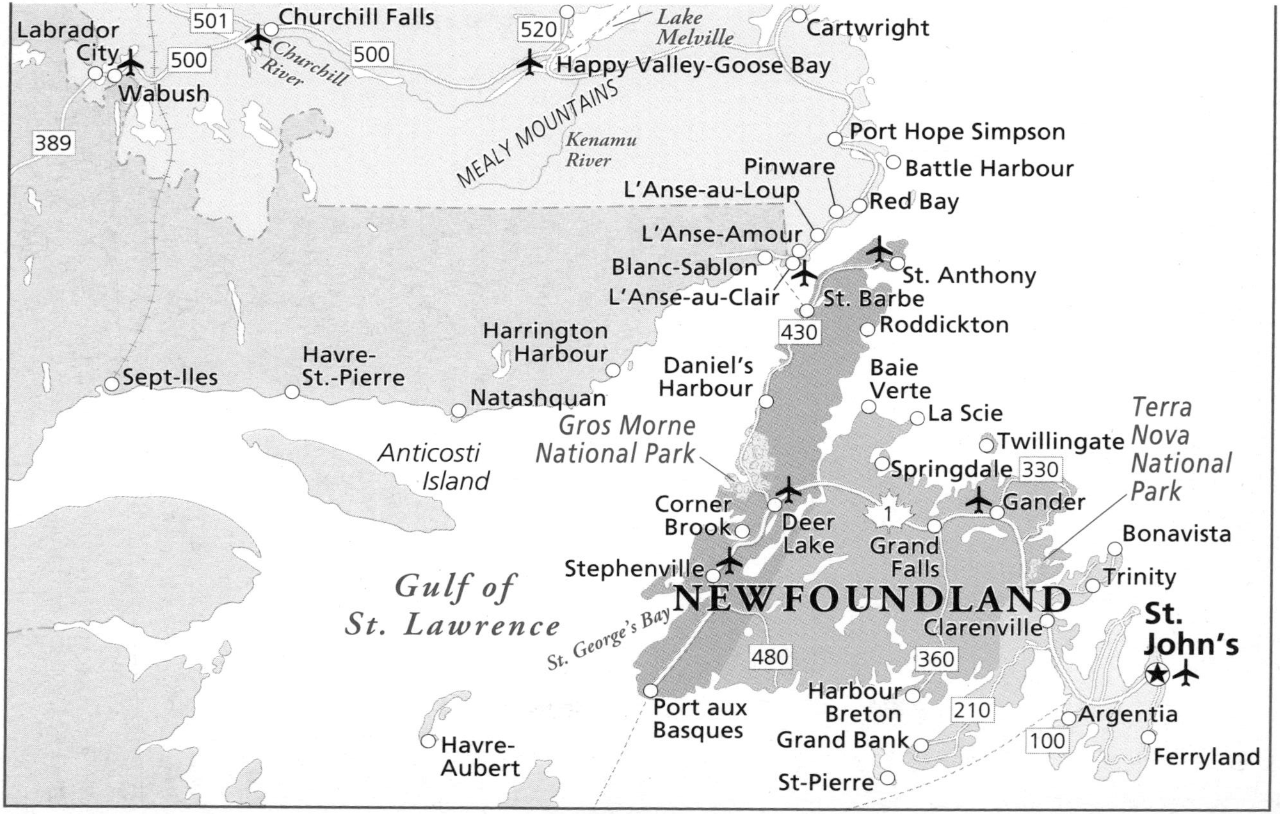

Labrador City
Wabush
389
500
501
Churchill Falls
Churchill River
500
520
Lake Melville
Cartwright
Happy Valley-Goose Bay
MEALY MOUNTAINS
Kenamu River
Port Hope Simpson
Battle Harbour
Pinware
L'Anse-au-Loup
Red Bay
L'Anse-Amour
Blanc-Sablon
L'Anse-au-Clair
St. Anthony
St. Barbe
430
Roddickton
Harrington Harbour
Havre-St.-Pierre
Sept-Iles
Natashquan
Daniel's Harbour
Baie Verte
La Scie
Gros Morne National Park
Anticosti Island
Twillingate
Terra Nova National Park
Springdale
330
Corner Brook
Deer Lake
1
Gander
Grand Falls
Bonavista
Stephenville
Trinity
Gulf of St. Lawrence
St. George's Bay
NEWFOUNDLAND
Clarenville
St. John's
480
360
Harbour Breton
210
Argentia
Port aux Basques
Grand Bank
100
Ferryland
Havre-Aubert
St-Pierre

Corner Brook, the province's second largest city, spills over steep hills to a large harbor. A popular ski resort and fishing in the Humber River are the main draws. **Stephenville to Port-aux-Basques** is a scenic 2-hour drive, with sections of highway hugging the ocean.

LABRADOR Almost two and half times the size of Newfoundland island, Labrador is the mainland portion of the province. It is best divided into four geographical and travel regions, which is how the region is presented in this book.

Labrador Straits, across the Strait of Belle Isle from the Northern Peninsula, is the most accessible region of Labrador. Sunken Spanish galleons, a restored outport village, and delicious bakeapple jams make this one of my favorite parts of the province. **Happy Valley–Goose Bay** are twin towns that serve as the commercial and transportation hub of Labrador.

Churchill Falls to Labrador West is the remote western portion of Labrador. Massive hydroelectric power stations keep the local economy humming, with the surrounding wilderness the domain of only the most adventurous travelers.

North Coast communities are linked to the outside world by a weekly ferry loaded with supplies and the occasional tourist looking for a beyond-the-ordinary adventure.

2 NEWFOUNDLAND & LABRADOR IN 1 WEEK

It is simply impossible to see all of Newfoundland and Labrador in 1 week. But you can get a taste of the province by following this itinerary, which starts and ends in St. John's but also takes in all the main points of interest within easy driving distance of the capital. For this itinerary, I assume you will be renting a vehicle at St. John's International Airport.

Day 1: Getting Oriented in St. John's

Make your way to **Signal Hill ★★★** (p. 99). Not only is the summit panorama a good way to get oriented with the city's layout, but from this single vantage point, you'll be able to search the Atlantic Ocean for icebergs, look down across the busy working harbor, and see out over downtown. Squeeze in a visit to the **Johnson Geo Centre ★★** (p. 99) on the way down the hill. **The Rooms ★★★** (p. 98) is not your usual stuffy museum, and it is well worth a couple of hours for its interesting approach to telling the story of the province's natural and human history. Monday through Thursday nights, I highly recommend joining a **St. John's Haunted Hike** (p. 106).

Day 2: Irish Loop

Leaving St. John's behind via the road to North America's most easterly point, **Cape Spear ★★** (p. 100), you're soon surrounded by the wildly rugged scenery for which Newfoundland and Labrador is famous. Continuing down the coast is **Ferryland,** where a 1621 settlement known as the **Colony of Avalon ★★** (p. 117) is carefully being unearthed by archaeologists. For something a little different, walk up to Ferryland's lighthouse, where **Lighthouse Picnics ★★★** (p. 117) will fill a basket of local goodies for you to enjoy on the surrounding grassy hillside. Continue around the Irish Loop to **Salmonier Nature Park ★** (p. 120), which is home to many of the birds and animals you would probably have seen in the wild if you had more time.

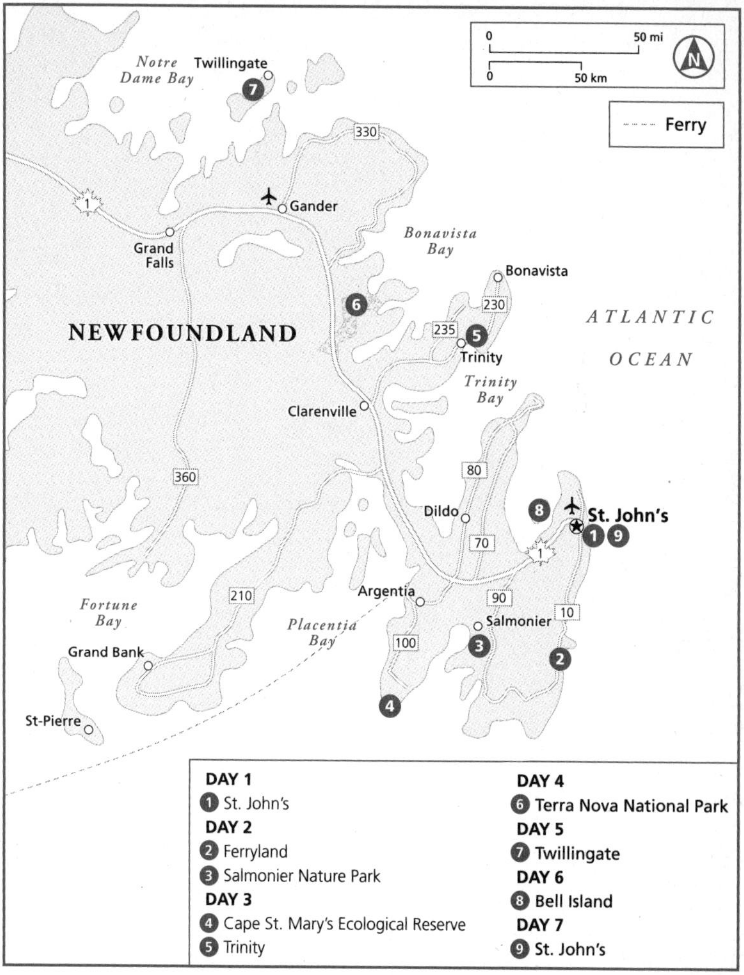

DAY 1
1 St. John's
DAY 2
2 Ferryland
3 Salmonier Nature Park
DAY 3
4 Cape St. Mary's Ecological Reserve
5 Trinity
DAY 4
6 Terra Nova National Park
DAY 5
7 Twillingate
DAY 6
8 Bell Island
DAY 7
9 St. John's

Day 3: Cape St. Mary's to Bonavista

Cape St. Mary's Ecological Reserve ★★★ (p. 122) is foggy 200 days a year, but this somehow adds to the appeal of seeing thousands of seabirds nesting on and flying around a sea stack rising just a few meters from the cliff-top lookout. Spend the rest of the morning driving up the Trans-Canada Highway to Clarenville, and then traveling east along the Bonavista Peninsula. Explore the charmingly historic streets of **Trinity** ★★★ (p. 135) before continuing north to Bonavista, where you get to soak up unequalled luxury at **Elizabeth J. Cottages** ★★★ (p. 140).

Day 4: Exploring Terra Nova

Drive across to **Terra Nova National Park** ★★ (p. 149), where you can take a boat tour of this little known park, searching out wildlife such as whales and eagle. Then choose between golfing, hiking, or simply soaking up the surrounding wilderness. Continue west to **Twillingate** ★★ (p. 165) for an overnight stay.

Day ❺: Iceberg Viewing

If it's late spring or early summer, I recommended making the effort to reach Twillingate for one reason—icebergs. Nowhere else in the world are icebergs as accessible as in local waters. Reserve a spot with **Twillingate Island Boat Tours** ★★★ (p. 168) to get out in the heart of iceberg territory. On the way out of town, step back in time at **Boyd's Cove Beothuk Interpretation Centre** (p. 165). You could spend the night of your fifth day in an anonymous hotel along the Trans-Canada Highway or continue on to the delightful **Inn by the Bay** ★★ (p. 124), overlooking Dildo Bay. ***Tip:*** Icebergs are not always present, so call ahead before driving out to Twillingate. If you don't go, spend the extra time on the Bonavista Peninsula or hiking in Terra Nova National Park.

Day ❻: Homeward Bound

The breakfast served at Inn by the Bay sets you up for a full day of sightseeing, starting with a drive along the Baccalieu Trail, passing coastal villages that are as charming as their names suggest (Heart's Content, Harbour Grace, Heart's Delight, Cupids). Then take Route 60 up the east side of Conception Bay to some surprisingly inviting beaches. If it's not beach weather, hop over to **Bell Island** (p. 128) for the afternoon. Spend your last night in Newfoundland and Labrador back in the capital at **Winterholme Heritage Inn** ★★★ (p. 89), a historic bed-and-breakfast on the edge of downtown.

Day ❼: Tying Up Loose Ends

Make one final trip into downtown to do some souvenir shopping. You can easily spend a couple of hours browsing the interesting shops along Water Street, but those at the north end of Duckworth Street are also worth visiting.

3 NEWFOUNDLAND & LABRADOR IN 2 WEEKS

This itinerary begins and ends in St. John's. I've organized it so you get the long trek across the province over and done with early, leaving you with 12 days to wind your way back to the capital.

Day ❶: Hit the Road

Arriving in St. John's the night before, you should rise early for the drive to Deer Lake, 640km (398 miles). Gander, halfway between the two, is a good lunch stop—and right on the highway is the **North Atlantic Aviation Museum** ★ (p. 163), perfect for a leg stretch. From Deer Lake, it's less than 1 hour's drive to **Rocky Harbour,** where you find accommodations for all budgets (p. 189).

Day ❷: Gros Morne National Park ★★★

A visit to the **Discovery Centre** (p. 192) will whet your appetite to get out and explore the park, so head to the **Tablelands** ★★ (p. 192) for a short walk through some of the oldest rocks on Earth. In the afternoon, join a boat tour of **Western Brook Pond** ★★★ (p. 193). It takes 40 minutes on foot to reach the dock, but once onboard, you'll be rewarded with the

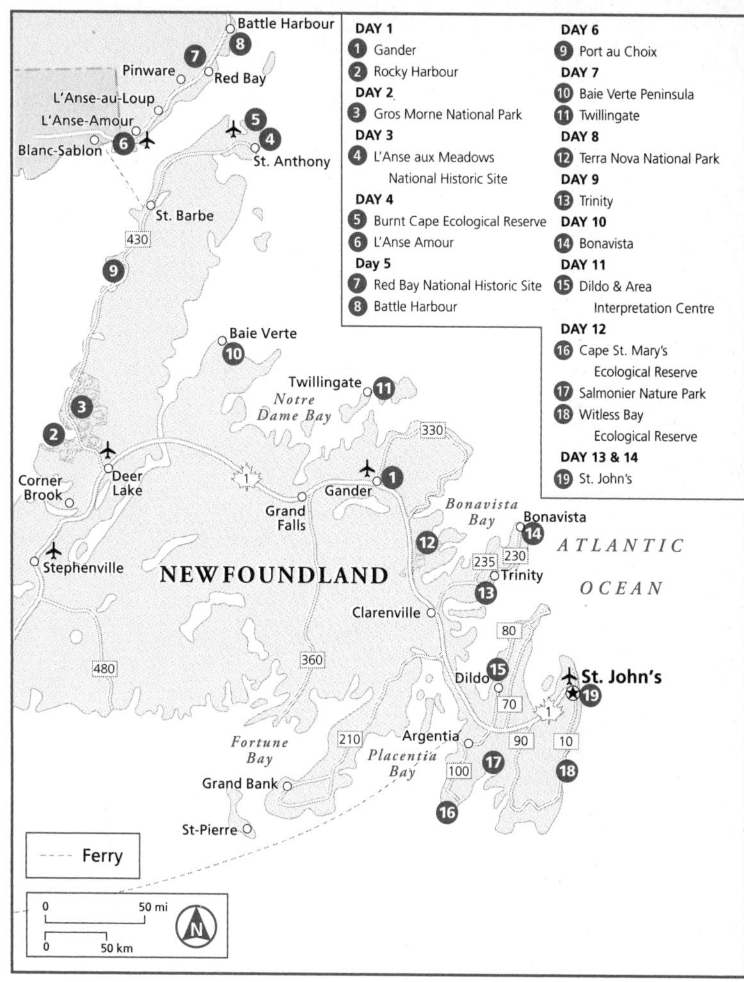

panorama of impossibly steep mountains rising from the lake. Continue to Cow Head and take in an evening performance of the **Gros Morne Theatre Festival** (p. 190).

Day 3: Viking Trail

Route 430 up the northern peninsula is known as the Viking Trail, and when you reach the end of the road, you'll find out why. Spend the afternoon at **L'Anse aux Meadows National Historic Site ★★★** (p. 205), learning about the Vikings who once called this barren knob of land home. Dinner at the **Norseman Restaurant ★★★** (p. 204) is a must.

Day 4: Labrador

There's no hurry to get up this morning, as the ferry from St. Barbe to Blanc Sablon doesn't leave until the early afternoon. Still, I recommend making the effort to rise early so as to squeeze in a visit to **Burnt Cape Ecological Reserve** ★★ (p. 206), underrated for its stark beauty. After the ferry ride, it's only a short drive up the Labrador Straits to **Lighthouse Cove B&B** ★ (p. 214), your lodging in L'Anse Amour, so take your time, stopping at the **Gateway to Labrador Visitor Centre** ★ (p. 212). After dinner walk out to **Point Amour Lighthouse** ★ (p. 214) in time to watch the last rays of light hit Atlantic Canada's tallest lighthouse.

Day ❺: More Labrador

Visit **Red Bay National Historic Site** ★★ (p. 217) to learn how three Spanish galleons finished at the bottom of the harbor. Drive to Mary's Harbour to catch the boat shuttle to **Battle Harbour** ★★★ (p. 218). Located on a rocky island, seemingly at the end of the world, this once-abandoned fishing village has been brought back to life, with a range of visitor services allowing outsiders to get a glimpse of life in an outport. Stay overnight on the island at **Battle Harbour Inn** ★ (p. 219).

Day ❻: Island to Island

Jump aboard the morning shuttle back to Mary's Harbour, drive to Blanc Sablon, and catch the ferry back across the Strait of Belle Isle. From St. Barbe, it's a 1-hour drive to Port au Choix. Here, **Port au Choix National Historic Site** ★★ (p. 197) protects an amazing 4,500 years of human history. The visitor center is interesting, but the **Phillips Garden Coastal Trail** ★★ (p. 197) gets you out into the field, where you can watch archaeologists at work. Continue south, bypassing the roadside motels of Deer Lake to stay at **Humberview Bed & Breakfast** ★★ (p. 183).

Day ❼: Deer Lake to Twillingate

Two weeks in the province means you don't miss anything major. But it also gives you the opportunity to get off the main tourist trail, and that is what Day 7 on the **Baie Verte Peninsula** is about. The turnoff is less than 100km (62 miles) northeast of Deer Lake, and before you know it, you'll be a world away from modern civilization. Official attractions aside—a miner's museum and the **Dorset Soapstone Quarry** ★ (p. 171), where you can see where and how the Dorset people mined soapstone—you'll be amazed at just how ruggedly remote this region is. Continue on to **Twillingate** ★★ (p. 165) for an evening cruise searching for icebergs with **Twillingate Island Boat Tours** ★★★ (p. 168).

Day ❽: Kittiwake Coast

It's a beautiful drive along the Kittiwake Coast to Gambo, and if you'd like to see how little the fishing villages dotting Route 330 have changed in the last century, plan on visiting **Barbour Living Heritage Village** ★ (p. 164) at Newtown. Spend the night at **Terra Nova National Park** ★★ (p. 149).

Day ❾: Terra Nova to Trinity

Go down to the waterfront interpretive center to learn about the park's natural history, and then walk across to the perfectly positioned **Starfish Eatery** (p. 154). Resist the temptation to order seconds of the delicious chowder, and you'll feel up to walking a section of the **Coastal Trail** ★ (p. 156). Drive to **Trinity** ★★★ (p. 135) and settle in for a 2-night stay.

Day ❿: Bonavista Peninsula

In Trinity, only a few historic buildings are open to the public, but for the most part, you get the most enjoyment out of simply wandering through the streets. After lunch, drive to **Bonavista** ★★ (p. 140), a surprisingly large town at the tip of the Bonavista Peninsula. Be sure to visit the local **lighthouse** ★★ (p. 141) for the dramatic setting and **Paterson Woodworking** ★ (p. 142) for a locally crafted souvenir. Back in Trinity, the antics at the **Rising Tide Theatre** (p. 138) will have you in stitches.

Day ⓫: Avalon Peninsula

Head south on the Trans-Canada Highway to Dildo. Once you've finished sniggering at the name, you'll find a picturesque fishing village and the **Dildo & Area Interpretation Centre** (p. 125), worth a stop for its portrayal of local history. Drive around the Baccalieu Trail to rejoin the Trans-Canada Highway near historic Brigus. Spend the night farther south at **Bird Island Resort** ★ (p. 121).

Day ⓬: Cape Shore and Irish Loop

Sure, you may have seen a moose on the northern peninsula and birds on your boat tour from Twillingate, but today is devoted to nature on a much larger scale. Even if you're not a keen bird-watcher, the sheer number of birds at **Cape St. Mary's Ecological Reserve** ★★★ (p. 122) will amaze you. A 1-hour drive north, at **Salmonier Nature Park** ★ (p. 120), it will be the variety of species that catches your attention. On an afternoon boat tour through **Witless Bay Ecological Reserve** ★★★ (p. 112), frolicking humpback whales are the attention getters. Spend this night in an oceanfront room at **Bears Cove Inn** ★★ (p. 114).

Day ⓭: St. John's

There are two places you won't want to miss in St. John's—**Signal Hill** ★★★ (p. 99) for harbor and ocean views and **The Rooms** ★★★ (p. 98) for its modern approach to displaying the province's long and colorful history. You've managed to fit a great deal into the last 2 weeks, so you deserve a treat. In this regard, spend an hour or two at **Spa at the Monastery** (p. 98), and then enjoy dinner at **Bacalao** ★★★ (p. 90).

Day ⓮: Leaving Newfoundland

Fly out of St. John's Airport. If time allows, detour north to the **Ocean Sciences Centre** ★ (p. 103), where admission to an outdoor pool of seals is free, and stop at the **Fluvarium** ★★ (p. 102) to catch a glimpse of the underwater world of a freshwater pond.

4 AN EXTENDED WEEKEND IN ST. JOHN'S

There are two scenarios that may have you looking for the best way to spend just a few days in St. John's—you have 2 weeks in Atlantic Canada and don't want to miss Newfoundland, or you've been attending a conference or sporting event in the capital and want to experience more than the inside of a boardroom or stadium. If you're in Canada on business, I'm sure the business hotel your boss put you up in has all the modern conveniences, but now is the time to pack your bags and move into one of the many heritage inns scattered through downtown.

Day ❶: Getting Acquainted with the City

Drive to the summit of **Signal Hill** ★★★ (p. 99) for city views. Get even higher by climbing the winding stairway of the Cabot Tower for a good way to get oriented with the capital's layout. On the way back down the hill, visit the **Johnson Geo Centre** ★★ (p. 99) to learn about the natural history of this ancient land. You will have spotted the distinctly shaped buildings of **The Rooms** ★★★ (p. 98) from Signal Hill. After lunch and once inside, you'll be even more wowed by the ultramodern displays of the provincial museum and gallery. The hub of evening entertainment is the lively **pubs of George Street** (p. 109), which fill nightly with the sounds of foot-stomping Newfoundland music.

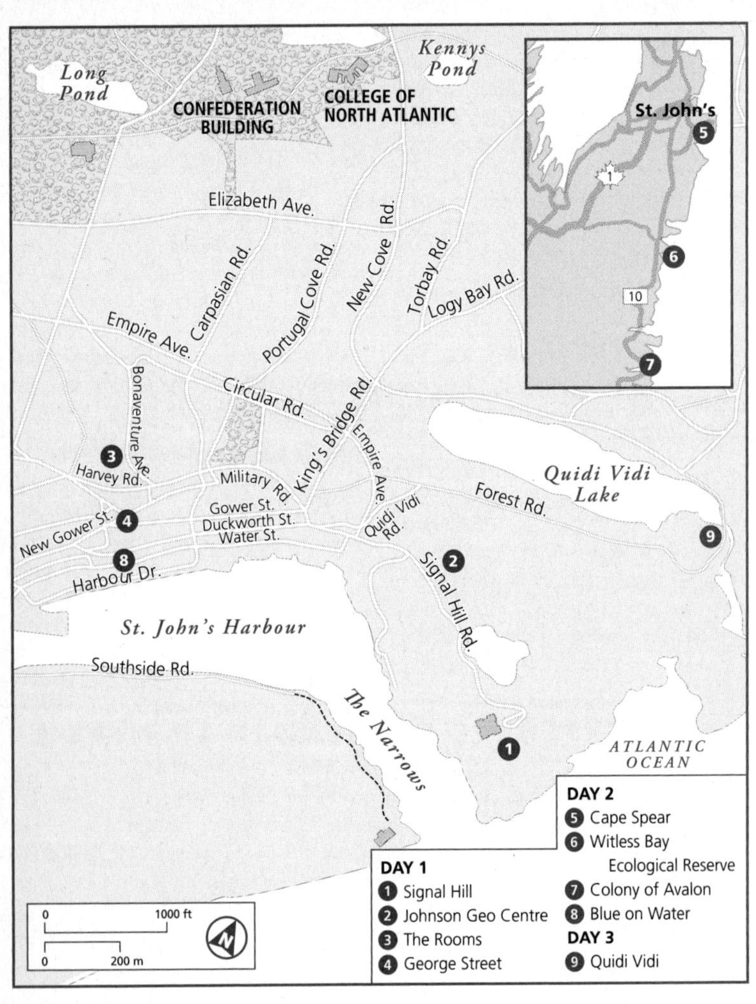

Day 2: Scenic Touring

Ferryland, less than 100km (62 miles) south of the city, is a good turnaround point for a day trip from the capital. But not so quick—there's lots to see along the way. First up is **Cape Spear** ★★ (p. 100), where the ocean views may be spectacular, but a stop here allows you to tell the folks back home you've stood at the easternmost point of North America. A boat tour to **Witless Bay Ecological Reserve** ★★★ (p. 112), with almost guaranteed sightings of humpback whales, should be next on your agenda. Order a picnic from **Lighthouse Picnics** ★★★ (p. 117) before taking in Ferryland's **Colony of Avalon** ★★ (p. 117) archaeological dig. You should be back in St. John's in time for your dinner reservation at **Blue on Water** ★★★ (p. 85).

Day ❸: Tying up Loose Ends

Take some time out from official attractions on your last morning in St. John's to admire the colorful homes along Gower Street, known locally as "Jelly Bean Row." Then, head to charming **Quidi Vidi** ★★★ (p. 100) to soak up the fishing village ambience. Back downtown, do your souvenir shopping on Water Street. If you have an afternoon flight, reserve a tee time at a local golf course; if golfing isn't your style, the walking trails of **Pippy Park** are a good leg stretcher.

5 EXPLORING THE WEST & LABRADOR

The northern peninsula is one of my favorite places in all of Canada, so I couldn't help but include this itinerary. It includes places you have seen pictures of, fishing villages that are just as you imagine they should be, and out-of-the-way attractions you will never forget. What it doesn't have are fancy hotels or fast-food restaurants—simply because there are none. This itinerary assumes that you are flying into and out of Deer Lake and have reserved a rental car at the airport.

Day ❶: Sunset over Lobster Cove Head

Chances are this day is spent in the air and changing planes to get to Deer Lake. But in summer, the sun doesn't set over Rocky Harbour's **Lobster Cove Head Lighthouse** ★ (p. 192) until late in the evening, so you can take advantage of the many scenic stops en route from the airport.

Day ❷: Gros Morne and Beyond

Take a morning boat tour on **Western Brook Pond** ★★★ (p. 193), allowing time to hike in to the boat dock from Route 430. The drive north from Gros Morne to Port au Choix takes well under 2 hours, so you'll have plenty of time to explore **Port au Choix National Historic Site** ★★ (p. 197), where thousands of years of human history unravel themselves. The town itself is a good overnight stop, if only so you can dine on local seafood at the **Anchor Café** ★ (p. 195).

Day ❸: Labrador Straits

The ferry trip across the Strait of Belle Isle takes just a couple of hours. Make your first stop across the other side at the **Gateway to Labrador Visitor Centre** ★ (p. 212). At L'Anse Amour, walk to the top of **Point Amour Lighthouse** ★ (p. 214) and spend a leisurely hour or so walking the Raleigh Trail. Catch the afternoon boat shuttle to **Battle Harbour** ★★★ (p. 218), which would look like the dozens of other outports (remote fishing villages) abandoned in the last 40 years, except that enterprising locals have spruced up the old wooden buildings, put up interpretive panels, and operate a variety of visitor services. **Battle Harbour Inn** ★ (p. 219) is where you stay overnight, taking advantage of being able to explore the village long after the day-trippers have left.

Day ❹: To St. Anthony

Catch the morning shuttle back to civilization and drive down the Labrador Straits to catch the ferry back across to Newfoundland. From St. Barbe, it's a 1-hour drive to St. Anthony. This town at the tip of the northern peninsula is filled with attractions related to Sir Wilfred Grenfell. Even if you're not familiar with the good doctor, you will marvel at his achievements in bringing health care and schooling to this remote part of the world through a visit to the **Grenfell Historic Properties** ★★ (p. 202).

Day 5: L'Anse aux Meadows

Take the morning tour with **Northland Discovery Boat Tours** ★★ (p. 203) in search of whales and icebergs, and you'll be out on the water before the wind comes up. Time-travel to the past at **L'Anse aux Meadows National Historic Site** ★★★ (p. 205), where Vikings established a village over 1,000 years ago. Across the road is **Norstead** ★★ (p. 205), a re-created Viking village complementing the historic site perfectly. Dinner at the **Norseman Restaurant** ★★★ (p. 204) will be a real treat; add to the experience by ordering lobster (you get to go across to the docks and pick your own).

Day 6: South along Route 430

Even if you don't rise early, you'll probably be one of the few visitors to **Burnt Cape Ecological Reserve** ★★ (p. 206). If you're interested in learning about the cape's ancient origins and many rare plant species, join a guided tour. On the drive back south along Route 430, you'll have plenty of time to stop at scenic fishing villages, ocean lookouts, and **Bird Cove Archaeological Dig** ★ (p. 198). Plan on overnighting at Cow Head so you can take in a performance of the **Gros Morne Theatre Festival.**

Day 7: Gros Morne National Park ★★★

The trail to the summit of **Gros Morne Mountain** (p. 184) takes most of the day, but summit views are phenomenal. If the difficulty of this hike is a little beyond you, there are many other options, such as combining a visit to the **Discovery Centre** ★ (p. 192) with a walk through the moonlike **Tablelands** ★★ (p. 192). Allow an hour to drive from the park back down to Deer Lake Airport, plus another 90 minutes for check-in procedures.

6 NEWFOUNDLAND & LABRADOR FOR FAMILIES

The golden rule for traveling families is not to try to fit too much into each day, which is why this itinerary, starting and ending in St. John's, keeps driving to a minimum. This itinerary is directed at families with preteens and teenaged children. I've made family-friendly lodging recommendations in this itinerary, but you should do your part, too—by making advance reservations.

Day 1: Settling into St. John's

Regardless of whether you have children or not, your first stop in St. John's should be the same—**Signal Hill** ★★★ (p. 99). The first to spot an iceberg wins a prize. Even if the children aren't captivated by the history of the hill, the silent cannons overlooking a harbor filled with ships make the visit worthwhile. On the way back into the city, plan on spending at least an hour at the **Johnson Geo Centre** ★★ (p. 99). The best city lodging for families is the **Holiday Inn St. John's Government Centre Hotel** ★ (p. 86), where children can splash around in the outdoor heated pool and eat free in the casual in-house restaurant.

Day 2: Exploring the Capital

There's no way children—or most adults—will want to miss the opportunity to get up close and personal with seals, so start out this day by visiting the **Ocean Sciences Centre** ★ (p. 103), where an outdoor pool is home to a half-dozen of these amusing mammals. Keep the nature theme going with a stop at the **Fluvarium** ★★ (p. 102), where you can watch pond life from the comfort of an underwater viewing chamber. If the weather is warm, head to **Bowring Park** (p. 104) for a swim in the outdoor pool or some fooling around on the adventure playground. It seems most children love trains, which makes the **Railway Coastal Museum** ★ (p. 97) popular.

Day 3: Irish Loop to Salmonier

Take a family photo at North America's easternmost point, **Cape Spear** ★★ (p. 100), then continue down the Irish Loop for a boat cruise through the whale-rich waters of **Witless Bay Ecological Reserve** ★★★ (p. 112). After lunch, make the short drive to **The Wilds at Salmonier River** (p. 119), a family-style resort with activities for everyone.

Day 4: To Terra Nova

The province's only wildlife park is **Salmonier Nature Park** ★ (p. 120). It should take well under 1 hour to walk the park's 3km (1.9-mile) loop trail, but with such animals as lynx, moose, and foxes playing hard-to-spot, allow at least 2 hours to take it all in. Then, drive to **Terra Nova Resort** ★★ (p. 153) for a 2-night stay. Spend this first afternoon at your leisure—golfing, swimming, playing tennis, or simply doing nothing at all.

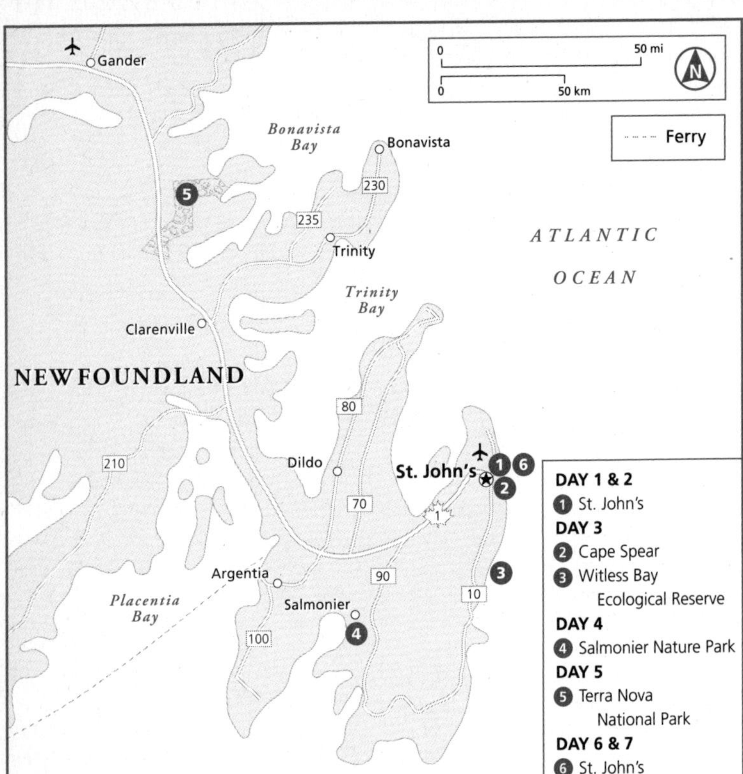

Day 5: Terra Nova National Park ★★

On a warm summer day, Sandy Pond comes alive with families relaxing on the sandy beach and swimming in the warm water. Those looking for something a little more educational should plan on a boat trip with **Coastal Connections** ★ (p. 155). Spend the afternoon at **Splash-n-Putt Resort** (p. 156), which combines water-slides with bumper boats, go-karts, and more.

Day 6: Return to St. John's

It will take a little over 2 hours for the drive back to St. John's, so stall for time by stopping at **Avondale Railway Station** (p. 125), where mini trains run along a section of narrow-gauge track.

Day 7: Leaving St. John's

If time allows, head downtown for some last-minute souvenir shopping. The **Downhome Shoppe & Gallery** (p. 107) has the widest selection of gifts.

St. John's

St. John's, the capital of Newfoundland and Labrador, is one of my favorite cities. It's full of old-world charm, new-world finesse, and the fresh salt smell of the sea.

The vistas and views in and around St. John's are spectacular. At the center of it all is the city's harbor. It was—and still is—the heart and soul of the city. Nothing has been more instrumental to the city's origin, growth, hard times, and return to prosperity than the cities connection to the sea. Downtown St. John's is concentrated along the harbor's western side, with steep streets lined by an enchanting mix of historic buildings and modern high-rises. Extending from the commercial core are residential streets, where you'll be enchanted by the colorful row houses standing tall in various shades of red, brown, yellow, blue, and green.

St. John's mystique comes from the wealth of history that looks down on the city from the surrounding cliffs. To one side, **Signal Hill** (now a National Historic Site), with its rich military history, stands proud, high atop the hill. Just across the Narrows (the protective entrance to the harbor), the 1810 lighthouse and World War II gun batteries at nearby **Fort Amherst** are reminders of past battles. And maritime history lives on in the fishermen and sailors who make their living much in the same way as their ancestors did more than a century ago.

Beyond these official attractions, you can immerse yourself in the past by staying at one of the city's delightful historic accommodations; spending time at The Rooms, a magnificent provincial museum; or, as generations of sailors have done, by simply pulling up a stool at a downtown pub. The goal of this chapter is to provide you with the tools to make your visit to St. John's a fun and fulfilling one. Just be sure to allow yourself time to see it all—especially if you visit during July and August, when St. John's is at its peak, with both the George Street Festival and the Royal St. John's Regatta.

The cultural and music scene in St. John's is unparalleled for a city this size. Indeed, many larger and supposedly more metropolitan centers would find it hard to compete with the range and quantity of St. John's homegrown talent. At many places, you can catch free (or very inexpensive) live local entertainment of excellent caliber.

St. John's is full of color—not just in the buildings, but in its people, who seem to take time to greet everyone they meet on the street. In a small city of about 102,000 residents, it's a lot easier to get to know others than it would be in larger centers.

Yet the city's "townies"—the nickname for those who live in St. John's, as opposed to the numerous outports throughout the province—are a special lot who seem to have treasured and preserved the art of knowing and caring about their neighbors more than many of us do.

Visitors are treated well in St. John's—much like long-awaited friends. And you'll find your fill of good restaurants, where the service is more than friendly and the food a treat for any palate. The wide range of choices for accommodations should please nearly every budget. And plenty of activities are available within an hour's drive of the city. As one of the oldest cities in North America, St. John's boasts a history that bursts with stories of pirate treasure, restless ghosts, and military prowess. Visit the "City of Legends" once, and I guarantee you'll find a way to return.

1 ESSENTIALS

GETTING THERE

St. John's International Airport (✆ **866/758-8581;** www.stjohnsairport.com) is a 3-hour flight from Toronto or Boston, a 4-hour flight from New York, and a 5-hour flight from London, England. Air Canada flies direct to St. John's from Halifax, Montreal, and Toronto, with connections from cities throughout the world made through the latter two hubs. The other major Canadian airline serving St. John's is WestJet from Halifax, Toronto, and Calgary (summer only).

Continental has daily flights between St. John's and Newark. Local airlines include Air Labrador and Provincial Airlines, both providing reliable links between the capital and points throughout the province. Upon arrival in St. John's you'll be pleased to find a modern airport with desks for all major rental-car companies, a choice of eateries, currency exchange, gift shops, and an information center. The airport is just minutes (6km/3¾ miles) and a relatively inexpensive cab ride (C$22.50 for one person, plus C$2.50 per extra person) to downtown.

Warning: If you're leaving St. John's on one of the early-bird flights (anywhere between 6–6:30am), you'll want to arrive at least 1½ to 2 hours before your scheduled departure. That's usually the busiest time of the day at the airport, and arriving early will save you from getting caught in congestion at the airport security checkpoint. The latest you should arrive at the airport for any domestic flight is 1 hour prior to departure.

Taking the **ferry** from Nova Scotia to Newfoundland is cheaper than flying, but it's a much more time-consuming endeavor. The routing that gets you closest to St. John's is a full 14-hour sailing from North Sydney to Argentia, followed by a 1½-hour drive to the city. But if you have the time, you can save a considerable chunk of change by **sailing** and **driving** your own car, versus flying and then renting a car on arrival. (Find more detail in "Getting There & Getting Around," in chapter 3.)

VISITOR INFORMATION

A **visitor information center** is located on the arrival level of St. John's International Airport. Here, you can pick up regional travel brochures, maps, and information; find out about accommodations; and even check out the most recent iceberg sightings. It's open daily 10am to midnight.

Downtown, the **St. John's Visitor Information Centre** is centrally located at 348 Water St. (✆ **709/576-8106;** www.stjohns.ca). It's open year-round Monday to Friday 9am to 4:30pm, with extended summer hours of 9am to 5pm daily. The marketing organization **Destination St. John's** (✆ **877/739-8899** or 709/739-8899; www.destinationstjohns.com) is a good source of trip-planning information.

Note: The Avalon Peninsula includes and surrounds St. John's and comprises about half the province's total population and many of its major attractions. The Avalon Peninsula outside of St. John's is covered in detail in chapter 6.

2 GETTING AROUND

From as far back as the early 1500s, life in St. John's has centered on its harbor. Indeed, in its early days, the city owed its existence to the British, Spanish, French, Portuguese,

Fun Facts Buried Treasure

Legend has it that in the 1940s, a dishonest bank employee stole tens of thousands of dollars and buried his loot in a laneway connecting New Gower and Water streets. The criminal was charged, found guilty, and spent 4 years in jail for the deed—only to discover upon his release that the laneway had been covered over with concrete during his incarceration. The money has never been recovered.

and other fleets, whose annual arrival signaled the beginning of another fishing season—usually for cod. Shops and local businesses seemed to spring from the water itself, so close were they to the city's teeming waterfront. Even today, most everything you'll want to see in St. John's will either be on, or just off, one of four streets.

Harbour Drive and Water, Duckworth, and George streets all run parallel to the waterfront. You'll find the boat tours, an opportunity to get close to all sorts of foreign ships, and most of the parking spaces in town along Harbour Drive, which runs adjacent to the harbor and is accessible off the Trans-Canada Highway (Rte. 1) leading into downtown from the west.

Most of the services (shops, financial institutions, post office, and so on) are on Water Street, the next street up from the waterfront, running the full length of the harbor. And you'll find the highest concentration of restaurants along Duckworth Street, 1 block farther up the hill. If you're looking for nightlife, about two dozen pubs can be found on George Street, a 2-block stretch of excitement between Water Street and City Hall.

BY FOOT

The streets of St. John's are ideal for walking. Buildings throughout the downtown area (especially along Gower St.) have brightly colored, beautifully restored historical facades. It's a perfect area for wandering: the air is invigorating, and there are many interesting diversions along the way to wherever you're heading.

Note: The city center is on a fairly steep incline, so if you have difficulty walking, you may want to stick to Harbour Drive and Water Street, which are relatively flat. By the time you get up to Duckworth Street, the incline gets more difficult to navigate. Between Duckworth Street and Lemarchant Road, there are places where you'd be grateful for a ski lift.

Another reason you may want to walk the city is that it's tricky navigating your way around by vehicle. St. John's has many one-way streets, quite a few hidden intersections (the one turning on to Harbour Dr. from the Quality Hotel on **Hill O'Chips** is especially tricky), and some crazy intersections where you have to do a roundabout to get where you want to go (watch out for one of these by the Sheraton). Plus, you may become absorbed by the wildly colored and intriguingly named buildings (such as the **Bread Pig**).

BY TAXI

Taxis in St. John's are fairly priced. Most rides about town will cost you under C$10. The biggest company is **Bugden's Taxi** (✆ **709/726-4400**). Others include **Co-op Taxi** (✆ **709/753-5100**) and **City Wide Taxi** (✆ **709/722-0003**). If you're planning to pay

Downtown St. John's

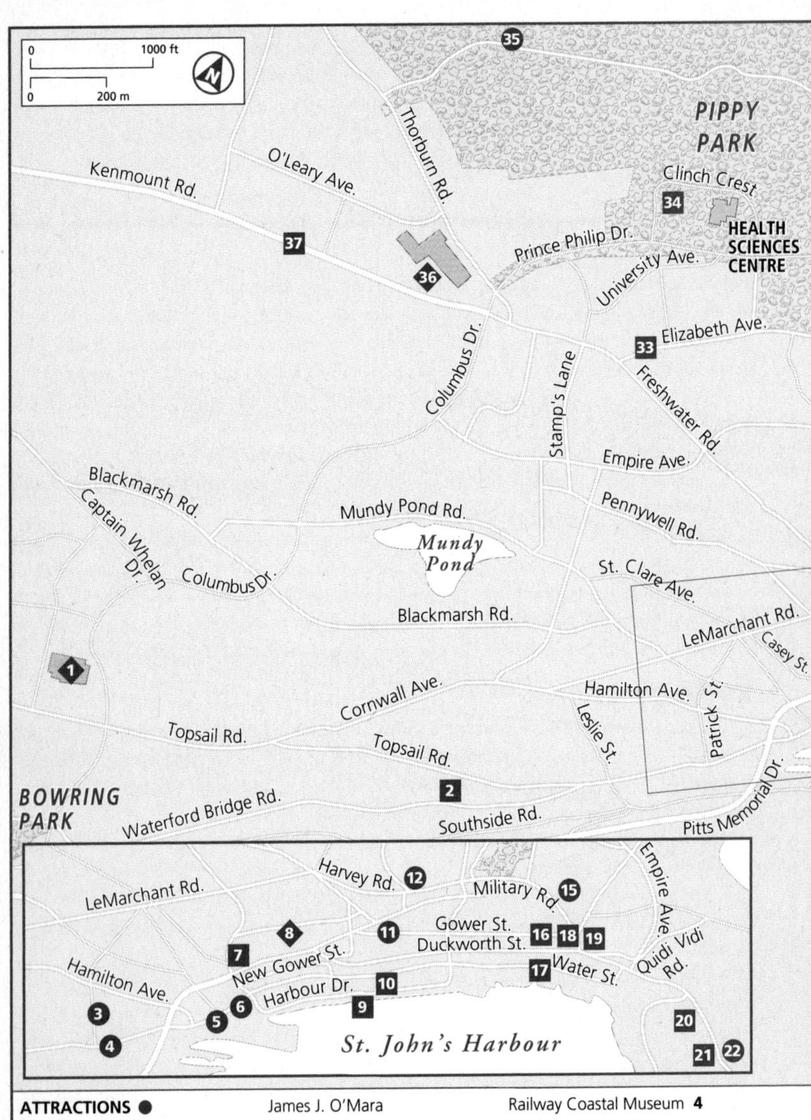

ATTRACTIONS ●

Anglican Cathedral of St. John the Bapist **11**
Basilica of St. John the Baptist **12**
Fluvarium **30**
Fort Amherst **23**
Government House **15**
James J. O'Mara Pharmacy Museum **6**
Johnson Geo Centre **22**
Marine Institute **29**
Memorial University Botanical Garden **35**
Newman Wine Vaults **5**
Quidi Vidi Village **25**
Railway Coastal Museum **4**
The Rooms **26**
Signal Hill National Historic Site **24**
Spa at the Monastery **3**

ACCOMMODATIONS ■

Banberry House **14**
Battery Hotel & Conference Centre **20**

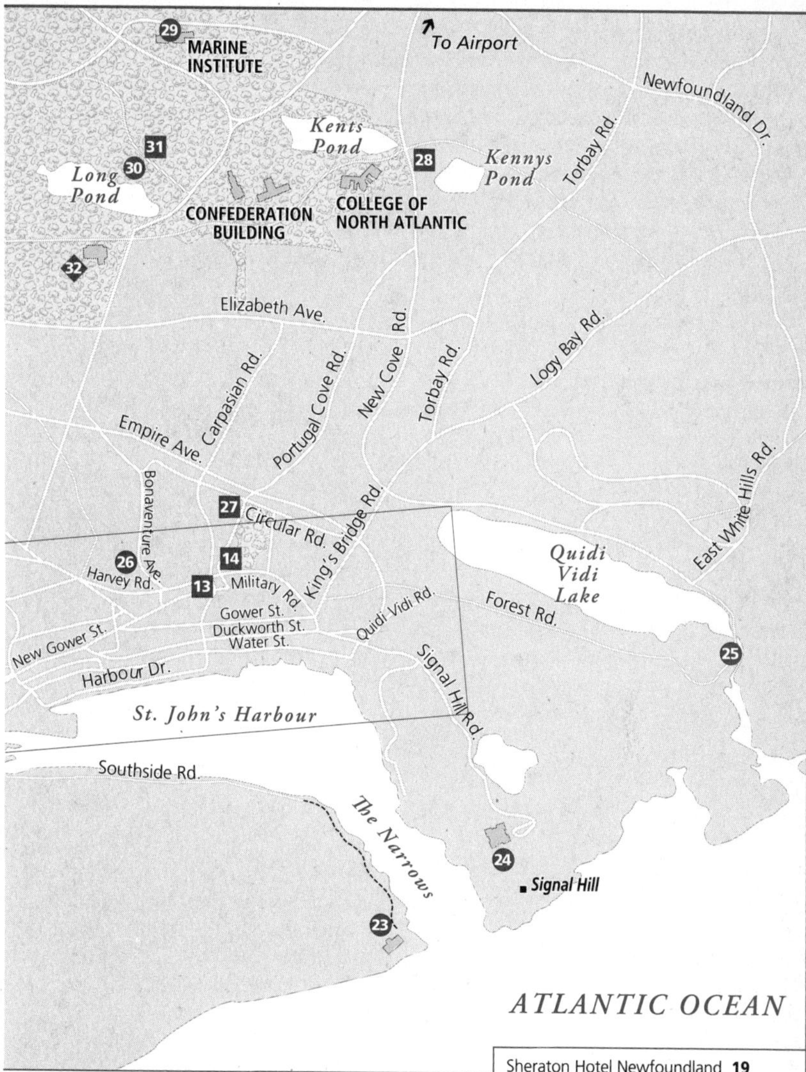

Blue on Water **10**
Bluestone Inn **13**
Courtyard St. John's **17**
Delta St. John's Hotel & Conference Centre **7**
Guv'nor Inn **33**
HI-St John's **16**
Holiday Inn St. John's Government Centre Hotel **28**
Leaside Manor **2**
McCoubrey Manor **18**
Memorial University Campus **34**
Murray Premises Hotel **9**
Oh What a View! **21**
Pippy Park Trailer Park **31**
Sheraton Hotel Newfoundland **19**
Traveller's Inn St. John's **37**
Winterholme Heritage Inn **27**

ENTERTAINMENT AND SHOPPING ◆

Avalon Mall **36**
Arts & Culture Centre **32**
Mile One Stadium **8**
Village Mall **1**

Moments Unforgettable Stories

You'll find that, regardless of which company they work for, most taxi drivers are exceedingly friendly. Many of them have a delightful Irish brogue, a sure hint of a marvelous storyteller who needs just a little encouragement to get started. One driver, named Sean, noted the time a passenger—after a wee bit too much fun on George Street—stumbled into his cab and promptly fell asleep. On awakening the passenger to find out where he lived, the groggy man threw C$20 on the seat, thanked Sean for the ride, and got out of the car right where he'd gotten in! It took some encouragement to get the man back in, and even more coaxing to find out where he lived, but Sean made sure his passenger was delivered safely home.

by credit card, be sure to call ahead before you get in the taxi to verify that credit cards—and your particular card—are accepted. Similarly, if you require an infant car seat, make sure you ask for one when you call for a cab—most taxi companies have at least a couple of vehicles equipped with that option.

BY BUS

As any experienced traveler knows, public transit is one of the cheapest and fastest ways to become acquainted with unfamiliar surroundings. St. John's doesn't have subways, streetcars, or passenger trains, but it does have an inexpensive public bus system, **Metrobus** (© **709/570-2020;** www.metrobus.com). Adults (including seniors) ride for C$2.25. Children ages 4 to 18 pay C$1.75; children 3 and under ride for free. You may find one of the 10-ride passes (C$20 adults, C$15 seniors and children) to be a bit more economical if you're planning to use the bus a lot; purchase these from major shopping malls or the Metro Transit Centre, at 245 Freshwater Road.

Note: Metrobus operates with cash-only, exact-change fare policy. Drivers do not carry change.

BY CAR

Get yourself a detailed city map and have your navigator guide you along the way, as driving in St. John's—despite the fact that it's a compact city—isn't the easiest. A lot of the streets in the capital city, as well as in most other communities throughout the province, are in desperate need of repair. According to some expert tellers of tall tales, there are potholes so big you could get lost in them. Unfortunately, after a few days driving around the municipal obstacle course, you start to believe them.

Note: Beware of the multitude of one-way streets, hidden and roundabout intersections, and the fact that streets change names at whim from one block to the next. The good thing is that it's not that difficult to find your way back on track, even if you do get lost or turned around, as the city isn't very large and traffic volumes are generally not a problem. Also, be aware that you may find a shortage of downtown parking during business hours and when there are special events taking place at Mile One Stadium.

Fast Facts St. John's

ATMs You'll find a number of financial institutions along **Water Street** in downtown St. John's. Check the phone book for other bank locations.

Business Hours See the "Fast Facts" chapter for a detailed listing of days that stores are closed. Most shops in the city are open weekdays for business from around 10am until 6pm, but individual store hours may vary. Malls are open 10am to 10pm. The malls and some shops are open Sundays from noon to 5pm. Banks are generally open weekdays 10am to 4pm, although some close at 3pm while others are open until 5pm.

Car Rentals All the major players have rental booths at the St. John's airport. See "Airline, Hotel, and Car Rental Websites," p. 231.

Climate St. John's has a temperate marine climate. See "When to Go," p. 34 for further details. Call ✆ **709/772-5534** for local updates or check out the Environment Canada website at **www.weatheroffice.gc.ca**.

Emergencies Call ✆ **911** in case of emergency to reach the police, an ambulance, or the fire department.

Internet Access All major hotels and most bed-and-breakfasts have in-room wireless or dataport Internet access. A recommended Internet cafe is **Classic Café East,** 73 Duckworth St. (✆ **709/726-4444**), open daily 7am to 9pm. **Starbucks/Chapters** at 70 Kenmount Rd. (✆ **709/726-0375**) also offers wireless Internet access. Also, free Internet service is available on computers at the following public libraries: **A. C. Hunter Library,** at the Arts and Culture Centre, 125 Allandale Rd. (✆ **709/737-2133**); **Marjorie Mews Public Library,** 18 Highland Dr. (✆ **709/737-3020**); and **Michael Donovan Public Library,** 655 Topsail Rd. (✆ **709/737-2621**).

Libraries See "Internet Access," above, or check out the website **www.nlpubliclibraries.ca**.

Newspapers The major newspaper in St. John's is The Telegram. The online version (www.thetelegram.com) offers many useful local links.

Post Office The main **Canada Post** outlet is at 354 Water St. (✆ **709/758-1003**). You can also find postal outlets in most **Shoppers Drug Mart** stores, for example at 430 Topsail Rd. in the Village Shopping Centre (✆ **709/368-6084**) and 141 Torbay Rd. (✆ **709/722-6270**).

Safety Whether you're gay, elderly, of a visible minority, or a woman traveling alone, you should feel secure walking the streets of St. John's. Street crimes are relatively rare. ***Warning:*** Be aware that because so many pubs are on George Street, the area can get quite rowdy late in the evening and is best avoided if you're not a pub-goer. (If you are, it can be a lot of fun!) Be sensible and lock your unattended vehicle anywhere in the city. Don't leave your purse or daypack unattended, and be alert to your surroundings, as you would when visiting anywhere.

Taxes An HST (harmonized federal and provincial sales tax) of **13%** is applicable to most purchases. St. John's has an **additional 3% tax on accommodations** within the city limits.

Telephone It costs C35¢ to make a local call from a pay phone. If you have a cellphone, you'll have no difficulty getting service while in St. John's. Call ✆ **411** for directory assistance.

Water St. John's tap water is fine for drinking. Bottled water is provided in many hotels and is available for purchase throughout the city.

3 WHERE TO STAY

St. John's offers a rich choice of accommodations, everything from a modest room in a local resident's home to upscale chain hotels. When it comes to historic lodgings, St. John's really shines. Not only are many of the best within walking distance of downtown, but prices are reasonable and the atmosphere always unstuffy and welcoming.

During peak season, which is generally late July to mid-August, the city books to capacity. This is when the Folk Festival, the George Street Festival, and the Royal St. John's Regatta all take place. If you like excitement, it's the best time to visit St. John's, but it can also be the most difficult time to secure accommodations. So plan well ahead whenever possible.

The listings in this guidebook include properties that stand out for a particular reason. For example, one is located next to the Folk Festival grounds; another is an aesthetic treat with its beautiful stained glass; and yet another is best known as a favorite hideaway for honeymooners. And to get away from strictly material amenities, one listing offers the friendliest hosts in the city. You get the picture.

If you're staying in St. John's for more than a few days, you may want to consider staying at more than one type of accommodations—say, a hotel and at least one heritage inn or B&B—to get a fuller flavor of the city's interesting range of offerings.

Type of accommodations may be more relevant in your decision-making process than strictly price, so I've grouped accommodations by type rather than price. I've used three broad categories to cover accommodations: **Hotels/Motels, Heritage Inns/B&Bs,** and **Hostels/Camping.** Depending on your individual preference, you can choose a particular property from within that category based on the price you want to pay and the amenities offered.

HOTELS & MOTELS

Battery Hotel & Conference Centre ★ An all-white, sentinel-like structure, the Battery at night appears to be an almost spectral image suspended above the city. Located on the way up to Signal Hill and a 5-minute walk from the Geo Centre, the Battery has unparalleled harbor views. And while the location is superb, it follows the standard impersonal script found in the majority of midrange hotels. The most striking amenities are the view, the natural Newfoundland courtesy of hotel staff, and a restaurant where you can soak up the harbor lights over baked salmon glazed with strawberries and cream.

There's ample free parking, and a business center in the lobby. There is no air-conditioning in the standard guest rooms, but the windows do open. Some rooms have whirlpool baths, and suites are fully equipped with kitchenettes.

100 Signal Hill Rd., St. John's. ✆ **800/563-8181** or 709/576-0040. Fax 709/576-6943. www.batteryhotel.com. 128 units. C$109–C$189 double. AE, DC, MC, V. Free parking. Pets welcome. **Amenities:** 2

restaurants; lounge; exercise room; indoor pool; sauna; walking trails. *In room:* TV w/pay movies, hair dryer, Wi-Fi.

Blue on Water ★ Leave history behind at Blue on Water, a small, centrally located boutique hotel that is as hip as it gets anywhere in Newfoundland and Labrador. The guest rooms are outfitted with all the amenities expected of an upscale hotel, including plush mattresses, flat-screen TVs, and luxurious bathrooms. Also notable is the street-level restaurant of the same name (see the "Where to Dine" section, below), which is open weekdays for breakfast and daily for lunch and dinner. On the downside, parking is in an outside public lot, and there is no elevator or bellhop service.

319 Water St., St. John's. ✆ **877/431-2583** or 709/754-2583. Fax 709/754-4380. www.blueonwater.com. 12 units. C$139–C$199 double. DC, MC, V. **Amenities:** Restaurant. *In room:* A/C, TV/DVD, CD player, minibar, Wi-Fi.

Courtyard St. John's ★★ Affiliated with the Marriott chain, the Courtyard offers smart and stylish guest rooms, with plenty of room to move around and as comfortable as those at the Sheraton and Delta. Request a room on the upper floors for harbor views. At the time of writing, Wi-Fi was only available in public areas of the hotel; guest rooms, however, have dataports.

131 Duckworth St., St. John's. ✆ **866/727-6636** or 709/722-6636. Fax 709/738-3775. www.marriott.com. 81 units. C$199–C$229 double. AE, DC, DISC, MC, V. Free parking; valet parking available for C$15 per day. **Amenities:** Restaurant; concierge; room service; Wi-Fi. *In room:* A/C, TV w/pay movies, fridge, hair dryer**Delta St. John's Hotel & Conference Centre ★** Adjacent to the convention center and Mile One Stadium, the Delta is an ideal choice for the business or individual traveler attending a function at any of these venues. It's also one of the closest accommodations to downtown shopping and nightlife, so you can shop 'til you drop, bring your parcels to your room, and be back in action within minutes. Part of an upscale Canadian chain, it's a modern hostelry easily recognized by the harbor-facing glass-walled exterior. Inside, you find midsize rooms filled with all the amenities needed for a comfortable stay, including in-house dining, a modern fitness facility, and an indoor pool. The Premier Rooms have harbor views. Of special note for those who like a little extra luxury are the Signature Club rooms, which, although the same size as standard rooms, come with such niceties as bathrobes and CD players, as well as thoughtful touches such as complimentary umbrellas.

120 New Gower St., St. John's. ✆ **888/890-3222** or 709/570-1614. Fax 709/570-1622. www.deltahotels.com. 403 units. C$195–C$385 double. AE, DC, DISC, MC, V. Underground, valet parking available for C$12 per day. **Amenities:** Restaurant; babysitting; children's programs; concierge; executive-level rooms; health club; pool; room service. *In room:* A/C, TV w/pay movies, hair dryer, Wi-Fi.

Guv'nor Inn You'd miss the Guv'nor on a quick drive-by because of its modest exterior, but this isn't one of those hotels you visit for its ambience. Its strongest feature is its location: minutes from Memorial University and within walking distance of the General Hospital Health Sciences Centre. The rooms are super spacious, although the furnishings are unremarkable. The in-house dining room is a British-style pub, with meal specials most nights. ***Note:*** The inn has no elevator, so anyone with heavy luggage or bad knees may have trouble with the stairs.

389 Elizabeth Ave., St. John's. ✆ **800/961-0092** or 709/726-0092. Fax 709/726-5921. www.guvnor-inn.com. 37 units. C$95–C$115 double; extra person C$10. AE, DC, MC, V. **Amenities:** Restaurant (see review p. 95). *In room:* A/C, TV, hair dryer, Wi-Fi.

Fun Facts **Remember When**

The original Hotel Newfoundland opened in 1926. With its steam heating, ballroom, and luxury accommodations, it was heralded in the news of the day as the ultimate in "artistic taste." Rooms cost C$18 per night for double occupancy; running water cost an extra C$7.

Holiday Inn St. John's Government Centre Hotel Kids With its own outdoor heated pool surrounded by deck chairs, as well as easy access to the 1.5-km (.9-mile) walking trail encircling Kent's Pond, a playground, and the best 18-hole mini-golf course in the city (Sir Admiral John's Green) all within a 5-minute walk, this hotel is the perfect accommodation for traveling families. If you request one of the motel-style rooms, you'll have the added bonus of being able to park your vehicle directly outside your door (great when small children fall asleep on the drive—you can carry them straight to bed). You also don't need to go searching for somewhere to eat—the in-house family-style restaurant is open long hours, and kids eat free.

180 Portugal Cove Rd., St. John's. ✆ **877/660-8550** or 709/722-0506. Fax 709/722-9756. www.holidayinn.com. 252 units. C$140–C$200 double. AE, DC, DISC, MC, V. Free parking. **Amenities:** Restaurant; lounge; babysitting; exercise room; pool (July–Aug only). *In room:* A/C, TV w/pay movies, fridge, hair dryer, minibar.

Murray Premises Hotel ★★ Finds A boutique hotel, the Murray Premises gets top marks for its excellent service and distinctive character. Built as a waterfront warehouse in 1846, the building has been completely transformed, with luxurious rooms filling the top two floors, complete with extras such as towel warmers, electric fireplaces, cordless phones, bathrobes, and marble bathrooms with jetted tubs. The original beamed ceilings, columns, and timber-slanted roofs add a rustic, cozy feeling to the otherwise contemporary rooms. Rates include a light breakfast.

If you can pull yourself away from the custom-made maple beds with gorgeous duvets and top-quality linens, you should take the time to discover the other businesses conveniently located under the same roof, including eating establishments, the province's best-stocked wine boutique, and an art gallery. The hotel is accessible from Water Street and Harbour Drive, which means you have both the downtown shopping district and the waterfront on your doorstep.

5 Beck's Cove, St. John's. ✆ **866/738-7773** or 709/738-7773. Fax 709/738-7775. www.murraypremiseshotel.com. 28 units. C$149–C$219 double. AE, DC, MC, V. Free parking. **Amenities:** 2 restaurants; limited room service. *In room:* A/C, TV/DVD, CD player, fridge, hair dryer, minibar.

Sheraton Hotel Newfoundland ★★ Still referred to as the "Hotel Newfoundland" among locals because of its longtime history under that name, the Sheraton Newfoundland stands alone as the best full-service hotel in town. Positives include everything from one of the city's best restaurants; a luxurious spa and fitness center; an art gallery; and Club Level executive rooms where guests that pay a little more enjoy the Sheraton Club Lounge, complete with complimentary breakfast and evening snacks, and a massive flat-screen TV. The only negatives are its lack of traditional charm and windows that don't open up and provide you with a whiff of that fresh sea air.

With more than 300 guest rooms on seven floors, the Sheraton is where royalty and other dignitaries stay while in St. John's. Traditional rooms have city views, while deluxe rooms face the harbor. For these and other rooms, check the Starwood website for specials, especially on weekends and outside of summer.

115 Cavendish Sq., St. John's. ✆ **800/325-3535** or 709/726-4980. Fax 709/726-2025. www.starwoodhotels.com. 301 units. C$289–C$429 double. AE, DC, DISC, MC, V. Free parking and valet parking available. **Amenities:** 2 restaurants, including Cabot Club (see review p. 92); lounge; babysitting; concierge; executive rooms; health club; pool; room service; spa. *In room:* A/C, TV, hair dryer, minibar, Wi-Fi.

Traveller's Inn St. John's Moderately priced, reliably clean, and uncomplicated accommodations that are perfect for the budget-conscious visitor. Because it's situated on one of the busiest streets in St. John's, you'll want to ask for a room at the back of the building, where the noise of passing traffic is less likely to keep you awake at night. The guest rooms are bright, spacious, and comfortably appointed. It also has one of the province's few outdoor pools, and as a bonus for families, children 18 and under stay free, and those 12 and younger eat free.

199 Kenmount Rd., St. John's. ✆ **800/261-5540** or 709/722-5540. Fax 709/722-1025. www.greatcanadianhotels.com. 99 units. C$89–C$119 double. AE, DC, MC, V. Free parking. **Amenities:** Restaurant; lounge; pool. *In room:* TV w/pay movies, hair dryer.

HERITAGE INNS AND BED & BREAKFASTS

Banberry House ★★ One of the best things about Banberry House is its location. When staying here, just a stone's throw from Bannerman Park, where the Folk Festival is held each summer, you can actually sit on the patio amid the potted plants and enjoy the music without ever leaving the yard. Built in 1892, immediately following the Great Fire, Banberry House boasts wonderful stained glass by the same craftsman whose work adorns the nearby Catholic Basilica of St. John the Baptist.

The guest rooms at the Banberry exhibit carefully preserved historical authenticity. One of the rooms has a four-poster bed and wood-burning fireplace. Some have the old-fashioned footed tubs, as well as shower stalls. The main-floor "Labrador Room" has an especially rugged feel to it, as well as a fireplace and views across the private garden. Upon rising in the morning, you are bound to be pleased with such local breakfast delicacies as *toutons* (fried bread dough that tastes much better than it sounds, especially topped with molasses), salt cod cakes, and bread-stuffed bologna. Everything is made on-site, and guests are guaranteed not to get the same breakfast twice if they're staying for a week or less, as a different specialty is featured each morning.

116 Military Rd., St. John's. ✆ **877/579-8226** or 709/579-8006. Fax 709/579-3443. www.banberryhouse.com. 6 units. C$139–C$169 double; off-season rates from C$99. AE, DC, MC, V. Free street parking. *In room:* TV.

Bluestone Inn This older, funky lodging in downtown St. John's is decorated with a wonderful selection of original art mingled with historical embellishments. It took owner Neil Oates a year and a half to dig out the original stone wall, which adds an old-world atmosphere to the wonderful breakfast/conference room, where guests enjoy local specialties such as partridgeberry pancakes. To unwind at the end of the day, you can enjoy a glass of wine and share stories with fellow travelers here or out on the street-front patio. The guest rooms are all very spacious. Room no. 1 is filled with dark wood and a more masculine feel. Some of the other rooms have a softer touch. All have Jacuzzis and many other amenities such as high-speed Internet, fireplaces, and a hotel-style telephone system. Self-contained units are available for longer stays.

34 Queen's Rd., St. John's. ✆ **877/754-9876** or 709/754-7544. Fax 709/722-8626. www.thebluestoneinn.com. 4 units. C$139–C$299 double. AE, MC, V. Free parking. **Amenities:** Lounge. *In room:* TV.

Leaside Manor ★★ A charming Tudor mansion situated in a quiet suburban location a 20-minute walk from downtown, Leaside Manor provides a peaceful and serene place to lay your head. The grounds are lovely, with gardens in full bloom if you're fortunate enough to visit during summer or early fall.

The most important thing to note about Leaside Manor is that the rooms vary considerably, both in rates and amenities. The Parker Suite is gorgeous, with a Jacuzzi beside the canopy bed. The spacious Signal Hill Suite is also nice, with full kitchen, a dining area, and a Jacuzzi. The Confederation Room, although nicely furnished in contemporary tone and equipped with plenty of reading material, as well as a DVD player, has a smallish bathroom.

All rooms include a complimentary full breakfast and parking. Tour planning assistance is offered, and fully equipped apartments are available for long-term stays at two additional locations.

39 Topsail Rd., St. John's. ✆ **877/807-7245** or 709/722-0387. Fax 709/739-1835. www.leasidemanor.com. 11 units. C$149–C$179 double. AE, MC, V. Free parking. *In room:* TV/DVD player, CD player, fridge, hairdryer, Wi-Fi.

McCoubrey Manor ★ Across the road from the Sheraton Hotel Newfoundland, McCoubrey Manor is a gracious Queen Anne–style home built in 1904. Now converted to an inn, it is quaintly nostalgic with black-and-white photos of the original owners throughout the home. Antique furnishings and log-burning fireplaces make this a cozy choice—especially during the colder months. The warm colors used to decorate McCoubrey Manor provide a comfortable ambience for the complimentary evening wine-and-cheese get-togethers hosted by the friendly owners. Some of the guest rooms have a view of the harbor; "Catherine's Haven" offers the romantic luxury of a double Jacuzzi, as well as a fireplace. Rates include a terrific breakfast of fresh fruit salad, muffins, loaves, homemade jams, and a choice of hot entrees.

6–8 Ordnance St., St. John's. ✆ **888/753-7577** or 709/722-7577. Fax 709/579-7577. www.mccoubrey.com. 6 units. C$139–C$199 double. AE, DC, MC, V. Free parking. *In room:* A/C, TV/DVD player, CD player, Wi-Fi.

Oh What a View! (Finds) A simple Newfoundland home has been converted to this welcoming bed-and-breakfast that is central to the attractions of Signal Hill and the restaurants you find within the Battery Hotel and Sheraton Hotel Newfoundland. A full breakfast is included, and the most expensive room has harbor views. The same owners rent out the nearby Harbour View Cottage, a two-bedroom home with a full kitchen and views that extend across the harbor to downtown, for C$150.

184 Signal Hill Rd., St. John's. ✆ **709/576-7063.** Fax 709/753-6934. www.ohwhataview.com. 4 units. C$75–C$150 double. MC, V. Free parking. Closed Dec–Mar. *In room:* TV/DVD player, Wi-Fi.

Points East It takes around 20 minutes to reach the century-old Points East cottage from St. John's International Airport, or a little longer from downtown. But friendly host Dr. Elke Dettmer will pick you up from either location, so for those without transport, the distance is not an issue. Upon arrival, you'll find a trim fisherman's home that has been given a fresh coat of paint and transformed into good-value accommodations. Perched on an oceanfront lot, the setting is nothing less than stunning, with a good chance of spotting icebergs in spring and whales in summer. The three guest rooms are simple, yet clean and comfortable; bathrooms are shared. Outside, you find plenty of spots to sit and soak up the view, or if you're feeling energetic, have Elke set up day hikes along the northernmost section of the East Coast Trail (p. 129). In fact, most guests stop by as part of a longer walking journey, with Elke and her accommodation partners all charging C$150 per person per night for accommodations, meals, and transfers as needed along the trail. Visit **www.trailconnections.ca** for details.

34 Sullivan's Loop, Pouch Cove. ✆ **709/335-8315.** www.pointseast.ca. 4 units. C$80 double. MC, V. Free parking. **Amenities:** Lounge.

Winterholme Heritage Inn ★★★ Anyone who appreciates fine craftsmanship and has a sense of history would enjoy staying at Winterholme, built in 1905 for the delightfully named Marmaduke Winter, who was a wealthy merchant. Sitting across the road from Bannerman Park, the property is now designated a National Historic Site—a wonderful example of Queen Anne Revival architecture, which was popular in Canadian house construction from the 1880s until about 1914, and truly breathtaking inside and out. The intricate woodwork, the lovely stained glass, and the spacious rooms are all special touches, but it's the English oak staircase that will leave you in awe. It's a piece of artwork in itself. Every guest room is different and offers its own charm. The six top-floor Attic Suites are built under the sloped roofline, but all are extremely spacious and equipped with luxuries such as a double Jacuzzi and fireplace, as are the larger suites on lower levels. A delicious full breakfast and parking are included in the rates; an on-site spa provides facials, massages, and pedicures.

79 Rennies Mill Rd., St. John's. ✆ **800/599-7829** or 709/739-7979. Fax 709/753-9411. www.winterholme.com. 11 units. C$159–C$249 double. AE, DC, MC, V. Free parking. **Amenities:** Spa. *In room:* TV/DVD player, hair dryer, Wi-Fi.

HOTELS AND CAMPING

Butter Pot Provincial Park ★ Along the Trans-Canada Highway 36km (22 miles) south of town, this beautiful tract of wilderness is just a taste of what you'll find throughout the province. "Butter pot" is the local name for a rounded hill; the summit of the most prominent of these within the park is reached by a trail that takes around 2 hours round-trip. Hikers are rewarded with sweeping views across the forested park. Add to the mix swimming, fishing, three playgrounds, and a summer interpretive program, and you'll find it hard to drag the family into the nearby city.

36km (22 miles) south of town beside the Trans-Canada Hwy. ✆ **709/458-2417.** www.env.gov.nl.ca/parks/parks/p_bup. 175 sites. C$15 per site. MC, V. Open mid-June to mid-Sept. **Amenities:** Shower, washroom, and laundry facilities; drinking water; kitchen shelter; dump station; picnic tables; firewood (C$6 per bundle); playgrounds; hiking.

HI-St. John's (Value) Affiliated with Hostelling International, which represents thousands of hostels around the world, HI-St. John's sits in the middle of "Jelly Bean Row," the famous street of colorful Victorian-era residences rising steeply above the harbor. (It's the dark turquoise house, sandwiched between the canary yellow and olive green homes.) The bright colors continue throughout the three-story building.

8 Gower St., St. John's ✆ **709/754-4789.** www.hihostels.ca. C$32 single, C$79 double. MC, V. Limited free parking. *In room:* Wi-Fi.

Memorial University Campus (Value) All budget-conscious travelers should know about the inexpensive accommodations available from mid-May to August through the Conference Office at Memorial University. Rooms are standard dormitory issue (single and twin rooms, all with linen supplied but no in-room TV or phone) with communal, gender-specific bathrooms. University residences are linked to the campus fitness facility, which has an indoor running track and Olympic-size swimming pool. The university is also on a main bus route and across the road from Pippy Park. All this in a quiet, park-like setting with mature trees and the added protection of campus security.

Register at the Conference Office, Room 316C, Hatcher House, Memorial University, Prince Philip Dr., St. John's. ✆ **709/737-7657.** Fax 709/737-6705. www.mun.ca/hfcs. C$33 single, C$54 double. MC, V. Parking C$4. **Amenities:** Exercise room; pool. *In room:* Wi-Fi, no phone.

Pippy Park Trailer Park Whether you're camping in a tent or a fancy RV, Pippy Park provides a wonderfully treed setting close to Memorial University and within minutes of downtown St. John's. Across the road is the Fluvarium, well worth investigating for its underwater angle on local pond life, while walking trails lead on in various directions, including one that encircles Long Pond. The campground comprises a mix of serviced and unserviced sites, and an overflow area needed for the busiest summer nights. Access from the Trans-Canada Highway is signposted from Exit 46.

Nagle's Place, St. John's. ✆ **877/477-3655** or 709/737-3669, or 709/737-3655 off-season. Fax 709/737-3303. www.pippypark.com. 216 sites. C$35–C$40 full service, C$30 semi-serviced, C$25 unserviced. MC, V. May–Sept, subject to weather conditions. **Amenities:** Dumping station; electrical, sewer, and water hook-up; general store; some sites with Wi-Fi; laundry facilities; hiking; pets allowed; playground; fully accessible shower and washroom facilities.

4 WHERE TO DINE

For such a small city, St. John's has some wonderful restaurants and a great variety of culinary adventures to choose from: traditional "Newfie" meals, wild game, expertly prepared seafood, Asian favorites, slick contemporary cooking—the list goes on. One of the most appealing things about dining in the capital is that you can enjoy local favorites—especially seafood—on all budgets, whether it's enjoying takeout fish and chips from along Freshwater Road or sitting in a contemporary setting such as Bacalao, enjoying perfectly prepared cod au gratin. The most sophisticated independent eating establishments are on Duckworth or Water streets, but several of the hotels also have great food.

Note: Smoking is banned in all public places, including restaurants and bars.

EXPENSIVE

AQUA Restaurant & Bar ★ CONTEMPORARY/CANADIAN Co-owner and chef Mark McCrowe has put together a rather exotic seasonal menu for this stylish downtown restaurant, with an interesting selection of oil paintings by local artists on the walls and fresh flowers adorning the bar. Specialties of the house include coconut curry seafood chowder and seared scallops with a side of lime yoghurt; both are listed as starters, but combined they make a perfect and affordable meal. I went for the apricot and jalapeno salad. Everything is made on-site and is fantastic, including the rich chocolate torte and the apple crisp smothered in caramel sauce. Lunch offers the same creative cooking at half the price. For example, a charbroiled caribou burger with soup or salad is just C$15.

310 Water St. ✆ **709/576-2782.** www.aquarestaurant.ca. Reservations recommended, especially during summer weekends. Main courses C$18–C$28 (sides extra). AE, DC, MC, V. Daily noon–2pm and 5:30–10pm.

Bacalao ★★★ NEWFOUNDLAND Meaning "salt cod" in Spanish, Bacalao is a gem of a restaurant that does a wonderful job of bringing the best out of Newfoundland's best known export, cod. And they do so using local ingredients as much as possible,

Dining Money Matters

You'll find a 13% harmonized sales tax (HST) added to your bill before tip, so at better establishments, you're looking at almost 30% (for tip and taxes) on top of the base price of your bill.

Most of the better downtown restaurants have mains in the C$25 to C$35 price range. If that's a bit steep for your budget, you can order a soup or salad followed by an appetizer as your entree, a more economical—yet satisfying—way to try the best restaurants without breaking the bank. Or you may want to save some of the more expensive places for lunch rather than dinner; many of these establishments offer basically the same menu at lunch, but for less money.

Another tip: To try as many restaurants as possible when you're on a limited schedule, why not restaurant hop? Ordering a soup or salad with a glass of wine in one restaurant and then heading to another for a hot appetizer or entree (and another glass of wine!), and maybe a third for dessert and coffee is a terrific way to try the offerings of a greater number of places. This works especially well on Duckworth Street, where you'll find several very good—yet varied—restaurants close together.

Wine: Wine prices in the capital tend to be higher than elsewhere in the province. It's not uncommon to pay C$10 to C$14 for a good glass of wine with dinner. Another somewhat more adventurous alternative is to go with the house wine, which can be as much as C$3 cheaper per glass.

including vegetables from organic farms scattered around the capital and seafood from local suppliers. The homegrown theme extends through all ingredients—mussels are steamed open in Quidi Vidi beer, and the caribou salad is drizzled with blueberry wine from the province's only winery. Even the bathroom hand soap is made by a St. John's company. As a dinner main, the cod au gratin topped with a creamy sauce and melted cheddar cheese is hard to fault. Other notable mains include seafood risotto and medallions of caribou with partridgeberry sauce. If you love fancy desserts, it's hard to choose between the Republic Mousse, which comes in the three colors of the Newfoundland flag, and the gooseberry Pavlova.

65 Lemarchant Rd. ✆ **709/579-6565.** www.bacalaocuisine.ca. Reservations recommended. Main courses C$21–C$34. AE, MC, V. Mon 6–10pm; Tues–Fri noon–2:30pm and 6–10pm; Sat–Sun 11am–2:30pm and 6–10pm.

Blue on Water ★★ SEAFOOD A bright, modern, almost Mediterranean setting sets Blue on Water apart from the city's other upscale dining rooms. Decorated in blue and white, this stylish space has well-spaced tables extending from the large window facing the main downtown shopping strip to a wooden bar along the back wall. I came for breakfast and had the smoked salmon eggs Benedict, which were excellent, and then came back for lunch with local company that swore by the scallop crepes. Dinner is a more elaborate affair. You could start by ordering phyllo-wrapped brie and grapes, and then get serious with honey and soy glazed pork tenderloin for a main. A thoughtful wine list rounds out one of the city's premier dining experiences.

319 Water St. ✆ **877/431-2583** or 709/754-2583. www.blueonwater.com. Reservations recommended for dinner. Main courses C$22–C$35. AE, MC, V. Mon–Fri 7:30–10pm, Sat 9am–11pm, Sun 9am–9pm.

Cabot Club ★ TRADITIONAL/CANADIAN Some may argue that the harbor view in itself is worth the hefty prices you'll pay in this magnificent dining room at the Sheraton Hotel Newfoundland, but after decades of standing alone as St. John's preeminent dining experience, the Cabot Club now competes with a rash of downtown upstarts. Still, you can be assured that the quality of service matches the impeccable quality of the food served here. Menu selection includes everything from grilled caribou brushed with a partridgeberry and molasses *demiglaze* to seasonal seafood prepared in classic European dishes. The desserts are so decadent that the locals order them to take home. If you're a chocolate lover, try the chocolate Italiano.

Sheraton Hotel Newfoundland, 115 Cavendish Sq. ✆ **709/726-4977.** Reservations recommended. Main courses C$27–C$43. AE, DC, DISC, MC, V. Daily 6–10pm.

Magnum & Steins ★ (Finds) MODERN/CANADIAN Billing itself as a creative dining experience, Magnum & Steins is also original when it comes to design, from your first glimpse of its audacious sidewalk presentation (oversize metal signage, floor-to-ceiling windows) to bold metallic interior accents, which include a steel-plated staircase leading to the upstairs dining room. But regardless of the artistic merit of your surroundings, they are no more (and no less!) than the perfect setting for the *pièce de résistance:* the food. Chef Antonio Esperanza creates each dish by blending layers of subtle flavor with complementary colors and extraordinary plate arrangement. The menu reflects modern trends extending from Toronto to California. Brie, leek, and apple in phyllo pastry sparkles as a starter while for a main, choices run from Dijon-crusted roast rack of lamb to cedar-planked maple salmon.

284 Duckworth St. ✆ **709/576-6500.** www.magnumandsteins.ca. Reservations recommended. Main courses C$28–C$35. AE, DC, MC, V. Mon–Fri noon–2pm; daily 6–9pm.

S at the Majestic ★★ (Finds) MODERN/CANADIAN Away from the main concentration of restaurants, the "S" stands for Social Dining, a big part of eating out for Newfoundlanders. While most St. John's eateries are happy to evoke the ocean theme, this establishment oozes urban chic under the same roof as a restored 1918 theater. The chef brings together the best regional ingredients, preparing them in simple, modern styles. Starters include roasted corn and lobster chowder or a much lighter duck, spinach, and pear salad. The braised lamb shank is one of the least expensive dinner mains; on the other hand, it's worth splashing out for the caribou tenderloin, cooked to perfection. Lunches are mostly under C$15, including venison meatloaf and the pulled pork sandwich.

390 Duckworth St., ✆ **709/722-8642.** www.majesticstjohns.com. Reservations recommended on weekends. Main courses C$22–C$38. AC, MC, V. Daily 11am–2:30pm and 5:30–9:30pm.

MODERATE

Nautical Nellies ★ PUB FARE From the road, this pub looks rather nondescript. But once inside, your eyes will quickly become accustomed to the dim lighting, and the friendly bar staff will welcome you with a choice of draft beers and a menu of traditional Newfoundland cooking. It's always crowded—especially from the start of Friday happy hour until closing. And, as you can tell from a quick conversation with any of those with Scottish, British, or Australian accents seated at the bar, it's the preferred hangout of visiting oil industry personnel. Why? Because it's the ideal place to have an ale and unwind, a true pub where staff know their regulars by name and drink preference. The food is excellently prepared and generously portioned—even at lunch, when one meal is probably enough for two people. Their pan-fried cod with sides of pork scrunchions and rice is delicious. The seafood chowder and crab spring roll appetizers are similarly tasty. ***Note:*** The pub gets so busy during happy hour that meals aren't served then.

201 Water St. ✆ **709/738-1120.** Reservations not accepted. Main courses C$12–C$18. AE, DC, MC, V. Meals served: Mon–Thurs and Sat 11:30am–3pm and 5–9pm; Fri 11:30am–3pm; Sun 11am–3pm.

Oliver's INTERNATIONAL Here, you'll find classic dishes served in Mediterranean-style comfort with cozy booths that are large enough for a group of friends and intimate enough for a romantic duo (although there are a couple of tables that are too close to their neighbor for comfort). The jambalaya pasta is a delicious medley of shrimp, chicken, and spicy sausage served over perfect al dente fettuccine. And the jumbo scallops marinara is a low-fat menu choice so sinfully tasty that you won't feel the least bit deprived. But my personal favorite is the seafood (shrimp and salmon) crepes smothered in a creamy dill sauce. Desserts such as the divine chocolate fudge cake will put your diet on hold. Oliver's wine list also deserves some attention. They stock more than 500 wines and select several different varieties to feature as their house wine of the day.

160 Water St. ✆ **709/754-6444.** Reservations recommended for dinner. Main courses C$17–C$30. AE, DC, MC, V. Sun–Fri 11am–10pm; Sat 10am–10pm.

Rumpelstiltskin's CANADIAN With a casual and informal atmosphere, and harbor views from some tables, this is a good choice for families looking for an inexpensive meal with predictable choices. Typical of hotel dining, the multipage menu has something for everyone, but with no real surprises: teriyaki chicken, creamy shrimp and scallop pasta, prime rib of beef, single-serve pizza, and more—lots more. Save room for one of their excellent desserts.

Quality Hotel, 2 Hill O'Chips. ✆ **709/579-6000.** Reservations not accepted. Main courses C$8–C$21. AE, DC, MC, V. Daily 7am–10pm.

Taste of Thai THAI In a typically modest St. John's commercial building is Taste of Thai, a warm retreat from the busy street out front. The setting is more traditional than you'd expect, and while the low Thai tables may not be comfortable to most, they add to the dining experience. The Thai Teaser takes the indecision away from choosing just a single appetizer. Among main course highlights is the green curry shrimp, while vegetarian and vegan choices such as the pad Thai have their fans with locals used to restaurants serving nothing but seafood.

179 Duckworth St. ✆ **709/738-3203.** Reservations recommended for dinner. Main courses C$12–C$17. MC, V. Daily noon–3pm and 5–9:30pm.

Velma's Place NEWFOUNDLAND Locals swear by Velma's for its traditional cooking, while many of the folk from elsewhere in the province swear it's the only place they'll eat when visiting the capital. And while Newfies may find Velma's well within their comfort zone, outsiders may be a little put off by a menu filled with deep-fried cooking that, in my humble opinion, is no better or worse than you can find in any small-town restaurant across the province. But it is what it is—a friendly, always-busy spot with moderately priced seafood. A hearty starter is the pea soup filled with salted beef; or stick with seafood and order cod cakes. For a main, a couple of platter-type combos provide

Fi' n' Chi'

Regardless of where you venture for finer dining, to fully immerse yourself in local cuisine, you should plan on having fish and chips at least a couple of times while in Newfoundland. You'll find Newfoundlanders are definite connoisseurs of this particular dish, judging each establishment by the texture of the batter and the crispness of the fries.

St. John's has some excellent places that specialize in *fi and chi* (pronounced locally as "fee and chee"; that's waiter-speak for fish and chips), with a concentration of casual places along Freshwater Road. The most famous is **Ches's,** at 9 Freshwater Rd. (© **709/726-3434**), which was started in the 1950s when Ches Barbour began selling fish harvested from his family's schooner. **Leo's,** at 27 Freshwater Rd. (© **709/726-2658**), and **Buddy's,** at 445 Newfoundland Dr. (© **709/722-3937**), are also recommended. At all these places, expect to pay around C$10 for two pieces of fish and generous serving of chips.

the opportunity to try a little of everything, including cod tongues. Desserts, such as the popular lemon meringue pie, are made daily.

264 Water St. © **709/576-2264.** Reservations not necessary. Main courses C$8–C$16. MC, V. Mon–Sat 8:30am–10pm; Sun 9am–10pm.

Zapata's MEXICAN Named for a leader in the Mexican revolution of 1910, Zapata's is the place to go when you're looking for a break from seafood. It caters to both locals and tourists, with a bright, splashy decor and tile-topped tables. The menu is filled with westernized Mexican dishes, including a delicious Mexican pizza and all the usual combinations of nachos, tacos, quesadillas, and enchiladas. A friendly wait staff and tasty margaritas add to the appeal of this popular restaurant.

10 Bates Hill. © **709/576-6399.** Reservations recommended for dinner. Main courses C$9–C$18. MC, V. Mon–Fri noon–2pm; Sun–Thurs 4:30–10:30pm; Fri–Sat 4:30pm–midnight.

INEXPENSIVE

Auntie Crae's ★★ NEWFOUNDLAND Step back in time while immersing yourself completely in Newfoundland culture at this unique establishment that combines a grocery store with Fishhook Neyle's Common Room. The former is filled with nostalgic provincial delicacies, such as canned meats, jams and preserves, and "nunny bags" (picnic baskets), as well as modern treats such as freshly ground coffee; muffins and savory bakery items fresh from the upstairs bakery; and cod chowder with two other daily soup choices. The adjacent common room is exactly as the name suggests—a room with two long tables where you can eat and socialize, and not necessarily in that order. Visitors are even allowed to bring their own food!

272 Water St. © **709/754-0661.** www.auntiecraes.com. Reservations not accepted. Light meals and snacks C$2–C$7. MC, V. Tues–Sat 8am–7pm.

Green Sleeves Pub, Lounge & Restaurant PUB FARE It's like having three restaurants in one, all offering the same menu but completely different dining experiences.

Fun Facts A Local Delicacy

Boiled corned beef and cabbage, along with potatoes, carrots, parsnip, turnip, and peas pudding (made from dried, split peas) was a dietary staple in Newfoundland in the days before modern refrigeration. It was also the favorite meal for Mr. Jiggs, a character in an American comic strip. Hence the nickname Jiggs Dinner. Traditional Jiggs Dinners appear on menus across the province, but if you're not feeling that adventurous, try the Jiggs Dinner cabbage rolls at Bacalao (see review p. 90).

The main floor is a pub—complete with boisterous patrons, local beers on tap, and video lottery terminals. Upstairs is a more subdued, civilized environment with table linens and table service. Outside is a multilevel open-air deck; the preferred choice for midday relaxation on a sunny afternoon. If you're in the mood for finger food, try the chicken wings. They're among the best in the city, with a dry-spice mix that's zesty on its own, or you can boost the zing with a mild, medium, or hot dipping sauce. For a more substantial main course, choose the chicken *savoyarde* (tender chicken breast with mushrooms and onions in a sour cream and bacon sauce, tossed with linguine). It's a house specialty. Live folk music on Sunday afternoons adds to the appeal.

14 George St. ✆ **709/579-1070.** Reservations not accepted. Main courses C$8–C$18. AE, MC, V. Mon–Sat 10:30am–9:30pm; Sun 10:30am–10pm.

Guv'nor Pub & Eatery PUB FARE You'll want to come here for the atmosphere of this very English-style pub. Although it can be moderately boisterous if a bunch of students are on hand (it's close to Memorial University), the comfortable booths give you enough space and privacy to still enjoy your meal. Menu selection is very broad, including local specialties such as deep-fried cod cakes and moose stew topped with mashed potatoes. The lasagna (served with garlic toast) is exceptionally good for pub fare. Mussels are discounted on Wednesday, and on Friday, prime rib is the specialty.

389 Elizabeth Ave. ✆ **709/726-0092.** Reservations not accepted. Main courses C$9–C$17. AE, MC, V. Sun–Mon 9am–11pm; Tues–Sat 9am–midnight.

Moo Moo's Ice Cream ICE CREAM If it's a warm day, you'll find hordes of locals gravitating to Moo Moo's. Housed in a building boldly painted to look like a black-and-white Holstein cow, Moo Moo's has excellent homemade ice cream. The orange-pineapple flavor is especially refreshing.

88 King's Rd. ✆ **709/753-0999.** Reservations not accepted. Single scoop C$4.50. MC, V. Daily 9am–11pm.

The Sprout ★ (Value) VEGETARIAN Widely regarded as the best vegetarian restaurant in the city, this small restaurant is always busy, even in a province known for its old fashioned meat-and-potatoes–style dining. This is mostly a testament to the owners, who have created a menu of simple, inexpensive meals that even meat-lovers find attractive. The whimsical names add to the charm—Give Peas a Chance (chickpea burger, and my personal favorite), Thai One On (pad Thai), and Me So Hungry (miso soup). Some meals are noted as vegan or gluten free, and everything is made from scratch.

364 Duckworth St. ✆ **709/579-5485.** Reservations not accepted. Main courses C$6.50–C$12. MC, V. Tues–Fri 11:30am–9pm; Sat 9am–10pm; Sun 9am–3pm.

Sweet Relic *Finds* BAKERY Ensconced in one of Newfoundland's oldest buildings, an 1804 former residence, this friendly little space is in a quiet area east of downtown toward Quidi Vidi. The coffee is freshly roasted, teas are carefully chosen by the owners, and the sweet treats—many of which follow the seasons, such as pumpkin cheesecake in fall—are baked fresh each morning. In addition to the modernized room set up as a bakery, there is a bookstore under the same roof.

42 Powers Court. ✆ **709/739-4223.** Reservations not accepted. Bakery items C$1.50–C$4.50. MC, V. Wed–Sat 10am–6pm; Sun noon–5pm.

5 EXPLORING ST. JOHN'S

Many of the capital city's most well-known attractions are within walking distance of downtown lodgings, while access to a few others—such as Fort Amherst, Signal Hill, Cape Spear, and Quidi Vidi—requires some sort of transportation. Unless you have mobility problems, the best way to explore the downtown area is on foot. In general, local motorists are courteous (they have to be because pedestrians have a tendency to just walk into traffic—especially downtown), so you don't have to worry about taking your life in your hands when you step off the curb. Another great thing is that walking doesn't cost anything, and many of the buildings you'll want to see or stop at require little to no cost for admission. So, take your time and enjoy what's around you.

Note: Downtown parking meters are strictly monitored, so you're best off parking in a lot if you're unsure of the amount of time you'll need. The maximum amount of time you can buy on a meter is 2 hours. Parking meters are free on weekends and after 6pm weekdays.

DOWNTOWN ATTRACTIONS

Anglican Cathedral of St. John the Baptist This National Historic Site was built between 1843 and 1885, with some reconstruction necessary following the Great Fire of 1892. The massive cathedral's Gothic architecture gives it a somewhat eerie presence, making the church an excellent meeting point for participants of the St. John's Haunted Hike, held late on summer evenings. (See more about this attraction in the "Walking Tours" section, later in this chapter.) A small museum is on-site. During July and August, you can include a stop in the Crypt Tea Room for a light meal (weekdays 2:30–4:30pm), prepared and served by parish members for C$7. On Wednesday, the church opens at 1:15pm for a free organ concert.

22 Church Hill (at Gower St.). ✆ **709/726-5677.** Call for the tour schedule.

Government House Completed in 1831 for the Governor of Newfoundland (the island was an independent democracy until it joined Canadian Confederation in 1949), Government House is one of the city's few architectural treasures to have survived the Great Fire of 1892. Built of locally quarried sandstone, it has a number of intriguing features, including a surrounding ditch that allows the basement to fill with natural light. The magnificent property reportedly cost four times more to complete than the U.S. White House (built the same year). Today, Government House is the official residence of Newfoundland and Labrador's lieutenant governor. The lovely grounds feature flower gardens and are an enjoyable place to have a relaxing stroll.

Military Rd., at King's Bridge Rd. ✆ **709/729-4494.** www.govhouse.nl.ca. Free admission. Grounds daily 9am–dusk

Up in Smoke

St. John's has been the victim of three "Great Fires." According to history, the first was actually a combination of two fires that took place in November 1817 (on the 7th and 21st). Together, they caused about C$4 million in damage and destroyed almost 400 homes. The second major conflagration happened in June 1946, again causing C$4 million in damage. But these were just sparks compared to the biggest fire of them all: the Great Fire of 1892. From a dropped pipe in a hay stable, the flames grew to nightmarish proportions. At its height, the heat was so intense it melted glass from windows throughout the city, most notably the Anglican Cathedral. When the smoke cleared, one-third of the city's population (10,000 people) were homeless.

James J. O'Mara Pharmacy Museum This Provincial Heritage Site is a good spot to visit if you've always been fascinated by pharmacies and the dispensing of prescription medicines. The building dates to 1895 and is particularly interesting because of its Art Nouveau/Art Deco amalgam design. It operated as a pharmacy from 1922 to as recently as 1986. Inside, you can see a set of original drugstore fixtures made in England in 1879 that found their way to St. John's and an assortment of antique apothecary bottles.

488 Water St. (at Brennan St.). ✆ **709/753-5877.** Free admission. July–Aug daily 10am–5pm; by appointment only the rest of the year.

Newman Wine Vaults These stone and brick vaults, constructed in the late 18th or very early part of the 19th century, were used by Newman & Co. (a British wine merchant) until at least 1893—possibly as late as 1914—to age their fine port. It started by accident in 1679, when a Newman's ship had been diverted to the island of Newfoundland to escape pirates and ended up storing its precious cargo in caves during that winter. When the crew returned to England with their port the following year, they discovered that its flavor had improved dramatically. Newman then began a cross-Atlantic custom of bringing its port to Newfoundland for aging in wine cellars, and eventually in these vaults, now a Provincial Historic Site. Allow yourself 20 minutes to explore.

436 Water St. (north side, just west of Springdale St.). ✆ **709/739-7870.** Admission by donation. Mid-June to Aug Tues–Sat 10am–4:30pm.

Railway Coastal Museum ★ Kids There's something strangely compelling about trains. Whatever it is, the mystique carries over to this museum, which is contained within the former Newfoundland Railway Station, a grandiose stone structure that was once the province's main railway station. Meticulously renovated, displays within the building tell the story of the narrow-gauge Newfoundland Railway, which operated between 1880 and 1988, and extended all the way from St. John's to Port aux Basques. Kids especially will be captivated by the 1940s passenger train diorama, as well as the automated train model. All aboard!

If you see a weary-looking backpacker arriving at the museum, don't be too surprised—this is the eastern terminus of the Trans Canada Trail, a transcontinental walking trail that is slowly nearing completion.

495 Water St. W. ✆ **866/600-7245** or 709/724-5929. www.railwaycoastalmuseum.ca. Admission C$6 adults, C$5 seniors and students, C$4 children 6–17, free for children 5 and under; C$13 families. June to mid-Oct daily 10am–5pm; mid-Oct to May Tues–Sat 10am–5pm, Sun noon–5pm.

Spa at the Monastery

If exploring the capital leaves you exhausted, let the **Spa at the Monastery** take you on a journey of renewal. The only facility of its kind in the province, this day spa has 40 well-trained staff eager to pamper you. The most popular treatments include the wonderful hydrotherapy (C$50); or you can purchase a Vitality Day Pass (C$50), which includes access to a soaking pool, plunge pool, sauna, and Jacuzzi. Reservations aren't just recommended, they're essential—unless you're lucky enough to step into a cancellation. The spa is at 63 Patrick St. (© **709/754-5800;** www.monastery-spa.com). Follow Water Street out of downtown to Patrick Street. Hours are Monday to Saturday 10am to 9pm, Sunday 10am to 6pm. A boutique, salon, and the Monastery Cafe (where they make some dynamite desserts) are on-site.

Basilica of St. John the Baptist The twin towers of the Basilica are a striking landmark in the city and can be seen rising high above its surroundings. You are free to tour this magnificent old stone church (a National Historic Site) of Romanesque design, built between 1841 and 1855, at any time other than during Mass, which is held Sunday at 8:30 and 11am, Monday at noon, Tuesday to Friday at 9am, and Saturday at 5pm. You are, of course, welcome to attend Mass.

The affiliated Basilica Museum, in an adjacent residence dating to 1856, holds a treasured collection of books, oil paintings, sacred vessels, and a massive oak table dating to the late 1800s.

200 Military Rd. © **709/754-2170.** www.thebasilica.ca. Free admission to the church; C$2 for anyone over 12 to tour the Basilica Museum. Museum June–Sept Mon–Sat 11am–4pm.

The Rooms ★★★ This cultural oasis—combining the provincial museum, art gallery, and archives—is the one place you just must visit while in St. John's. Located on a hill above downtown, the design of The Rooms pays tribute to the traditional lifestyle of Newfoundland and Labrador. "Fishing rooms" were buildings along the shoreline where fish were processed and where nets and other fishing equipment were stored. While the design has historic connotations, the interior is contemporary and slick, with state-of-the-art technology used to tell the story of Newfoundland and Labrador's natural and human history. The main display area is Connections: This Place and Its Early Peoples, which tells the story of human habitation that began when the last Ice Age ended 9,000 years ago. Another point of interest is that Fort Townshend, the site of The Rooms, is itself an archaeological treasure, as a late-18th-century strategic fortification and also once the residence and seat of early Newfoundland governors. An exhibit dedicated to the fort's history leads outside to the actual grounds.

A portion of The Rooms is devoted to the **Provincial Art Gallery,** which has the same hours as the main museum and is included in admission. It is the province's largest public gallery, housing more than 7,000 works on two floors. The emphasis is on contemporary Canadian art (but there's only a small sampling of this on display), including traditional and mixed media. The permanent collection features major works by nationally recognized artists, as well as hooked mats made by women who live in the many outport communities throughout Newfoundland and Labrador.

9 Bonaventure Ave. ✆ **709/757-8000.** www.therooms.ca. Admission C$7.50 adults, C$5 seniors and students, C$4 children 6–16, free for children 5 and under; free admission for everyone Wed 6–9pm and Nov–May on the first Sat of every month. June to mid-Oct Mon–Tues and Thurs–Sat 10am–5pm, Wed 10am–9pm, Sun noon–5pm; mid-Oct to May Tues–Sat 10am–5pm, Sun noon–5pm.

SIGNAL HILL

Take Duckworth Street east through downtown, pass below the imposing Sheraton Hotel Newfoundland, and you'll soon find yourself on Signal Hill Road, which leads to two attractions.

Johnson Geo Centre ★ (Kids) What better place than the Rock to have a world-class geology center? But this is much more than a rock exhibit. A glass-walled elevator carries you three stories underground to the floor of the main reception hall, where you are greeted by an oversize 3-D display of the solar system. Your next stop is the Geo Theatre for a dramatic presentation (with voice-over by actor Gordon Pinsent) on plate tectonics and continental formation. From there, it's impossible not to be intrigued by the exposed bedrock along one side of the cavernous room. Water bottles encourage you to spray the wall—thereby revealing the nuances of the 550-million-year-old granite. The main display areas are divided into four themes: Our Planet, describing how the Earth was formed; Our Province, telling the story of Newfoundland and Labrador's 4-billion-year natural history; Our People, dedicated to explaining human relationships to the natural world; and Our Future, which touches on subjects such as energy needs of generations to come. Allow a minimum of 1 hour to visit—more if anyone in your party has a fascination with the natural world.

175 Signal Hill Rd. ✆ **866/868-7625** or 709/737-7880. www.geocentre.ca. Admission C$11.50 adults, C$9 seniors and students, C$5.50 children 5–17, free for children under 5; C$28 families. Mid-May to mid-Oct Mon–Sat 9:30am–5pm, Sun noon–5pm. Closed mid-Oct to mid-May.

Signal Hill National Historic Site ★★★ Rising 183m (600 ft.) above the entrance to St. John's Harbour, this is the city's granite guardian. The harbor and city views alone make a drive to the top worthwhile, but as a National Historic Site, it also has much significance as a lookout post. The military history of this site is well explained at the informative Interpretive Centre halfway up the hill. You'd be wise to stop here and learn about the site before you head to the next level. Between the Interpretive Centre and the top of Signal Hill, you'll find a restored cannon battery pointed seaward, much as it was when it was necessary to protect the settlement from marauding pirates or warring nations.

At the top of the hill is Cabot Tower, a stone tower built in 1897 to commemorate the 400th anniversary of John Cabot's landing at St. John's. Inside, displays tell the story of the site, including that of Guglielmo Marconi, who received the first transatlantic wireless message from the hill in 1901. On the tower's second floor, ham-radio enthusiasts operate a small station through summer. While visitors can access the roof of the Tower, it's not advisable on windy days—particularly not with children. The winds here can get very high and could literally pull a small child out of your arms.

Try to time your visit to take in the Signal Hill Tattoo, held below Cabot Tower 4 days a week during the summer (Wed, Thurs, Sat, and Sun) at 11am and 3pm. The colorful artillery and military drumming display takes you back to the days when this site was of paramount importance to the safety of St. John's.

If you're feeling really energetic, and I mean *really* energetic, you can tackle the 896-step descent that skirts the seaward side of Signal Hill. The view from the trail is breathtakingly beautiful. But don't be deceived: It's also very dangerous. If you do the complete walk, there are sections where only 1.5m (5 ft.) of terra firma and an iron chain hammered into the rock separate you from a 61m (200-ft.) drop. Not recommended for children, pets, or acrophobics.

Signal Hill Rd. ✆ **709/772-5367.** www.pc.gc.ca. Admission to the Visitor Interpretation Centre and Cabot Tower C$3.90 adults, C$3.40 seniors, C$1.90 children. May 15–Oct 15 daily 10am–6pm; Oct 16–May 14 Mon–Fri 8:30am–4:30pm. Cabot Tower closed mid-Jan to Mar.

QUIDI VIDI ★★★

Pronounced "kiddee viddee," the historical fishing village of Quidi Vidi quite literally has something for everyone. Its namesake, Quidi Vidi Lake, is the site of the Royal St. John's Regatta (see more about this in the "Festivals & Special Events" section, below).

A self-guided walking trail around Quidi Vidi Lake provides information about the local history and the opportunity to enjoy the outdoors. Plan to spend at least half a day in Quidi Vidi Village. It's just minutes from the modern world of downtown St. John's, yet a historical world away. One of the highlights is Mallard Cottage, at 2 Barrows Rd., which dates to 1750, making it North America's oldest cottage. Across the tiny, picture-perfect harbor, your imagination will be captured by the sheds and stages seemingly suspended from the side of a cliff. They are accessible only by boat.

Quidi Vidi Battery At this Provincial Historic Site, you can learn more about the military presence in old St. John's. The Battery was first erected in 1762 by the French. It was later rebuilt by the British and has been restored to around 1812. The knowledgeable interpretive guides in period costume make history come alive.

Cuckhold's Cove Rd., Quidi Vidi. ✆ **709/729-0592.** Admission C$3 age 13 and up. Mid-June to early Sept daily 10am–5:30pm.

Quidi Vidi Brewery If you're a beer drinker, consider a tour of Quidi Vidi Brewery, a microbrewery offering seven great brews. The Iceberg Beer, made from water melted from icebergs, is the brewery's most unique offering. The QV is a pretty standard lager and is the brewery's most popular beer. If you're looking for something really different, try the Cranberry Cloud. It's uniquely refreshing on a hot summer day.

35 Barrows Rd. ✆ **800/738-0165** or 709/738-4040. www.quidividibrewery.ca. Call ahead for tour times and costs.

SOUTH SIDE OF THE HARBOR

Cape Spear ★★ Cape Spear is the most easterly point in North America and protected as a National Historic Site for its lighthouse, which was built in 1832. The lighthouse keeper's residence has been restored and allows a glimpse of daily life at this remote outpost in the mid-1800s. History aside, the cape is worth visiting for its naturally dramatic setting. You may be amazed at how different its weather can be from that in the city—it's situated just 15 minutes and 11km (6¾ miles) south of St. John's, but you may feel as much as a 10°C (25°F) temperature difference. Be sure to bring a sweater or jacket along with you. Allow at least 1½ hours to tour the Visitor Interpretation Centre, lighthouse, and gift shop—more if you'd like to linger and watch for whales along the coast.

Cape Spear Rd. (heading out of town, Water St. provides access to Cape Spear Rd.). ✆ **709/772-5367.** Lighthouse tour C$4 adults, C$3 seniors and children. Grounds open year-round; guided lighthouse tours

Step Back in Time at Petty Harbour/Maddox Cove

If you don't have the time or resources to tour the outlying regions of the province, try to make it to Petty Harbour/Maddox Cove. It's only a 15-minute drive from the capital city, and a favorite stop for visitors touring Cape Spear.

Petty Harbour is the most picturesque part of the community, a fact recognized by filmmakers, who have used the town as a backdrop for a number of feature films *(Orca, A Whale for the Killing,* and *John and the Missus).* As you can tell from the number of boats around the harbor, as well as the old-time wooden wharves, this is a vibrant fishing community—and has been for more than 500 years. Even the name reflects its maritime heritage (Petty is derived from the French word "petite," meaning "small").

In Petty Harbour, **Chafe's Landing,** 11 Main Rd. (✆ **709/747-0802**), is a great place to stop for lunch. In an 1878 home along the main street, this friendly little cafe takes full advantage of local seafood, with a cod-filled seafood chowder and a snow crab sandwich that are hard to resist. The village also has an interesting antiques-and-flea-market shop by the town's bridge. **Herbie's Olde Shoppe** is a craft store worth visiting just so you can see its interior: Until 2001, it was a traditional and working rural grocery.

To get to Petty Harbour/Maddox Cove, take Route 11 (Cape Spear Rd.) south from downtown St. John's.

mid-May to mid-Oct daily 10am–6pm. Visitor Interpretation Centre open mid-May to Aug daily 8:30am–9pm; Sept to mid-Oct daily 10am–6pm.

Fort Amherst The former lighthouse keeper's house at the Fort Amherst light station has been privately restored and now houses a small museum, photo gallery, craft shop, and a lovely tearoom with a breathtaking view. Local military, lighthouse, and community history is interpreted in each room. The original lighthouse at this spot was put into operation in 1813 and was the first on the island of Newfoundland. The current structure dates to 1952. Fort Amherst is across the Narrows from Signal Hill—a reminder of just how much protecting St. John's must have needed in its early days. It takes a bit of an effort to get there but makes for a pleasant outing.

Prosser's Rock Boat Basin. ✆ **709/368-6102.** Admission C$2.50. June–Sept Mon–Fri noon–8pm, Sat–Sun 10am–8pm. Traffic to Fort Amherst is restricted because of the narrowness of the road and lack of parking. You can park at Prosser's Rock and walk the rest of the way. It's not a difficult walk, but be aware of it. To get there, go west on Water St. until you reach the turnoff for Cape Spear Dr., at the intersection of Leslie and Water sts. Turn left at the traffic light; go over the bridge, then turn left again. This will take you along the south side of the harbor and to Prosser's Rock.

ACADEMIA

Don't be put off by the heading—the local university holds something of interest for everyone. Established in 1925, the Memorial University of Newfoundland sprawls across a wide swath of land adjacent to Pippy Park on the north side of downtown. The student population is 17,000, and it employs over 3,000 full-time staff. Although no general campus tours are offered, many departments operate their own visitor programs.

Finding Your Lucky Rock

While in the area of the Ocean Sciences Centre, be sure to stop in at **Middle Cove Beach** and look for your lucky rock! Many Newfoundlanders believe that finding a stone with a complete white line (the white line is calcite) around it will bring you good luck. And finding one with a double white line is said to bring you double the luck.

Fluvarium ★★ (Kids) If you're interested in what's underwater in the local freshwater ponds, the Fluvarium is a great place to visit. Within this distinctive octagonal building, you'll learn about three distinct freshwater habitats and see a free-range fish habitat, a deepwater display of brown trout, and many interactive displays. You're looking through a glass wall at the underwater world outdoors, so it's best not to visit immediately after a rain, as the water will be cloudy and visibility poor. Allow no less than 1½ hours to visit, more if you'd like to enjoy the surrounding hiking trails, including one leading along Rennies River to Quidi Vidi Lake (see "Quidi Vidi," above). Feeding time is at 4pm, so it's best to arrive around 3pm.

Nagle's Place, off Allandale Rd. ✆ **709/754-3474.** www.fluvarium.ca. C$5.50 adults, C$4.50 seniors and students, C$3.50 children 5 and up, free for children under 5; C$18 families. Summer daily 9am–5pm; rest of year Mon–Fri 9am–5pm, Sat–Sun noon–5pm.

Marine Institute Affiliated with the Memorial University of Newfoundland, the Marine Institute teaches everything from fishing techniques to sea rescue. You can see the world's largest flume tank, where actual-size fishing gear is lowered: From the amphitheater observatory, it's like looking into a huge aquarium. There's also a marine simulator room where captains are trained and tested. Computer screens at the institute can simulate various harbors from around the world, creating virtual storms and causing the floor to move while students navigate their way on the screens. Both rooms are extremely interesting if in use, but not nearly as exciting if you happen to visit while nothing is scheduled. Also of note is the Marine Institute Bookstore, open weekdays 8:30am to 4pm.

155 Ridge Rd. ✆ **800/563-5799** or 709/778-0200. www.mi.mun.ca. Free tours conducted during the summer. Call in advance for reservations or to see what's happening that day.

Memorial University Botanical Garden If you're curious about the province's flora, you should make your way over to the 110-hectare (272-acre) Botanical Garden, much of which is set aside as a nature reserve. The garden is linked to the main campus by walking trail and accessible by road via Nagle's Place. Plants are tastefully arranged by theme—one section is devoted to boreal species, another to wetlands. I found the barrens garden most interesting, and it made visiting the barrens at places such as Burnt Cape Ecological Reserve (see "Northern Peninsula" in chapter 8) more meaningful. There are also walking trails that take you down to Oxen Pond, passing signs describing native plants and how early settlers used them. Give yourself a couple of hours to enjoy the setting. The on-site gift shop is filled with floral-themed arts and crafts with a tea room open daily for light snacks and afternoon tea.

306 Mt. Scio Rd. ✆ **709/737-8590.** www.mun.ca/botgarden. Admission C$6 adults, C$4 seniors and students, C$2.50 children ages 6–18, free for children 5 and under; C$12 families. May–Sept daily 10am–5pm; Oct–Nov daily 10am–4pm. Closed Dec–Apr.

Ocean Sciences Centre ★ Finds Kids Just a short 5km (3-mile) drive from St. John's, you'll find the Ocean Sciences Centre, an oceanfront research facility for studying ocean ecology, oceanography, and fisheries. The building itself is not open to the public, as it is strictly a research facility, but outside, you can see seals joyfully frolicking in large outdoor tanks with student interpreters on hand to answer questions—all for free.

Marine Lab Rd. (take Rte. 30 [Logy Bay Rd.] onto Marine Dr. to get to Marine Lab Rd.). ✆ **709/737-3706.** www.mun.ca/osc. Summer Visitor's Program runs June–Aug daily 10am–5pm.

6 FESTIVALS & SPECIAL EVENTS

The atmosphere in St. John's is festive year-round, but especially so during the first week of August, when you'll find the province's three largest events—the **Newfoundland & Labrador Folk Festival,** the **George Street Festival,** and the **Royal St. John's Regatta**—happening simultaneously.

George Street Festival One word best describes the George Street Festival—*wild!* If you don't like crowds, loud music, and lots of noise, best not to visit George Street prior to the regatta (see below). That's when you'll find bands playing on the street and in the 20 pubs and clubs that occupy this 2-block stretch of rowdy-dom. But if you *do* like great music—and standing shoulder-to-shoulder with your fellow enthusiasts—check it out!

Not just for the 19-to-25 crowd, over a 6-day period in early August, the George Street Festival provides cheap—but great—entertainment of most music types, from rock to bluegrass, country, and Celtic, and for all ages. George Street is closed off for the festival, but once you've paid the admission charge, you're allowed to freely walk on the street—beer in hand—until 3am. But navigating your way down the street can be tough. Not just from the amount of beer you're likely to consume, but because it's difficult to find a place to walk. It's as crowded—and rowdy—as you'll find any evening on Bourbon Street in New Orleans (perhaps except during Mardi Gras). Check the website or drop into any George Street pub for a schedule of performers. At other times of year, visit **www.whatsongeorge.com** for entertainment schedules at the pubs along this busy street.

George St. (between Queen's Rd. and Bate's Hill). ✆ **709/685-9232** or 709/576-5990. www.georgestreetfestival.com. Day passes C$15 per person.

Newfoundland & Labrador Folk Festival This festival is most rewarding because of its size. It's not like many larger festivals throughout North America, where you're one very small part of a massive sea of fans, waving with excitement in the wind. At this festival, the crowds are smaller and the performances more personal.

The event takes place the first full weekend in August, beginning on Friday night and concluding with singing of the **"Ode to Newfoundland"** on Sunday evening. The Ode was the national anthem of Newfoundland, when it was an independent nation, and was written by Sir Cavendish Boyle while he was Britain's governor of Newfoundland between 1901 and 1904.

Most of the entertainment is top-notch local and of a bluegrass or Celtic nature. In addition to the main stage hosting well-known performers, smaller stages provide the chance to listen to quality music in a more personal environment. There are booths where you can purchase the performers' music, as well as watch artisans blowing glass and turning woodcrafts. Others are selling pottery, jewelry, dyed silks, and T-shirts. Reasonably priced food can be purchased at booths on-site, and, of course, there's the expected beer tent, where you can purchase beer, wine, or coolers. You can't take your alcoholic beverage out of the beer tent, but you can see the stage and hear the music from the open-sided tent.

Bannerman Park (enter from Military Rd.). ✆ **866/576-8508** or 709/576-8508. www.nlfolk.com. Regular weekend pass C$50adults, C$25 seniors and children 12–18; evening and afternoon sessions C$15 adults, C$10 seniors and children 12–18; free for children under 12.

Royal St. John's Regatta This is the event of all events in St. John's. And it's the only civic holiday in all of North America that's weather dependent! The Regatta started in 1825 and is the oldest continuous sporting event in North America. The excitement centers on a day of fixed-seat rowing races in six-man (or -woman) sculls. It's normally held on the first Wednesday of August—if you wake up that morning and the weather is windy or wet, the best thing to do is turn on the radio or TV to find out whether the Regatta has been postponed. If it's on, head down to Quidi Vidi Lake and have yourself a great time.

The action centers on teams of rowers challenging one another in a series of races. You'll also find dozens of food booths, games of chance, rides for the kids, and small items such as jewelry for sale. Moo Moo's homemade Newfoundland ice cream has a booth offering delicious treats. Another local favorite is the Hiscock's Wedge Fries truck from Grand Falls. Make sure to try the grilled shish kabob (marinated pork cubes skewered with onions). Where else can you get a country-fair atmosphere with free entertainment, free admission, and a day's worth of inexpensive family fun within 5 minutes' drive of a city's downtown?

Quidi Vidi Lake (take King's Bridge Rd. to Lakeview Ave.). ✆ **709/576-8921.** www.stjohnsregatta.org. Free admission. First Wed of Aug, weather permitting. Races run continually from 8:30am–6pm. Parking can be a problem; be prepared for a long walk.

7 OUTDOOR ACTIVITIES

The city of St. John's is full of parks and a great place to enjoy the outdoors. Whether you just want to take a leisurely walk and smell the flowers or you're looking to be educated along the way, there are a number of good options from which to choose. The city is small, so seeing it on a big motor-coach tour should be a last resort. (That mode of travel is best reserved for touring other regions of the province and will be touched on in subsequent chapters.) To best enjoy the full flavor of St. John's, take a walk or a carriage ride, and see the city slowly—as it should be seen.

If you're a golfer, you'll be pleased to learn that Newfoundland and Labrador has a number of fine courses and that some of them can be found right in St. John's. The best-groomed 18-hole course in the city is the Osprey (one of two courses at Clovelly), but if you want more of a challenge, look to the Admiral's Green, located in Pippy Park. For an online guide to the province's golf courses, visit **www.golfnewfoundland.ca**.

PARKS & GARDENS

Bowring Park Bowring Park is the city's preeminent green space. It has a river and brook running through it, ducks swimming happily about, and pigeons doing their best to make a mess of the lovely bronze statues. There's a whimsical statue of Peter Pan (it's a replica of the same statue that stands in the Kensington Gardens of London) alongside the pond that, while beautiful to look at, has a melancholy history. It's actually a memorial for

Grand Concourse

Straddling three municipalities, Grand Concourse is the name given to the network of walking trails that link every park, pond, and river within city limits. It's a wonderful concept, one that is still under construction, but with much of the signage already in place. Most of the downtown trails are along paved sidewalks, but beyond the central business district, popular paths include the 3.8km (2.4-mile) Rennie's River Trail, linking the Fluvarium and Quidi Vidi Lake, and the 1.5km (.9-mile) loop around Kent's Pond. One of many local businesses involved is the Newfoundland-themed grocery store Bidgoods (see p. 106), which is linked to the trail system and was prominent in creating nearby Bidgood Park, where a boardwalk leads across wetlands. Free trail maps are available at the information center, or visit **www.grandconcourse.ca**.

a little girl who had loved the park, but who, along with her father, was tragically shipwrecked. The park also contains a tribute to St. John's military history, with a number of commemorative war plaques to read. Bowring Park also offers a large adventure playground, an outdoor swimming pool, tennis courts, picnic grounds, walking trails, and cross-country ski trails and tobogganing in the winter.

Southwest of downtown on Waterford Bridge Rd. ✆ **709/576-6134.** Free admission. Daily 9am–10pm.

Pippy Park Northwest of downtown, adjacent to the Memorial University of Newfoundland, this park features a peaceful pond where you can rent canoes or kayaks. There's a playground and mini-golf for the kids, two golf courses, camping, picnic grounds, hiking trails, a botanical garden, and the Fluvarium (see "Exploring St. John's," earlier in this chapter). Locals regard Long Pond as excellent for city bird-watching, and the occasional moose has even been sighted in the park. You'll pass the expansive park many times on your travels in and around the city.

Take Kenmount Rd. to Thorburn Rd. or Prince Philip Dr. ✆ **709/737-3655.** www.pippypark.com. Free admission. Daily dawn–dusk.

WATERSPORTS

Swimming in the ocean off St. John's is definitely not recommended. Not only is the water bone-chillingly cold, but the seas are often rough and the coastline rocky. The water of Conception Bay, on the west side of the city, is slightly more tempting, and you'll often see locals splashing around on warmer days at sandy Chamberlains Beach (Conception Bay South) and Lance Cove (Bell Island). If these options don't sound too enticing, head to Bannerman Park Swimming Pool, on Bannerman Road (✆ **709/576-7671**). This outdoor facility is open July and August daily 11am to 7pm.

Ocean Quest If you can put up with the cold water, scuba diving in and around St. John's has lots going for it, including an abundance of shallow-water shipwrecks and extremely clear water. Based on the edge of Conception Bay, a 20-minute drive southwest of St. John's, Ocean Quest covers all bases. It takes certified divers on day trips to local wreck sites, has stylish waterfront accommodations, offers full rental packages, and even has its own diving school. In addition to diving activities, the company offers cod-fishing charters (C$65), boat tours in Terra Nova National park, and overnight charters along the east coast.

17 Stanley's Lane, Conception Bay South. ✆ **866/623-2664** or 709/834-7234. www.oceanquestadventures.com. C$230 for a half-day boat diving, inclusive of gear rental and barbecue lunch; C$1,400 for 5 days diving, 7 nights accommodations, and airport transfers.

Wilderness Newfoundland Adventures Based at Cape Broyle, a 45-minute drive south of downtown, this company conducts sea kayaking tours that take in an amazing number of natural attractions. The highlight is paddling around icebergs that occasionally come to rest near the shoreline. But even without icebergs, seeing whales, puffins, sea caves, and waterfalls will not disappoint. Tours include rental and basic instruction. A good source of information for kayakers heading to St. John's is the website **www.kayakers.nf.ca.**

Harbour Rd., Cape Broyle (a 45-min. drive south of St. John's on Rte. 10). ✆ **888/747-6353** or 709/579-6353. www.wildnfld.ca. C$59 2½-hr. tour, C$89 4-hr. tour. Overnight options also offered, including a 7-day trip each June to Iceberg Alley for C$3,360. Transportation from St. John's extra.

WALKING TOURS

St. John's Haunted Hike If you're not afraid to delve into the dark side and want to be spooked a little, take this evening stroll with the Reverend Thomas Wyckham Jarvis, Esquire. Sunday and Monday, the Sinners and Spirits tour is the more macabre of the two options, with stories of murders and public hangings recounted. The Ghost and Ghoulies tour, Tuesday through Thursday, is a little toned down, but still full of drama. Regardless of which tour you join, come with an open mind and hope for a foggy night for the full effect.

Meet at the west entrance of the Anglican Cathedral on Church Hill. ✆ **709/685-3444.** www.hauntedhike.com. Tour prices are C$10 per person; cash only. June–Sept Sun–Thurs at 9:30pm.

8 SHOPPING

St. John's has a lively shopping scene, with local arts and crafts that hold a seafaring theme always popular as souvenirs. Touristy shops line Water Street, but if you're looking for bargains, you might have to venture away from downtown and into suburbia, where the locals shop. One such suburb is The Goulds, where you'll find **Bidgood's,** one of the most comprehensive places in St. John's to shop for traditional food products (see below for more information).

Suburban malls are generally open Monday to Saturday from 10am until 9pm, Sunday noon to 5pm. Close to downtown is **Avalon Mall,** at 48 Kenmount Rd., which has more than 100 stores and services, including movie theaters and a grocery store. Avalon Mall is accessible by Metro bus nos. 3, 4, 9, 14, and 15. **Village Shopping Centre** is at 430 Topsail Rd. and has 100 stores and services, including Sears and Shoppers Drug Mart. The location is very accessible by bus if you don't have wheels. (Bus nos. 1, 2, 5, 7, 8, 11, 12, 21, 22, and 25 all stop at the mall.)

Bidgood's ★★ What will you find at Bidgood's? Just about everything! It's basically a family-run supermarket, but so much more. "Bidgood's Cottage Crafts" (at the back of the store) has a noteworthy collection of Newfoundland and Labrador crafts and books—and at very reasonable prices. "Bidgood's Cove" is a section of the store where you will find a vast array of traditional Newfoundland foods, all prepared on-site and of the same quality you'd find in the home of a Newfoundlander. You can buy (or just look at!) such local delicacies as seal flipper pie, cod heads, and caribou or rabbit pies.

On shelves throughout the store, you'll also find many local products, such as Bidgood's own wonderful jams (try the bakeapple) and a huge selection of Purity products, such old-fashioned candy and tasty ginger cookies. There's a lunch bar in the store, where you can grab the inexpensive daily special to eat in or take out (the turkey potpie, on Tuesday, is just C$3.50). There's even a playground for the kids, to keep them amused while you shop. And the store is in picturesque dairy farm country, only a 20-minute drive from downtown.

Rte. 10 (just off Old Bay Bulls Rd.), Goulds. ✆ **709/368-3125.** www.bidgoods.ca. Mon–Sat 9am–9pm; Sun 11am–5pm.

Devon House Craft Centre Probably the best-known craft shop in the city, Devon House offers a great selection of Newfoundland handicrafts at very reasonable prices (jewelry, sculpture, silk painting, hooked mats, model boats, and so on). It's a nonprofit venture operated by the Craft Council of Newfoundland and Labrador. Every product in the store has been vetted by the council for its exceptional quality and artistic merit. Devon House is below the Sheraton Hotel Newfoundland on Duckworth Street. Don't overlook the upstairs showroom, where you'll find the larger and more eclectic pieces.

59 Duckworth St. (below the Sheraton Hotel Newfoundland). ✆ **709/753-2749.** www.craftcouncil.nl.ca. Mon–Wed and Sat 10am–5pm; Thurs–Fri 10am–8pm; Sun noon–5pm.

Downhome Shoppe & Gallery This is a one-stop shop where you can choose from a wide selection of videos, books, music, souvenirs, and gifts. They claim to have the world's largest collection of "Newfoundlandia," and after a few glances around the place, you'll likely agree. It's definitely worth a look. A unique offering is the *Household Almanac & Cookbook,* which provides a good assortment of traditional recipes, in addition to household hints and home remedies.

303 Water St. ✆ **888/588-6353** or 709/722-2970. www.shopdownhome.com. Mon–Fri 9:30am–8:30pm; Sat 10am–6pm; Sun noon–5pm.

Fred's Records You can pick up recordings of Newfoundland music everywhere from gas stations to grocery stores, but Fred's is the place to search out the real thing. Here you'll find an amazing collection of new and used recordings, as well as the occasional live performance by local or touring musicians.

198 Duckworth St. ✆ **709/753-9191.** www.freds.nf.ca. Mon–Fri 9:30am–9pm; Sat 9:30am–6pm; Sun noon–5pm.

Living Planet The screen printing is done on eco-friendly clothing material. The bright artwork featured on some T-shirts is tasteful and eye-catching, while other designs are most definitely politically incorrect—making them all the more popular.

197 Water St. ✆ **709/754-9300.** www.livingplanet.ca. Mon–Sat 9:30am–5:30pm.

Nonia Nonia is a nonprofit, volunteer-driven network founded by the Newfoundland Outport Nursing & Industrial Association (NONIA). Unique products include hand-knit baby bonnets, booties, tuques, mittens, and lots and lots of sweaters in all sorts of designs. Plus, they'll do special orders on request.

286 Water St. (at George St.) ✆ **877/753-8062** or 709/753-8062. www.nonia.com. Mon–Sat 9:30am–5:30pm.

The Outfitters In the heart of downtown, this is a great place to get equipped for the wilderness of Newfoundland and Labrador. The store stocks a range of top-notch recreational clothing; climbing equipment; everything you need for a sea kayaking trip; camping gear, such as tents and sleeping bags; as well as guides and maps. Tents, kayaks, and snow sports equipment are available to rent.

220 Water St. ✆ **800/966-9658** or 709/579-4453. www.theoutfitters.nf.ca. Mon–Wed and Sat 10am–6pm; Thurs–Fri 10am–9pm; Sun noon–5pm.

Pollyanna Art & Antiques Along an eclectic strip of shops, Pollyanna is filled with antiques, most notably furniture, jewelry, pottery, and paintings. Upstairs is a gallery of contemporary art.

214 Duckworth St. ✆ **709/726-0936.** www.pollyannagallery.com. Mon–Sat 11am–5pm.

The Rooms Gift Shop Within the province's premier museum, The Rooms Gift Shop strives to offer merchandise related to the province, locally made whenever possible. The section of books is particularly strong, while there is also a great selection of kid-friendly souvenirs.

9 Bonaventure Ave. ✆ **709/757-8061.** www.therooms.ca. June to mid-Oct Mon–Tues and Thurs–Sat 10am–5pm, Wed 10am–9pm, Sun noon–5pm; mid-Oct to May Tues–Sat 10am–5pm, Sun noon–5pm.

Woof Design This is the place to go if you want one of those great Newfoundland sweaters like the one Kevin Spacey wore in *The Shipping News.* Woof Design specializes in the design and production of mohair, wool, and angora sweaters and accessories. All of their sweaters are handcrafted in Newfoundland homes by independent craftspeople, using domestic knitting machines; expect to pay around C$140 each. The accessory items are hand-knit, hand-crocheted, or woven.

181 Water St. ✆ **709/722-7555.** www.woofdesign.com. Mon–Sat 9am–5:30pm.

GALLERIES

Christina Parker Gallery Built in the 1930s and originally occupied as a canning factory, this somewhat funky gallery features an eclectic mix of visual art in an open, spacious environment. All the artists featured are contemporary artists from Newfoundland and Labrador. Highlights include landscape paintings by Cliff George, recycle art by Peter Drysdale, impressionistic photography by Peter Wilkins, and dyed silk art by Diana Dabinett, who is responsible for the beautiful silk art hanging at the Fluvarium.

7 Plank Rd. ✆ **709/753-0580.** www.christinaparkergallery.com. Mon–Fri 10am–5:30pm; Sat 11am–5pm.

Emma Butler Gallery This is a more traditional gallery, with a wonderful selection of classic art. Blue-chip artists such as Christopher and Mary Pratt and David Blackwood—Canada's foremost printmaker—are well represented. Blackwood's etchings provide an excellent visual history of Newfoundland and Labrador. You'll also be impressed by the work of lesser-known artists such as Jeanette Meehan, whose oil paintings depict the bright side of Newfoundland. The gallery also handles several international artists from countries that include the U.S., France, and Russia. You will find many pieces by Jean-Claude Roy, a French artist who comes to Newfoundland and Labrador every year to paint. Emma will ship your purchases worldwide.

111 George St. W. (between Waldegrave and Springdale). ✆ **709/739-7111.** www.emmabutler.com. Tues–Sat 11am–5pm and by appointment.

Lane Gallery If you're interested in photography, don't miss the Lane Gallery. Don Lane strictly sells and exhibits his own work, but don't think that's limiting. As a native of the city, he knows where—and how—to get the best shots. His photographs of icebergs are simply breathtaking. If you're looking for a photograph to hang on your wall that will always remind you of just how beautiful this province is, drop in to visit the Lane Gallery, situated on the main floor of the Sheraton. Prices range from C$100 for smaller prints to over C$1,000 for larger pieces.Sheraton Hotel Newfoundland, 115 Cavendish Sq. ✆ **877/366-5263** or 709/753-8946. www.lanegallery.com. Mon–Fri 9am–5pm; Sat 10am–5pm.

9 ST. JOHN'S AFTER DARK

St. John's may be the oldest European settlement in North America, but it has a very young population. The average age of a "townie" is 35 to 44. That translates into a very active nightlife. In fact, it's said that the city has the highest concentration of pubs per capita on the continent! You'll find great live music playing everywhere, as well as a good selection of dinner theaters and other cultural offerings. So, don't wear yourself out during the day. You'll miss too much at night!

GEORGE STREET & SURROUNDS

This is where you want to be if you're looking for the local pub scene. Within a 2-block stretch, you'll find about 20 establishments eager to draw you a pint. Keep in mind that it gets wildly busy on weekends—especially during the academic year at Memorial University—so plan to arrive early if you want to get in to a certain place. ***Note:*** Lines can be long on Thursday, Friday, and Saturday nights, so bring your umbrella and, in winter, wear warm clothing and boots so you don't freeze. Once you get in, you're bound to have a great time, no matter which of these establishments you choose.

Sundance Bar & Grill, George Street at Adelaide (✆ **709/753-7822**), is the largest and most contemporary facility and boasts the George Street Beer Market, with a wide selection of beers on tap. It's especially popular on summer weekend afternoons, when local bands play out in the largest beer garden east of Montreal. Very welcoming to visitors is **Trapper John's** (2 George St.; ✆ **709/579-9630**), a pub well known for its "screeching-in" ceremony, which allows you to become an honorary Newfoundlander. **Turkey Joe's** (7 George St.; ✆ **709/722-5757**) is for the just-turned-19 (and barely dressed) set that's heavy into the latest music trends. **Bridie Molloy's** (5 George St.; ✆ **709/576-5990**) has a great outdoor patio and traditional Irish music. **O'Reilly's** (13 George St.; ✆ **709/722-3735**) is an institution. It's the most popular Irish pub on the strip. The music will have you tapping your toes, but you can expect to have them squished on the minuscule dance floor. **Kelly's Pub** (25 George St.; ✆ **709/753-5300**) has live entertainment every weekend and no cover charge.

A couple of blocks north from George Street are two more good choices, both traditional and lively, but without the raucous crowds associated with their George Street neighbors. **Nautical Nellies** (201 Water St.; ✆ **709/738-1120**) has a distinct maritime theme (including a scale model of the *Titanic*), a menu filled with local specialties, and friendly bar staff. Across the road is **Erin's Pub** (186 Water St.; ✆ **709/722-1916**), a low-key, very Irish drinking spot with Celtic artists performing most nights.

OTHER OPTIONS

If you're looking for a quieter, more relaxing atmosphere, try the **Windsock Lounge** (161 Water St.; ✆ **709/722-5001**), which (as the name suggests) has a distinct aviation theme, including oversized model aircraft hanging from the ceiling and difficult-to-decipher signs leading into the washrooms. This downtown piano bar features local performers Thursday to Saturday. Similarly stylish is **Narrows Lounge,** within the Sheraton Hotel Newfoundland (115 Cavendish Sq.; ✆ **709/726-4980**). Here, you can sip a cocktail overlooking the greenery of a cavernous atrium.

The **Ship Inn** on Solomon's Lane (access from 265 Duckworth St.; ✆ **709/753-3870**) is the most famous drinking establishment in the city. It's a rather dark but lively pub with a history that boasts many well-known writers and artists as frequent customers. The Ship Inn is known for hosting literary events, such as book launches and readings, so you just never know what—or whom—you'll find when you drop in. Expect live jazz, blues, reggae, rock, or folk Thursday through Saturday and poetry readings on Monday.

Another unique and interesting option is the **Crow's Nest,** located next to the War Memorial (between Water St. E. and Duckworth St.; ✆ **709/753-6927;** www.crowsnestnf.ca). Here, you'll find a periscope from a German World War II sub as part of the decor! The only drawback is that the Crow's Nest offers limited hours of operation: Tuesday to Thursday 4:30 to 7:30pm; Friday, lunch is served from noon to 2pm and they remain open until 10pm; Saturday 2 to 8pm; and closed Sunday and Monday. In business since 1942, the Crow's Nest is a private officers' club, but visitors to the city are welcome to drop in. A "smart casual" dress code is in effect, with summers being a bit more flexible.

The **Resource Centre for the Arts** presents entertaining comedy and alternative theater at the newly renovated LSPU Hall (3 Victoria St. at Duckworth St.; ✆ **709/753-4531;** www.rca.nf.ca). The building itself has been designated a registered heritage structure, and you'll find an art gallery downstairs.

If you like classical music, see if the **Newfoundland Symphony Orchestra** is playing while you're in town. Call ✆ **709/722-4441** or visit **www.nso-music.com** for an online schedule of performances and corresponding ticket prices. The season runs mid-September through early April, with most performances at either the Arts & Culture Centre on Prince Philip Drive or Cook Recital Hall on the university campus..

Avalon Peninsula

If your visit to Newfoundland allows for a mere week or so, you really have time to see only one region of the province—St. John's and the surrounding Avalon Peninsula.

The Avalon not only includes the capital, St. John's (see chapter 5), but also is home to half the entire provincial population, whom you'll find living in the many tiny coastal communities dotted throughout this charming and picturesque region. Using St. John's as a base, you can plan day trips around the Avalon Peninsula or, better still, pack your bags for an overnight stay.

Wildlife is a major attraction throughout Newfoundland and Labrador, but nowhere is it as accessible and as concentrated as on the Avalon Peninsula. **Witless Bay,** immediately south of St. John's, is the summer playground of more than 5,000 humpback and minke whales, as well tens of thousands of entertaining puffins. Farther south, and seemingly perched at the edge of the world, is **Cape St. Mary's Ecological Reserve,** where an offshore sea stack provides a summer home for 60,000 seabirds. Meanwhile, back on the mainland, herds of caribou migrate through the interior.

Most of the population lives in historic coastal communities, with **Ferryland,** first settled in 1621, the oldest of them all. It's an easy day trip from St. John's south to Witless Bay and Ferryland, but there are many reasons to travel farther, none more inviting than the wild coastal scenery that changes at every turn. Around the **Irish Loop,** the fossils of **Mistaken Point Ecological Reserve** are world renowned; along **Baccalieu Trail,** the village of **Brigus** has changed little in a century or more; and around **Conception Bay, Bell Island** attracts history buffs for its mine tours and diving enthusiasts for its shipwrecks. For hiking enthusiasts, the **East Coast Trail** has special appeal. Divided into 19 manageable sections, it extends from the outskirts of St. John's south to Trepassey, a total distance of 220km (137 miles).

Services on the Avalon Peninsula may be more limited than you are used to, but the region is more touristy than the rest of the island. Most villages have at least one accommodation and eatery, with more choices south of St. John's along the Irish Loop than elsewhere in the region.

VISITOR INFORMATION

The Visitor Information Centre at St. John's Airport has information on the Avalon Peninsula. It's open from 10am to midnight, 7 days a week. For pre-trip planning, you can contact **Destination St. John's** (✆ **877/739-8899** or 709/739-8899; www.destinationstjohns.com). The websites **www.southernavalontourism.ca** and **www.northernavalon.com** are also useful.

1 IRISH LOOP

If your time is limited (say, 1 extra day in St. John's), choose the Irish Loop for a day trip. Around 320km (199 miles) in total, the loop is a series of connected highways south of St. John's that pass the jumping-off point for whale-watching, an active archaeological dig, dozens of picturesque fishing villages, a wonderful golf course, and the opportunity to get up close and personal with many of the province's mammals.

As you stop at the various communities that comprise the Irish Loop, you may be surprised at the very strong Irish accent of the Newfoundlanders who call this region home. Most of the people who live here are direct descendants of the Irish who settled this area hundreds of years ago. And because many of the communities have been somewhat isolated until recent times, the Irish heritage has remained vibrant and the accent kept nicely intact.

ESSENTIALS

Getting There

To reach the 320km (199-mile) Irish Loop from St. John's, take Route 2 (Pitts Memorial Dr.) out of town, and then head south via Route 3, which will lead you to **Route 10,** forming the first section of the Irish Loop. You can make a slight detour onto Route 11 and stop in at **Cape Spear** (p. 100) or **Petty Harbour** (p. 101) along the way.

From the west, you can access the Irish Loop by taking Highway 1 to Route 13 (the Witless Bay Line), and then heading east to hook up with Route 10 between Bay Bulls and Witless Bay.

Back on Route 10, **Bay Bulls**—the northern gateway to Witless Bay Ecological Reserve—is reached 40km (25 miles) south of St. John's. Next up is **Ferryland,** site of the Colony of Avalon, an active archaeological dig. Continuing south, **Cape Race** is worth the detour, if you're interested in shipwrecks and the history of the *Titanic.*

Around the coast, as the highway turns back north, you'll arrive at **St. Vincent's,** a seaside community whose waters are known as a favorite dining spot for humpback whales. At St. Vincent's, Route 10 becomes **Route 90** (also known as the Salmonier Line) and carries on to **Salmonier,** home to one of the province's finest golf courses and **Salmonier Nature Park,** which itself is home to a variety of animals you probably won't see in the wild.

Visitor Information

You should have a detailed highway map and travel literature in hand before heading out from St. John's. Once you get into the smaller communities, services are more difficult to find, and they operate shorter hours. There are, however, visitor centers offering localized information at Bay Bulls, Ferryland, and Salmonier Nature Park.

For trip-planning information, contact the **Southern Avalon Tourism Association** (© **877/700-5667** or 709/334-2609; www.southernavalontourism.ca).

WITLESS BAY ECOLOGICAL RESERVE ★★★

Extending from **Bay Bulls** in the north to **Bauline East** in the south, Witless Bay Ecological Reserve was established to protect North America's largest puffin colony, which is at its peak April through mid-August. In addition to 520,000 of the province's official bird, the reserve provides a summer home for over two million other seabirds, as well as humpback and minke whales. If you're visiting in spring, icebergs are a spectacular bonus. The actual reserve is offshore, protecting coastal water and four uninhabited islands. Access to the reserve is by tour boat from the village of Bay Bulls, although island landings are not permitted.

Heading south from St. John's, the village of Bay Bulls will probably be your first stop on your way round the Irish Loop. It's a vibrant community of striking contrasts—rural

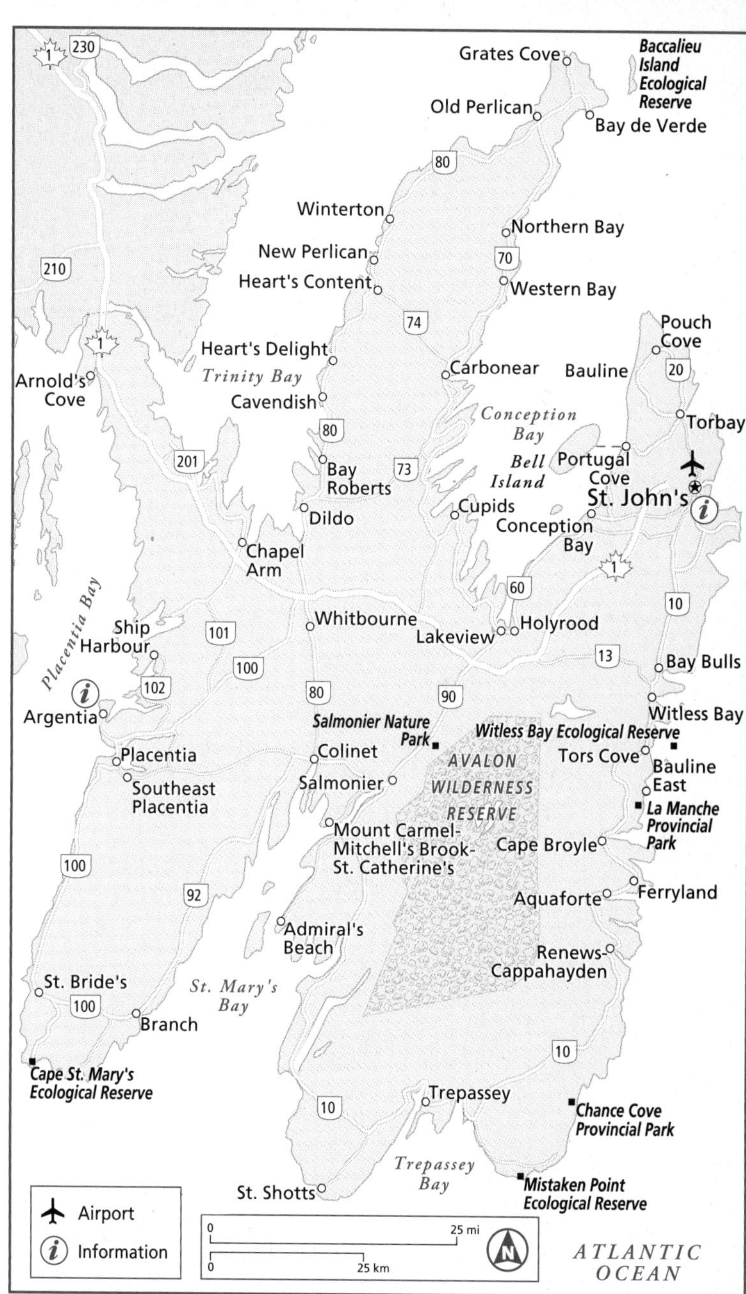
Grates Cove
Baccalieu Island Ecological Reserve
Old Perlican
Bay de Verde
Winterton
Northern Bay
New Perlican
Heart's Content
Western Bay
Pouch Cove
Heart's Delight
Trinity Bay
Arnold's Cove
Cavendish
Carbonear
Bauline
Conception Bay
Torbay
Bell Island
Portugal Cove
Bay Roberts
St. John's
Cupids
Dildo
Conception Bay
Chapel Arm
Placentia Bay
Ship Harbour
Whitbourne
Lakeview
Holyrood
Bay Bulls
Argentia
Salmonier Nature Park
Witless Bay
Witless Bay Ecological Reserve
Placentia
Colinet
AVALON WILDERNESS RESERVE
Tors Cove
Bauline East
Southeast Placentia
Salmonier
La Manche Provincial Park
Mount Carmel-Mitchell's Brook-St. Catherine's
Cape Broyle
Ferryland
Aquaforte
Admiral's Beach
Renews-Cappahayden
St. Bride's
St. Mary's Bay
Branch
Cape St. Mary's Ecological Reserve
Trepassey
Chance Cove Provincial Park
Trepassey Bay
St. Shotts
Mistaken Point Ecological Reserve
Airport
Information
0
25 mi
25 km
N
ATLANTIC OCEAN
230
1
210
201
80
70
74
73
60
20
10
13
101
100
102
90
92

attitude and architecture stand side by side with a strong commercial and industrial base—but for you, the visitor, it's the departure point for the ecological reserve.

Where to Stay

Bears Cove Inn ★★ Guests at this oceanfront lodging have a choice of comfortable rooms in a modern home. Some rooms face the garden, others offer a sweeping ocean panorama; or choose an apartment with a small but well-stocked kitchen. Unlike many bed-and-breakfasts in Newfoundland, Bears Cove has a delightful contemporary ambience, which extends from the en suite bathrooms to polished hardwood floors. Rates include a gourmet breakfast.

15 Bears Cove Rd., Witless Bay. ✆ **866/634-1171** or 709/334-3909. www.bearscoveinn.com. 7 units. C$129–C$179 double. MC, V. *In room:* TV/DVD player, Wi-Fi.

Celtic Rendezvous Cottages by the Sea ★ (Finds) Living up to its name, this oceanfront mini-resort pays homage to the endless harmony of surf and sky. Each of the five cottages has a huge kitchen and dining table, large sitting area, and outdoor patio. The two-bedroom Luxury Cottage comes with its own bedside jetted tub. In addition to the free-standing cottages is a row of 12 motel-like rooms, all of which open to an ocean-facing deck. One unit is wheelchair accessible. There is room for 12 RVs. Sites have electrical hookups and ocean views, but no privacy. Other facilities include a grocery store, a restaurant with sweeping ocean views, laundry facilities, and a covered barbeque area, where guests can cook up a feast of fresh seafood.

Main Rd., Bauline East. ✆ **866/334-3341** or 709/334-3341. www.celticrendezvouscottages.com. 17 units. C$89 motel room double; C$139–C$249 cottage double; C$25 RV site. DC, MC, V. Pets allowed. **Amenities:** Restaurant; Internet. *In room:* TV, hair dryer, kitchen (cabins only).

Elaine's B&B by the Sea ★ If you like kids, kittens, warm welcomes, and hearty breakfasts, try Elaine's, set on a charming seaside meadow, with 150m (492 ft.) of ocean frontage overlooking Bird Island and a panoramic view of Witless Bay Ecological Reserve. Late May and early June is the prime time for iceberg-watching from the backyard swing. If you're really lucky, your morning view just might include a distant whale waving its tail fluke. It's a large, modern home, with big windows to take advantage of the view. Modest though comfortably spacious guest rooms and firm mattresses work in conjunction with the invigorating power of sea-salt air to ensure one of the most restful sleeps imaginable. It's worth paying C$10 extra for the room with the best ocean view. The owners arrange evening bonfires down on the beach and offer their guests 90-minute whale-watching tours in a rigid-hulled Zodiac for C$55.

Lower Loop Place, Witless Bay. ✆ **709/334-2722.** www.elainesbythesea.com. 6 units. C$75–C$85 double, including breakfast. V. Free parking. *In room:* TV, no phone.

La Manche Provincial Park For overnight and/or day use, La Manche Provincial Park offers hiking, canoeing, swimming, and bird-watching opportunities. The highlight for me is the abandoned fishing village of La Manche (destroyed by a winter storm in 1966), which is reached in around 30 minutes on foot from the campground (the trail begins by Site 59). Each of the campsites has a picnic table, fireplace, garbage can, and parking. You will have to stock up on supplies before you arrive, as there is no convenience store on-site, nor are there shower or laundry facilities.

Rte. 10 (53km/33 miles south of St. John's). ✆ **800/563-6353** or 709/685-1823. www.env.gov.nl.ca/parks/parks/p_lm. 70 sites. Campsites C$15. Open mid-May to mid-Sept. **Amenities:** Trout angling; day-use facilities; drinking taps and pit toilets located throughout the park; hiking trails; interpretation program; outdoor freshwater swimming; picnic sites; playground. Firewood is C$5 per bundle.

The Sights & Sounds of Ireland

The **Southern Shore Folk Arts Council** (✆ **888/332-2052** or 709/432-2052; www.ssfac.com) provides a variety of entertainment from a restored building in downtown Ferryland that's been painted a nationalistic Irish green.

June through September, the association puts on **dinner theater** a few nights a week (call for dates and times). For C$42, you get a three-course meal and entertainment that brings the village's Irish heritage to life.

The **Shamrock Festival** offers lively music with traditional Irish/Newfoundland flavor. It's held outdoors, right in the middle of town, with some of the biggest names in Newfoundland music taking to the stage over the 2 days of the fourth weekend of July. Entry costs C$10 per day; those that don't want to pay fill the adjacent hillside with blankets and chairs—quite a sight!

Exploring Witless Bay Ecological Reserve

Each of the following operators is listed here because of certain unique characteristics, but others are around if the choices below are booked to capacity. Tours run from May to September and last around 2 hours. They are very weather dependent, so call before leaving St. John's to confirm that you'll be going.

For general information on the reserve, visit **www.env.gov.nl.ca/parks/wer/r_wbe**.

Gatherall's Puffin & Whale Watch (✆ **800/419-4253** or 709/334-2887; www.gatheralls.com) operates a high-speed catamaran that departs one to seven times daily from Bay Bulls. Because the boat travels at high speed, you spend less time getting to and from the best viewing sites, and more time watching the whales and puffins. There's enough seating for 100 passengers in the heated cabin, but if you prefer the wind in your hair, you can stand outside on the top deck. Cost is C$56 adults, C$49 seniors, C$19 children 9 to 17, and C$8 children 8 and under.

Also departing from the Bay Bulls waterfront, **O'Brien's** (✆ **877/639-4253** or 709/753-4850; www.obriensboattours.com) is justifiably popular. It's like getting two events for the price of one: a world-class marine adventure and a heck of a party, too. The 2-hour tour takes you aboard a two-level passenger vessel where you'll hear—and sing along to—lively Irish Newfoundland folk music; drink screech; have lots of fun; and get to see whales, puffins, and icebergs. Prices are similar to Gatherall's. O'Brien's also offers a zippy 2-hour Zodiac trip that will get you close to the Spout, sea caves, sea stacks, and more. These trips are C$85 per person. This trip is not recommended for really young kids. Transfers from downtown St. John's hotels are C$25 per person.

FERRYLAND

With almost 400 years of European settlement to its credit, **Ferryland,** 75km (47 miles) south of St. John's, is one of the oldest communities in North America. It's also the site of an ongoing excavation of a 17th-century settlement known as the Colony of Avalon. It's a unique archaeological dig in that local residents live in the midst of the pick-and-shovel activity.

Lighthouses

You'll find many lighthouses as you make your way around Newfoundland and Labrador. They have been protecting seafarers since 1813, when the first lighthouse was built and operated by volunteers at Fort Amherst at the mouth of St. John's Harbour. Other lighthouses were built after the formation of Newfoundland's Lighthouse Board in 1832. Most of those colorful lighthouses or their replacement structures still stand. The Cape Bonavista Lighthouse is of prime significance as the place where continental Europeans first landed in Newfoundland. And the Point Amour Lighthouse on the Labrador Straits, first illuminated in 1858, is the tallest in Atlantic Canada. It is now automated, as are most of the lighthouses in the province, but their history remains alive and of prime significance to residents and visitors hoping to gain a deeper understanding of this seafaring province.

Many lighthouses are open to the public, with exhibits related to the fishery, the naval history and shipwrecks, and the strong people who have built this land. Some lighthouses have been made even more appealing to visitors, including the 1871 **Ferryland Lighthouse,** where you can order a picnic lunch to enjoy on the grassy headland. For something really unique, plan on an overnight stay at the **Quirpon Lighthouse Inn.**

Where to Stay & Dine

Colony Café ★ SEAFOOD This dining experience offers Continental flavor while overlooking the archaeological dig. The enterprise, in a building once occupied by a fish plant, began as a simple coffee shop. Customer demand forced those modest plans to be upgraded to a full-service restaurant, although aside from a custom-painted historical mural, the ambience is uninspiring. Seafood is the specialty, with cod dominating the menu. This mild fish is easily overpowered by excessive accoutrements, and is prepared accordingly. A tantalizing whiff of a passing bowl of seafood chowder will have you salivating for more. Give in to temptation. I guarantee you won't be disappointed.

Rte. 10, Ferryland. ✆ **709/432-3030.** www.thecolonycafe.ca. Reservations recommended for dinner. Main courses C$14–C$27. MC, V. May–Sept Mon–Thurs 11am–8pm, Fri–Sun 9am–8:30pm. Closed the rest of the year.

Hagan's Hospitality Home B&B The house isn't an architectural masterpiece, nor will the decorating scheme win any awards, but everything beyond that is extraordinary. Both in portion and flavor, the generous cooked breakfast epitomizes homemade perfection. But even that pales in comparison to the warmth and friendliness of your host, the delightful Rita Hagan. Her perpetual smile and musical brogue more than make up for any splendor lacking from her listed amenities. With a mug of tea in your hand and one of her timeless stories in your ear, you'll feel as privileged as royalty.

Rte. 10, 8km (5 miles) southwest of Ferryland in Aquaforte. ✆ **709/363-2688.** 2 units. C$60 double; 10% discount for seniors. Rate includes lunch and full breakfast. No credit cards. Free parking. **Amenities:** Room service; TV lounge. *In room:* No phone.

Lighthouse Picnics ★★★ LIGHT FARE From the archaeological dig, walk up onto the headland, and Ferryland Lighthouse will soon come into view. Built in 1870, this classic red-and-white lighthouse was abandoned until 2004, when enterprising locals spruced up the exterior and began using it as a store, providing picnic baskets for visitors. You can order goodies as simple as muffins baked in-house, or as extravagant as gourmet sandwiches, imported cheeses, crab cakes, and salad. The strawberry shortcake is an absolute must. Picnic baskets come with thoughtful extras, such as blankets and books, which encourage visitors to linger longer on the surrounding grassy headland.

Ferryland Lighthouse, Ferryland. ✆ **709/363-7456.** www.lighthousepicnics.ca. Picnic baskets C$12–C$35. MC, V. Mid-June to late Sept Tues–Sun 11:30am–5pm.

Exploring Ferryland

Colony of Avalon ★★ The reason you'll want to visit Ferryland is for the opportunity to immerse yourself in the history of this living archaeological dig. Located in the heart of the village, the site is composed of two parts—the modern Interpretation Centre and the actual dig site. Start at the interpretation center. Watch the short documentary and then view artifacts from the first successful planned colony in Newfoundland, including everything from coins to cannonballs. Visitors are welcome to view the second-floor Conservation Laboratory, where the cataloging and reconstruction of artifacts takes place (weekdays 8am–4:30pm). An on-site gift shop sells local crafts and reproductions of 17th-century items from the colony. Outside is an interesting garden filled with the same herbs as the first settlers would have planted.

You're then ready to take a 1½-hour guided tour (or a more leisurely self-guided tour) of the village settled in 1621 by Sir George Calvert (who later became Lord Baltimore). On the guided tour, you'll learn about the world's first flushable toilet (we have clogs to thank for artifacts found in the "pipe") and walk on the oldest cobblestone street in British North America.

Rte. 10, Ferryland. ✆ **877/326-5669** or 709/432-3200. www.colonyofavalon.ca. Admission C$7.50 adults, C$5.50 seniors and students; C$15 families. Mid-May to June and Sept to early Oct daily 8:30am–4:30pm, July and Aug daily 8:30am–7pm.

TREPASSEY & SURROUNDS

Midway round the Irish Loop, you'll come to the small fishing village of Trepassey, a good place to stop for the night if you find yourself at Mistaken Point late in the day. The location is somewhat remote, but there are advantages to that: you're right in the heart of caribou country. ***Warning:*** Be aware that this area is prone to heavy fog, so be careful when driving, as the animals frequently cross the road. Trepassey's historic claim to fame is as the place where Amelia Earhart launched her cross-Atlantic flight in 1928. The town has a small museum with a commemorative display featuring photos of the famous aviator during her visit to the town, but the real highlights are the ecological reserve and the views from **Cape Race Lighthouse.**

Where to Stay & Dine

Northwest Lodge Bed & Breakfast Hosts Harold and Marie Pennell offer safe, clean, and economical accommodations in a family environment. Marie is noted for her homemade jams (and her cooking, in general), and Harold has loads of stories about his days as a lighthouse keeper at nearby Cape Race. Although comfortable, the rooms alone won't lure you here (they're almost filled to capacity by a bureau and double bed). You'll

Fun Facts Graveyard of the Atlantic

With its perpetual fog and rock-studded shore, it's no wonder the area of the southern Avalon around Cape Race is called the **"Graveyard of the Atlantic."** Records show 365 ships have gone down between Renews Harbour and Cape Pine. Cape Race is in the center between these two points. If you're interested in maritime history and prepared for travel along a rough access road, plan on visiting **Cape Race Lighthouse,** operating since 1856. It has the largest lighthouse lens in North America. You can tour the lighthouse and its museum for C$3. In the museum, you'll find a small *Titanic* display, highlighting the Cape Race connection to the doomed ship (this is where the SOS signal from the sinking luxury liner was received). Although the lighthouse is automated, there is a lighthouse keeper in residence, and students provide interpretive services in the summer. To make advance arrangements for your trip to the lighthouse, stop by the **Portugal Cove South Visitor Centre** or call ✆ **709/ 438-1100.**

be far more impressed by the leaping salmon in the nearby river, as well as the chance to get up close and personal with the resident caribou herd.

Rte. 10, Trepassey. ✆ **877/398-2888** or 709/438-2888. www.bbcanada.com/bbnorthwest. 4 units. C$85 double. MC, V. Free parking. *In room:* TV, no phone.

Trepassey Motel & Restaurant If all you need are clean sheets, a roof over your head, and a shower in the morning, this is an excellent choice roughly halfway around the Irish Loop (around 2 hr. from St. John's). Treat yourself to breakfast in the motel restaurant. Not only is the food reasonably priced and well prepared, but the dining room's floor-to-ceiling windows provide a view that'll be the highlight of your stay.

111–113 Coarse Hill, Trepassey. ✆ **709/438-2934.** www.trepasseymotel.com. 10 units. C$80 double. AE, MC, V. Free parking. **Amenities:** Restaurant. *In room:* TV, no phone.

To Cape Race

From Trepassey, backtrack to Portugal Cove South and make the turn south to Cape Race. You'll pass Mistaken Point on the 30km (19-mile) drive to Cape Race.

Mistaken Point Ecological Reserve This is the only place in the world where Precambrian animal fossils are so abundant that they cover exposed areas the size of tennis courts. If you're into fossils, you'll appreciate the area's key importance to paleontologists as the home of 560-million-year-old fossils. They are the world's oldest known multi-celled creatures, living in the ocean before animals had developed skeletons.

Before heading out to the site, make a stop at the **Portugal Cove South Visitor Centre** (✆ **709/438-1100**), a modern building filled with displays describing the importance of the site. It's open May through October daily 10am to 6pm. Admission is free. The center also organizes inexpensive tours, which leave on demand. From Portugal Cove South, allow around 25 minutes to drive to the end of the road, and then 45 minutes to walk across open fields to the fossil bed. The site has no signage, so unless you've join a tour, you're on your own. ***Note:*** Fossil collecting is prohibited. ***Warning:*** The unpaved access road is rough, and the parking lot for the fossil bed is not well marked; drive carefully and keep your eyes peeled for the small and faded sign.

Turn off Rte. 10 at Portugal Cove South. ✆ **709/438-1100.** www.env.gov.nl.ca/parks/wer/r_mpe. Free admission. Accessible year-round during daylight hr., weather permitting.

ST. VINCENT'S

The tiny village of St. Vincent's, 38km (24 miles) west of Trepassey in the beautiful Peter's River Valley, is the place to be between June and August if you want to see humpback whales **lunge feeding.** The whales launch their bodies right out of the water—mouths wide open—and fill themselves with capelin (small fish similar to smelt, which are a favorite dinner for the whales). The whales like it here because the water is deep, even close to shore, and these conditions attract more capelin. More capelin, more whales. Nature being nature, there are no promises that you'll see the whales feeding, but they've been doing so with some regularity the past few years; if you're patient the chances are good. To help you pass the time while you wait for the whales, a food stand sells souvenirs and serves fish and chips right on the beach.

You can also stop by the **Fisherman's Museum,** on Route 90 across from the visitor center (✆ **709/525-2798**). It is housed in the early 1900s home of a local fishing family. You can examine all sorts of artifacts from a traditional fisherman's home, including an example of the **Newfoundland Thermos**—a bottle wrapped in a sock that would contain the fisherman's special blend of hot tea mixed with hooch. Upstairs is an interesting collection of handmade carpentry tools. The museum is open July and August daily 10am to 5pm. Admission is by donation.

SALMONIER

This little village, 57km (35 miles) north of St. Vincent's on Route 90, is just a dot on the map, but nearby is a resort-style golf course and the province's only wildlife park.

Where to Stay & Dine

The Wilds at Salmonier River Ample accommodations choices await you at this resort, geared more to golf enthusiasts than luxury-seeking travelers. You can choose from 39 standard hotel-style rooms or a three-bedroom, self-contained chalet. The latter provides more privacy and is a better choice for families or small groups wanting to be together. ***Hint:*** The chalet books up early, so try to reserve well in advance, especially for summer weekends. Hotel rooms come in five configurations, including the Honeymoon Suite, which has a king-size bed, jetted tub, fireplace, fridge, and views across the pool to the golf course.

The Wilds is set on the beautiful Salmonier River and nestled in a hilly, wooded area. With the outdoor swimming pool, the golf course, and nearby Salmonier Nature Park, you'll have plenty of opportunity to enjoy the great outdoors. And the complimentary supervised kids' program (for ages 5–14) means you'll be able to have some time to yourself.

Caddie's Cookhouse, overlooking the golf course and river, is open daily for breakfast, lunch, and dinner. The menu is as predictable as you'd expect at a family-oriented resort, with something to please everyone and prices to please whoever's paying. The weekend breakfast buffet (C$13) is an especially good value.

Rte. 90, Salmonier Line (Hwy. 1 to Exit 35). ✆ **866/888-9453** or 709/229-5444. www.thewilds.ca. 39 units C$139–C$199 hotel room double; C$350 chalet. AE, DC, MC, V. **Amenities:** Restaurant; lounge; pool; babysitting; children's program; golf course. *In room:* TV.

Avalon Wilderness Reserve

A large chunk of the interior between routes 10 and 90 is protected as the Avalon Wilderness Reserve, home to the most southerly herd of woodland caribou in the world. Numbering less than 50, the herd was almost extinct in the 1960s. But numbers have rebounded, and today, around 2,000 animals inhabit the remote region. The reserve is total wilderness, with no services and only a few old service roads passing through. An overnight hiking trail, beginning from Salmonier Nature Park, is for experienced backcountry hikers only. Lucky for the less adventurous, the caribou are occasionally seen along the surrounding highways, most often along Route 90. For more information and details on permits required for hiking, visit **www.env.gov.nl.ca/parks/wer/r_aw**.

Exploring Salmonier

Salmonier Nature Park ★ Kids Finds This peaceful and calming nature reserve is operated by the provincial government. Because it's a rehabilitation facility for injured and orphaned birds and animals, you'll find the guest list to be constantly changing—the goal of the park is to release as many of the creatures as possible back into the wild. For those who will never be able to survive the wild again, the park serves as a comfortable hospital or retirement home. As you stroll along the park's 3km (1.9-mile) wheelchair- and stroller-friendly boardwalk, you'll see moose, lynx, owls, bald eagles, and arctic fox in specially developed enclosures that represent their natural habitat. In addition to the resident mammals, approximately 100 species of birds and 175 species of plants have been recorded in the park—including the pitcher plant, Newfoundland and Labrador's provincial flower. Benches are strategically situated along the way so you can rest, enjoy a snack, or just marvel at nature. Some of the residents are shy, so call ahead for feeding times, knowing that a small bribe will coax the animals out of hiding. Allow at least an hour for your visit.

Rte. 90 (12km/7½ miles north of Salmonier). ✆ **709/229-7189.** www.env.gov.nl.ca/snp. Free admission. June–Aug daily 10am–6pm; Sept Mon–Fri 10am–4pm.

The Wilds This 18-hole golf course has made the greatest of efforts to preserve the native woodlands long before we decided it was fun to whack a small white ball around with a shiny club. You'll find waterfalls and small creeks running throughout the course, and if you're lucky, you just may see a moose crossing a fairway (the big brown fellows have been known to hang around the 16th green and the woods lining the 7th hole).

Because it's only minutes from Salmonier Nature Park, one parent can take the kids to the park while the other has a round of golf. Better yet, if you're staying overnight at The Wilds at Salmonier River, you can avail of the childcare program so that everyone gets to play. You'll find a restaurant, pro shop, club rentals, and a driving range at the golf course.

The Wilds at Salmonier River, Rte. 90 (Hwy. 1 to Exit 35). ✆ **709/229-9453.** www.thewilds.ca. C$45–C$55 for 18 holes; C$34 for a power cart.

2 CAPE SHORE

Circling the extreme southwest corner of the Avalon Peninsula, the Cape Shore provides access to **Cape St. Mary's Ecological Reserve,** the province's best bird-watching spot. Even if you're not an avid birder, you'll be awed by the number of gannets that inhabit Bird Rock. In fact, the symbol for the Cape Shore Route is one of our fine feathered friends because this region is a birder's paradise. Also along the way is Argentia, where ferries from North Sydney (Nova Scotia) dock. Argentia is the site of a now-deserted U.S. naval base.

ESSENTIALS

Getting There & Around

The Cape Shore driving route branches off Route 90 near Salmonier. It loops south past Cape St. Mary's to St. Bride's, and then parallels the eastern side of Placentia Bay to Argentia. From St. John's, the entire loop is a little over 400km (249 miles). Taking the winding road into consideration, it's a full day trip from the capital.

Note: The provincial travel literature tells you it will take only 2 hours to get to Cape St. Mary's from St. John's, but allow 3 hours. The road is narrow, with lots of hairpin curves through gorgeous hilly countryside. It's not just difficult driving—you won't *want* to rush! If you've just come off the ferry at Argentia and your first destination is Cape St. Mary's, head south 75km (47 miles) along Route 100. It's a lovely coastal drive, and you'll be there in about an hour. If you're heading from Argentia to St. John's, take Route 100 north to the Trans-Canada Highway (Rte. 1), which will take you directly into the heart of the city in a little more than 90 minutes.

Visitor Information

If you arrive in this region by way of **ferry** from Nova Scotia, plan on stopping at the **visitor center** in Argentia (✆ **709/227-5272**). It is open hours that coincide with the ferry's arrivals and departures. You can also pick up brochures and information about the region at the **Cape St. Mary's Visitor Centre** (✆ **709/277-1666**).

WHERE TO STAY

Tourist accommodations and services are not as developed along the Cape Shore Route as you'll find in neighboring regions, mainly because fewer communities are along the way, with virtually nothing along Route 92 from North Harbour to Branch. The community of **St. Bride's** is the largest one nearest to Cape St. Mary's and it is still very small.

Bird Island Resort (Kids) This family resort with spectacular oceanfront property is as easy on your eyes as your pocketbook. The two-bedroom efficiency units offer full

Navigating Newfoundland

It can be confusing driving around Newfoundland, as you'll often find that a street or highway starts out with one name or number, and then changes without notice. That's why it's critical you have a detailed highway map before heading out on any road trip in the province.

kitchen facilities equipped with all the dishes, glasses, and appliances you could need—so you don't have to worry about the expense of a restaurant. There's a small fitness center to help you stay in shape for your day at the on-site beach, and a convenience store is within walking distance. The Mannings, who own and operate the place, are a considerate family who pay attention to the details that make Bird Island Resort such a popular establishment. This is the closest accommodations to Cape St. Mary's.

Rte. 100 (Main Rd.), St. Bride's. ✆ **709/337-2450.** www.birdislandresort.com. 20 units. C$69 double; C$109 efficiency units. AE, MC, V. **Amenities:** Exercise room. *In room:* TV, kitchenette.

Rosedale Manor B&B ★★ One of the finest bed-and-breakfasts to be found on the Avalon Peninsula, Rosedale Manor is a restored heritage home with well-manicured gardens overlooking the ocean. Located a short drive from Argentia, it's also a handy overnight stop for arriving or departing ferry passengers. The stylish rooms are outfitted with handcrafted Newfoundland-made furniture, and some (such as the Osprey Room) enjoy water views. Instead of in-room televisions, guests congregate in the living room. But it is the breakfast that is most memorable. Unusual for the province, the emphasis is on ingredients such as free-range eggs and bread made daily with organic whole grains. Even the jams and preserves are made with berries grown in the surrounding garden.

40 Orcan Dr., Placentia. ✆ **877/999-3613** or 709/227-3613. www.rosedalemanor.ca. 5 units. C$79–C$99 double. MC, V. Free parking. *In room:* Wi-Fi.

EXPLORING THE CAPE SHORE

Cape St. Mary's Ecological Reserve ★★★ Even if you're not a keen birder, visiting Cape St. Mary's is a must. The reserve protects the breeding ground of 24,000 northern gannets, 20,000 common murres, 2,000 thick-billed murres, 20,000 black-legged kittiwakes, and more than 200 northern razorbills. The birds are only part of the attraction—the cliff-top setting is also spectacular. Upon arriving at the cape, just east of St. Bride's and a 3-hour drive from St. John's, your first stop should be the Interpretive Centre, where you can familiarize yourself with the types of birds you'll be seeing.

From the center, it's a 1km (½-mile) walk across subarctic tundra to the lookout point for **Bird Rock.** It will take you 15 minutes if you're a fast walker, 30 minutes if you take the time to appreciate the sights along the way. This 100m-high (328-ft.) sandstone sea stack is separated from the mainland by only a few meters. You'll be standing high atop a rock roughly equivalent in height to Bird Rock itself, where thousands of northern gannets can be seen courting, nesting, and feeding.

Tip: Be sure to bring a weatherproof jacket and nonslip footwear for the walk. And remember that this is a site to protect wildlife—not humans—so be sure to hang on to children when you are hiking near the edge of the cliff. You'll also want to be extra cautious when the fog rolls in, which happens around 200 days each year (May and June are particularly foggy).

15km/9¼ miles east, then south off Rte. 100 from St. Bride's. ✆ **709/277-1666.** www.env.gov.nl.ca/parks/wer/r_csme. Free admission; 1½-hour guided tour to Bird Rock C$7. Trail to Bird Rock open year-round; Interpretive Centre mid-May to early Oct daily 9am–5pm.

Castle Hill National Historic Site This barren, oceanfront site between Placentia and Argentia protects the foundations of French fortifications dating to 1662. The site, overlooking Placentia Bay, was chosen for its strategic location above rich fishing grounds, but the land itself was poor and self-sufficiency impossible. By 1713, when sovereignty to Newfoundland was handed over to Great Britain, the fort's usefulness waned. Unless you happen to be in the area or arrive in the province by ferry via Argentia, I wouldn't recommend making the journey specifically to visit Castle Hill. It's a long drive, and the attraction isn't as impressive as some other more readily accessed sites—Signal Hill in St. John's, for instance.

Rte. 100, between Placentia and Argentia. ✆ **709/227-2401.** www.pc.gc.ca//eng/lhn-nhs/nl/castlehill/index.aspx. Admission C$4 adults, C$3.50 seniors, C$2 children; C$10 families. Mid-May to mid-Oct daily 10am–6pm.

3 BACCALIEU TRAIL

Baccalieu may seem an odd word to find in Newfoundland. However, it's actually a derivation of an old Portuguese word for salted cod, and once you've spent any time in the province, you realize the historical importance of cod.

The Baccalieu Trail extends up an arm of the Avalon Peninsula, one that separates Conception and Trinity bays. You may also hear this region referred to as Northern Avalon.

Brigus, not far from the Trans-Canada Highway, is a scenic highlight. Except for the pavement, you'll think you've stepped back in time. You'll walk beneath the arching branches of aging trees gracefully overhanging the narrow streets. You'll explore the gentle paths meandering over stony escarpments and nod to the locals as they go about their daily business around immaculately maintained old-style homes, some flanked by the ordered rows of vegetable gardens. If you're driving out to Brigus from St. John's, allow 45 minutes via the Trans-Canada Highway (Rte. 1).

Beyond Brigus are a multitude of fishing villages with enchanting names such as Heart's Content, Harbour Grace, Heart's Desire, Heart's Delight, Cupids, and Blow Me Down. Each bend of the coastline brings with it a different personality.

ESSENTIALS

Getting There

The gateway to the Baccalieu Trail is Exit 31 of the Trans-Canada Highway, 70km (43 miles) west of St. John's. From this point, it's 16km (10 miles) north to Brigus and 44km (27 miles) north to **Carbonear,** the largest town along the trail. The western access is near **Whitbourne,** at Route 80, which follows the coast of Trinity Bay and extends north at **Grates Cove** before continuing south along the coast of Conception Bay (as Rte. 70) and ending back at the aforementioned Exit 31. The entire loop is 214km (133 miles); if you cut across the peninsula at Carbonear on Route 74, the distance is 140km (87 miles).

Visitor Information

Although there are no official visitor centers along the Baccalieu Trail, the accommodations and attractions detailed below are a good source of information. Another contact is the **Northern Avalon Tourism** (✆ **709/596-3474;** www.northernavalon.com).

WHERE TO STAY

Blazing Horizon Cottages Driving north beyond Dildo, you quickly reach Whiteway, a small community overlooking Trinity Bay. In town, with a prime waterfront location, are the four Blazing Horizon Cottages, each with a full kitchen and its own picnic table and fire pit. Part of the same complex is **Brown's Restaurant,** open daily for breakfast, lunch, and dinner. Look for a menu filled with seafood favorites, including delicious seafood chowder. Both the cottages and the restaurant have ocean views, with distinctive Shag Rock easily identified just offshore.

Route 80, Whiteway. ✆ **866/998-7829** or 709/588-7829. www.blazinghorizoncottages.com. 4 units. C$129–C$169 double. Each additional person C$20. MC, V. Free parking. Closed Nov–Apr. **Amenities:** Restaurant; Wi-Fi. *In room:* TV/DVD player, kitchen.

The Brittoner Value This beautifully restored 1840s saltbox-style home in the heart of Brigus is not flush with amenities, but its central location makes it perfect for sightseeing. As a bonus, there are hiking trails nearby, tennis courts across the street, and a deck that's the perfect setting for a delicious outdoor breakfast. It overlooks a lovely pond that's home to a playful family of ducks.

12 Water St., Brigus. ✆ **709/528-3412.** www.bbcanada.com/4385.html. 3 units. C$75–C$85 double. No credit cards. Closed Nov–Apr. Pets allowed. **Amenities:** Playground. *In room:* No phone.

Fong's Motel If you prefer the anonymity of a motel room, as opposed to a bed-and-breakfast, Fong's is a decent choice while touring the Baccalieu Trail. Fong's offers a motel, restaurant, banquet room, and lounge. Guest rooms are simple and sparse, but they're spacious, with large windows and full bathrooms. It's conveniently located right off the highway, near the edge of town.

143 Columbus Dr., Carbonear. ✆ **709/596-5114.** 16 units. C$70–C$80 double. AE, DC, MC, V. Free parking. **Amenities:** Restaurant, lounge. *In room:* TV.

Inn by the Bay ★★ This exquisite waterfront lodging overlooks Dildo Bay from the historical fishing village of Dildo, named one of Canada's 10 prettiest towns. Dating to 1888, the inn is operated by Todd Warren, an enterprising young man with extensive experience in the hospitality industry. It shows, because Todd doesn't miss a beat. The finest of feather duvets and pillows adorn the tastefully furnished rooms. And each room has a private bathroom, as well as its own decorative personality.

Todd's abilities as a chef make the meals at the in-house Sea Level Dining Room a real treat. In addition to the full breakfast, specialties (such as mussels served in a caramelized sauce) are an example of the gourmet four-course dinners guests can enjoy for an additional C$39 per person. Rates include a full breakfast.

78 Front Rd., Dildo. ✆ **888/582-2167** or 709/582-3170. www.innbythebaydildo.com. 7 units. C$89–C$199 double. AE, DC, MC, V. Off-street parking. Closed Mid-Dec to Apr. From Exit 28 of the Trans-Canada Hwy. follow Route 80 12km/7½ miles north to Dildo. **Amenities:** Restaurant. *In room:* TV/DVD player, Wi-Fi.

NaGeira House ★ Just over an hour's drive from St. John's (via the Trans-Canada Hwy. to Rte. 70), you'll find the full-service community of Carbonear and this welcoming bed-and-breakfast, a registered heritage structure. NaGeira's gives you a wide choice of distinctively decorated rooms. One room has an in-room whirlpool bath; another has a mahogany four-poster bed. And all rooms have down duvets and en-suite bathrooms. The exquisite woodwork sets the tone for a quiet and relaxing stay, complemented by the inn's fireplaces and library. The quiet location, well-manicured gardens, and exemplary service make this a great place to stay while in the area.

7 Musgrave St. (off Rte. 70, and also accessible from Rte. 74 if coming across the peninsula from Heart's Content), Carbonear. ✆ **800/600-7757** or 709/596-1888. www.nageirahouse.com. 4 units. C$99–C$149 double. AE, MC, V. Free parking. *In room:* TV.

WHERE TO DINE

You'll get wonderful meals at the locations listed above, but if you're looking for a snack, light meal, or picnic lunch, here are a couple of reasonably priced options that are worth checking out.

Kountry Kravins 'n' Krafts LIGHT FARE This quaint little cafe serves reasonably priced lunches at a few indoor tables or outside on the small deck overlooking Dildo Bay. Alternatively, the friendly staff will make a picnic lunch for you to enjoy along the road. They have a fairly limited light-lunch menu, and the offerings (particularly the sandwiches) aren't great, but the setting is picturesque, and it's worth stopping in, at least to see the terrific selection of local crafts they have for sale.

Front Rd., Dildo (across the street from the Interpretive Centre). ✆ **709/582-3888.** www.dildosouvenirs.com. Reservations not accepted. Lunch C$7. MC, V. Mid-May to mid-Sept daily 9:30am–9:30pm; mid-Sept to mid-May daily 11am–8pm.

The Country Corner LIGHT FARE While exploring Brigus, drop in to the Country Corner for lunch. The chowder combo gets you a delicious bowl of cod chowder and a serving of blueberry crisp, along with a beverage and a tea biscuit. They also sell a nice assortment of Newfoundland souvenirs and gifts.

14 Water St., Brigus. ✆ **709/528-1099.** Reservations not accepted. Lunch C$6–C$14. AE, MC, V. May–Oct daily 10am–6pm.

EXPLORING THE BACCALIEU TRAIL

Avondale Railway Station (Kids) Just south of Brigus on Route 60, you'll find a gem of a museum located in Newfoundland's oldest railway station (ca. 1864). It features five static railway cars, including a snowplow, CN A913, diesel locomotive, baggage/kitchen car, a working dining car, and a caboose. What excites most railway buffs about Avondale is that it is the site of the last remaining mainline track of the Newfoundland Railway and a prime example of the old narrow-gauge track. The museum runs a few small railcars on the track for kids and their parents over the 2km (1¼ miles) of narrow gauge.

Rte. 60, Avondale Access Rd. ✆ **709/229-2288.** Free admission. July–Aug daily 11am–5pm.

Baccalieu Island Ecological Reserve This remote seabird reserve is largely inaccessible due to its steep, high cliffs and treacherous shoreline. The reserve itself contains Baccalieu Island, located off the tip of the northwest Avalon Peninsula near the tiny outport of **Bay de Verde.** It's the largest seabird island in Newfoundland and Labrador, measuring approximately 6km (3¾ miles) long and 1km (½ mile) wide. Between June and August, the island is home to approximately 3.3 million pairs of Leach's storm petrels, the world's largest such colony. Eleven seabird species breed on Baccalieu Island.

You can learn more about the birds and the reserve by visiting the **Bay de Verde Heritage House,** in Bay de Verde. Built in 1896 for a local merchant, this imposing house (no longer a home) has an exhibit devoted to Baccalieu Island, as well as displays cataloguing the life of early settlers.

Museum is on Rte. 70, Bay de Verde. ✆ **709/596-3474.** www.env.gov.nl.ca/parks/wer/r_bie. Admission by donation. June–Sept Mon–Sat 11am–5pm, Sun 1–6pm.

Dildo & Area Interpretation Centre This is a surprisingly impressive heritage site, considering the diminutive size of both the facility and its host community. Inside a restored waterfront building, you'll find a historical account of Dildo Island and the people, such as the Maritime Archaic Indians, who called it home. There's also a display on the history of the local cod fishery and a touch tank filled with smaller ocean critters. Outside is a replica of a giant 8.5m-long (28-ft.) squid that was caught in local waters in 1933. It has seen better days, but is still interesting for its sheer size. Most of the items on display have been donated by members of the community. A half-hour should be sufficient to tour this facility.

Front Rd., Dildo. ✆ **709/582-3339.** Admission C$2 adults, C$1 children; C$5 families. June–Sept daily 10am–6pm.

Grates Cove The tiny outport of Grates Cove (pop. 250) is at the very northern tip of the land finger separating Trinity Bay from Conception Bay. Here, you will find the remains of rock walls used from the late 1700s to the late 1800s to separate and protect vegetable gardens and livestock. The walls extend for over 65 hectares (161 acres) and are plainly visible to anyone walking through the community. To really appreciate the extent of the walls, follow the walking trail to the summit of Big Hill, behind the community.

Note: Grates Cove has no restaurant—or even a place to get a cup of tea (unless you're lucky enough to be invited to the home of one of the locals). Apart from the rock walls and a small art studio on Main Road, there is really very little to see or do here. There is no signage to provide an interpretation of the rock walls, nor are there guided tours. They are, however, an interesting (and free) viewing spectacle.

Rte. 70, 12km (7½ miles) north of Bay de Verde.

Hawthorne Cottage National Historic Site Built in 1830, Hawthorne Cottage, in the lovely community of Brigus, is one of the few remaining examples of the picturesque cottage *orné*—translated from French, this means it's nicely decorated. But it's more than that. The home once belonged to Captain Bob Bartlett (the world-famous Newfoundland-born Arctic explorer) and contains interesting artifacts from Bartlett's journeys to the Arctic during the early 20th century. As you walk through the house, you'll hear recordings that explain the historic importance of fishing and sealing to Brigus residents. You'll also see local period artifacts and textiles in their original setting, including the various upstairs bedrooms and kitchen. Be sure to visit the lovely commemorative sculpture in the shape of a ship's sails that has been erected in honor of Bartlett, on the harbor near the Brigus Tunnel.

Irishtown Rd., Brigus. ✆ **709/753-9262.** www.pc.gc.ca/lhn-nhs/nl/hawthorne/index.aspx. Admission C$4 adults, C$3.50 seniors, C$3 children; C$10 families. Mid-May–Sept Wed–Sun 9am–5pm; July–Aug daily 9am–7pm. Wheelchair accessible.

Heart's Content Cable Station This provincial historical site commemorates the importance of the transatlantic cable that made communications between Europe and North America near-instantaneous. After the failure of two earlier attempts, a permanent transatlantic telegraph cable was landed here in 1866. The station houses equipment and interpretive displays that explain the role Heart's Content played in the world of communications for nearly 100 years. I was fascinated by the replica of the original Victorian cable office, as well as the storyboards describing how engineers of the day were able to overcome the many difficulties associated with laying a sub-sea electrical cable between the two continents.

Rte. 80, Heart's Content. ✆ **709/583-2160.** Admission C$3 for ages 13 and up. Mid-May to late-Sept daily 10am–5:30pm.

Rodrigues Winery If you've looped around the Baccalieu Trail and find yourself back on the Trans-Canada Highway with some extra time, this is an interesting stop.

Located near the village of **Markland** (south of Whitbourne), Rodrigues was established in 1993 as Newfoundland and Labrador's first winery. It's surprising to find that there are indeed wineries in Newfoundland, and even more impressive to learn that this one has won several awards with its fine vintages.

A variety of wines are made from local berries such as bakeapple, partridgeberry, blueberry, raspberry, and other special blends. I especially liked the bakeapple and partridgeberry wines for their tartness. They also distill a super-sweet pear brandy, as well as fruit-flavored vodka. Take a free tour, sample the different varieties, and take some home as tasty souvenirs.

Rte. 81, Markland. ✆ **709/759-3003.** www.rodrigueswinery.com. July–Aug daily 9am–4:30pm; Sept–June Mon–Fri 9am–4:30pm.

4 CONCEPTION BAY

Conception Bay is on the back doorstep of St. John's and, if you've been following the order of this chapter, will complete your tour of the Avalon Peninsula. If you're in St. John's and want a break from city sightseeing, a drive to Conception Bay makes a great day trip, as the town is rich in maritime history and spectacular scenery. I recommend you make the journey to **Bell Island,** an enjoyable 20-minute ferry ride from the community of Portugal Cove.

Conception Bay (the actual body of water) was named by the Spanish in the 1700s in honor of a religious holiday relating to the Immaculate Conception. The Bay has a colorful history and was home to pirates during the 17th and 18th centuries. **Kelly's Island,** just offshore from Conception Bay South, was a popular stopover for pirates and is the rumored hideaway of buried treasure.

ESSENTIALS

Getting There & Around

If you take Route 40 (Portugal Cove Rd.) from downtown St. John's, you'll pass the airport and quickly find yourself in **Portugal Cove.** Portugal Cove Ferry Terminal is where you catch the Bell Island Ferry. The ferry, which carries passengers and vehicles, can't be booked in advance—it's filled on a first-come, first-served basis. **Conception Bay South** is a much larger, full-service community of about 20,000 people, accessible by taking Route 2 off the Trans-Canada Highway.

Just a bit farther south, you'll come to **Holyrood,** a picturesque community at the junctions of routes 90, 62, and 60. Its location makes it a convenient place to lay your head while touring around the Avalon.

WHERE TO STAY

Beachside B&B ★ Sunny Conception Bay South is said to have the best weather on the Avalon, so if you're affected by the weather, you might like to choose this location. Beachside is also a great location if you don't have a vehicle but would still like to stay outside the city, as guests are offered free pickup from St. John's Airport.

All guest rooms are modern and have en-suite bathrooms. The spacious Celebration Suite has a double Jacuzzi and private deck overlooking the ocean. The least expensive rooms have a slight Victorian-era feel. In addition to the standard breakfast fare, you'll also be treated to local specialties that include *toutons,* moose or caribou sausages, and salt

Tips Money-Saving Tip on Accommodations

Staying close to but outside of the city limits can save you—not only on the basic rates, but also on taxes. Smaller facilities with three rooms or fewer are not required to charge tax, so you save yourself an additional 17% off rates that are (in some cases) already lower than within the city.

fish (when available). Don't be surprised if your hosts, Pat and Jerdon Reid, ask you to join in a friendly Newfoundland sing-along—it's a happy and musical household. Wisemans Lane (off Gully Pond Rd.), Kelligrews, Conception Bay South. ✆ **866/834-0077** or 709/834-0077. www.beachside-bb.nf.ca. 7 units. C$69–C$149 double. MC, V. Free parking. *In room:* TV.

EXPLORING CONCEPTION BAY

You'll find the Conception Bay area to be a splendid outdoor retreat, offering spectacular scenery, photographic sunsets, an abundance of marine life, and even the odd iceberg. With three shipwrecks piled on top of one another in shallow water offshore, Conception Harbour offers terrific diving opportunities. Just be aware that the clarity of the water changes when the algae are in bloom.

Conception Bay—and the water around Bell Island, in particular—is an excellent place for **scuba divers** to explore shipwrecks and take a closer look at torpedoed ore carriers. You'll also discover the abundance of native marine life. **Ocean Quest,** 17 Stanley's Rd. (✆ **866/623-2664** or 709/834-7234; www.oceanquestadventures.com), based at Conception Bay South, leads the way as a charter operator. They run full day trips aboard the M/V *Ocean Quest,* with the cost of C$230 per person, including two dives, rental equipment, and a hot lunch. If you think the water may be a little chilly for your liking, a dry suit rental is an additional C$20. The boat itself is modern and well equipped, with amenities such as hot showers, restrooms, a barbecue, a dive platform for easy access to the ocean, a flying bridge for sightseeing, and even a tender (a smaller boat) for exploring shallow coves.

Back on shore, Ocean Quest has a dive shop, a certified learning facility complete with indoor pool, and comfortable accommodations (C$150–C$175 double, including a light breakfast).

Bell Island

The largest of several islands in Conception Bay, Bell Island measures about 9km (5½ miles) by 3.5km (2¼ miles). There's quite a bit to see and do on the island, including diving, bird-watching, hiking, and touring. Be sure to take note of the mining murals that adorn many of the town's buildings.

At the island's south end is Lance Cove, where you can see firsthand evidence of World War II. It was here on September 5, 1942, that German U-boats sank two Canadian ships, the *Lord Strathcona* and the *Rose Castle,* along with many other British and French ships during the war. Two of these were the British *Saganaga* and the French *PLM 27,* where 69 lives were lost. Efforts are being made to protect the wreck sites.

Visit **www.bellisland.net** for detailed information about services on Bell Island.

Getting There

To get to Bell Island, take Portugal Cove Road west from downtown St. John's. This road ends at Portugal Cove Ferry Terminal. From here, the round-trip fare is C$6.25 per vehicle and driver. Seniors and their vehicles pay C$5. Additional adult passengers are C$2.25 and seniors C$1.75. The trip takes only 20 minutes, and the ferries run frequently during the summer from as early as 6am until midnight, less often at other times of the year. There are permanent residents of Bell Island who regularly commute to St. John's to work—so the service is dependable, but it can still be influenced by the weather.

Tip: In order to avoid lines, it's recommended not to travel from the island to Portugal Cove in the morning nor try to get to the island during the late afternoon rush hours.

You can reach the **Bell Island Terminal** at ✆ **709/488-2842** and the **Portugal Cove Terminal** at ✆ **709/895-3541.** See **www.bellisland.net** for the online ferry schedule.

Exploring Bell Island

No. 2 Mine & Museum The most popular attraction on Bell Island is this mine, located a short drive along Main Road from the ferry terminal. From 1895 until 1966, more than 78 million tons of iron ore were mined here, the world's largest submarine (underground) iron-ore mine. The mine's museum contains interesting artifacts, as well as masterful photos taken by world-famous photographer Yousuf Karsh. Karsh, who is known for his uncanny ability to portray the inner character of his subjects, has captured on film the grit and determination of Bell Island's iron-ore miners. You can also take a 1-hour walking tour of the underground mine, but dress warmly.

Main Rd., Bell Island. ✆ **709/488-2880.** www.bellisland.net/no2mine. Admission and tour C$10 adults, C$8 seniors, C$3 children under 12; C$5 for museum entry only. June–Sept daily 11am–7pm.

5 EAST COAST TRAIL

For the avid hiker, the East Coast Trail will be the Avalon Peninsula's most magnetic attraction. The trail takes you 220km (137 miles) along North America's easternmost coastline. Some sections are difficult, requiring overnight excursions. Other parts are easy—and short—enough for someone in moderate shape.

The trail is open year-round and extends along the coast from Fort Amherst in the north to Cappahayden in the south. A trail south from Cappahayden to Trepassey exists, but there is little or no signage. (At completion, the trail will extend from Topsail Beach in the north to Placentia in the south—a total distance of 540km/336 miles.) There is no fee for walking the East Coast Trail, nor do you need to book a time for your journey.

Serious hikers use the services operators affiliated with **Trail Connections** (see below) to arrange accommodations and transportation, allowing overnight excursions. But most visitors are content to walk a short length of trail as a day hike. Closest to the capital, **Deadman's Bay Path** begins at Fort Amherst (see p. 101) and winds along high cliffs for 11km (6.8 miles) to the village of Blackhead. The most spectacular stretch is the **Spout Path,** a 16km (10-mile) expanse linking Shoal Bay in the north to Bay Bulls in the South. It is rated as difficult and strenuous. The namesake highlight is the **Spout,** a wave-driven geyser that shoots saltwater 60m (197 ft.) into the air. You'll also have the opportunity to view sea stacks (stand-alone stone pillars rising from the sea), a cast-iron lighthouse, and a couple of abandoned settlements along the way. Where the Spout Path ends at Bay Bulls, the easier 7.3km (4.5-mile) **Mickeleen's Path** begins. It loops around a high headland, with the opportunity for hikers to see whales in the offshore Witless Bay Ecological Reserve. The abandoned village of **La Manche** is also along the section of East Coast Trail south from Tors Cove, but it can be reached much more easily from the end of La

Tips Hiking Tips

Keep these suggestions in mind before setting out on the East Coast Trail (or anywhere in the province, for that matter):

- When hiking in damp weather, be careful stepping over logs, as they can be very slippery when wet.
- Always bring rain gear along with you as the weather can—and does—change at whim. Also, layer your clothing so you can enjoy the sun's warmth when it comes out.
- If you have a bad back or weak knees, take along a walking stick, as it helps take some of the pressure off those areas.
- Never hike alone. Always travel with at least one companion, as well as an emergency pack with a flashlight and flares. And be sure to let someone know where you're going and when you expect to return.

Manche Road. From the village site, cross the bridge, and you're on the official trail and seemingly a million miles from civilization.

ESSENTIALS

Your best resource is the **East Coast Trail Association** (✆ **709/738-4453;** www.eastcoasttrail.com). They can advise you about renting hiking equipment from any number of outfitters in the St. John's area if you don't want to bring (or don't have) your own. They also sell two volumes of comprehensive guidebooks covering the main trail. Alternatively, for C$33 you can purchase a set of 19 waterproof topographic maps—also available through the ECTA website. The association also organizes guided day hikes; check the website for a schedule and other helpful information such as carpool arrangements from St. John's.

Another good resource is **Trail Connections** (✆ **709/335-8315;** www.trailconnections.ca), an association of accommodations and eco-tourism service providers for hikers. For a reasonable fee, a member of Trail Connections will provide trail transfers, make bag lunches geared especially for hikers, provide bed-and-breakfast accommodations, and set you up with dinners. The daily rate for the Trail Connections service is C$150 per person.

If you plan to hike the East Coast Trail and want to do a little kayaking at the same time, get in touch with **Stan Cook Sea Kayak Adventures** (✆ **888/747-6353** or 709/579-6353; www.wildnfld.ca), which is based out of a converted general store at Cape Broyle. One- and two-person kayaks are available; there are even special kayaks that can accommodate children too young to paddle. Experienced guides ensure beginners get thorough on-shore instruction before they head out on the water, and the sheltered environment of the harbor makes it an ideal experimental paddling ground. Guided kayaking is C$59 for 2½ hours, C$89 for 4 hours, and C$129 for a full day of kayaking and hiking. The company also offers the opportunity to paddle with whales for C$129 for 4 hours. As well, their "GO & Tow" program allows paddlers to return via motorboat, which leaves more time to spend in the adjacent Witless Bay Ecological Reserve. Tours are C$99 for 2½ hours, C$129 for 4 hours.

7

Eastern Region

The Eastern Region of Newfoundland and Labrador is the smallest region of the province, but it would be a mistake to equate the depth of its attractiveness to its diminutive size.

On the **Bonavista Peninsula,** you'll find the twin communities of **Trinity** and **Bonavista.** Bonavista is the fabled landing spot of old-world explorer John Cabot, while Trinity is renowned for its historically accurate architectural restorations.

Turning to the region's polar opposite, the **Burin Peninsula,** you'll discover a seemingly barren area that is really a treasure-trove of glacial deposits and the favored stamping grounds of 16th-century privates and privateers. Their modern-day equivalents can be found in the rum-runners who still smuggle bootleg hooch from the French colonies offshore.

Yes, France's border actually extends this far across the Atlantic, to the tiny islands off the south coast of Newfoundland—**St. Pierre** and **Miquelon.** You can get there by plane or via passenger ferry from the town of **Fortune,** at the foot of the Burin Peninsula.

Clarenville is the region's figurative center of gravity. It's roughly halfway between the Bonavista and Burin peninsulas, and is the main service center for the area. For that reason, it's not so much a destination as it is a base for exploring the rest of the region.

Although I've said elsewhere that I'm generally following the same regional divisions as the provincial tourism guide, that's not entirely true in this section. The provincial tourism guide stops the Eastern Region boundary at Port Blandford, but I'm stretching it as far west as Glovertown. Why? Because you're more likely to tour this area from a Clarenville base than from the doubly distant town of Grand Falls–Windsor. Between the two towns is **Terra Nova National Park.** Not as well known as Gros Morne, this park also presents a more subdued landscape than its western cousin. Its sandy freshwater pond, children's interpretive programs, less strenuous walking trails, and nearby urban attractions make it more appropriate as a family vacation destination. That said, it still has backcountry appeal for the more adventurous souls.

If you are lodging in any of the communities just outside the park, a full-day tour of Terra Nova will give you a very good idea of what the park has to offer. But if you're camping, the scenery and terrific outdoor facilities can keep you occupied for a full week and more.

1 BONAVISTA PENINSULA

From the picture-perfect village of Trinity, to roadside vendors of hand-picked seasonal berries, to a singularly unique railway loop (the only one of its type in North America), to a replica of a 500-year-old sailing ship, exploring the Bonavista Peninsula will be a highlight of your time in Newfoundland. Although you can easily make the return trip in a single day, you'll really need at least 2 days to enjoy the multitude of services and attractions you'll find here.

While you'll undoubtedly head to the anchor attractions of the Bonavista Peninsula, there are other, less-well-known points of interest that also deserve attention. Like the enticingly named Tickle Cove (after Bonavista, it's thought to be the oldest settlement on the peninsula) or James Leo Harty House in Duntara (a prime example of a traditional outport home, built by the great-grandson of the village's founder). There's also Elliston—the root-cellar capital of the world. Although they look like fairy dwellings, root cellars are merely holes dug into the side of a hill for winter storage of dried meats and root crops. Encased as they are by the hill itself, with roofs of grass and wildflowers, you won't recognize a root cellar from any angle except front-on. That's when you see the door. Another not-so-main attraction is Port Union, the only union-built town in North America. Sir William Coaker, leader of the Fishermen's Protective Union, established the town in 1916, in an attempt to ensure fishermen were paid a fair price for their catch. The moral of the story: You're on the Discovery Trail, so don't restrict yourself to the roads most traveled.

Nor should you limit yourself to summer touring. The weather of early fall (Sept to mid-Oct) is generally very favorable, requiring just a light jacket and pants. You won't want to come here after the end of October, however, as many of the attractions and even accommodations close for the winter.

ESSENTIALS

Getting There

The southern gateway to the Bonavista Peninsula is Clarenville, a 2-hour drive northwest of St. John's (189km/117 miles) on the Trans-Canada Highway (Rte. 1). From the Argentia ferry terminal, Clarenville is a 1½-hour drive. From Clarenville, Route 230 winds its way 114km (71 miles) along the peninsula to the town of Bonavista. The other main attraction in the area is Trinity, which lies just off Route 230, 73km (45 miles) from Clarenville.

From the west, the Trans-Canada Highway enters Terra Nova National Park 80km (50 miles) southeast of Gander. From this point, it's 48km (30 miles) south through the park to Port Blandford, where Route 233 cuts across the southern end of the peninsula to join Route 230.

Visitor Information

You'll find visitor information in Clarenville at the office of the **Discovery Trail Tourism Association,** 54 Manitoba Dr. (✆ **866/420-3255** or 709/466-3845; www.fallfordiscovery.com).

On the peninsula itself, most accommodations hand out tourist information, as does the **Trinity Interpretation Centre** in Trinity (✆ **800/563-6353** or 709/464-2042), open mid-May through late September daily 10am to 5:30pm, and the **Ryan Premises National Historic Site** in Bonavista (✆ **709/468-1600**), open mid-May through mid-October daily 10am to 6pm.

Getting Around

Roads throughout this region are in comparatively good condition (not really an endorsement when you consider the potholes and their black-patch spawn that dominate so many of the province's highways).

Tip: Within the historical communities of Bonavista and Trinity, park your car and travel on foot. Not only does the diminutive size of these towns make for an enjoyable

Bonavista
Bonavista Bay
Keels
Catalina
Port Union
Duntara
Salvage
Burnside
Eastport
Red Cliff
Traytown
Gloverown
Trinity East
Trinity
TERRA NOVA NATIONAL PARK
Charlottetown
Lethbridge
Trinity Bay
Port Blandford
Thorburn Lake
Clarenville
Hickman's Harbour
St. Jones Within
Hillview
North West Brook
Goobies
BAY DU NORD WILDERNESS RESERVE
Swift Current
Garden Cove
Woody Island
Bay L'Argent
Petite Forte
Fortune Bay
Placentia Bay
Garnish
Frenchman's Cove
Frenchman's Cove Provincial Park
Marystown
Burin
Grand Bank
Fortune
St. Lawrence
MIQUELON (France)
St-Pierre
ST. PIERRE (France)
ATLANTIC OCEAN
Information
Ferry
0
25 mi
25 km
320
330
310
235
230
233
232
231
205
204
201
1
360
361
362
364
210
215
100
222
220

walking tour, but you'll find that the narrow breadth of the streets (paths, really, in some sections) makes driving a less-than-pleasurable experience.

Warning: Be aware that children may be playing on or very near the highway: extra caution is advised when traveling along the smaller routes. You may be startled to find kids playing basketball—complete with a portable hoop—right on the highway!

CLARENVILLE

For those preferring to stay in a full-service community, Clarenville is a large (by Newfoundland standards) center and the home of roughly 5,200 residents. It has full-service hotels, a hospital, banks, a couple of fair-size shopping malls, and other major services.

Clarenville itself has little of interest in the way of attractions. About 5 minutes along the Trans-Canada Highway northwest of Clarenville, you'll find **White Hills Resort** (© **877/466-4559** or 709/466-4555; www.discoverwhitehills.com), with a triple chairlift accessing 12 downhill trails, 30km (19 miles) of groomed cross-country trails, and on-hill lodging. Lift tickets are C$29 for a half-day and C$39 for the full day.

Where to Stay & Dine

Clarenville Inn ★ Kids This is a family-oriented hotel easily recognized by the larger-than-life inflatable crustacean flanking the front lawn (except during the winter months, when Larry the Lobster goes into hibernation). Last renovated in 2006, the guest rooms are larger than most, with the choice of one king or two double beds, and some with distant views of Trinity Bay. The suite—there's just one—is extra spacious and offers two bedrooms and a jetted tub. But it is the other amenities that make this hotel a hit with families—most notably, an outdoor heated pool surrounded by comfortable outdoor furniture.

Random Sound Restaurant ★, the Clarenville Inn's on-site restaurant, is above average for a hotel dining room, with elegant surroundings and well-presented food. Lunch

Clarenville's Geese

Each spring and fall, Canada geese migrate across the North American continent between warmer southern climes and nesting grounds as far west as British Columbia and as far north as remote Arctic islands. For some birds, an annual stop are the wetlands and waterways around Clarenville. But this hasn't always been the case.

In the 1920s, local resident Clyde Tuck bought a breeding pair of geese to town and began nurturing their young, going so far as to keep them indoors through the harsh months of winter. As time went by, the flock grew considerably, and he built pens for them. When Newfoundland joined the confederation in 1949, a federal law came in effect prohibiting keeping geese as pets, although locals continued to feed the geese through winter.

Today, descendents of Tuck's geese can be seen each spring and fall at Lower Shoal Harbour, just outside Clarenville. The best place to look for them is the causeway, where a walking trail is dotted with interpretive signs, one of which tells the delightful story of Tuck and geese.

prices average C$10; dinner mains range from C$17 to C$24. Specialties of the house include seafood and prime rib.

134 Trans-Canada Hwy., Clarenville. ✆ **877/466-7911** or 709/466-7911. Fax 709/466-3854. www.clarenvilleinn.ca. 63 units. C$95–C$165 double. AE, DC, MC, V. Free parking. **Amenities:** Restaurant; lounge; pool. *In room:* A/C, TV, hair dryer.

St. Jude Hotel ★ Almost directly across the blacktop from the Clarenville Inn is the low-slung, three-story St. Jude Hotel. While the former is ideal for the traveling family, this hotel caters to those with disabilities and to business travelers. Not only is the entire hotel wheelchair friendly, but there's also a specially designed room for people with physical disabilities. You can kick back with your favorite beverage in the warm surroundings of the Republican Lounge (or out on the patio) or pick something from the all-ages recreational reading material in the decently stocked guest library. The standard guest rooms at the St. Jude are cheery and slightly more contemporary than across the road at the Clarenville Inn: small worktable with chair, plain but solid furnishings, and color-matched prints on the wall. For double your money, you can have the best suite in the house (complete with separate sitting room, and whirlpool built for two).

Rte. 1, Clarenville. ✆ **800/563-7800** or 709/466-1717. Fax 709/466-1714. www.stjudehotel.nf.ca. 63 units. C$95–C$170 double. AE, DC, MC, V. Ground floor parking. **Amenities:** Restaurant; lounge. *In room:* A/C, TV, hair dryer.

TRINITY ★★★

It's sure to be love at first sight in Trinity (pop. 350), a famously picturesque village overlooking Trinity Bight, 73km (45 miles) east of Clarenville along Route 230. Here, you'll find a passionate regard for the past embodied in an almost unanimous community-wide celebration of historically accurate home restoration. From the picket fences, vertical slider windows, vegetable gardens, and distinctive signage, it's obvious that Trinity takes pride in its history. And why not? It was a crucial pioneer settlement in the province, with some of the first clergy, doctors, and professional tradesmen in Newfoundland.

Where to Stay & Dine

Lodging in Trinity is limited to a number of small inns and bed-and-breakfasts. In summer especially, make reservations well in advance.

Artisan Inn ★★ Originally from Holland, ambitious owner Tineke Gow has transformed a number of Trinity's most historic structures into tourist accommodations. Most notable of these is the Artisan Inn, a classic two-story wooden waterfront building holding two guest rooms. The Cove View Room is slightly smaller than the Trinity Room, but has water views. It's well worth the extra C$36 to upgrade to the Ocean Shore Apartment. Located adjacent to the main house, it features a full kitchen, king bed, TV/VCR combo, small library, and best of all, a private waterfront deck outfitted with a propane barbeque. All three are furnished with locally crafted furniture, which blends perfectly with the welcoming ambience throughout.

49 High St., Trinity. ✆ **877/464-7700** or 709/464-3377. www.artisaninntrinity.com. 3 units. C$119–C$155. Closed Nov–Apr. AE, DC, MC, V. **Amenities:** Restaurant.

Campbell House ★ Adjacent to the Artisan Inn and also operated by Tineke Gow, Campbell House is a first-class hospitality home, epitomizing traditional styling and old-world refinement. It was built more than 150 years ago in conventional saltbox form (a popular Newfoundland house design, the saltbox features a main rectangle-shaped front section with gabled roof, sloping down to a single-story appendage out back). Once inside, you'll love the exposed brickwork in the dining area and be drawn to touch the crockery displayed in the open-face cupboard (back away from the blue-patterned serving tray—it's a hand-painted antique). Moving to the upstairs bedrooms (each has its own private bathroom, but not all are en suite), you'll delight in the low-by-today's-standards ceilings and the romance of old-fashioned washbasins. With the four-poster bed, fireplace, bureau, and cheval mirror, some people might think the rooms crowded, but I prefer the term "cozy."

If you like the sound of the atmosphere at Campbell House and the Artisan Inn but require more privacy, you'll want to stay at one of Gow's other Trinity properties: **Gover House** (C$275) and **Lighthouse View** (C$230). Both are heritage-style vacation homes with similar amenities to those you'll find at the main house. The two-bedroom Gover is right on the waterfront. It is also the more "feminine" of the two properties, with dainty floral-patterned wallpaper and comforters. With water views, Lighthouse View has a more dominant color scheme, and a sleeker, Euro-design kitchen.

High St., Trinity. ✆ **877/464-7700** or 709/464-3377. www.trinityvacations.com. 3 units. C$119–C$250. Closed Nov–Apr. AE, DC, MC, V.

Eriksen Premises ★ A haute-atmosphere establishment that couldn't decide if it wanted to be a high-class B&B or a gourmet restaurant, so it became both. Originally the home of a 19th-century merchant, the Eriksen Premises shows what it was like to live in outport high society 200 years ago. Furnished with authentic period pieces, including Victrolas and handmade washbasins, this Mansard-style home deliberately evokes Victorian charm. But the real extravagance is in the fine-dining room, where gourmet treats are served with classical flair (think of succulent scallops in a white-wine sauce and a piano concerto softly filling the background). No reservations necessary, as seating is on a first-come, first-served basis. Lunches range from C$6.50 to C$11, and dinners are C$15 to C$24. The restaurant is open May through October daily 8am to 9pm. Also at the inn is Polly's Pantry (open daily through the summer season for light lunches), an old-fashioned ice cream parlor, and a gift shop.

Rte. 230, Trinity. ✆ **877/464-3698** or 709/464-3698. www.trinityexperience.com. 7 units. C$95–C$135. Each additional person or rollaway cot C$15. Rates include breakfast. AE, MC, V. Free parking. Closed Nov–Apr. **Amenities:** Restaurant.

Fishers' Loft Inn ★★★ It's a 5-minute road trip outside Trinity proper to the favored destination of visiting movie stars. Dame Judi Dench and Kevin Spacey stayed at Fishers' Loft during filming of *The Shipping News* (in separate rooms, of course). With good reason: On the exterior, it fits in well with the local architecture, but inside, it has

Tips **Best Seat in the House**

For the best possible view of Trinity, stroll over to Courthouse Road, behind the Royal Bank. Climb the hill, following the hiking trail to the top, where you'll be rewarded with an incredible view of Trinity Bay. Do it just before sunset, when the soft pre-dusk lighting produces picture-perfect colors, leaving you with a visual memory to last a lifetime.

Camping on the Bonavista Peninsula

If you prefer natural over man-made history, pitch your tent at **Lockston Path Provincial Park** (✆ **709/464-3553;** www.gov.nl.ca/parks/parks)—a provincially run campground with 36 semi-serviced and 20 fully serviced campsites sheltered by fir trees, and a lakefront beach for swimming. The lower-numbered campsites are closest to the water, while nos. 40 to 57 have the advantage of being beside a wheelchair-accessible comfort station with laundry and shower facilities, as well as a dumping station. Overnight rates are C$15 to C$23.

Lockston Path Provincial Park is 6km (3¾ miles) from Port Rexton on Route 236—about a 15-minute drive from Trinity. The woods grow close to the road on this unpaved route, so keep a sharp eye out for moose.

the world-class flavor you'd expect from its cosmopolitan owners. John and Peggy Fisher are from England and Ottawa, Ontario, respectively. The former professional restorers brought their talents to Port Rexton in 1990, when they decided to turn their summer home into a year-round residence. Their handiwork is evident in each of the 20 distinctive guest rooms, which are scattered through eight buildings, all of which have a big-screen view of the mini islands scattered along the shore of Trinity Bay. The spacious guest rooms feature handcrafted furniture hinting at old-world austerity, but the down-filled duvets are pure luxury where it counts the most. Also notable is the original art decorating public spaces and guest rooms.

The royal treatment becomes even more evident in the dining room, where the in-house cooks create culinary artistry with seafood, berries collected locally, and vegetables and herbs from the surrounding garden. The nightly menu is several steps ahead of the fare you'll find in most inns this size: garden greens with lime vinaigrette, herb-crusted salmon and roasted vegetables, and chocolate torte with blueberry *coulis.* ***Tip:*** Plan on splurging on the meal package—this is the place you've been saving for.

Mill Rd., Port Rexton. ✆ **877/464-3240** or 709/464-3240. www.fishersloft.com. 20 units. C$112–C$206 double; modified American plan C$248–C$342 double. Discounts for multi-night stays in May and Oct. AE, DC, MC, V. Free parking. Closed Nov–Apr. **Amenities:** Restaurant; lounge. *In room:* TV.

Exploring Trinity

Begin your Trinity Village visit at the **Trinity Interpretation Centre** (✆ **709/464-2042**). Here, you'll get a one-page map naming each of the significant sites (convenient in a town where so many of the buildings look like heritage structures). From there, your next stop should be the Lester-Garland Premises, located in the former general store. Take a look at the original 1896 ledger to see the names and purchases made by residents of the time. Nearby, Lester-Garland House was built in 1819, making it Newfoundland's first brick home. Hiscock House, a 1910 restoration, represents a typical merchant's household, complete with fancy furnishings. Next door to that is a craft shop that closes at 5:30pm, so try not to arrive too late in the day or you may be disappointed. At the Green Family Forge, marvel at the work of early blacksmiths, while The Cooperage is the summer home of a cooper, who creates magnificent woodturnings using restored machinery.

Random Passage

If you're a movie buff, you've probably already seen the movie *The Shipping News* and know that it was filmed in Trinity Harbour. But *Random Passage*, based on the novels *Random Passage* and *Waiting for Time*, by Bernice Morgan, was filmed 14km (8¾ miles) from Trinity, south along Route 239 in **New Bonaventure.**

Travelers can still visit the **film set** (✆ **709/464-2233;** www.randompassagesite.com), which includes a number of early-1800s houses, a church, school, and fishing stages and flakes (wooden structures upon which fish was traditionally dried and salted). With its weathered gray dwellings and denuded spruce trees for fencing, this re-created settlement depicts the hardships of living in a world without running water or electric heat, physically cut off from the world, dependent on a merciless sea for its people's livelihood. Set tours run June through mid-October daily 10am to 5pm and cost C$8 for adults, C$6 for seniors, C$4 for children 5 to 16, and C$16 for families.

The various historical sites are open mid-June to September daily 10am to 5:30pm. A pass for all sites is C$7.50 for adults. Children 12 and under are free. For more information, visit the website of the Trinity Historical Society (www.trinityhistoricalsociety.com). ***Tip:*** The admission pass is valid for more than 1 day, so plan on dividing your visits up between other activities.

Note: The historical experience is so well integrated within the community it's easy to forget that people really live here. When you see someone hanging out clothes or eating supper, remember they're not historical interpreters—they're residents. Say hello, but respect their privacy.

Trinity After DaA trip to Trinity wouldn't be complete without treating yourself to a performance of the **Rising Tide Theatre** (✆ **888/464-3377** or 709/464-3232; www.risingtidetheatre.com), a professional theater company since 1978. Between mid-June and mid-September each year, the company puts on a number of performances in an outdoor seaside venue. It costs C$24 for one of the regular plays in the program, and C$38 for the dinner theater. You'll find the Rising Tide box office in the Rising Tide Arts Centre, near the waterfront.

Rising Tide's prime offering is the **New Founde Lande Trinity Pageant** ★, the anchor event of Trinity's Summer in the Bight Theatre Festival. Actors move from one historical site to another throughout the town, telling a story as they go. There are times when the wind and passing traffic overwhelm the actors' voices, but these impressive improv artists usually find a way to integrate such minor technicalities into the script. The pageant is held from early July until Labour Day on Wednesday and Saturday, departing the Interpretation Centre at 2pm. Tickets are just C$15.

If you're not into live theater but love live music, put on your dancing shoes and shuffle over to **Twine Loft** (High St.; ✆ **709/464-3377**), where there's a packed program of musicians performing through summer. On Wednesday evenings at **Rocky's Place** (✆ **709/464-3400**), just up the road from the Twine Loft, fiddlers Kelly Russell and

Baxter Wareham, along with folklorist Tonya Kearley get together for Dance Up (a lively mélange of folk music and step-dancing). While you're welcome to sit back and enjoy the show, audience participation is a given. Don't worry about not knowing the steps—the music itself has a way of telling you how to move. The action starts at 10pm.

Outdoor Pursuits

If you're looking for a more active adventure than you'll find at the local museum, invigorating outdoor activities are easy to find in and around Trinity.

If you're into **hiking,** you'll really enjoy the network of walking trails that lace the peninsula, all of which are easily accessed from Trinity. The nine trails, ranging in length from 3km (1.9 miles) to 17km (11 miles), are all well signposted. One of the most interesting is the **British Harbour Trail,** which starts at New Bonaventure. After 2km (1.2 miles), an old cart road reaches the abandoned outport village of Kerley's Harbour. From this point, the trail narrows and traverses a remote stretch of coastline for 4km (2.5 miles) to British Harbour, a fishing village that was abandoned in the 1950s.

Visitors staying at Fishers' Loft Inn will find themselves within walking distance of the trail head for the **Sherwink Coastal Trail.** In a little over 5km (3.1 miles), the trail passes through dense forest, along oceanfront cliffs, and across berry-filled barrens. The 17km (11-mile) **Maberly Trail** retraces the footpaths traditionally used by early European and aboriginal settlers who searched out partridgeberries, blueberries, and bakeapples on the oceanfront barrens between Little Catalina (Rte. 230) and Maberly (Rte. 238). This trail also accesses a remote stretch of sand at Flower's Brook Cove.

Ask at your local lodging for a map, or visit the **Discovery Trail Tourism Association** (www.fallfordiscovery.com) for links to local hikes.

Atlantic Adventures Set sail for an all-in-one yachting adventure, whale-watching tour, dinner theater, and port exploration. Your host Art Andrews (former CBC radio personality) leads a 2-hour nature cruise aboard his 14m (46-ft.) ketch-rigged sailing boat *Atlantic Adventurer.* It's a glorious feeling to be standing on the large forward deck, feet braced on the plank floor, hands gripping the railing, and all 60 sq. m (646 sq. ft.) of sail stretching to catch the wind. With each graceful dip of her prow, you feel the salty sting of pure freedom. You may even find yourself in the company of a curious humpback, finback, or minke as you head into one of the narrow harbors leading to an abandoned fishing port. In late spring and early summer, icebergs are occasionally spotted. ***Tip:*** When you're back at the marina, allow time to browse through the Dock Art Gallery & Craft Shop, highlighting the work of local artists.

Departures on demand from Dock Marina May–Oct. ✆ **709/464-2133.** www.atlanticadventures.com/tours.htm. 2-hour cruise C$104 per person for 2 passengers, C$52 per person for 3 or more.

Enjoying a Newfoundland Boil-Up

Boil-ups are a traditional Newfoundland way to enjoy a sunny summer afternoon—the equivalent of the North American picnic with sandwiches, and lemonade or iced tea. But in Newfoundland, the beach boil-up generally includes boiling the kettle for a cup of tea and having a bun or slice of homemade bread with it.

BONAVISTA ★★

At the tip of the Bonavista Peninsula and the site where *continental* Europeans first touched North American soil more than 500 years ago (the Vikings were here first; you can read about that in chapter 9), Bonavista is an almost full-service community. It has a hospital, pharmacy, gas station, and banking services, but little in the way of accommodations (apart from a couple of B&Bs and a small motel). That being the case, it's best to think of Bonavista as a half-day excursion from Trinity, or Trinity–Bonavista as a full-day trip from Clarenville.

Where to Stay & Dine

Elizabeth J. Cottages ★★★ An unexpected slice of luxury at the end of the road, these two spacious two-bedroom cottages enjoy an absolute oceanfront setting on the edge of town. Styled on the Newfoundland saltbox style of home, the cottages are anything but traditional. The units fill with natural light and come with unexpected niceties such as handcrafted sleigh beds fitted with Egyptian cotton sheets, plush bathrobes, and baskets of breakfast provisions. Other highlights are a modern entertainment system, polished hardwood flooring, a private deck and barbecue, and a well-equipped kitchen.

Harris St., Bonavista. ✆ **866/468-5035** or 709/468-5035. www.elizabethjcottages.com. 2 units. C$274 double. Reduced rates in spring and fall. MC, V. Closed Nov–Apr. *In room:* TV/DVD player, kitchen.

Harbour Quarters Inn ★ Built in 1920 as headquarters for a fish exporting business, this downtown waterfront building has been transformed into Harbour Quarters Inn. The lower floor is filled by Skipper's Restaurant (see below), while the two upper floors hold 10 regular rooms and one suite. All are smartly decorated and come with modern en suite bathrooms and locally crafted furniture. Ask for a room that faces the harbor. The suite spreads across both sides of the top floor. Also notable is the elevator, which is a rarity in these parts.

42 Campbell St., Bonavista. ✆ **709/468-7982.** www.harbourquarters.com. 11 units. C$139–C$229 double. Rates include continental breakfast. AC, MC, V. **Amenities:** Restaurant. *In room:* TV.

Skipper's Restaurant (Value) NEWFOUNDLAND On the lower level of Harbour Quarters Inn and beside Ryan Premises, this dining room is as close to the water as you can be without getting wet. It offers a lovely, unobstructed view of Bonavista Harbour,

"O Buena Vista!"

These were the words uttered by Italian explorer Giovanni Caboto (aka John Cabot) on his first sight of Cape Bonavista on June 24, 1497. He and his 20-man crew had been sailing into the unknown for 5 tense weeks, wondering if at any minute they were going to fall off the edge of the Earth. They were on a mission, funded by King Henry VII of England, to investigate whatever lands they might find by sailing west from Europe across the Atlantic. The underlying hope was that they would discover a shorter passage to the Far East. Instead, Cabot found a new founde lande teeming with fish reportedly so plentiful they filled a net at a single dip. Whether Cabot's cry of *"O buena vista!"* ("Oh, beautiful sight!") expressed his appreciation for the view or relief that he and his near-mutiny crew had finally found land remains shrouded in history.

Fun Facts Getting to Know the Puffin

The official feathered mascot of Newfoundland and Labrador is the puffin, a penguin-size bird roughly 30cm (12 in.) tall with a large white face and prominent, colorfully striped beak. Also known as the "sea parrot," puffins are excellent swimmers and divers. Their flying, however, is decidedly less graceful.

coupled with a traditional food menu at reasonable prices. At breakfast, be adventurous and try *toutons* (fried dough smothered in molasses). During lunch and dinner, try the chowder, with hearty chunks of seafood; it may seem a tad expensive, but it's well worth it. The chicken and broccoli casserole is a hit with locals, or try something lighter, such as the Caesar salad. Skipper's has a full liquor license and boasts a historic ambience, as well as friendly service.

42 Campbell St., Bonavista. ✆ **709/468-7982.** Reservations recommended for dinner. Main courses C$13–C$21. MC, V. June–Sept daily 7am–10pm. Closed Oct–May.

Exploring Bonavista

Cape Bonavista Lighthouse ★★ A leisurely 3km (1¾ miles) through the town of Bonavista is Cape Bonavista, site of a photogenic red-and-white-striped lighthouse. Interpreters dressed in 1870s costume will guide you through this beautifully restored facility, with its 9m-high (30-ft.) central stone tower (housed inside the building). The attention to historical detail is exquisite, from the warmth of the kitchen woodstove to the toys in the children's bedroom. After viewing the living quarters of the former lighthouse keeper, his assistant, and the assistant's family, you head up the steps to the top of the tower. From here, you can see puffins flitting around nests burrowed into various granite cliffs. The view is magnificent, but you may still be disappointed—it's all just for looks these days; an automated light is mounted atop a metal tower constructed alongside the lighthouse.

When you've finished the inside tour, take an hour or two to explore the marshy grounds around the site itself. Climb to the hill above the parking lot, where you'll discover a miniature pond and sandpipers searching for insects in the mud while bluebells tinkle in a light breeze and a whale snorts in the distance. Turn to the left and walk across the barrens to the municipal park, where you'll find a statue of John Cabot. Along the way, you may be lucky enough to sight the low-growing orange-red berry known as the bakeapple. Also called a cloudberry, it grows only in this province and Norway.

Cape Shore Rd., Cape Bonavista. ✆ **709/468-7444.** C$3 for ages 13 and up. Same admission gets you into the Mockbeggar Plantation. Mid-May to Sept daily 10am–5:30pm.

Dungeon Provincial Park Located on the tip of the Bonavista Peninsula near the Cape Bonavista Lighthouse is Dungeon Provincial Park, a natural scenic wonder. The Dungeon is a collapsed sea cave with a natural archway carved out by ocean movement. It looks like someone—or something—literally sucked the land down into the ocean through the dual "straws" formed by the arches. Situated on what is locally known as "Backside," on a scenic but bumpy gravel road (approximately 2km/1¼ miles off Rte. 235), complete with pasture land for horses, cows, and sheep, a trip to the Dungeon makes for a nice diversion.

Cape Shore Rd., Cape Bonavista. June to Sept. Closed Oct–May.

Wonderful Woodwork

While at the Ryan Premises, check out the unique wooden furnishings and collectibles handcrafted by Mike Paterson of **Paterson Woodworking** ★, a company based in nearby Upper Amherst Cove. If you're intrigued by Paterson's display of period reproductions at the Ryan Premises, drive down Route 235 to his shop and see his range of products from C$30 to C$3,000. Call ✆ **709/445-4341** or visit www.patersonwoodworking.com for showroom hours or to request a copy of their catalog.

Matthew Down at the harbor, you can board (but you can't sail on) a 20th-century reconstruction of John Cabot's 15th-century ship, the *Matthew.* Start your visit at the Matthew Legacy Visitor Interpretation Centre, where exhibits tell the story of Cabot's journey and the extraordinary effort that went into building the replica of his famous ship. Then, join a 30-minute tour of the ship, led by costumed interpreters who provide a fascinating insight into the trials faced by Cabot and his crew as they sailed the wild waters of the Atlantic in the very close quarters of a 19m (62-ft.), three-masted, wooden caravel. Imagine yourself as one of the 21 people who lived and worked on just such a ship for the 5-week crossing—manually pumping the bilge, struggling for sleep, surrounded by caged livestock, living on salt fish and ale—and you'll come a lot closer to understanding why Cabot was so grateful to make landfall at Bonavista.

Roper St., Bonavista. ✆ **877/468-1497** or 709/468-1493. www.matthewlegacy.com. C$7.50 adults, C$7 seniors, C$3 children 6–16, free for children 5 and under; C$17 family. Mid-June to late Sept daily 10am–6pm.

Mockbeggar Plantation Provincial Historic Site Although it's 300 years old, this waterfront property has a more recent event to thank for its Provincial Historic Site status. In March 1946, two of the most important political figures of the day met here to plot strategy for the upcoming referendum that would decide whether Newfoundland joined the Canadian Confederation. Gordon Bradley and Joseph R. "Joey" Smallwood agreed that, if successful in getting a majority vote in favor of Confederation, Smallwood would become premier and Bradley would become Newfoundland's first cabinet minister in Canada's federal government. Aside from being silent listeners to secret political machinations, the walls of Mockbeggar show how the upper class of the time lived, offering quite a contrast from the very basic lifestyle common to most residents of the fishing villages. Highlights include a stained-glass window inside the main house that depicts the *Matthew,* as well as an old-fashioned carpentry shop and cod-liver oil factory. Allow at least 30 minutes at this site, or a little longer if you request a free guided tour.

Mockbeggar Rd., Bonavista. ✆ **709/468-7300.** C$3 adults. This admission also gets you into the Bonavista Lighthouse. Mid-May to Sept daily 10am–5:30pm.

Ryan Premises National Historic Site ★ There's nothing grand or ostentatious about this cluster of five historic white, red-trimmed, wooden structures with sharply angled roofs on the Bonavista waterfront. And that's exactly why those interested in local history should include them on their itinerary. The understated drama of their purpose-built design gives new life to the daily interactions of 19th-century fishermen and merchants. When you walk through the former offices, look at the figures logged on the old ledger. Fishermen would sell their fish to the merchant and get paid in goods from the company store, owned by the same merchant to whom they had sold their fish. Rarely did this barter system work to the fishermen's advantage, with more than one of them going to an uneasy grave because they died indebted to the merchant.

As you wander around the site, you'll encounter plank floors and sawdust, thick-beamed building supports, and the unmistakable scent of salt fish. You'll watch videos, read storyboards, and speak to costumed reenactors demonstrating how the fishery brought Newfoundland and Labrador into the global economy hundreds of years before e-commerce, NAFTA, or the WTO. There's a gift shop on-site and a restaurant next door.

Rte. 235, Bonavista Harbour. ✆ **709/468-1600.** www.pc.gc.ca/lhn-nhs/nl/ryan/index.aspx. C$4 adults, C$3.50 seniors, C$2 children; C$10 family. Mid-May to mid-Oct daily 10am–6pm.

2 BURIN PENINSULA

It's a long and lonely drive for most of the 198km (123 miles) from the time you turn off the Trans-Canada Highway at Goobies to Grand Bank, near the tip of the Burin Peninsula. Those with limited time will want to concentrate on the Bonavista Peninsula (see above) before continuing westward to Terra Nova National Park. But with an extra day or two, the natural charm of the Burin will begin to shine through. It's a place where you must stop and pause to take it all in—ancient rocks deposited by retreating glaciers that are now scattered across the barren landscape, the stand of birch mirrored in a ripple-free pond, or the circling flight of a bald eagle on the hunt. And a people who'll smilingly acknowledge your presence, often stopping in the middle of whatever they're doing to say hello and help you on your way. The Burin Peninsula throbs with under-acknowledged beauty. Whether or not you see it is up to you. Approximately 60% of the peninsula's 27,000 residents live in one of the five major communities of Burin, Fortune, Grand Bank, St. Lawrence, and Marystown, the communities discussed in this section.

ESSENTIALS

Getting There

Route 210 (also referred to as the Burin Peninsula Hwy. or Heritage Run) spurs south of the Trans-Canada Highway at Goobies, 162km (101 miles) west of St. John's. If you're traveling east to west across the island, take the left turn onto Route 210 just past the Irving gas station (watch for the giant statue of Morris the Moose out front). Route 210 will take you all the way to Marystown, the largest community on the Burin Peninsula. Past Marystown, a looped highway takes you to the coastal communities around the foot of the Burin Peninsula (see the map on p. 133).

Visitor Information

Information about sites along the Heritage Run is available from the **Heritage Run Tourism Association** (✆ **709/279-1887;** www.theheritagerun.com), which has an office in Marystown, at 1 Centennial Rd., in the lighthouse-shaped building located at the entrance to town. The office is open from mid-June to mid-September daily 9am to 9pm. You'll also find visitor information centers in **Goobies,** at the Irving gas station, at the intersection of routes 210 and 1 (✆ **709/542-3239**); and in **Fortune** (✆ **709/832-3031**), near the waterfront Customs Office. Hours at this location coincide with the arrival and departure of the St. Pierre ferry.

Moments Ghosts of Days Gone By ★★★

A common theme in Newfoundland and Labrador culture is the dreaded necessity of having to leave someone or something you love (usually for economic reasons). In certain cases, entire towns, known locally as "outports," have been abandoned. Such is the case with Woody Island. Except for a handful of seasonal fishing families, this once-prosperous community of 400 became a ghost town after the provincial government's resettlement programs of the 1960s.

But unlike most other outports, the island has been reinvented as **Woody Island Resort,** a tourist destination—one that gives outsiders the opportunity to understand the indestructible connection that ties Newfoundlanders to their anchor, the Rock. You may at first marvel that anyone would want to live so far away from the rest of the world, but you'll soon come to understand the Newfoundlander's love of place.

Your first stirrings of empathy come to life with lodge-owner Loyola Pomroy's stories of days gone by (Pomroy was born on another resettled island—Merasheen—38km/24 miles south of Woody Island). Then, standing beside the cracked stone monuments and simple wooden crosses of uncles, parents, children, and sisters long gone but not forgotten, you feel the magnetic pull of this land. You smell it in the smoke of your beachside bonfire. It seeps into your bones as you hike in the footsteps of families and friends who will never again tend to their sheep or vegetable gardens. It becomes part of you with every breath of salt air and every glimpse of naked foundation. By the end of your visit, you may well find yourself on the upper deck of the *Merasheen,* fixated on that final glimpse of departing land, unexpected tears of bereavement mingling with the ocean spray.

Woody Island welcomes visitors between May and November. The 2-day, 1-night package costs C$165 per person, with discounts for seniors and children. This includes boat transfers from Garden Cove, accommodations in guest rooms that reflect the simple tastes of residents from decades ago, and all meals. For more information or to make reservations, contact **Woody Island Resort** (✆ **800/504-1066** or 709/364-3701; www.woodyi.com).

Visitor information for the French islands of St. Pierre and Miquelon is available from **St. Pierre Tours Ltd.,** at 5 Bayview St. in Fortune (✆ **800/563-2006** or 709/832-0429; www.spmtours.com). ***Note:*** When visiting the islands, you must have a passport and the same documentation as though you were visiting France (which means a visa for the citizens of many non-European countries).

Getting Around

The local tourism association divides the Burin Peninsula into four regions, each traversed by a different numbered highway, beginning with Route 210, which extends all the way to Marystown, the region's major center on the east coast of the Burin Peninsula. This part of the route is known as **Mariner Drive.** The connecting route from Marystown south through routes 222, 221, and 220 to Point May is known as **Captain Cook Drive.** The portion of Route 220 that takes you around the bottom of the peninsula to Point May is **Captain Clarke Drive.** The segment of Route 220 that takes you to Fortune (where you catch the ferry to the French islands of St. Pierre and Miquelon) and nearby Grand Bank is appropriately known as the **French Island Drive.**It's all a bit confusing—with the route changing its name and number at nearly every bend in the road—but apart from a couple of very short side routes that branch off from Route 210–220, it's all one road and you can't get lost.

Note: You'll find far fewer services for visitors in this region than on the Avalon or Bonavista peninsulas. Be sure to plan ahead and pack snacks or a lunch, especially if you're traveling in the evening or on a Sunday, when services may be closed. The same advice goes for filling up your gas tank. Don't assume that just because you'll soon be arriving at a village that there is a gas station, or that it will be open if you're arriving outside of daytime business hours.

GOOBIES TO MARYSTOWN

As you begin your journey along Route 210, you'll leave the fast pace of the Trans-Canada Highway at Goobies, a small community of 250 residents 162km (101 miles) northwest of St. John's. Goobies is your gateway to the Burin Peninsula.

Marystown, the major regional commercial center of the Burin Peninsula with 5,600 residents, is 144km (89 miles) southwest of Goobies. It doesn't sound that far, but if you look at the map, you'll see it isn't a straight drive.

A little over halfway between Goobies and Marystown on Route 210, Route 212 spurs west to the community of **Bay L'Argent.** This is the departure point for a passenger-only ferry to **Rencontre East** and **Pool's Cove,** two isolated outports. While Pool's Cove is accessible by road, the 1-hour-and-45-minute passenger ferry is the only way into or out of Rencontre East, home to 160 people. It's a land of lush green hills, gravel roads, fishing boats, wooden wharves, and friendly locals. The ferry travels back and forth between Bay L'Argent–Rencontre East–Pool's Cove two to three times per day. One-way fare is C$4.25 per adult and C$2.25 per child or senior. For more information and schedules, contact Provincial Ferry Services (✆ **709/535-6244;** www.tw.gov.nl.ca/ferryservices).

Where to Stay & Dine

You aren't going to find much in the way of accommodations or restaurants between Goobies and Marystown. Which means you either eat at the Irving Restaurant in Goobies (it's typical Irving, with clean bathroom, booth seating, slow service, and filling food at a reasonable price), or you wait for the bigger selection in Marystown. ***Tip:*** While you can function on low fuel for a few hours, your car can't. It's a good idea to fill your tank in Goobies before beginning the next 144km (89 miles) to Marystown.

Audrey's Restaurant NEWFOUNDLAND Like so many small-town restaurants across the province, Audrey's dishes up hearty portions of predictable fare at reasonable prices from a low-slung red brick building right beside the highway. Local favorites (think cod cakes or pan-fried cod tongues) are under C$17, as are sweet and sour chicken balls, while burgers and sandwiches are all under C$10. There's a separate menu for children and a takeout counter for those in a hurry.

13 Church St., Grand Bank. ✆ **709/832-0131.** Reservations not accepted. C$8–C$17. MC, V. Daily 11am–8:30pm.

 Kilmory Resort ★★ You'll pay more here than for the standard rent-a-cabin, but it's worth it. Kilmory Resort is one of the best cottage getaways in the province. Overlooking Piper's Hole River, an extension of Placentia Bay, the setting is filled with opportunities for outdoor recreation. You can fish for trout from the resort wharf, or get serious by chasing salmon in nearby rivers. Motorboats can be rented for exploring local waterways. Back on land, be sure to take a stroll to the top of the hill overlooking Swift Current as the view is spectacular—especially in the fall, when the foliage turns intense shades of reds and oranges. If you enjoy winter sports, Kilmory Resort is a great place for snowmobiling, as well as cross-country skiing. Adding to the appeal are the cabins themselves. Private decks with a barbeque and water views, overstuffed furnishings, floor-to-ceiling pine interiors, and full kitchens all contribute to the enjoyment of your stay.

Rte. 210, Swift Current. ✆ **888/884-2410** or 709/549-2410. www.kilmoryresort.com. 21 units. C$109–C$179 double; additional person C$10. Free parking. **Amenities:** Pool. *In room:* Kitchen.

Marystown Hotel The best thing about the Marystown Hotel is its location—you're just 70km (43 miles), about 40 minutes, from the St. Pierre ferry, and Marystown is a central point for exploring the Burin Peninsula. Bilingual service is offered, and the hotel has a pretty good restaurant (see below). Although thoroughly revamped in 2005, the guest rooms themselves are standard for the brand (bland decor, comfortable beds, desk)—if you've seen one, you've seen them all.

76 Ville Marie Dr., Marystown. ✆ **866/612-6800** or 709/279-1600. www.marystownhotel.com. 133 units. C$79–C$129 double. AE, DC, MC, V. Free parking. Pets allowed. **Amenities:** Restaurant; lounge. *In room:* TV, kitchenette, Wi-Fi.

P.J. Billington's Restaurant INTERNATIONAL Decorated with a theme corresponding to the colorful rum-running history of the Burin Peninsula area, Billington's has a casual, relaxed, and friendly atmosphere. The best value of the day is at breakfast: you can have a complete breakfast with toast, hash browns, scrambled eggs, bacon or bologna, juice, and tea or coffee for C$5.50. The rest of the day, the menu offers a mix of standard North American family restaurant fare, along with such local specialties as fish cakes for breakfast and raspberry-glazed salmon in the evening.

Marystown Hotel, 76 Ville Marie Dr., Marystown. ✆ **709/279-1600.** Reservations not required. Main courses C$9–C$21. AE, DC, MC, V. Mon–Sat 7am–11pm; Sun 8am–9pm.

Trailside Motel If you've made your way as far as Goobies (about a 1½-hr. drive from St. John's) and would like to stay for the night before you head down the Burin Peninsula, the Trailside Motel will give you a comfortable place to lay your head and get a home-cooked meal in a friendly atmosphere. The guest rooms—although clean, with comfortable beds and private, three-piece bathrooms—are best suited for a brief stopover.

Rte. 1, Goobies. ✆ **877/542-3444** or 709/542-3444. Fax 709/542-3445. www.trailsidemotel.com. 13 units. C$65–C$75 double. AE, MC, V. Large parking area. **Amenities:** Restaurant; lounge. *In room:* TV.

Exploring Marystown

As the Burin Peninsula's main service center, Marystown's economy revolves around a fish plant and a shipyard. In addition to enjoying the local scenery, there are a couple of low-key attractions worth visiting. **Marystown Museum** (✆ **709/279-1462**), on Ville Marie Drive, is open from late May to September. Displays are composed of artifacts collected throughout the peninsula and provide an interesting interpretation of the area's nautical-themed history. On a hill overlooking town and the harbor is the other worthwhile curiosity—a 5m-high (16-ft.) statue of the Virgin Mary.

Finds A Little Bit of France, Just Off the Coast of Newfoundland

The islands of **St. Pierre** and **Miquelon** provide a tantalizing tidbit of France—242 sq. km (93 sq. miles) to be exact—just 75 minutes away by ferry from Fortune, or a short flight from St. John's.

Roughly 7,000 French-speaking citizens live in the French territory, which is made up of three islands. Most of the population is centered on the town of St-Pierre, on an island of the same name. Here, the narrow streets are lined with colorful houses; and you'll find the assorted boutiques, the French pastry shops *(Ah, les croissants! Les baguettes! C'est magnifique!)*, and the wonderful restaurants worth the trip. You'll need to be on full alert as you walk through the shopping district, as the Minis seem to race along at a speed out of proportion to their size.

You can take day trips to St. Pierre by passenger-only ferry, or you can plan for a longer stay so as to better soak up the French *joie de vivre*. Contact **St. Pierre Tours** (✆ **800/563-2006** or 709/832-0429; www.spmtours.com) to book the ferry and to make accommodation reservations. The ferry departs Fortune July to early September Monday to Saturday at 7:30am. The round-trip costs C$99 for adults and C$50 for children. **Air Saint Pierre** (✆ **709/726-9700;** www.airsaintpierre.com) charges C$277 round-trip from St. John's and C$522 round-trip from Halifax.

Once on the island, there are many touring options, including bus, mini-train, bicycle, and horseback. For independent travel, visit the **St. Pierre and Miquelon visitor's site** (**www.st-pierre-et-miquelon.com**), which will provide you everything you need to know, as well as interesting current affairs and the story of how the islands finished in French hands.

Note: St. Pierre time is 30 minutes ahead of Newfoundland time (this is important to remember when looking at your departure time from the island). You'll also find getting around on the islands expensive. Think France. Canadian money is accepted, but all prices will be quoted in euros. At press time, C$1 = 0.65€.

BURIN

Detouring off Route 210 onto secondary Route 221, you'll arrive in **Burin,** a community of about 3,000 residents. This stretch of coast boasts quite a colorful seafaring history. The famous navigator and cartographer Captain James Cook spent five summers navigating the coast of Newfoundland between 1763 and 1767. His goal was to create the first accurate maps of the area, complete with sailing directions and advice on safe anchorage. Captain Cook used one of the best vantage points in the Burin area to keep an eye out for smugglers, illegal French fishing boats, and French and American mercenaries called privateers. The **Captain Cook Lookout** in Burin bears the explorer's name.

In town, **Burin Heritage Museum** (✆ **709/891-2217**) is an impressive facility, with 12 display rooms that pay tribute to the community's seafaring past. It has a gallery for art and traveling exhibits, a craft shop and tearoom, and is open from late May through early October, daily 10am until 6pm, with extended hours during July and August to 8pm. Admission is by donation.

FRENCHMAN'S COVE

This tiny village, 25km (16 miles) west of Marystown on Route 213, is home to a 9-hole golf course, a small provincial park with swimming and a playground, and a couple of recommended accommodations.

Where to Stay

Frenchman's Cove Provincial Park This is a quiet, picturesque, family-oriented facility with forested campsites within walking distance of the beach, town, and golf course.

Frenchman's Cove. ✆ **709/826-2753.** www.env.gov.nl.ca/parks/parks/p_fc. 76 sites. C$15 per site. Closed Sept 17–May 14. **Amenities:** Swimming; boat rentals; fishing; drinking water; picnic sites; fire pits; playground.

Grand Fairways Resort From the provincial park and golf course, it's just a 5-minute walk to Grand Fairways' fully equipped two-bedroom chalets with rustic styling and handcrafted furniture. You'll also find a pullout couch for additional sleeping quarters. Each cabin has a gas barbecue and private lot with a large grassed backyard. There is one fully accessible unit. Be sure to bring all the supplies you'll need, as there is no local grocery store.

Rte. 210, Frenchmen's Cove. ✆ **866/826-2400** or 709/826-2400. www.grandfairwaysresort.com. 6 units. C$98 double. AE, DC, MC, V. Free parking. **Amenities:** Playground. *In room:* TV/DVD player, kitchen.

Long Ridge Cottages If you can't get into the Long Ridge Cottages, try the Grand Fairways Resort and vice versa: Accommodations-wise, they are quite similar. Like Grand Fairways, these are fully equipped two-bedroom housekeeping units. The main difference is the view. Grand Fairways has a more private, wooded setting, while Long Ridge offers spectacular ocean views from less-private cabins. The cottages are fully winterized and open year-round, making them an excellent four-season retreat. Accommodations are spacious and very modern, with pine log interiors.

Long Ridge Place, Garnish. ✆ **709/826-2626.** www.longridgecottages.com. 4 units. C$95 double. AE, MC, V. Free parking. Take Rte. 210 to Rte. 220, then to Rte. 213. **Amenities:** Playground. *In room:* TV, kitchen, Wi-Fi.

GRAND BANK

Continuing southwest from Frenchman's Cove takes you to Grand Bank, home to around 2,700 residents. The community is most noteworthy because of its connection to the Grand Banks fishery, excellently depicted in the murals that adorn the Provincial Seamen's Museum.

Where to Stay

The Thorndyke ★★ Historical character comes to life on the walls of this old sea captain's home. Built in 1917 by Captain John Thornhill, the home is named after one of Thornhill's fishing schooners. When completed, the Captain didn't host a housewarming party—he hosted a wall-signing party. To this day, you'll find the signatures of early-20th-century sea captains scribbled on the Thorndyke's wall. The house is an excellent example of Queen Anne architecture, with a "widow's walk," or belvedere, on the roof that guests are allowed to use. Back in the seafaring days, wives of the fishing captains would stand on the roof to watch for the flags of the incoming schooners. While the kitchen is thoroughly modern, the rest of the house is maintained in its original condition. You'll find evidence of that early-1900s character in the antique furnishings and

Cod Fishing and the Grand Banks

You may have heard of the "Grand Banks" off the southeast coast of Newfoundland, once considered the richest cod fishing grounds in the world. The town of Grand Bank, on the west coast of the Burin Peninsula, was named in honor of the region's fishing heritage, much of which is well explained in the Provincial Seamen's Museum.

If you'd like to see just how dangerous fishing on the Grand Banks can be, watch the George Clooney movie *The Perfect Storm.* The film depicts the tragedy faced by so many longliner fishing boats that never made it back from a trip to the fish-filled waters. It's based on the book *The Perfect Storm: A True Story of Men Against the Sea,* by Sebastian Junger, about Grand Banks fishermen from Gloucester, Massachusetts.

four-poster beds gracing most of the seven guest rooms, and especially in the bridal suite, with its canopy bed and brass-fitted claw-foot tub. And being served with genuine crystal glasses really brings home the elegance of a more refined time. Don't take that the wrong way: this isn't a stiffly formal establishment. You can come and go as you please at the Thorndyke, and even make yourself a late-night snack in the kitchen.

33 Water St., Grand Bank. ✆ **709/832-0820.** www.thethorndyke.com. 7 units. C$65–C$95 double. Rates include full breakfast. MC, V. Free parking. Closed late Sept–Apr. *In room:* No phone.

Exploring Grand Bank

Provincial Seamen's Museum In a striking building originally used as a pavilion for the 1967 World Expo in Montreal and reopened after extensive renovations in 2010, you'll find a large collection of models and paintings of the schooners so important to the heritage and settlement of the peninsula. It will take you at least an hour to see all the exhibits—more if you're really into fishing and seafaring history. On the building, you'll find the largest mural in Atlantic Canada, depicting a 1930s Newfoundland fishing village.

54 Marine Dr., Grand Bank. ✆ **709/832-1484.** C$3 for ages 13 and over. May to late-Oct daily 9am–4:45pm.

3 TERRA NOVA NATIONAL PARK ★★

Terra Nova ("new land") is Newfoundland's first and more accessible national park. The main visitor center is 240km (149 miles), or about a 3-hour drive, northwest of St. John's, and about 76km (47 miles) southeast of Gander.

If you were to give the province's two national parks human personalities, Gros Morne would be an extreme sports enthusiast while Terra Nova would be the family guy driving a minivan. But while Terra Nova doesn't possess the striking scenery you'll find in Gros Morne, it is still a beautiful park with great camping and some excellent naturalist programs. If you have just 2 weeks in Newfoundland, you can probably see Terra Nova, the Avalon Region (including St. John's), and the Eastern Region (ends just outside Terra Nova) without feeling rushed.

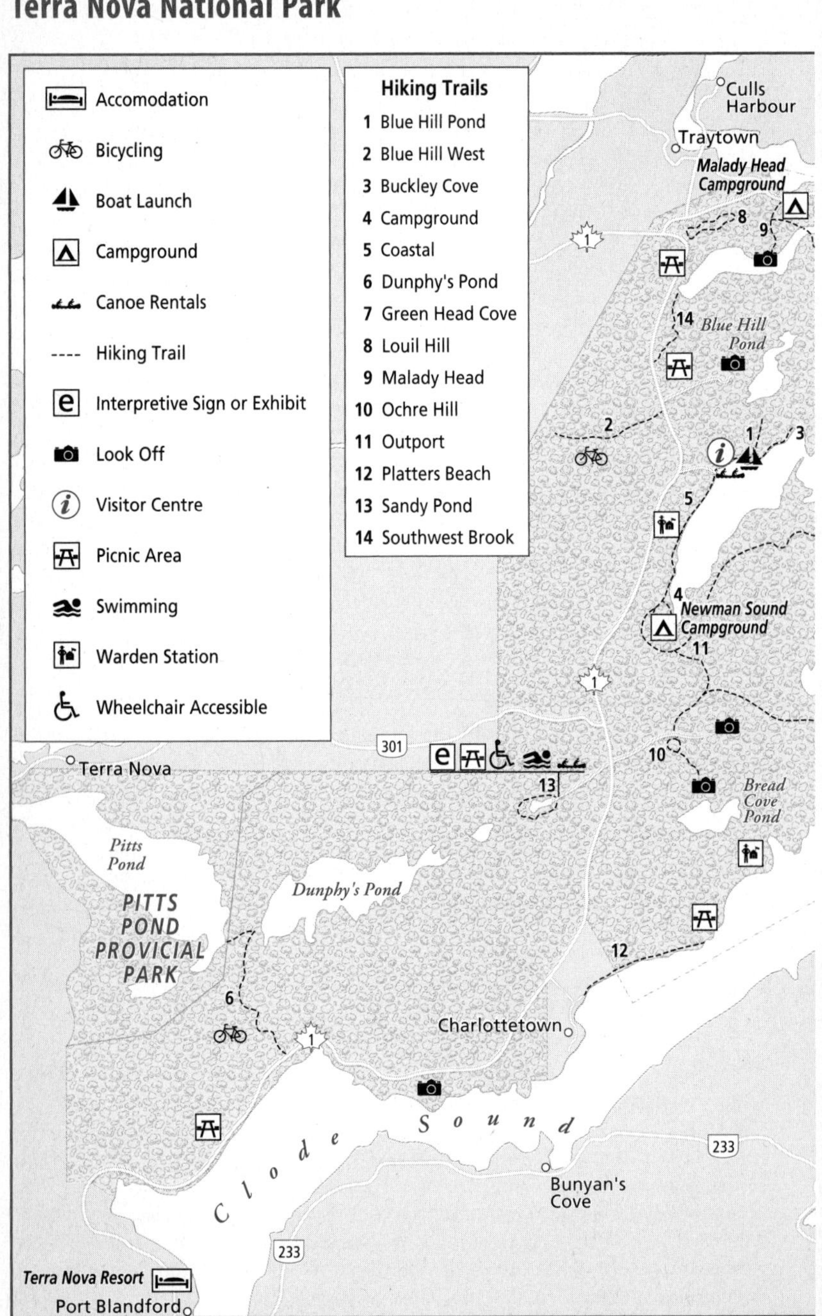
Accomodation
Bicycling
Boat Launch
Campground
Canoe Rentals
Hiking Trail
Interpretive Sign or Exhibit
Look Off
Visitor Centre
Picnic Area
Swimming
Warden Station
Wheelchair Accessible
Hiking Trails
1 Blue Hill Pond
2 Blue Hill West
3 Buckley Cove
4 Campground
5 Coastal
6 Dunphy's Pond
7 Green Head Cove
8 Louil Hill
9 Malady Head
10 Ochre Hill
11 Outport
12 Platters Beach
13 Sandy Pond
14 Southwest Brook
Culls Harbour
Traytown
Malady Head Campground
Blue Hill Pond
Newman Sound Campground
Bread Cove Pond
Terra Nova
301
Pitts Pond
PITTS POND PROVICIAL PARK
Dunphy's Pond
Charlottetown
Clode Sound
233
Bunyan's Cove
Terra Nova Resort
Port Blandford

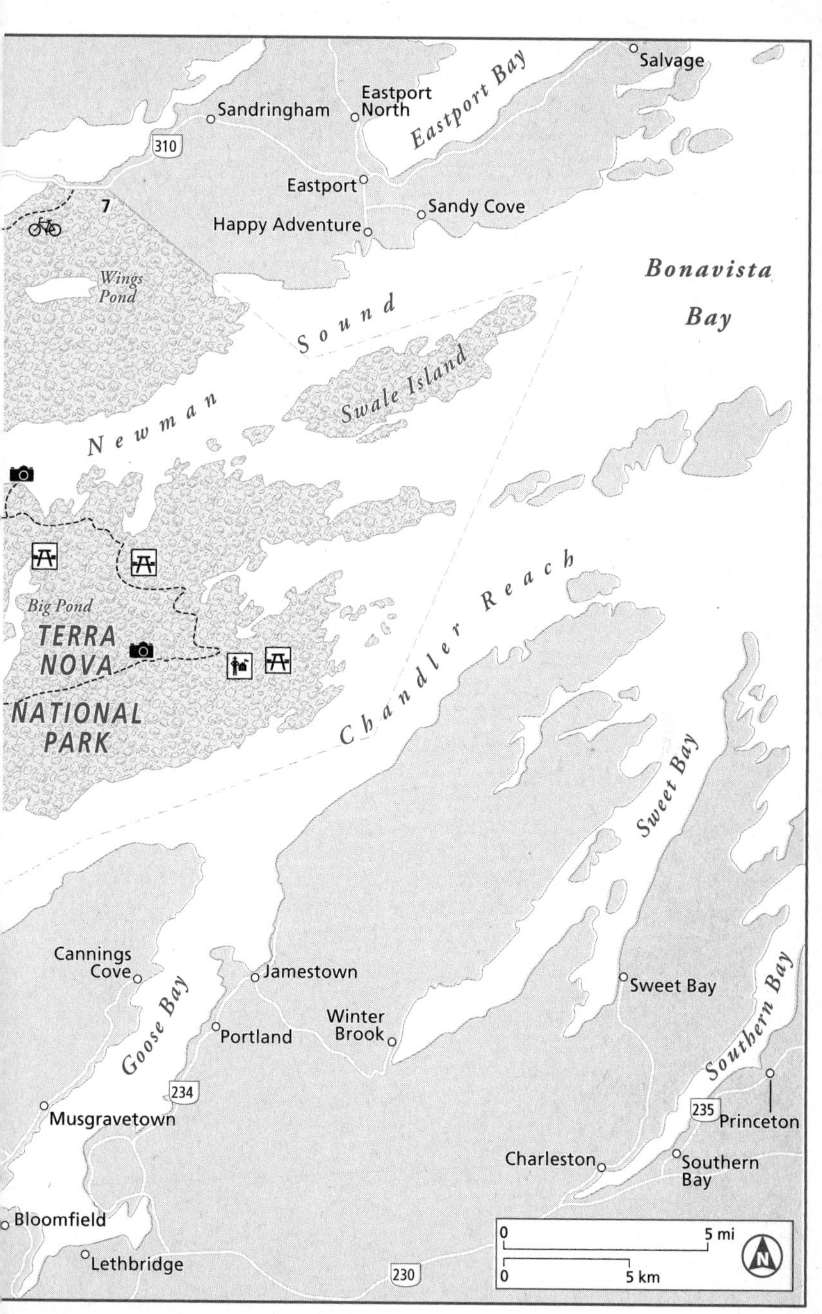
Salvage
Eastport North
Sandringham
Eastport Bay
310
Eastport
Sandy Cove
Happy Adventure
7
Wings Pond
Bonavista Bay
Newman Sound
Swale Island
Chandler Reach
Big Pond
TERRA NOVA NATIONAL PARK
Sweet Bay
Cannings Cove
Jamestown
Goose Bay
Winter Brook
Portland
Sweet Bay
Southern Bay
234
Musgravetown
235
Princeton
Charleston
Southern Bay
Bloomfield
Lethbridge
230
0
5 mi
0
5 km
N

ESSENTIALS

Getting There

Terra Nova National Park is conveniently located along the Trans-Canada Highway (Rte. 1), so if you're driving across the province, you'll go straight through it. It's located in the Eastern Region about 80km (50 miles) northwest of Clarenville. Along the 48km (30-mile) stretch of the Trans-Canada Highway within the park are numerous side roads leading into the park, including to small lakes, the main information center, and two campgrounds.

Visitor Information

You can obtain visitor information for the park at the **Visitor Centre** (✆ **709/533-2801**). Set on Newman Sound, this facility is the hub of Terra Nova National Park. Hours are daily 9am until 7pm in summer, and daily 10am to 5pm mid-May to late June and September to mid-October. The facility is closed mid-October to mid-May.

There is no visitor information available at the Charlottetown or Traytown entrances to the park, and it will take you 15 minutes to drive to the Visitor Centre from the Charlottetown entrance.

For general information about Terra Nova, visit **Parks Canada**'s website at www.pc.gc.ca/eng/pn-np/nl/terranova/index.aspx.

If you're planning to tour the park, you'll need to purchase a pass. A day pass, valid until 4pm following the day of purchase, costs C$6 for adults, C$5 for seniors 65 and over, C$3 for children 6 to 16, and free for children 5 and under. The family rate is C$15. If you plan on spending lots of time in Canada's national parks, the National Parks of Canada Pass might be best for you: C$68 for adults, C$58 seniors 65 and over, C$34 children 6 to 16, and free for children 5 and under. There is a family rate of C$137. Valid for 1 year from the date of purchase, it will get you into national parks across Canada. ***Note:*** You don't need a Parks Canada vehicle pass if you're just driving through the park and do not stop.

The park's visitor's guide, *Terra Nova Sounds,* will be quite useful in planning your visit and choosing which trails and campgrounds are best suited to you.

You can obtain general information about most communities near the park and private services available in and around the park from the **Kittiwake Coast Tourism Association.** Call them at ✆ **709/256-5070** and ask for a copy of the *Kittiwake Visitors' Guide,* or find all the same information online at **www.kittiwakecoast.ca**.

Getting Around

The best way to explore the park is on foot, but you will need a vehicle to travel between trail heads and the information center. The Trans-Canada Highway (Rte. 1) bisects the park from north to south. The road is good, also making it relatively easy traveling for the cyclist. In July and August, this road has heavy traffic with quite a few RVs that may slow things down a bit. But that's okay, as you should be watching your speed and looking out for wildlife. There are quite a few moose in the park, so take extra precautions at dusk or dawn, avoiding night travel, if possible.

Over the past few years, Terra Nova National Park has made many of its facilities and programs accessible to visitors with physical disabilities. A heavy-duty all-terrain wheelchair is available at no charge from the park's Nature House. It's not motorized, so someone still has to push it, but this amenity allows visitors with disabilities to tour and enjoy many areas of the park that may otherwise be inaccessible to them.

Pocket-size FM "Easy Listener" receivers are available for those with a hearing impairment. Closed-captioned audiovisuals are shown at the Nature House.

WHERE TO STAY

Other than park-administered campgrounds and the sites near the park gates at the southern and northern access points, there are no visitor accommodations within the expanse of the park, but as it's only 50km (31 miles) from one end of the park to the other, this shouldn't be a problem.

Clode Sound Motel & Restaurant *Value* You're bound to feel at home once you step through the door of this family-run establishment. Nellie Cunningham, the friendly hands-on manager, ensures you have a quality visit—whether you're dropping in for lunch, or staying with them for a week. Many small touches make the Clode Sound special. The smell of fresh bread and the apple pies made from apples grown on their property, the fresh-cut flowers on each dining table from the flower gardens that adorn the grounds, and the smiling staff—all will help make you glad you found this tiny haven just off the Trans-Canada Highway, 16km (10 miles) north of the southern entrance to the park. The accommodations are aging but well maintained. Each of the fully equipped housekeeping units has access to a picnic table and barbecue pit. The peaceful yet convenient location is what makes this property stand out. You're surrounded by the wilderness of Terra Nova National Park and have access to activities such as whale- and bird-watching, sea kayaking, hiking, and golf.

Part of the complex is Clode Sound Restaurant, open May to October daily 8am to 9pm. It serves up the usual array of cooked breakfasts, while the rest of the day, cod tongues and scrunchions provide local flavor.

Rte. 1, Charlottetown. ✆ **709/664-3146.** www.clodesound.com. 17 units. C$90–C$160 double. MC, V. Closed Nov–Apr. **Amenities:** Restaurant; pool; tennis court; playground. *In room:* TV, kitchen.

Terra Nova Resort ★★ *Kids* If you love to golf and you have kids, the Terra Nova Resort is a wonderful vacation destination. Twin Rivers, the resort's 18-hole golf course, has been voted one of the top 50 in Canada. Its challenging layout and water views make the greens fees of C$57 an excellent value. Adding to the appeal for parents is the Children's Recreation Program (included with the room rates), which includes games, supervised swimming, treasure hunts, and craft-making, as well as supervised lunches. Other facilities include an outdoor heated pool, walking trails, a playground, tennis courts, a basketball court, and mini-golf.

Guest rooms are nicely furnished in a solid, rustic style and are notably soundproof, considering the number of children you'll find scurrying about. As none of the guest rooms comes with cooking facilities (even the efficiency units have just a fridge and microwave, no stove), you'll probably eat at least one meal in the on-site Clode Sound Dining Room. But don't worry, they don't take advantage of their culinary monopoly. The surroundings are business-casual elegant, with golf-course views and thick wooden beams running overhead to remind you that you're in a lodge. Mains on the wide-ranging menu are C$14 to C$27, with children's meals under C$10. It is open daily 7am to 11am and 5pm to 10pm.

Rte. 1 (3rd exit to Port Blandford, if you're arriving from the south). ✆ **709/543-2525.** Fax 709/543-2201. www.terranovagolf.com. 83 units. C$128–C$249 double. AE, DC, DISC, MC, V. **Amenities:** 2 restaurants; lounge; babysitting; 2 golf courses; pool; room service; tennis courts; playground. *In room:* A/C, TV.

Terra Nova Hospitality Home ★ Value Beyond the south end of the park, at the turnoff to Port Blandford, this is the place to make reservations if you're looking for genuine Newfoundland hospitality. There are accents so thick and so studded with motherly endearments, you'd almost think you were staying in a private outport home—especially when you wake to the smell of fresh-baked bread. As homespun as it is, it's also a very professional, full-service resort with three distinct accommodations options. You can choose from the economical B&B, spacious suites, or self-contained cottages.

The winterized two-bedroom cabins are excellently maintained and spotlessly clean (with a little squeezing, two families could share one of the cottages by using the sofa bed). The main feature of the B&B has nothing to do with its six guest rooms. It's the sauna—small, yes, but still a sauna. For just C$75 a night, you can sweat the small stuff and then retire to your private bathtub to soak your cares away. In a separate building, the suites hold king-size beds, Jacuzzi tubs, and gas fireplaces.

Rte. 1, Port Blandford. ✆ **888/267-2333** or 709/543-2260. Fax 709/543-2241. www.terranova.nfld.net. 19 units. B&B: C$75 double. Cabins: C$115 double. Inn: C$125–C$145 double. AE, DC, MC, V. Free parking. **Amenities:** Restaurant. *In room:* A/C, TV, kitchen.

WHERE TO DINE

Each of the accommodations detailed above has food services, but for setting and casual ambience, my pick for a meal is the Starfish Eatery, the only place to eat within the park boundary.

Starfish Eatery SEAFOOD When you've finished learning about the park at the Visitor Centre, grab a free map, take a seat at this adjacent cafe, and start planning your itinerary. Perfectly located overlooking Newman Sound, this homey cafe even has a few outdoor tables. The simple cooking includes pan-fried scallops and hearty chowders.

Visitor Information Marine Centre. ✆ **709/533-9555.** Reservations not necessary. C$5–C$10. MC, V. May to mid-Oct daily 10am–6pm.

CAMPING IN TERRA NOVA

If you are equipped, camping is the best way to really appreciate Terra Nova. Park staff members operate an excellent outdoor theater program, with nightly events at the beachside campfire circle built from natural logs.

In addition to the camping fees detailed below, a national parks pass (see "Visitor Information," above) is required for all campers.

Malady Head Campground If you're looking for a secluded campground, this one provides a quiet, natural setting for campers wishing to experience nature without human frills. There are numerous hiking trails in the area, and sightseeing is good on the "Road to the Beaches." One other great thing about this campground is that it doesn't book up like Newman Sound, so if you arrive without a reservation, chances are that you'll still get into Malady Head. A National Parks Pass is required to enter the campground.

Glovertown (Rte. 1 to Rte. 310). ✆ **709/533-2801.** 99 sites. C$22 per site. AE, MC, V. Closed early Sept to late June. **Amenities:** Wooded sites; heated washrooms with flush toilets; wheelchair accessible; playground; fire pits; kitchen shelter; hiking trails.

Newman Sound Campground ★ This is by far the largest campground in the park, with 356 campsites, and it's my recommended destination as it has fully serviced and treed lots. Only 66 of the sites are fully serviced with electricity, so if this is a requirement, be sure to book as far in advance as possible through the **Parks Canada camping**

reservation system (✆ **877/737-3783;** www.pccamping.ca); there is an additional charge of C$11 for this service. Check-in time is 1pm; checkout time is 11am. Quiet hours are enforced beginning at 11pm. You can camp here year-round, but the electricity is turned on only from May through October.

Newman Sound is 30km (19 miles) from the south entrance of the park and is linked to the Visitor Centre by a hiking trail.

Rte. 1 to Newman Sound. ✆ **709/533-2801.** 356 sites. C$26–C$30 per site. AE, MC, V. **Amenities:** Heated washrooms with showers and flush toilets; wheelchair accessible; grocery store; snack bar; laundry services; dumping station; playground; community fire pits; kitchen shelter; hiking trails; interpretive programs; kids' activity center; campfire programs.

EXPLORING TERRA NOVA

The landscape of the park varies from the rugged cliffs and sheltered inlets of its coastal region (which takes in Clode Sound and Newman Sound, fjords that are extensions of Bonavista Bay), to the rolling hills of the boreal forest and the bogs and ponds that jointly make up the park's inland region. Terra Nova's "Fingers of the Sea" provide many scenic vistas and give the park about 200km (124 miles) of shoreline.

As with other parts of Newfoundland, much of your Terra Nova visit will be determined by your interests and the weather. As Newfoundland has "weather with an attitude," your plans may have to be altered without choice and with little advance notice.

If you're not into hiking or formal tours, one of the park's highlights is **Blue Hill,** the highest point in the park, at 199m (653 ft.). You must take a short, somewhat washboarded, gravel road to get here, which may be difficult for RVs and low-riding vehicles. But once at the top, you'll get a lovely view of the finger fjords. If you're feeling energetic, take the short drive to Ochre Hill, the site of an ancient volcano, and climb the lookout tower for another great view of the finger peninsulas and the Visitor Centre.

The **Junior Naturalist Club** ★ makes the park a hit with families. The program is geared toward kids 5 to 13, who get a chance to learn about nature in a fun, hands-on way. Visit the Nature House at Newman Sound Campground for more information. It is open July and August 10am until 5pm.

Coastal Connections ★ This company provides an easy way to leave the land behind and take to the waters of Newman Sound. But be aware that sailings are occasionally canceled due to inclement weather or high winds. The captain is Jan Negrijn, who has decades of experience in local waters, It's nice to be in good hands, and Negrijn is certainly knowledgeable about the area.

The tours provide an educational experience that enables you to see parts of the park you can't see from shore. Depending on the time of your visit, you will be able to spot and learn about icebergs, whales, bald eagles, and other wildlife. The 2½-hour Discovery Tour concentrates on searching out humpback and minke whales, soaking up the pristine scenery, and learning about the park's natural and human history. The Coastal Connections' boat, the M/V *Coastal Explorer,* is a stable 12m (39-ft.) vessel that is also used for scientific expeditions. It has a covered area and a washroom.

Visitor Centre. ✆ **709/533-2196.** www.coastalconnections.ca. C$65 for adults, C$35 for children 17 and under. MC, V. Tours depart mid-May to early Oct daily at 9:30am and 1pm.

Visitor Centre ★ An impressive facility overlooking Newman Sound just off Route 1. This is worthy not only as a stand-alone attraction, but also as the place from which you'll take a boat or kayak tour, and from where you can access the Coastal Trail.

Kids Splashtacular! ★★

Before you say goodbye to the Eastern region, give the kids a treat by spending a day at the largest water park in the province. **Splash-n-Putt Resort** borders the Trans-Canada Highway just outside Terra Nova National Park's northern boundary in Glovertown. And except for some overly aggressive go-kart drivers (they must think they're at the Clarenville Dragway), it makes for great family fun. There's a 91m (299-ft.) waterslide, 18-holes of mini-golf, a .5km (.3-mile) go-kart track, a miniature go-kart track, electric bumper cars, bumper boats, swimming pools, and a kiddies' recreation complex. A Splash Pass day pass (including two go-kart rides, three bumper car rides, two bumper boat rides, and unlimited use of all other park activities) costs C$44. Camping is free with admission. ***Tip:*** Try going to the park after 5pm, when you can buy an evening pass for C$22. For more information, call ✆ **709/533-2541** or visit www.splashnputt.com.

The facility has three display areas: the wet lab, the theater, and the marine exhibit. The marine exhibit is great for children, as they can learn about and touch various live marine creatures in the touch tank. They can even conduct an experiment in the Wet Lab with guidance from an interpreter. There is also a children's activity center, gift shop, and cafe (with outdoor patio). Give yourself about 1½ hours to tour the complex before you head out and explore.

Terra Nova (10km/6¼ from the western entrance). ✆ 709/533-2801. Admission is free once you have purchased a park pass. Mid-May to late June and Sept to mid-Oct daily 10am–5pm; late June to Aug daily 9am–7pm.

TERRA NOVA OUTDOOR ACTIVITIES

Hiking

If you like hiking, you're in luck. Terra Nova has 100km (62 miles) of hiking trails with various levels of difficulty, as well as three trails designated for mountain bikes.

The Visitor Centre is the starting point for a number of trails, including a 3.5km (2.2-mile) trail through the forest to **Blue Hill Pond.** At the pond, you'll find a boardwalk leading through wetlands and a short sandy beach. Allow 1 hour each way.

One of the nicest hiking trails is the 4.5km (2.8-mile) **Coastal Trail** linking the Visitor Information Marine Centre to Newman Sound Campground. Allow around 90 minutes each way. About halfway along, you'll pass by Pissing Mare Falls—not spectacular by any means, but a soothing place to listen to the water trickling down the rocks as you relax on a bench and smell the fresh air. Depending on the time of your visit, you may see the dogberry in bloom and the "old man's beard" lichen hanging from the trees. Old man's beard is also called "traveler's joy"—it's an indication of clean air in the areas where it grows. It's edible, but beware—it acts as a natural laxative!

Campers staying at Malady Head Campground find an evening stroll along the 1km (.6-mile) **Green Head Cove Trail** enjoyable. In just 20 minutes, they find themselves surrounded by seabirds at an abandoned bridge spanning Southwest Arm. Also starting from the campground, the 2.5km (1.6-mile) **Malady Head Trail** is relatively flat until a final short ascent to a lookout with sweeping views across Southwest Arm.

Sandy Pond

Sandy Pond is the place to be on a hot sunny day. Here, you'll find a sandy beach safe for swimming and watersports. The water is shallow, so it's great for small children. And you can rent boats and surf bikes—a surfboard that you bicycle on. Boat rentals cost C$5 for a half-hour and C$28 for a full day. If you can drag yourself away from the water, take the time to walk the 3km (1.9-mile) walking trail that encircles the lake. There are also ice-cream sales and a small concession at the beach that's open mid-June to Labor Day daily 10am to 6pm.

8

Central Region

If all you see of the massive landmass between Terra Nova National Park and Deer Lake is what you glimpse from behind your windshield on the Trans-Canada Highway, you're going to be disappointed. For 4 hours of driving, it's nothing but spruce, birch, pine, scattered ponds, and boreal bog. So, if you're planning to just drive straight through, pack a pillow and designate another driver. But consider yourself warned: You'll miss the best of Central Newfoundland if you don't detour from the main highway.

The two largest towns of Central Newfoundland, Gander and Grand Falls–Windsor, are on the Trans-Canada Highway, and both offer a wide range of services for highway travelers. At **Gander,** it's worth devoting time to a couple of flight-related attractions, while **Grand Falls–Windsor** is home to excellent salmon fishing. But to experience the best of Central Newfoundland, plan on leaving the main highway behind and detouring along the **Kittiwake Coast,** especially to the town of **Twillingate,** known for the numerous icebergs that can be seen just offshore. The thrill of passing by these great castles of the sea in a tour boat provides an outdoor experience that's hard to duplicate. The peninsula also boasts white-sand beaches, perfect away-from-it-all picnic spots, a town cobbled together by inter-island bridges, and the re-creation of a Beothuk community. Lying offshore is **Fogo Island,** a delightful destination that receives few visitors, but those who do make the effort are rewarded with experiencing a slice of Newfoundland life that hasn't changed in generations.

Even more remote than the Kittiwake Coast is the South Coast, made up of isolated fishing communities, some of which are accessible only by passenger ferry.

Information centers are located in Gander and Great Falls–Windsor, but for travel beyond the Trans-Canada Highway, you should make plans in advance. This includes accommodation and tour reservations.

1 GANDER

The story of Gander's founding is a classic tale of putting the cart before the horse. A world-class international airport was built here in 1938—before anyone lived here! Residents, services, and accommodations came later. Even though the town has since expanded in size and raison d'être (with a population of 12,000, it's now one of the main service centers in the region), much of its history and cultural character remain entwined with the transportation industry.

ESSENTIALS

Getting There

Outside of St. John's, Gander is the transportation hub of the province. You'll need to travel Route 1 and pass through Gander, whether you've come off the ferry at Port aux Basques in the Western Region and are heading toward St. John's, or are making your way west toward Gros Morne from Argentia or St. John's. It's a straightforward drive from either direction, so you couldn't get lost unless you tried. You can also fly to **Gander International Airport** (✆ **709/256-6666;** www.ganderairport.com) with Air Canada from St. John's and Halifax. The oversized airport has a cafe, gift shop, information desk, and car rentals (Avis, Budget, National, and Thrifty).

Visitor Information

The **Gander Tourist Chalet** (✆ **709/256-7110;** www.gandercanada.com) is on the south side of the Trans-Canada Highway in town. It's open late May through September daily 8am to 8pm. A limited amount of visitor information is also available at Gander International Airport.

Getting Around

With no public transit system in town, rent a vehicle or be prepared to pay C$12 for a taxi to take you the 5km (3 miles) from the airport to downtown, where you'll find most of the hotels and services. There are only five main thoroughfares in Gander (plus the Trans-Canada Hwy., which borders the town to the south), with side streets intersecting one or more of them—you'll be navigating like a pro in no time.

WHERE TO STAY

Next to St. John's, Gander has the highest density of hotel rooms in the province. In addition, you'll find a good selection of restaurants and other services for travelers. That said, you won't come across the assortment of charming historical properties that are in St. John's or some of the smaller communities.

BlueWater Lodge & Retreat ★★ **Finds** The focus of this wilderness lodge west of town is four-season outdoor enjoyment. In winter, spring, summer, or fall, BlueWater Lodge can arrange activities for it all, such as canoeing and scuba diving, kayaking and hiking, or snowshoeing and snowmobiling. After a busy day of roaming, retire to the coziness of the lodge's character-filled dining room for a satisfyingly simple three-course feast made from fresh produce and seasonal berries. Toast your day with a glass of wine by the magnificent stone hearth while watching the crimson farewell of a fading sun magnified in the still waters of the nearby lake. Finally, return to your comfortable guest room, with its exposed logs, cheery fabrics, and comfortable bed, to snuggle under a fluffy duvet for the most stress-free sleep you'll ever have. ***Tip:*** This is not a family vacation destination; BlueWater is best suited to adult guests, as families will need to book at least two rooms.

Rte. 1 (30km/19 miles west of Gander and 3km/1¾ miles east of the Rte. 340 Notre Dame Junction). ✆ **709/535-3003.** www.relax-at-bluewater.ca. 10 units. C$125 double. AE, MC, V. Free parking. **Amenities:** Restaurant; lounge.

Comfort Inn The units may be somewhat sterile, but you can always count on the chain to provide clean, comfortable guest rooms at reasonable prices. It's a modern two-story building, offering drive-up rooms with either two double beds or a king, and some very spacious kitchenette units (C$10 extra). A continental breakfast (hot drinks, toast, cereal, muffins, bagels, and more) is included in the rates. Plus, the Comfort Inn is home to Jungle Jim's restaurant (see below).

112 Trans-Canada Hwy., Gander. ✆ **877/424-6423** or 709/256-3535. www.choicehotels.ca. 64 units. C$119–C$129 double. Rates include continental breakfast. Senior discount 20%. AE, DC, MC, V. Free parking. **Amenities:** Restaurant; exercise room. *In room:* A/C, TV, kitchenette, Wi-Fi.

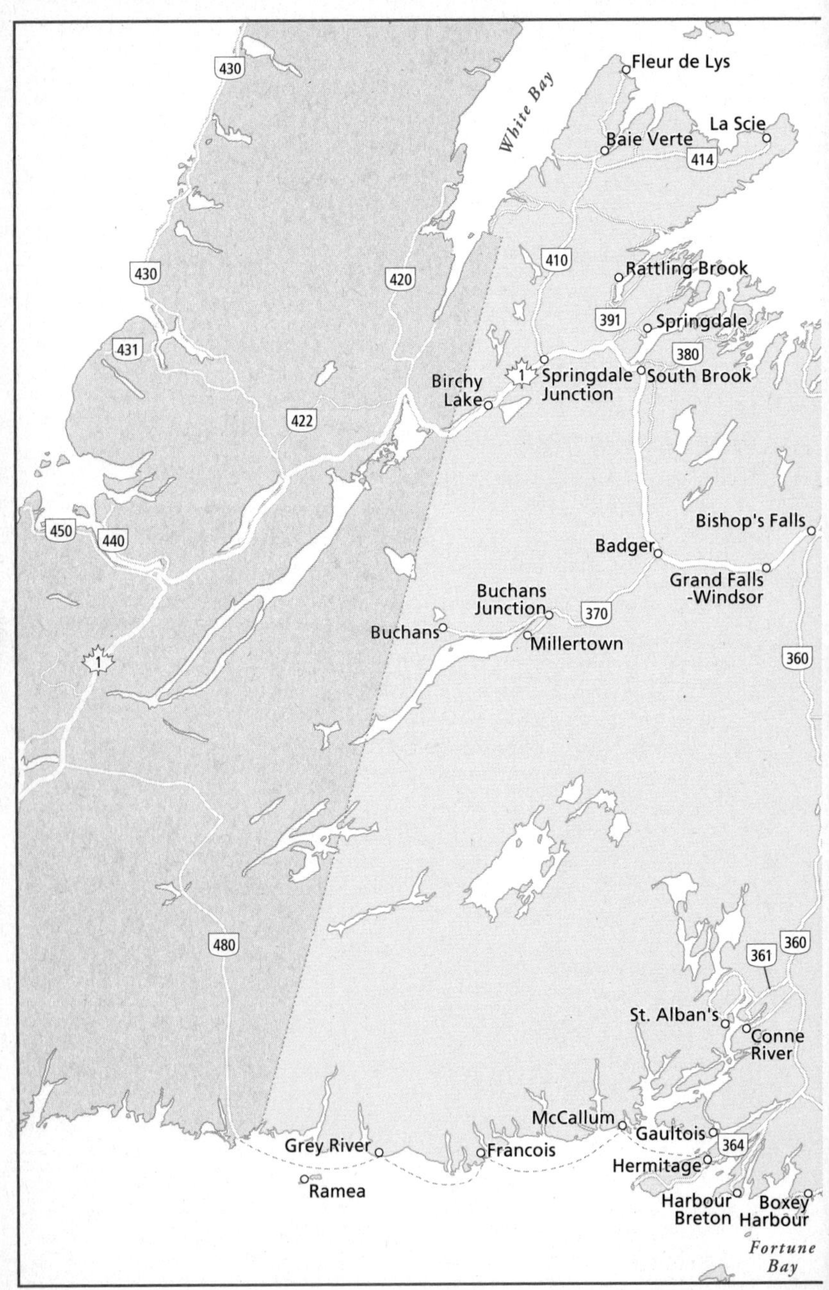
430
Fleur de Lys
White Bay
La Scie
Baie Verte
414
410
Rattling Brook
430
420
391
Springdale
431
380
1
Springdale Junction
South Brook
Birchy Lake
422
Bishop's Falls
450
440
Badger
Grand Falls -Windsor
Buchans Junction
370
Buchans
Millertown
1
360
480
360
361
St. Alban's
Conne River
McCallum
Gaultois
364
Grey River
Francois
Hermitage
Ramea
Harbour Breton
Boxey Harbour
Fortune Bay

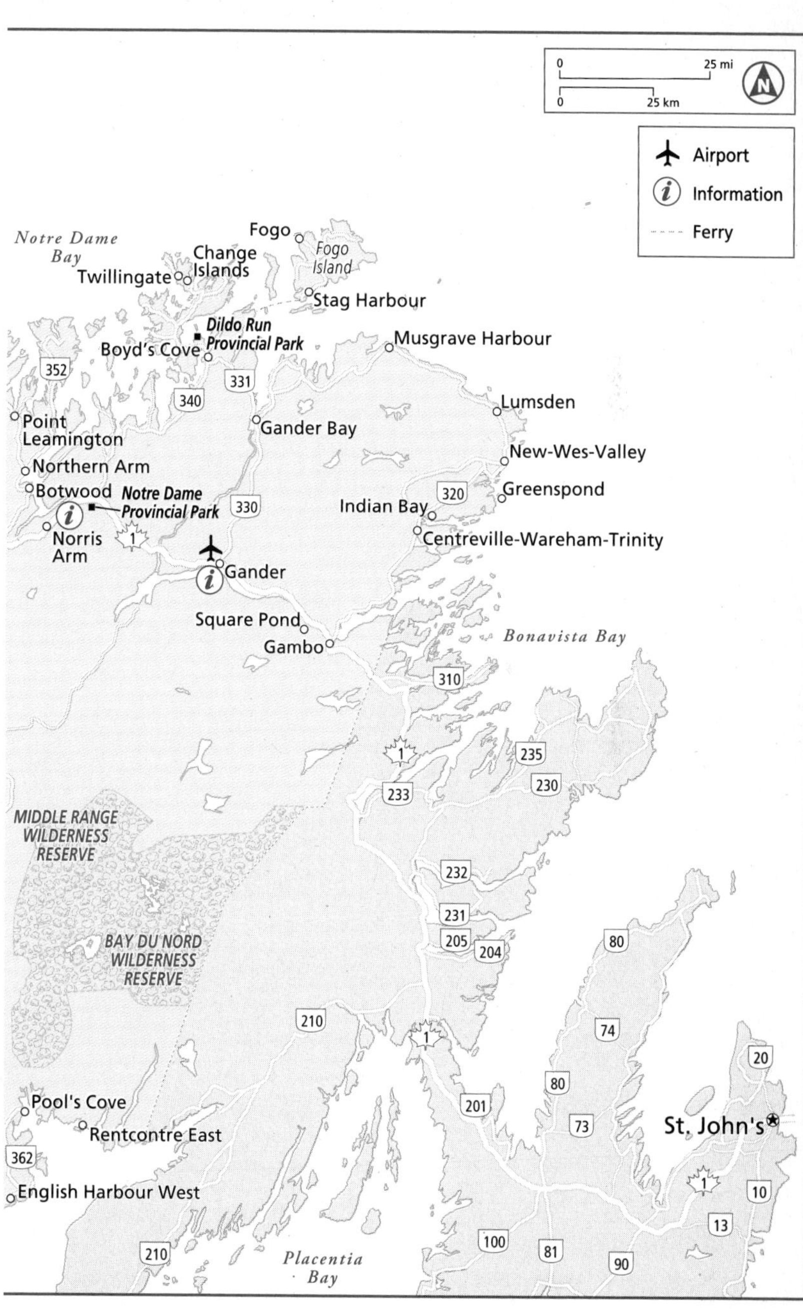

0
25 mi
0
25 km
Airport
Information
Ferry
Notre Dame Bay
Fogo
Fogo Island
Change Islands
Twillingate
Stag Harbour
Dildo Run Provincial Park
Boyd's Cove
Musgrave Harbour
352
331
340
Lumsden
Point Leamington
Gander Bay
New-Wes-Valley
Northern Arm
Botwood
Notre Dame Provincial Park
330
320
Greenspond
Indian Bay
Norris Arm
1
Centreville-Wareham-Trinity
Gander
Square Pond
Gambo
Bonavista Bay
310
1
235
233
230
MIDDLE RANGE WILDERNESS RESERVE
232
231
205
204
80
BAY DU NORD WILDERNESS RESERVE
210
1
74
20
80
Pool's Cove
201
73
St. John's
Rentcontre East
362
1
10
English Harbour West
13
100
81
90
210
Placentia Bay

Hotel Gander Catering to the convention crowd, this is the biggest accommodation in town, with a location that begs a trip to the two nearby shopping malls. The guest rooms are comfortably appointed, with bedside sitting areas that can be either convenient work spaces or cozy conversation corners. Among their 152 rooms, they have just one Jacuzzi suite. Alcock & Brown's, the on-site eatery, has a split personality: simultaneously fun and formal (see "Where to Dine," below), while Tomcats Bar & Grill opens to a delightful patio. ***Tip:*** The Superior Rooms are worth the extra C$15, for the contemporary look and brighter decor.

100 Trans-Canada Hwy. (Rte. 1). ✆ **800/563-2988** or 709/256-3931. www.hotelgander.com. 148 units. C$105–C$155 double. AE, DC, MC, V. **Amenities:** Restaurant; lounge; exercise room; pool; limited room service; spa. *In room:* A/C, TV, hair dryer, Wi-Fi.

Irving West Hotel Smaller than Hotel Gander but with rooms of a similar standard, the Irving West has the bonus of an outdoor heated pool. Other pluses are rooms with balconies and a lounge with live music and drink specials. The walk to downtown Gander takes just 5 minutes.

1 Caldwell St., Gander. ✆ **709/256-2406.** 62 units. C$111–C$120 double. Rates include continental breakfast. AC, MC, V. Free parking. **Amenities:** Restaurant; lounge; pool. *In room:* A/C, TV, Wi-Fi.

WHERE TO DINE

Alcock & Brown's CANADIAN Named after the two airmen who made the first nonstop aerial crossing of the Atlantic, Alcock & Brown's is appropriately decorated with caricatures of the famous duo. The funky cartoon-character wall hangings signal an informal bonhomie that's made even more evident by the brown-paper table coverings and complimentary crayons. But wait, there's more here than meets the eye: There's also a quieter, more upscale eating area custom-made for intimate dining. The menu reflects the restaurant's dual personality, with burgers and chips sharing space with grown-up dishes such as bruschetta salmon in a creamy dill sauce. Make sure you leave room for dessert, especially the whimsically named Chocolate Moose. Not only is it a perfectly velvety smooth concoction, it comes with its own antlers! Sunday brunch, served 11:30am to 1:30pm, is a bargain at C$14 per person.

Hotel Gander, 100 Trans-Canada Hwy. (Rte. 1). ✆ **709/256-3931.** www.hotelgander.com. Reservations recommended for dinner. Main courses C$15–C$23. AE, DC, MC, V. Sun 7am–1:30pm and 5–9pm; Mon–Sat 7am–2pm and 5–10pm.

Giovanni's LIGHT FARE In a setting as hip as it gets in Newfoundland, Giovanni's is a great place for coffee made from freshly ground beans, Italian sodas, grilled panini (several different varieties are available), fruity salads, biscotti, and other tasty treats. Centrally located in the heart of downtown, Giovanni's faces Town Square, with a couple of outdoor tables to enjoy warm summer days.

71 Elizabeth Dr. ✆ **709/651-3535.** Reservations not accepted. Main courses C$6–C$14. MC, V. Mon–Wed 7:30am–6pm; Thurs–Fri 7:30am–10pm; Sat 9am–10pm; Sun noon–5pm.

Jungle Jim's INTERNATIONAL Part of a 23-strong homegrown restaurant chain, Jungle Jim's is a good choice for casual family dining. The safari-style bamboo decor, patio lights, and stuffed jungle animals provide plenty of distractions for energetic youngsters. The extensive menu includes a variety of Mexican-style dishes (nachos, burritos, fajitas, and tacos) as well as steaks, hamburgers, pasta, and salad. Tribal Feasts, designed to share, are an especially good value.

112A Trans-Canada Hwy. ✆ **709/651-3444.** www.junglejims.ca. Reservations not accepted. Main courses C$12–C$19. AE, DC, MC, V. Daily 11am–11pm.

EXPLORING GANDER

Let your spirits soar in Gander. It's as easy as checking out one of these aviation attractions.

AeroSmith Inc. You've heard of boat tours, bus tours, and even walking tours. Why not an airplane tour? It's not cheap (their Cessna 185 floatplane charters for C$260 per flight hour), but since the plane can hold three passengers, you can share the cost with fellow travelers. Allow a couple of hours for a decent tour—not of just the Gander area, but the entire Central region.

Gander International Airport, James Blvd. ✆ **888/999-2376** or 709/651-3222. www.aerosmithinc.com.

Festival of Flight Gander's biggest annual brouhaha is held through the first week of August. It's a full week of family entertainment, much of it centered on the namesake theme. The schedule includes community breakfasts, suppers, and barbecues, as well as model airplane demonstrations, kite-flying, and fireworks. There are buskers, pub nights, craft sales, a demolition derby, and a parade.

Various venues. ✆ **877/919-9979** or 709/651-5927. www.gandercanada.com. Some events are free; others charge a nominal entrance fee.

North Atlantic Aviation Museum ★ This museum, Gander's main attraction, is on the south side of the Trans-Canada Highway as it passes through town. You shouldn't have any problem finding it: The front of the building has an airplane tail sticking out of it. The museum is both a record of Gander's growth and a timeline for aeronautical evolution. Aircraft on display include a 1938 Lockheed Hudson Mk III, which was used for coastal reconnaissance; an F101 Voodoo Canso fighter plane; a DeHavilland Tiger Moth biplane; a Beech 18-S, which was one of the world's first corporate airplanes; a 1933 Montreal-built PBY-5A flying boat, which was one of the most common aircraft that refueled at Gander during the airport's heyday; and a homemade Rutan Quickie, with a cockpit so small that the pilot had to fly lying down (no wonder he donated it to the museum!).

Rte. 1 (between the Tourist Chalet and James Paton Memorial Hospital). ✆ **709/256-2923.** www.naam.ca. C$5 adults, C$4 seniors and youth ages 5–15, free for children under 5. July–Aug daily 9am–6pm; Sept–June Mon–Fri 9am–5pm.

Silent Witness Memorial On the east side of town, a side road winds down to this poignant memorial, marking the site of Canada's worst air disaster. On December 12, 1985, Gander Airport was a scheduled refueling stop for a DC-8 flight carrying the U.S. 101st Airborne Division (best known as the Screaming Eagles), who were returning home from a United Nations peacekeeping mission in Sinai. The plane, with 248 soldiers and an eight-member crew, crashed shortly after takeoff between the Trans-Canada Highway and Gander Lake. A group of statues—an American soldier and two children—backed by Canadian, U.S., and Newfoundland flags, overlooks the lake.

4km (2½ miles) east of Gander (signposted to the south). No phone.

---

2 KITTIWAKE COAST

Many communities along the remote stretch of coast north of Gander were isolated until as recently as the 1960s, when causeways were constructed between the Twillingate, Change, Chapel, and New World islands to the mainland.

The best-known community along the north coast is **Twillingate,** a picturesque haven for viewing the many icebergs that float into Notre Dame Bay. It has about 5,000 residents and numerous services, including a regional hospital.

En route to Twillingate, you'll come to the village of **Musgrave Harbour** and the coastal stretch to **Lumsden,** where you'll find Newfoundland's best beach. A few kilometers farther along, you'll arrive in **Newtown.** It's known as the "Venice of Newfoundland" because it's built on a series of tiny islands joined by bridges.

ESSENTIALS

Getting There

Several routes run north of the Trans-Canada Highway (Rte. 1) to the communities along the Kittiwake Coast. If you leave the Trans-Canada at Gambo for Route 320, you're in for a leisurely coastal drive that'll take you past Newtown and the Barbour Living Heritage Village, as well as the beach at Lumsden and other assorted outport settlements. If you continue west along Route 320, it becomes Route 330 at Cape Freels. Keep going until you reach the intersection at Gander Bay South, and you'll have a choice between heading south to Gander along Route 330 or continuing north to Twillingate. Returning to the Trans-Canada Highway from the Kittiwake Coast, take Route 340, from where it's 46km (29 miles) east to Gander and 50km (31 miles) west to Grand Falls–Windsor. There is no public transportation along the Kittiwake Coast.

Visitor Information

The **Kittiwake Coast Tourism Association** (✆ **709/256-5070;** www.kittiwakecoast.ca) is a useful resource that can provide information about the northeastern part of the Central Region, including the Notre Dame Bay area. For information specific to the Twillingate area, click through the links at **twillingatetourism.ca**.

GAMBO TO TWILLINGATE

Turning off the Trans-Canada Highway at Gambo, you pass the following attractions on the 260km (162-mile) run to Twillingate. Accommodations are few and far between, so plan on continuing to Twillingate for the night or traveling this route as a day trip from Gander.

The following sights are listed from east to west.

Barbour Living Heritage Village ★ *Finds* You'll want to spend at least 2 hours exploring this re-created fishing village (ca. 1900), perched along the weathered shore of Newtown (listed as New-Wes-Valley on many maps). The sights and sounds, as well as the look and feel, of the Barbour Living Heritage Village proclaim its historical authenticity. The buildings represent the prosperous mercantile premises, owned by the Barbour family, which played an important role in the local sealing industry. In addition to the Barbour family buildings, the historic park includes a Methodist schoolhouse, craft shop, restaurant, visitor information center, sealing interpretation center, theater, art gallery, wooden stage used for drying fish, liver factory, and other smaller buildings.

In July and August, the village hosts the Seabird Theatre Festival, a dinner theater filled with local color. The actors' accents tend to be exaggerated Newfoundland, so you may have some problem understanding the dialogue. Dinner, which approximates a traditional potluck meal, is a serve-yourself affair featuring such items as cod au gratin, fish-'n'-brewis, beet salad, mustard salad, potato salad, ham, turkey, caramel tart, partridgeberry pie, and Jell-O. The theater, restaurant, and craft shop are wheelchair accessible.

Rte. 330 to Newtown. ✆ **709/536-3220.** www.barbour-site.com. C$7 adults, C$6 seniors, C$3 children 6–18, free for children 5 and under; C$15 families. Theater performances are an additional C$10 adults,

C$8 seniors, C$4 children 6–18, free for children 5 and under; C$21 families. Dinner extra. June 15–Oct 15 daily 10am–6pm. Closed Oct 16–June 14.

Boyd's Cove Beothuk Interpretation Centre Little is known about the Beothuk people because—unlike other native groups—they avoided Europeans. Boyd's Cove has particular significance because it offers more evidence about their way of life than any other site on the island. Among the items recovered at the archaeological dig are iron nails that have been refashioned into arrowheads and other tools. The nails weren't the result of trade, but of Beothuks scavenging through the debris left behind by seasonal European fishers. The life of these now-extinct people (the last known Beothuk died in 1829) is depicted in the construction and contents of the wigwam-shaped Interpretation Centre, as well as along the 1.5km (.9-mile) walking trail leading to the excavation site of several Beothuk houses that date between 1650 and 1720.

Rte. 340 (70km/43 miles north of Gander and 40km/25 miles south of Twillingate). ✆ **709/656-3114.** www.heritage.nf.ca/aboriginal/beo_boydscove.html. C$4 age 13 and up, free for children 12 and under. June to late-Sept daily 10am–5:30pm.

Fisherman's Museum A short distance past Newtown is Musgrave Harbour and its Fisherman's Museum. You'll find this location especially interesting if you've been to Port Union (on the Bonavista Peninsula). This two-story, oversize fishing shed was built as a general store in 1910 by Sir William Coaker, founder of the Fishermen's Protective Union. The Fisherman's Museum has an interesting collection of artifacts related to the fishery (like a fish-splitting table and weighing machine). On an external side wall, you'll see a fascinating mural depicting the way fishing traditions have progressed from past to present.

Rte. 330, Musgrave Harbour. ✆ **709/655-2119.** C$4 age 13 and up, free for children 12 and under. Late June to Aug Sun, Tues, and Thurs–Sat noon–6pm.

TWILLINGATE ★★

During the 1800s, Twillingate was the most active and prosperous seaport on the North Coast. Even today, you'll find a picturesque town of 2,800, with a broader range of services here than in many of its neighboring communities.

If you're keen on seeing icebergs, the best time to come is late spring and early summer. If you're most interested in whales, the summer months provide your best chances. So, if you come in late June or early July, you just may catch a glimpse of both these natural wonders floating about in Notre Dame Bay.

Twillingate is an Anglicized version of the community's original French name, "Toulinguet," which is also the name of a group of islands off the French coast near Brest. The French fishermen evidently saw a similarity between their homeland and this lovely Newfoundland community.

Where to Stay & Dine

Cabins by the Sea (**Value**) The price is definitely right for these simple but adequate 2-bedroom family getaways. The location is ideal, with picnic tables outside the cabins and recreational facilities just a short walk away. By foot, you're 2 minutes from a playground and 3 minutes from the indoor swimming pool in the Twillingate Recreation Centre. One of the cabins is wheelchair accessible. No pets allowed. ***Warning:*** Watch children closely, you're just 30m (98 ft.) from the ocean.

11 Hugh Lane, Twillingate. ✆ **709/884-2158.** www.cabinsbythesea.com. 7 units. C$80 per unit. AE, MC, V. *In room:* TV.

Dildo Run Provincial Park The amenities are typical of provincial park campgrounds throughout Newfoundland and Labrador: Each of the 55 well-spaced campsites comes with a picnic table and fire pit. A newer washroom complex has showers and flush toilets. Drinking-water taps are conveniently located throughout the park, as are some less-than-fresh pit toilets. ***Tip:*** Ask for a campsite that's away from a pit toilet. You don't want to be caught downwind.

Facilities aside, it's the location that gives every provincial park its character. In this instance, the lovely seacoast setting offers the opportunity to see growlers and "bergy bits" (iceberg chunks that might float ashore), as well as whales. You can also see quite a few of the 365 islands in Dildo Run from the lookout point, which is reached along the 3km (1.9 miles) of hiking trails. This is a wonderful location for kayaking and canoeing.

Rte. 340, Virgin Arm. ✆ **709/629-3350.** www.env.gov.nl.ca/parks/parks/p_dr/index.html. 55 sites. C$15. MC, V. Closed Sept 17–May 30. **Amenities:** Day-use facilities; showers; drinking water (taps); kitchen shelters; dumping station; laundry facilities; picnic sites.

Harbour Lights Inn Located across the road from the ocean, this three-story home was built in the 1820s and has been beautifully restored to offer guest accommodations in nine rooms. Two rooms have jetted tubs, but all are comfortable and filled with old-fashioned charm. Out front is a covered veranda from where you can watch fishing boats making their way back to port or relax in the sitting room with a book from the collection of local literature. Rates include a cooked breakfast. For those without laptops to take advantage of the Wi-Fi, there's a computer for guest use. This is a nonsmoking establishment.

189 Main St., Twillingate. ✆ **877/884-2763** or 709/884-2763. www.harbourlightsinn.com. 9 units. C$109–C$139 double. MC, V. Free parking. Closed mid-Oct to Apr. *In room:* TV, hair dryer, Wi-Fi.

Toulinguet Inn Bed & Breakfast Beautifully located overlooking the ocean, Toulinguet Inn is also a short distance from a coin laundry, bank, restaurants, walking trails, and the departure point for boat tours. Inside this traditional 1920s Newfoundland home, you'll find a kitchen replete with antique collectibles; my personal favorite is an old-fashioned cast-iron stove. There are two spacious queen-size units and one smaller room with twin beds; all three have private bathrooms.

Toulinguet's welcoming character also deserves attention. From the minute you pull into the driveway, it's like you're a long-lost friend or favorite cousin. You feel it in the radiant greeting at check-in, you smell it in the just-washed sheets upon the bed, and you

Fun Facts Nightingale of the North

Born in Twillingate in 1867, Georgina Ann Stirling was the daughter of Ann Peyton and Twillingate's first doctor, William Stirling. The clarity of her powerful soprano voice was apparent at a young age and her wealthy father sent her first to Toronto and later to Paris to train as an opera singer. Under the stage name Marie Toulinguet, she became one of the most famous singers of her time, performing in Italy, Washington, and New York. Tragedy struck at the peak of her career in the form of a serious throat ailment, thus ending her operatic dreams. She returned to Twillingate, where she lived until she died of cancer in 1935. A 2m ($6^1/_2$-ft.) stone monument near St. Peter's Church marks her burial spot.

Fogo Island

While nearby Twillingate gets most of the attention, hulking Fogo Island, a 45-minute ferry trip from the Kittiwake Coast, lies beyond the well-worn tourist path. Named by the Portuguese "Fire Island" for fires lit by resident Beothuk people, there are few official attractions. Instead, take your time to appreciate the understated natural beauty, to marvel at local lifestyles that haven't changed in generations, and to make conversation with friendly locals.

The ferry from the mainland docks at Man-O-War Cove, from where a narrow 40km (25-mile) road loops across the island to connect 11 communities, none home to more than a few hundred residents. The first community reached is Seldom, where the Marine Information Centre is housed in a former cod liver oil factory. It is open daily June to September 9am to 8pm. For the best views, drive to the summit of Burnt Point, which overlooks the village to the south.

Lying in the shadow of distinctive Brimstone Head, the Town of Fogo enjoys a stunning oceanfront setting and is surrounded by water on all sides. The island road system ends at delightfully named Tilting, where a distinctive Irish flavor is apparent. Most surprisingly, nearby Sandy Cove Beach is exactly that—a beautiful white sand beach that is surely one of the most beautiful in Canada.

Ferries to Fogo Island depart 10 to 12 times daily from Farewell, which is well signposted along Routes 331 and 335 from Gander Bay. The round-trip fare for the 45-minute trip is C$17 for a vehicle and driver, plus C$5.50 for each additional passenger. No reservations are necessary. Visit **www.tw.gov.nl.ca/ferryservices** for more information.

It's possible to visit as a day trip from Twillingate or Gander, but for the full effect, plan on staying at **Foley's Place B&B** (✆ **709/658-7244;** www.foleysplace.ca). This trim, 100-year-old home with 4 en-suite rooms, is in Tilting at the far end of the road. Rates are C$75 double, including breakfast.

taste it with every bite of your homemade breakfast muffin. Smoking is permitted outside, on the porch, in the garden, or on the second-story balcony. This is a popular location, so be sure to book ahead as far as possible.

56 Main St., Twillingate. ✆ **877/684-2080** or 709/884-2080. www.bbcanada.com/9127.html. 3 units. C$80 double. Rates include expanded continental breakfast. Closed mid-Oct to mid-May. *In room:* No phone.

Exploring Twillingate

The main reason to visit Twillingate is to take a boat tour in search of whales and icebergs, but there are a number of things to see and do while you're in the region. The landscape is starkly beautiful and well worth exploring along a number of signed walking trails. The 2km (1.2-mile) **Top of Twillingate Trail,** starting from south of town at Manuels Cove, climbs steadily to a point where the view puts the town and surrounding convoluted coastline into perspective. You can also explore along the oceanfront by taking trails leading from Long Point Lighthouse (see below) to **Sleepy Cove** and along sandy **French Beach** to intriguing rock formations.

Fish, Fun & Folk Festival

Folk-music enthusiasts will want to mark their calendars for the third week in July, when Twillingate is home to one of the largest and best established folk festivals in the province. Activities include a parade, a beach bonfire, helicopter rides, a craft fair, and (of course) lots of great music and fellowship. Unlike many other folk festivals, this one's musical entertainment takes place indoors, meaning it won't be affected by inclement weather. Prices vary per activity. For more information, visit **www.fishfunfolkfestival.com**.

Long Point Lighthouse A must-see in the Twillingate area is one of the last manned lighthouses in the province—the Long Point Lighthouse, built in 1876. The lighthouse is not open to the public, but is still worth the drive because of its dramatic setting, especially if you arrive around sunset, when its red and white stripes take on new, softer shades. Across the parking lot from the lighthouse is the **Long Point Interpretation Centre,** home to an exhibit that explains the connection between the area's natural and human history, as well as a small gift shop and tearoom.

A pleasant walking trail leads down from the lighthouse to **Sleepy Cove,** a short stretch of rocky beach. Allow 20 minutes for the round-trip.

Rte. 340, north of Twillingate. ✆ **709/884-2247.** Opens on demand for tours mid-May to mid-Oct daily 9am–9pm.

Twillingate Island Boat Tours ★★★ Set sail with Cecil Stockley, the self-appointed "Iceberg Man of Twillingate." Stockley has been chasing bergs for more than 20 years and says he has a sixth sense that enables him to track the sometimes-elusive sea castles. This is a smaller vessel than you'll find used by the competition, but "Cec" takes a more educational approach to his tours, making this the best choice for anyone who wants an in-depth interpretation of what they are seeing. The 2-hour boat tours run three times daily. Also allow time for visiting the Iceberg Shop (which is also the tour departure point) for its collection of stunning berg photography.

50 Main St., Twillingate. ✆ **800/611-2374** or 709/884-2242. www.icebergtours.ca. C$50 adults, C$32 children 15 and under. Departures May 1–Sept 30 daily 9:30am, 1pm, and 4pm. Evening tours leave on demand.

3 GRAND FALLS–WINDSOR

There's always been an unofficial rivalry between Gander and Grand Falls–Windsor. Both communities are service centers, but they have very different personalities. Grand Falls–Windsor has fewer services for travelers, but it has a longer, stronger history, as evidenced by its numerous heritage properties.

Grand Falls–Windsor is the home of Canadian actor Gordon Pinsent, who starred with Julie Christie in *Away From Her.* But that's not all the town has to brag about. *Chatelaine* magazine, a popular Canadian publication, once named Grand Falls–Windsor one of the top places to live in North America because of its community spirit, natural beauty, and friendly residents (obviously, climate was not a factor).

ESSENTIALS

Getting There

Grand Falls–Windsor is the approximate halfway point between St. John's and Port aux Basques. To be exact, it's 428km (266 miles) west of St. John's, 476km (296 miles) east of the ferry terminal at Port aux Basques, and 91km (57 miles) west of Gander International Airport.

Visitor Information

The **Grand Falls–Windsor Visitor Information Centre** (✆ **888/491-9453** or 709/489-6332; www.townofgrandfallswindsor.com) is located along Route 1 on the west side of Grand Falls–Windsor. The centre is open May 1 to October 15, daily 9am to 9pm.

WHERE TO STAY & DINE

Carriage House Inn ★ All it needs are a few climbing vines, and you'd swear it was straight from a Norman Rockwell painting. Even without the encircling greenery, Carriage House Inn is pretty as a picture. The covered veranda, gabled roof, and 2.4-hectare (6-acre) wooded property give it the presence of a cozy country retreat. Which is exactly what it is. You'll want to relax in the porch swing with a book from the library, or soak in the sun on the spacious patio deck. Inside, you can't go wrong with any of the nine nicely furnished guest rooms with varying bed sizes and amenities—all are impressively clean, with freshly scented linens and private bathrooms.

181 Grenfell Heights, Grand Falls–Windsor. ✆ **800/563-7133** or 709/489-7185. www.carriagehouseinn.ca. 12 units. C$79–C$119 double. Rates include breakfast. V. Free parking. *In room:* AC, TV/DVD player, hair dryer, no phone.

Mount Peyton Hotel It's not the only game in town, but it is the largest. The Mount Peyton is a Central Newfoundland institution that is one of the only full-service hotels west of the capital. In the main building, a staid structure dating to the 1960s, are 101 midsize hotel-style rooms with unremarkable decor and amenities that include air conditioning and Wi-Fi. Across the road are the remaining units, a mix of park-at-your-door motel rooms and efficiency units with basic but adequate kitchens. In the main lodge, you can choose from three dining options: Clem's Dining Room, offering a mix of local and standard North American hotel fare; Peyton Corral Steakhouse, with mains in the C$16 to C$25 range; and an English-style pub, with a menu to match and live music on weekends.

214 Lincoln Rd., Grand Falls–Windsor. ✆ **800/563-4894** or 709/489-2251. www.mountpeyton.com. 149 units. C$90–C$135 double. MC, V. **Amenities:** 2 restaurants; lounge. *In room:* A/C, TV, hair dryer, kitchenettes, Wi-Fi.

Riverfront Chalets ★★ Owned by the same couple that operate Rafting Newfoundland (see below), these four magnificent wooden chalets enjoy a wilderness setting west of Grand Falls–Windsor, with the Exploits River flowing through the property. Each unit features two separate bedrooms, a large bathroom with jetted tub, a full kitchen, a living area with a wall-mounted LCD TV, and a deck with your own private barbeque. The units sleep four comfortably, but a sofa bed allows the option of two additional guests.

Aspen Brook, 19km (12 miles) west of Grand Falls–Windsor. ✆ **709/486-0892.** www.raftingnewfoundland.com. 4 units. C$199 per unit. MC, V. Free parking. *In room:* TV/DVD player, kitchen, Wi-Fi.

Sanger Memorial RV Park Some people call it camping, but purists will scoff as they turn over in their sleeping bags. Why? Because it's a campground where no tents are allowed, only RVs and trailers. Sanger Memorial has a good range of amenities, including private showers and washrooms, accessible facilities, and 24-hour security. The camping lots are large and full-service, with 15- to 50-amp hookups. It's right on the river and just minutes from downtown Grand Falls–Windsor.

Trans-Canada Hwy. (Rte. 1; Exit 20 to Scott Ave.), Grand Falls–Windsor. ✆ **709/489-8780,** or 709/489-7350 for off-season bookings. 45 sites. C$24. MC, V. Closed mid-Sept to mid-June.

EXPLORING GRAND FALLS–WINDSOR

There are a number of activities and events to please visitors to the Grand Falls–Windsor area: everything from hiking and fishing to snowmobiling and cross-country skiing. For information about any of the events, call ✆ **709/489-0450.**

Exploits Valley Salmon Festival During this 5-day mid-July event, the resident population triples to approximately 60,000 (keep this in mind when booking accommodations). The festival kicks off with a salmon dinner, "Newfie Night," live music, a craft fair, and lots of family fun. The highlight of the festival is the Salmon Festival Concert, which features well-known Canadian artists of contemporary, country, and traditional music.

Various locations. www.salmonfestival.com. Admission C$5, Newfie Night C$30, Salmon Festival Concert C$35.

Queen Street Dinner Theatre Running from early July to the end of August, the Queen Street Dinner Theatre features a number of enthusiastic local performers. Don't let their youthful appearance fool you: Their stage presence has a maturity far beyond their years. There are both evening and daytime performances. The daytime shows are considerably cheaper than the evening dinner shows and offer an economical option to see a great performance for less cash.

5 Queen St. ✆ **877/822-7469** or 709/489-6560. www.andco.nf.ca. Reservations recommended. Tickets C$15–C$38 adults, C$12–C$32 seniors and students.

Rafting Newfoundland ★ This adventure operator combines first-class guides and dazzling scenery in an unforgettable day trip. Experience the thrill of white-water rafting as you battle the surging waters of the Exploits River. Plus, it's full family fun—the ultimate antidote for teenage ennui. For those with paddling experience, the company rents canoes and kayaks, and offers shuttle services to various points through the region. ***Note:*** The company is based out of Aspen Brook, 19km (12 miles) west of Grand Falls–Windsor.

Tours take place at various locations throughout the Exploits Valley. ✆ **709/486-0892.** www.raftingnewfoundland.com. C$99 for a 1-day rafting or canoeing tour. Canoes ($50 per day) and kayaks ($35 per day) available for rental.

Salmonid Interpretation Centre See salmon in midair, as they jump from rung to rung on the "salmon ladder," making their way upstream to their spawning grounds. At this interesting facility, located on the Exploits River 4km (2½ miles) from downtown Grand Falls–Windsor, highlights are the underwater viewing windows, where you can see salmon in their natural habitat, and the live exhibits of brook trout, sticklebacks, and eels. The center is fully wheelchair accessible and has a restaurant and small gift shop.

Cross the bridge over the Exploits River to reach the Salmonid Interpretation Centre. ✆ **709/489-7350.** C$4 adults, C$2.50 children. Mid-June to mid-Sept daily 8am–8pm.

4 BAIE VERTE PENINSULA

Also known as the **Dorset Trail,** the peninsula accessed from Springdale Junction off the Trans-Canada Highway doesn't have an abundance of services or attractions, but what it does have is worth seeing—especially the **Baie Verte Miner's Museum,** in the village of Baie Verte, and the **Dorset Soapstone Quarry,** 28km (17 miles) up the road in Fleur de Lys. Because it's a 2-hour trip from Grand Falls–Windsor to Baie Verte, you should plan to stay the night in the area so you can take in the two main attractions, as well as spend a few hours cruising along the coast.

ESSENTIALS

Getting There

From Grand Falls–Windsor, continue west on the Trans-Canada Highway for 92km (57 miles) to Springdale Junction, where Route 410 spurs north up the Baie Verte Peninsula. From the Trans-Canada, it's 62km (39 miles) to the community of Baie Verte. Continuing north for 29km (18 miles), you reach Fleur de Lys, at the northern tip of the peninsula.

Visitor Information

The **Baie Verte Visitor Information Centre** (✆ **709/532-8090;** www.townofbaieverte.ca) is right on Route 410 at the junction of Route 412 as you enter town. This is the same building housing the Miners' Museum. It is open daily during July and August, from 9am to 9pm.

WHERE TO STAY

Dorset Country Inn Located in the center of Baie Verte, this welcoming inn has eight rooms, each with a private bathroom, and a delightfully homespun atmosphere. Your host, Teri Boterman, will do everything she can to make you feel comfortable—so you'd better not come here if you don't like being pampered. The common area lounge has a TV.

3 Hoskins Terrace, Baie Verte. ✆ **877/532-8095** or 709/532-8075. 8 units. C$65–C$80 double. Rates include a full breakfast. AE, MC, V. *In room:* TV.

EXPLORING BAIE VERTE PENINSULA

Baie Verte Miners' Museum ★ You won't have to dig too deep to find this goldmine of information about the region's rich mining heritage. The building is immediately evident because of its distinctive double A-frame shape. Inside, there's a simulated mining tunnel leading to the museum, which contains an interesting collection of artifacts that date back to the first European mine built here in 1860. Among the things you'll see outside the museum is the first train in the province, used for the now-defunct Terra Nova mine.

Rte. 410 to Baie Verte. ✆ **709/532-8090.** C$3 adults. June–Sept daily 9am–9pm.

Dorset Soapstone Quarry ★ At the northernmost tip of the northernmost community on the Baie Verte Peninsula, you'll find a little-known Provincial and National Historic Site. But don't mistake its obscurity as a measure of its worth: The Dorset Soapstone Quarry is an incomparable link to the people who lived here more than 1,000 years ago. Inside the Interpretation Centre, you'll see examples of the soft-stone cooking pots used by the Dorset natives.

There are four hiking trails around the site. If your time is limited, choose the one to the main quarry. This well-marked walking trail is flanked by waving wildflowers, and along the way, you can see where the Middle Dorset people carved out pots and lamps. Here, you'll see archaeologists at work as they continue to uncover artifacts. ***Note:*** Look, but don't touch. Rather than accidentally destroy archaeological evidence, watch from the designated viewing platform.

Rte. 410, Fleur de Lys. © **709/253-2126.** Admission by donation. Mid-May to mid-Oct daily 6am–8pm.

5 SOUTH COAST

The southern coastline of Central Newfoundland—also known as the **"Coast of Bays"**—is missed by most visitors because of its remoteness. Route 360 will take you into the area, but you have to take a small ferry if you want to visit many of the tiny outport communities, as they are not accessible by road. It's isolated, primitive, beautiful, and totally unspoiled by commerce and tourism.

ESSENTIALS

Getting There

From 19km (12 miles) east of Grand Falls–Windsor, Route 360 begins its long and lonely trek south, dead-ending after 208km (129 miles) at the town of Harbour Breton. Around 40km (25 miles) before Harbour Breton, Route 364 branches southwest to Hermitage, from where ferries depart for all points west.

Visitor Information

The **Coast of Bays** website (**www.coastofbays.nl.ca**) has information that will help plan a trip to the South Coast.

Getting Around

Passenger-only ferries provide the only link to the outside world for a string of communities between Hermitage in the east and Rose Blanche in the west. The service operates year-round, although the schedules change with the seasons. Per sector, the 1½-to-2-hour ride between communities costs up to C$8 for adults and C$4 for seniors, children, and students. Visit **www.tw.gov.nl.ca/ferryservices** for more information.

The adventure begins in the village of **Hermitage.** The first ferry stop is **McCallum**—a community married to land and sea by both livelihood and geography. You'll have half an hour in this picturesque place, which is barely enough time to capture it on film. But don't worry, you'll have a 75-minute stopover on the return trip. Next up is **François** (pronounced "Franceway"). It's a breathtakingly rugged village (pop. 120) tucked into the shadow of 207m-high (679-ft.) hills. There are no roads in François: the main street is an extra-wide wooden boardwalk. Houses are built in ascending order, with the most congested area around the waterfront and increasingly fewer dwellings as you move uphill. You'll have to spend the night here, as the ferry doesn't move down the line until 7:30am the next day.

Then, you're off on a 2-hour sail to **Grey River,** another fishing village of fewer than 150 residents. You won't have any problem getting to meet the locals, as many of them have a habit of coming to greet the boat. From Grey River, you'll have to decide whether to turn back or continue on to Ramea and Burgeo on a different ferry, one that sails from Rose Blanche to Grey River via Burgeo.

Conne River Mi'kmaq Reserve

For an experience unlike any other on the island, visit the Miawpukek Band in Conne River—180km (112 miles) from Grand Falls–Windsor on Route 360. They are a proud, independent, visionary people, reveling in their native heritage while simultaneously embracing modern society. You may be surprised—even disappointed—by the modern bungalows, retail stores, cars, trucks, and ATVs. Don't be. Underlying these 21st-century appendages is a deeply rooted respect for the land and each other. You see it in the design of their native crafts, and you hear it in the tales of their unique customs (like planting trees in lieu of headstones as a way to remember a lost loved one).

Time your visit to coincide with the annual **Powwow,** a 4-day event usually held the first week in July. It combines sacred ritual with tribal dance, as well as communal feasting and elder wisdom. Non-natives are allowed to participate in most ceremonies. Free camping and trailer sites are available on the Powwow site on a first-come, first-served basis. There is no entry fee to the Powwow, but participants are asked to contribute to the daily potluck feasts. For more, visit Conne River online at **www.conneriver.com**.

HARBOUR BRETON

Harbour Breton (pop. 1,900) is the largest and one of the oldest communities along the South Coast. It has a hospital, a bank, and a beautiful beach at Deadman's Cove, where on a clear day, you can see the French islands of St. Pierre and Miquelon in the distance. Since the late 1700s, the folks of Harbour Breton have depended on the local fishery as a source of work and money, but in 2005, the local fish-processing plant closed, putting 350 locals out of work. The closure spurred the community to look beyond the ocean for economic stimulus, and as a result, the local focus turned to tourism—the Elliott Premises waterfront buildings were refurbished to hold craft shops and a marina, a kayak launch was developed, interpretive panels were placed through town, and a walking trail to the lighthouse was upgraded. And then, in late 2006, the processing plant reopened!

A good source of information on the town is **www.harbourbreton.com**.

Where to Stay & Dine

Southern Port Hotel ★ This facility is so flawlessly organized and charmingly operated, you'll think you've walked into a fairy tale. And in a way, you have. The hotel is a relatively new (2002), single-story, fully accessible facility overlooking the town. Each of the clean, comfortable, and spacious guest rooms comes with its own private bathroom. All are designated non-smoking. In the hotel restaurant, a light breakfast is available daily for just C$3.50. Lunch is offered weekdays only, and dinner is offered daily.

96 Canada Dr., Harbour Breton. ✆ **709/885-2283.** www.southernporthotel.ca. 16 units. C$87–C$90 double. MC, V. Free parking. **Amenities:** Restaurant; lounge; limited room service. *In room:* TV, Wi-Fi.

Exploring Harbour Breton

Sunny Cottage is a good place to start a walking tour of Harbour Breton, but you should also take time to explore Elliot Premises, also along the waterfront. Although it's not an official museum, there's a display room here, a workshop where you may see local craftspeople at work, and a theater that hosts occasional live performances.

Sunny Cottage The grandest building in town is a wonderful 1909 Queen Anne–style home that offers displays on fishing, resettlement, and the home's original merchant residents. Guides dressed in period costumes will take you on a guided tour; in the kitchen, you'll be able to sample freshly made traditional delicacies. The harbor-front setting and lovely gardens add to the charm of this attraction. Sunny Cottage currently serves as the area's tourist information center.

Rte. 360 to Harbour Breton. ✆ **709/885-2425.** Free admission. Late May to early Sept Mon–Fri 9am–5pm, Sat–Sun 1–5pm.

Tradition by the Sea In mid-July, Harbour Breton hosts this lively celebration of traditional life along the South Coast. The annual festival begins with a beach party at Deadman's Cove and continues with a variety of activities, such as dory races, that demonstrate the distinct culture of this area. Other highlights include traditional music, dancing, and food; games of chance; cotton candy; and festivities for the kids. Prices vary per activity.

Activities staged at various locations throughout Harbour Breton. ✆ **709/885-2354.** www.harbourbreton.com.

Western Newfoundland

If you're traveling in an east-west direction across the island, Western Newfoundland is the grand finale to a wondrous adventure. If, however, this is your entry point to Newfoundland, it's an enticing prelude to an unforgettable vacation. Either way, it's a memory in the making.

From the ferry terminal at Port aux Basques, the wide, easy-driving Trans-Canada Highway winds north along the coast, past slumbering rivers and pastoral prettiness. You'll encounter world-class salmon fishing on the renowned **Humber River,** the best downhill skiing east of the Canadian Rockies at **Marble Mountain,** and Newfoundland's last francophone stronghold on the **Port au Port Peninsula.**

Just over 260km (162 miles) north of Port aux Basques and 200km (124 miles) west of Grand Falls–Windsor is the transportation and service hub of **Deer Lake.** It's also the point of decision. You either leave the Trans-Canada to follow Route 430 along the **Northern Peninsula,** or you stay on the Trans-Canada and head east across the island toward St. John's.

North of Deer Lake is **Gros Morne National Park,** a UNESCO World Heritage Site and the undisputed highlight of Western Newfoundland. Its cloud-shrouded mountains, glacial fjords, endangered species, and granite upheaval make it an outdoor adventurer's delight. Try to give yourself at least 2 days in Gros Morne—more if you're camping or backpacking.

It's almost 400km (249 miles) from Gros Morne to the north end of the northern peninsula, but it's well worth the journey. The peninsula is where you'll find **Port au Choix National Historic Site,** the known home of four distinct ancient cultures, and **L'Anse aux Meadows,** where Vikings settled more than 1,000 years ago.

Along the way, you're likely to see moose—lots of moose. The peninsula is home to the largest percentage of the province's plentiful and impressively racked creatures. The area around St. Anthony is also a good place to see icebergs if you're visiting later in the summer.

1 PORT AUX BASQUES TO STEPHENVILLE

Port aux Basques is at the southwestern end of Route 1. The community gets its name from its French heritage, as this region was originally settled by Basque fishermen who came to Newfoundland in the 1500s. Today, Port aux Basques has around 4,500 residents and is home to a Marine Atlantic ferry terminal, which receives year-round ferry service from North Sydney, Nova Scotia. The community is also referred to as Channel–Port aux Basques.

North of Port aux Basques is Stephenville (pop. 5,500), a good base for exploring the lovely Port au Port Peninsula or Barachois Pond Provincial Park, both just minutes away from town.

ESSENTIALS

Getting There

Stephenville is 796km (495 miles) west of St. John's, 77km (48 miles) southwest of Corner Brook, and 166km (103 miles) north of Port aux Basques.

Port aux Basques is 218km (135 miles) south of Corner Brook. Most people who come here do so because of its ferry terminal. (See the "Getting There" section of chapter 3 for full details on the Nova-Scotia-to-Port-aux-Basques ferry.) Unlike the utilitarian North Sydney terminal in Nova Scotia, the Port aux Basques docking area and terminal site features a romantically lit harbor entrance and a dramatic blasted-rock approach. And, although significantly smaller in size, the Port aux Basques waterfront is more visitor-friendly than the one in St. John's.

Visitor Information

Port aux Basques' **Visitor Information Centre** (✆ **709/695-2262)** is on the Trans-Canada Highway, 4km (2½ miles) from the ferry terminal, at the turnoff to downtown. The center is open June to August daily from 9am until 10pm. Through summer and the rest of the year, it also opens for all ferry arrivals.

WHERE TO STAY

Barachois Pond Provincial Park (Kids) Beside Route 1, 20km (12 miles) east of Stephenville is one of Newfoundland's most scenic and best-maintained provincial parks. Glorious natural eye candy combines with a host of family fun for an unparalleled outdoor adventure. Activities in this 3,500-hectare (8,649-acre) park include lake swimming, water-skiing, boating, and fishing for both brook trout and salmon. There are also two sandy beaches (one is sheltered from westerly winds, the other from easterly breezes), as well as boat and canoe rentals. The most enjoyable of three hiking trails is the 4km (2.5-mile) Erin Mountain Trail. Beginning at the bridge spanning the lake, the trail starts out as a boardwalk. This section, to a lookout over the lake, is excellent for families. The upper half of the trail is recommended for experienced hikers because it's a tougher climb through brush and barren rock. Allow 2 hours one way. The park also has an excellent interpretive program that includes guided walks and campfire sing-alongs.

Trans-Canada Hwy. (Rte. 1) to Barachois Pond Provincial Park. ✆ **800/563-6353** or 709/649-0048, off season 709/635-4520. www.env.gov.nl.ca/parks/parks/p_bp. 150 sites. C$12. MC, V. Open mid-May to mid-Sept. Closed mid-Sept to mid-May. **Amenities:** Freshwater swimming; boat rentals; convenience store; day-use facilities; dumping station; laundry facilities; showers.

Cape Anguille Lighthouse Inn ★★ (Finds) For a completely different experience, consider spending the night in this lighthouse keeper's home, which sits high atop cliffs on Cape Anguille. The adjacent lighthouse is still in operation—and your hosts are the keeper Leonard Patry, who was born at the lighthouse, and his family. The guest rooms are simple yet clean and practical. It's worth the extra C$10 for those with ocean views. In keeping with the get-away-from-it-all theme, the rooms do not have televisions or phones. Meals are available with advance notice. ***Tip:*** Bird-watchers will love the cape and adjacent Codroy Valley, with over 200 species recorded, and some (such as great blue herons) at the northern extent of their range.

Turn off Trans-Canada Hwy. at Doyles, 37km (23 miles) north of Port aux Basques to Cape Anguille. ✆ **877/254-6586** or 709/634-2285. www.linkumtours.com. 6 units. C$100 double. Rates include full breakfast. MC, V. Free parking. Closed Nov–Apr. *In room:* No phone.

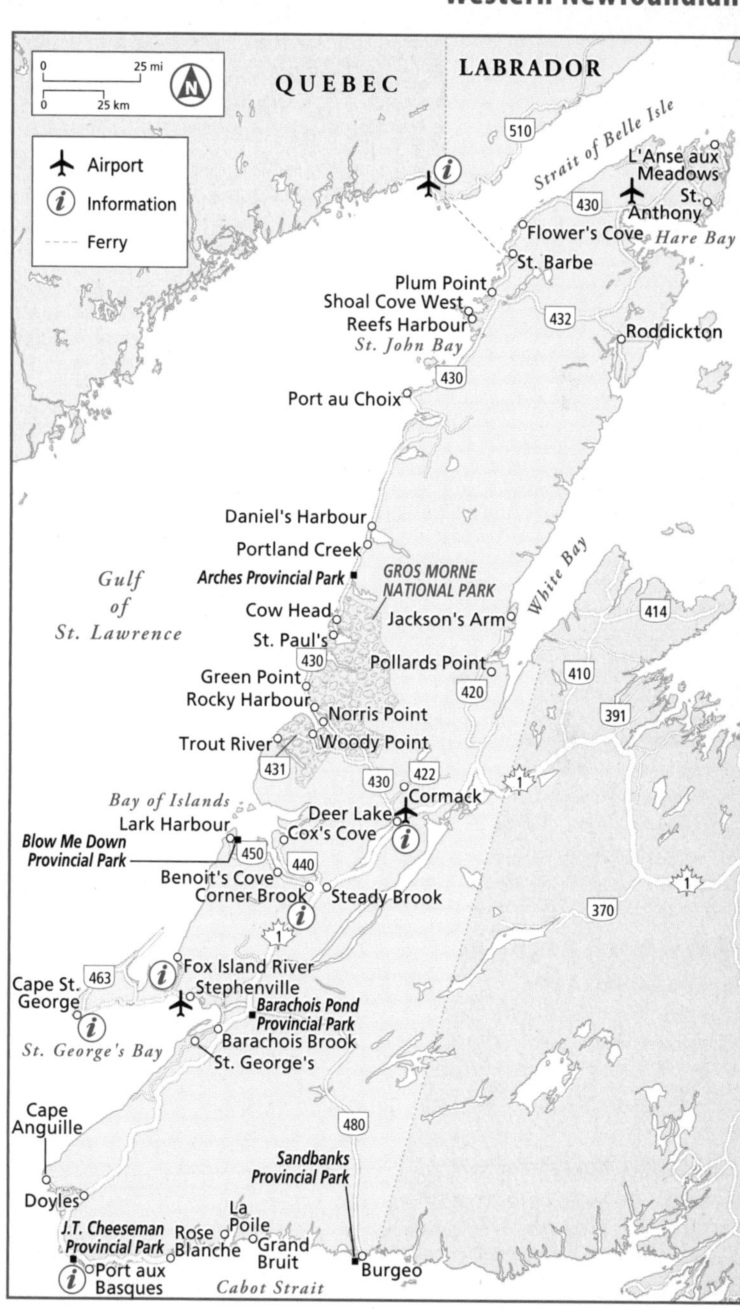

0
25 mi
0
25 km
N
Airport
Information
Ferry
QUEBEC
LABRADOR
510
Strait of Belle Isle
L'Anse aux Meadows
St. Anthony
430
Flower's Cove
Hare Bay
St. Barbe
Plum Point
Shoal Cove West
Reefs Harbour
St. John Bay
432
Roddickton
430
Port au Choix
Daniel's Harbour
Portland Creek
Gulf of St. Lawrence
Arches Provincial Park
GROS MORNE NATIONAL PARK
White Bay
Cow Head
Jackson's Arm
414
St. Paul's
430
Pollards Point
Green Point
410
420
Rocky Harbour
Norris Point
391
Trout River
Woody Point
431
430
422
Cormack
1
Bay of Islands
Deer Lake
Lark Harbour
Blow Me Down Provincial Park
Cox's Cove
450
440
Benoit's Cove
Corner Brook
Steady Brook
1
370
1
Fox Island River
Cape St. George
463
Stephenville
Barachois Pond Provincial Park
Barachois Brook
St. George's Bay
St. George's
Cape Anguille
480
Sandbanks Provincial Park
Doyles
J.T. Cheeseman Provincial Park
Rose Blanche
La Poile
Grand Bruit
Port aux Basques
Burgeo
Cabot Strait

Holiday Inn Stephenville Stephenville's largest hotel is ideally situated for shopping (it's connected to the town's shopping plaza), golfing at Harmon Seaside Links' 18-hole golf course, and touring the Port au Port Peninsula. The slightly dated decor of the guest rooms is more than made up for by their super-spacious layout.

44 Queen St., Stephenville. ✆ **800/465-4329** or 709/643-6666. www.holidayinnstephenville.com. 47 units. C$105–C$152 double. AE, MC, V. Free parking. **Amenities:** Restaurant; lounge. *In room:* A/C, TV, hair dryer.

Hotel Port aux Basques If you're looking for the closest accommodations to the ferry terminal in Port aux Basques, this is it. Formerly a Holiday Inn, this pleasant hotel is regularly renovated and modernized. The single and double rooms are unremarkable, with three suites—each with separate bedrooms and one with a kitchen—providing better value. The on-site casual restaurant specializes in generous helpings of seafood and has a kids' menu. Hotel Port aux Basques is within walking distance of shopping, churches, a railway heritage site, a cinema, a hospital, and recreational facilities. The hotel is wheelchair accessible.

1 Grand Bay Rd., Port aux Basques. ✆ **877/695-2171** or 709/695-2171. www.hotelpab.com. 50 units. C$90–C$140 double. Family, seniors, and off-season discounts available; kids stay free. AE, DC, MC, V. Free parking. Pets accepted. **Amenities:** Restaurant; lounge; exercise room. *In room:* TV, hair dryer.

WHERE TO DINE

Emile's Pub and Eatery CANADIAN Located within the Holiday Inn, Emile's has a reputation among locals for delivering reliably good food. Some of their more popular offerings are homemade soups—especially the rich and chunky seafood chowder. They also make great hot wings and cod dishes, and have lunchtime sandwich specials. Emile's has a lounge, as well as a separate section for families with children.

44 Queen St., Stephenville. ✆ **709/643-6666.** Reservations recommended for dinner. Main courses C$12–C$22. AE, MC, V. Mon–Thurs 7am–10pm; Fri 7am–11pm; Sat–Sun 8am–midnight.

Hartery's Family Restaurant ★ Value NEWFOUNDLAND If you're looking for a more traditional Newfoundland atmosphere and a good meal, I recommend Hartery's. They serve a large variety of dishes and are well known for their traditional "Jiggs Dinner" (boiled beef and cabbage), served all day Thursday and a steal at C$9. They also serve a very nice seafood platter for C$25.

109 Main St., Stephenville. ✆ **709/643-2242.** Reservations recommended for Thursday Jigg's Dinner. Main courses C$8–C$25. MC, V. Mon–Fri 9am–9pm; Sat–Sun 11am–9pm.

EXPLORING STEPHENVILLE & PORT AUX BASQUES

Harmon Seaside Links Originally built for U.S. servicemen based at the local Air Force base, this 18-hole course has all the elements of a Scottish links course, including wide fairways lined with fescue grass and ocean views. The course has club and power-cart rentals, as well as a driving range.

Off Rte. 460, Stephenville. ✆ **709/643-4322.** www.harmonseasidelinks.com. Greens fees C$35. Closed Nov–Apr.

Stephenville Theatre Festival The Stephenville area has several festivals during the summer, the most popular of which is the professional theater festival that runs during July and August. The venue itself is interesting to visit. Outside are impressive murals, while an interior gallery features changing art exhibits, often with a Newfoundland theme.

Stephenville Arts and Culture Centre, 380 Massachusetts Dr., Stephenville. ✆ **709/643-4553.** www.stf.nf.ca. Tickets for main-stage productions are C$24 adults, C$22 seniors, and C$10 children.

Finds The Last French Stronghold

West of Stephenville along Route 460 is the **Port au Port Peninsula,** Newfoundland's only remaining French region. The original settlers were reportedly Cape Breton Acadians who moved here in the 18th century. Until the last 50 years, geographic isolation and a rural economy protected the language and customs of this small francophone population.

Each August, the people of Cap Sainte-Georges and surrounding communities hold "Une Longue Veillée," a folk festival that celebrates their French heritage. In recent years, this festival has attracted traditional musicians, singers, and dancers from all over the province and a host of visitors and performers from the Maritime provinces, Quebec, and the French islands of St. Pierre and Miquelon.

Places to see include **Our Lady of Mercy Church and Museum** in Port au Port West (✆ **709/648-9236**), the largest wooden structure in the province; **Our Lady of Lourdes Grotto,** in the town of Lourdes, which in addition to the religious monument, also features a beautiful flower garden and an 1800 man-of-war cannon; and the **Lewis Hills,** which include the 814m (2,671-foot) The Cabox, the highest point in Newfoundland.

It takes 2½ hours to drive around the loop of the peninsula and back to Stephenville—if you don't stop. But if you take your time and enjoy the breathtaking cliff-hanging vistas, consider it a full day's outing. ***Note:*** There aren't a lot of services for travelers in the area. It's best to tank up before you head out, and pack a picnic lunch or have a big breakfast that will do you until you return to your post for the night. For more information on the peninsula, contact the **Port au Port Economic Development Association** (✆ **709/642-5831;** www.nfld.net/paped).

2 CORNER BROOK

Its proximity to the open waters of the Gulf of St. Lawrence makes Corner Brook a favorite stopover for cruise ships sailing Canada's east coast. That's just one of many appealing aspects to Corner Brook's spectacular location. The community is in a hilly lowland region surrounded by the Long Range Mountains—a continuation of the Appalachian belt stretching up from the New England states—so the natural beauty is stunning.

Corner Brook has been called the "Forest Capital of Canada," so it's no surprise to find one of the world's largest integrated pulp and paper mills here. Too bad it spoils the view of the Humber Arm, but the mill provides a very important and much-needed source of employment to the community's 21,000 residents.

ESSENTIALS

Getting There

Corner Brook is 53km (33 miles) southwest of Deer Lake along the Trans-Canada Highway (Rte. 1) and 218km (135 miles) north of the Port aux Basques Ferry Terminal. It's 687km (427 miles) west of St. John's.

Visitor Information

Corner Brook Tourist Chalet, located at 11 Confederation Dr. (✆ **709/634-5831;** www.cornerbrook.com), provides information on all of Western Newfoundland. The center is open year-round, from June 15 to September 15 daily from 9am until 9pm, and the rest of the year Monday to Friday from 9am until 5pm.

WHERE TO STAY & DINE

There are quite a few places to stay and eat in Corner Brook, but I always prefer spending the night at one of the appealing Steady Brook lodgings, included in this section, 12km (7½ miles) north of town at the base of Marble Mountain.

Glynmill Inn ★ The professional confidence of the staff and the understated dignity of the foyer tell you that this is the most prestigious property in Corner Brook. This traditional Tudor-style hotel overlooking its namesake pond is within a 10-minute walk of downtown Corner Brook. Built as a guesthouse for executives of the pulp mill back in 1924, the Glynmill Inn has been thoroughly modernized. The inn carries an Olde-English theme throughout public spaces (think dark wood furnishings and gilded picture frames). Guest rooms have a similar theme, with the standard rooms on the small side and some suites with separate bedrooms.

The Glynmill is home to two restaurants. The elegant **Wine Cellar** dining room specializes in steak and seafood, while the casual and moderately priced **Carriage Room** restaurant dishes up traditional Newfoundland favorites such as cod tongues with scrunchions (save room for a generous slice of partridgeberry pie). The former is open daily for dinner, while the latter is open daily 7am to 9:30pm.

1 Cobb Lane, Corner Brook. ✆ **800/563-4400** or 709/634-5181. www.glynmillinn.ca. 81 units. C$114–C$190 double. AE, DC, MC, V. Free parking. **Amenities:** 2 restaurants; lounge; exercise room. *In room:* A/C, TV, fridge (some), hair dryer.

Greenwood Inn & Suites The only hotel right downtown, this hostelry has a little more style than other choices in Western Newfoundland. Elegant tile floors, leather furnishings, and a dramatically curving staircase are among the features that grace the open reception area of the hotel. Amenities include an oversize whirlpool, fitness facility, underground heated parking, and the only hotel swimming pool in town. Guest rooms are midsize and regularly renovated; some have two double beds, others have king-size beds. The Executive Suites have upgraded everything, and Family Suites include bunk beds for the kids. If you don't feel like splurging at the Bay of Islands Bistro (see below) across the road, the on-site **Crown & Moose** has a large selection of beers on tap and is a reliable dining choice for well-priced pub fare.

48 West St., Corner Brook. ✆ **800/399-5381** or 709/634-5381. www.greenwoodcornerbrook.com. 102 units. C$104–C$145 double. AE, DC, DISC, MC, V. Underground parking garage. **Amenities:** Restaurant; lounge; exercise room; pool; room service; sauna. *In room:* A/C, TV.

Marble Inn Resort ★★ (Value) Marble Inn is on the banks of the Humber River 12km (7½ miles) north of Corner Brook—within walking distance of the alpine resort. The maroon-colored cedar-shake cottages range in size from one to four bedrooms. Amenities and services differ from unit to unit, with some having full kitchens and others having kitchenettes. Several have a fireplace and Jacuzzi. ***Hint:*** The cottages have a distinctive woodsy feel and are best suited for families, but for a slice of luxury, choose one of the two-bedroom riverside suites, which feature stainless steel kitchen appliances, comfortable living areas, and laundry facilities. Some units come with a Jacuzzi or fireplace.

Madison's Grill, the resort's restaurant, is an excellent choice for dinner, even if you have rented a kitchen-equipped unit. The healthy, wide-ranging menu offers something for everyone, including family-friendly choices such as a whole lasagna for four people. It's open daily for dinner and Sunday for lunch.

21 Dogwood Dr., Steady Brook, 12km (7½ miles) north of Corner Brook. ✆ **877/497-5673** or 709/634-2237. www.marbleinn.com. 12 cottages, 7 inn rooms, 9 suites. C$119–C$299 cottages; C$139 inn rooms; C$329 suites. Midweek and off-season discounts apply. Inquire about ski-pass discounts. MC, V. **Amenities:** Restaurant; exercise room; pool; sauna; playground; guided tours; ski packages. *In room:* TV/DVD player, kitchen/kitchenette.

Marblewood Village Resort ★ Here, at the foot of Marble Mountain, you'll find ultimate convenience and deluxe accommodations, designed with winter visitors in mind. You can ski or snowboard from the doorstep of your very own luxury chalet. Each of the adjoining units is styled along modern, clean lines with dramatic cathedral ceiling, pine-and-marble fireplace, and private sun deck or patio. With the fully equipped kitchen (even down to the microwave and dishwasher) and top-quality linens, staying here is like taking the comforts of home with you on vacation. ***Tip:*** Because it's part of a ski resort, winter is high season, so check the resort website for summer deals (rooms were renting for C$99 midweek in July during the research for this edition).

8 Thistle Dr., Steady Brook. ✆ **888/868-7635** or 709/632-7900. www.marblemountain.com. 24 units. C$129–C$349 per unit. AE, DC, MC, V. *In room:* TV, kitchen, electric fireplace, Wi-Fi.

Bay of Islands Bistro ★★ CONTEMPORARY/CANADIAN Bay of Islands Bistro is one of the best restaurants west of the capital—it has an innovative menu with a wide range of offerings. This is the high-caliber kind of restaurant you'd expect to find in a major city, and a wonderful find in a smaller city such as Corner Brook. On a rather uninspiring main street, the setting, in a renovated residence surrounded by bland buildings, is also a surprise. The emphasis is on local and seasonal produce and seafood, which is given a modern makeover and beautifully presented. Also notable is the professional service. The dinner prices are higher than you'll find in most other restaurants in town, but lunches, including gourmet sandwiches, are well priced.

13 West St., Corner Brook. ✆ **709/639-3463.** Reservations recommended. Main courses C$17–C$33. AE, DC, MC, V. Tues–Thurs noon–9:30pm; Fri–Sat noon–10:30pm; Sun noon–9:30pm.

EXPLORING CORNER BROOK

Corner Brook has a couple of attractions, but it's also worth considering the coastal drive along the southern side of the Humber Arm. Route 450 begins right in town and passes a string of fishing villages en route to Lark Harbour, at the end of the road 50km (31 miles) from town. Aside from admiring the coastal panorama, allow time for a stop in delightfully named **Blow Me Down Provincial Park,** where the Bay of Islands spreads out to the north, and to the south, you can easily spot the barren rust-colored peaks of the Blow Me Down Mountains. Allow 3 hours for the round-trip.

Corner Brook Museum & Archives A former courthouse/telegraph office/customs house now finds life as a regional museum, a good place to while away an hour or so on a rainy day. The collection of approximately 1,000 items highlights the town's forestry, and pulp and paper industries, the lifestyle of the aboriginal people who once lived here, and leisure time as displayed through antique skis and toboggans. In addition to enjoying the intriguing photos depicting life in Corner Brook at the turn of last century, you'll be captivated by the century-old artifacts (like the Nestlé floor-model hair-perming machine: it looks like Medusa on wheels). If nostalgia overwhelms you, compare the push-button modern clothes washer to the crank-handle wringer washer. It gives you a completely new perspective on the "good old days."

2 West St., Corner Brook. ✆ **709/634-2518.** www.cornerbrookmuseum.ca. C$5 adults, C$3 children 12–17, free for children 11 and under. July–Aug daily 9am–5pm, Sept–June Mon–Fri 9am–4:30pm.

Marble Mountain Resort ★★★ Atlantic Canada's biggest and best winter resort destination. Rising steeply from the Humber River, Marble Mountain has a peak elevation of only 546m (1,791 ft.), but receives an amazing 5m (16 ft.) of snowfall per year. There are 37 runs, ranging from novice to expert, with 27 groomed trails, seven mogul runs, and three runs through glades of trees. Freestylers are catered to with a half-pipe, snocross park, and terrain park. Marble Mountain operates a high-speed detachable quad chair, two more quad chairs, and a platter lift. Not only will the steepness of the slopes catch your eye, so will the magnificent post-and-beam day lodge, where you find multiple eateries, a ski school, and a rental shop.

While winter is most definitely high season, it's also worth stopping by in summer. A short but steep trail leads to photogenic Steady Brook Falls (allow 30 min. for the round-trip), while the super-fit who slog their way to the summit of Marble Mountain will be rewarded with sweeping mountain and river views. This trail takes around 2 hours to complete.

Rte. 1, Steady Brook, 12km (7½ miles) north of Corner Brook. ✆ **888/462-7253** or 709/637-7601. www.skimarble.com. Lift pass C$49 adults, C$37 seniors and students, C$25 children 12 and under. Ski lifts operate late Dec to early Apr.

3 DEER LAKE

Deer Lake is the transportation hub of Western Newfoundland. Here, you head either north to Gros Morne and the Northern Peninsula, east to St. John's, or south to Corner Brook and the Nova Scotia ferry. The community has a population of about 5,000 residents and offers a good range of services, including an airport. The airport is especially convenient if you fly into St. John's, drive across the province, and don't want to drive all the way back to St. John's to catch a return flight.

ESSENTIALS

Getting There

If you're coming from Port aux Basques and traveling north along the Trans-Canada Highway (Rte. 1), it's a 3-hour drive to Deer Lake. From the east, it's 637km (396 miles) between Deer Lake and St. John's. And, if you're heading south from St. Anthony on Route 430, it's a 443km (275-mile) drive to Deer Lake.

Or you can just bypass the driving altogether and fly directly into **Deer Lake Regional Airport** (✆ **709/635-3601;** www.deerlakeairport.com), 3km (1¾ miles) northeast of town. This large, modern airport is serviced by Air Canada, Air Labrador, Provincial Airlines, and WestJet. Four car-rental agencies have outlets at the airport (Avis, Budget, Hertz, and National), and an information desk is located by the baggage carousel. Other airport services include Wi-Fi, a gift shop, a restaurant, and an ATM.

Visitor Information

Deer Lake Visitor Information Centre (✆ **709/635-2202;** www.town.deerlake.nf.ca) is along the Trans-Canada Highway (Rte. 1), beside the Irving gas station. It's open June to September daily 8am to 8pm.

WHERE TO STAY

Deer Lake Motel Conveniently located on the Trans-Canada Highway, this handy motel is nothing special, although a 2004 renovation had yet to show the wear and tear of previous guests when I checked in for this edition. The on-site restaurant has a pleasant decor, quiet ambience, and predictable food at reasonable prices. The dining room is thankfully free of the most common restaurant mistake: Tables are spaced sufficiently far apart to allow for private conversations.

15 Trans-Canada Hwy. (Rte. 1), Deer Lake. ✆ **800/563-2144** or 709/635-2108. www.deerlakemotel.com. 54 units. C$85–C$166 double. AE, DC, MC, V. Free parking. **Amenities:** Restaurant; cafe; lounge. *In room:* A/C, TV, hair dryer.

Driftwood Inn Dating to the 1950s and with a vaguely Tudor exterior, this distinctive accommodation is away from the noise of the highway yet close to downtown. Guest rooms are smallish and a little on the dark side, but reasonable rates make up for these shortcomings. The cozy atmosphere with rustic styling is enhanced by the friendly service of the super-accommodating staff.

3 Nicholsville Rd., Deer Lake. ✆ **888/635-5115** or 709/635-5115. www.driftwoodinn.ca. 25 units. C$89–C$156 double. MC, V. Free parking. **Amenities:** Restaurant; lounge. *In room:* TV, Wi-Fi.

Humberview Bed & Breakfast ★★ (Finds Overlooking the river and within walking distance of the town's most popular beach, this lodging is in a modern estate-style home in an upscale neighborhood. The aptly named Grand Suite is 76 sq. m (818 sq. ft.) of elegant intimacy, with its own sitting area and four-poster bed. Not only does the en-suite bathroom have a Grecian-style Jacuzzi flanked by twin columns, it also has a bidet. The other six rooms are less ostentatious but equally comfortable. Rounding out the stylish setting is a sitting room, complete with piano. It would be easy to be intimidated if not for the warm hospitality of owners Bronson and Irene Short. Still, you can't help but feel you have to be on your best behavior (this is, after all, a private home—not an impersonal hotel).

11 Humberview Dr., Deer Lake. ✆ **888/635-4818** or 709/635-4818. www.thehumberview.com. 7 units. C$109–C$149 double; C$10 additional person. Rates include hot breakfast. MC, V. Take Exit 15 off the Trans-Canada Hwy and head north. *In room:* TV, Wi-Fi, no phone.

WHERE TO DINE

Irving Big Stop Family Restaurant (Value DINER Like so many casual Newfoundland restaurants, this busy restaurant on the main highway through town combines typical no-frills North American diner cooking with local specialties. A "Jiggs Dinner" (corned beef and cabbage), served every Thursday for C$8, attracts hordes of locals. The kids will likely be thrilled at the sight of Howley, Newfoundland's Biggest Moose—a huge moose statue in the front of the building. There are no alcoholic beverages served, and smoking is not allowed.

Trans-Canada Hwy. (Rte. 1), Deer Lake. ✆ **709/635-2129.** Reservations not accepted. Main courses C$8–C$18. AE, DC, MC, V. Daily 24 hr.

Jungle Jim's (Kids INTERNATIONAL This casual, safari-style restaurant at the Driftwood Inn is part of a Newfoundland restaurant chain that has expanded as far west as Alberta. Because of their long hours, it's a great place to eat if you're looking for a late-night meal. Specialties include stir-fry, barbecue ribs, and spicy chicken wings. The funky "jungle" surroundings and children's menu make this an ideal family restaurant (a welcome change in a sea of ultra-fast-food choices).

3 Upper Nicholsville Rd., Deer Lake. ✆ **709/635-5054.** www.junglejims.ca. Reservations not accepted. Main courses C$8–C$18. AE, DC, MC, V. Sun–Tues 11am–11pm; Wed–Sat 11am–11:30pm.

EXPLORING DEER LAKE

Deer Lake (the actual lake) has one of the nicest sandy beaches in Newfoundland. Behind the beach, you'll find a lovely park and scenic walking trail. To get there, take the Nicholsville Road exit from the Trans-Canada Highway. The town also serves as a base for salmon fishing on the Humber River. Some of the best local fishing holes are within **Sir Richard Squires Memorial Provincial Park,** 8km (5 miles) northwest on Route 430 and then 47km (29 miles) north on Route 422. Even if you don't want to dangle a line, it's worth driving out to this park to see **Big Falls** (this is the name by which the park is known to locals)**,** where you can see the salmon jumping right out of the water. The best time to witness this natural wonder is in late June and early July, when water flow is at its highest. Other features include two short hiking trails, a playground, and salmon fishing.

Newfoundland Insectarium ★ (Kids The highlight of Deer Lake is the Insectarium, just north of town on Bonne Bay Road. If you like butterflies, this place is a must-see, with many specimens, including the impressive Blue Morpho. There's also an observation hive where you can watch thousands of honeybees going about their busy day—and be a breath away from live scorpions and tarantulas (safely enclosed by thick glass). If you're one of those people who like to get up close and personal with creepy crawlies, the staff will be happy to oblige by putting a live tropical leaf insect in your hand. This is one of only two such facilities in Canada (similar to sections of the American Museum of Natural History). It comes with a nice walking trail, an ice-cream shop, and a unique bug-themed gift shop. An elevator facilitates wheelchair access to all three levels.

Rte. 430 to Bonne Bay Rd., Reidville. ✆ **709/635-4545.** www.nfinsectarium.com. C$10 adults, C$8.50 seniors, C$6.50 children 5–14. July 1–Aug 31 daily 9am–6pm; mid-May to June and Sept to mid-Oct Mon–Fri 9am–5pm, Sat 10am–5pm, Sun noon–5pm.

4 GROS MORNE NATIONAL PARK ★★★

Gros Morne is larger than life, bordered by the Long Range Mountains and tapering to 90m (295-ft.) oceanic depths mere meters from shore. In between is an unbelievable biotic richness: old-growth forests, coastal lowlands, glacier-scarred landscapes, and a place where continents collided. The best way to really appreciate it is via a boat tour, hiking, rock climbing, skiing, or snowmobiling. In short, you have to get out there!

Unless you're the hardy type, the weather may hamper your enjoyment of the park. Between the prevailing southwest winds and the proximity of the Gulf of St. Lawrence, there is, on average, precipitation every 2 days during the summer months. From late September (for the higher elevations) on through the winter months, that dripping wetness translates into an impressive snowfall—up to 1,000 centimeters (394 in., or 33 ft.) in some areas, making Gros Morne ideal for backcountry skiing.

The weather in Gros Morne can be quite unpredictable, so be prepared with clothing for all types, and be sure to get a pre-trip orientation from a park warden before you head off into the backcountry. You'll find hiking trails for every experience level, with the most difficult being the 16km (10-mile) trail to the summit of Gros Morne Mountain, the highest peak in the park at 850m (2,789 ft.). ***Warning:*** Pay special attention to prudent food handling when picnicking, camping, or hiking the backcountry so that you're not surprised by a hungry black bear.

ESSENTIALS

Getting There

The park entrance is 30km (19 miles) northwest of Deer Lake along Route 430. From this point, it's an additional 40km (25 miles) to Rocky Harbour, the park's main service center. From farther afield, it's 340km (211 miles) to Rocky Harbour from the ferry terminal at Port aux Basques and 640km (398 miles) to the park from St. John's. Alternatively, you can fly into Deer Lake from Halifax, St. John's, Toronto, or Montreal, and rent a car (see "Deer Lake," above).

Visitor Information

The most comprehensive information on Gros Morne is available in the park's **Discovery Centre** (✆ **709/458-2417**), on Route 431 near the community of Woody Point. It's open mid-May to June daily 9am to 5pm; July to August daily 9am to 6pm (until 9pm Sunday and Wednesday); and September to early October daily 9am to 5pm. The main **Park Visitor Centre** (✆ **709/458-2066**), near Rocky Harbour, is open mid-May to late June daily 9am to 5pm; late June to early September daily 9am to 9pm; and early September to October daily 9am to 5pm. You can also get information at the **park entrance kiosk,** on Route 430 near the southeastern entrance to the park at Wiltondale. The kiosk does not have a telephone and is open mid-May to mid-October daily 10am until 6pm.

Parks Canada publishes a wonderful visitor's guide called the *Tuckamore,* which provides detailed information about services in and around the park. You'll be given a copy upon paying your entrance fee; you can also get the same information online at **www.pc.gc.ca/grosmorne**.

For information about privately run services in the communities bordering the park (a number of towns, such as Rocky Harbour, are fully encompassed by the park), contact **Newfoundland & Labrador Tourism** (✆ **800/563-6353** or 709/729-2830; www.newfoundlandlabrador.com). **Gros Morne National Park**'s website (**www.grosmorne.com)** also provides information about commercial services in the area, such as tour operators and accommodations.

All park visitors must pay an entry fee. A day pass is C$10 for adults, C$8 for seniors 65 and over, C$5 for children 6 to 16 years, and free for children 5 and under. Family passes are C$20. If you're continuing up the northern peninsula from Gros Morne, consider the **Viking Trail Pass,** which covers park entrance for 1 week, as well as admission to four national historic sites along the northern peninsula. The cost is C$44 for adults, C$36 for seniors 65 years and over, C$22 for children 6 to 16, free for children 5 and under, and C$89 for families. Your park entrance fee gives you access to park services, including the wonderful Discovery Centre.

Getting Around

Gros Morne National Park is almost divided in two by Bonne Bay. The community of Wiltondale (gas station, lodging), 30km (19 miles) northwest of Deer Lake, is at the head of the bay, at the fork of the road where Route 431 branches out from Route 430.

Route 430 takes you north to Rocky Harbour and along the park's western coast, while Route 431 branches in an easterly direction to the southern side of Bonne Bay and ends at the picturesque fishing village of Trout River. You'll need to take Route 431 if your destination is the Tablelands, and camping or hiking at Lomond or Trout River Pond. Route 431 is also the location of the park's Discovery Centre, an absolute must-see if you are to make the most of your visit to Gros Morne.

Boat Tour

Campground

Discovery Centre

Group Campground

Interpretive Sign or Exhibit

Outdoor Theatre

Pay Phone

Picnic Area

Primitive Camping

Swimming

----- Hiking Trail

Park Visitor Centre

Wheelchair Accessible

Hiking Trails

1 Bakers Brook Falls
2 Berry Head Pond
3 Berry Hill
4 Berry Hill Pond
5 Broom Point
6 Coastal (Green Point)
7 Green Gardens
8 Gros Morne Mountain
9 Lobster Cove Head
10 Lomond River
11 Lookout Hills
12 Old Mail Road
13 Snug Harbour
14 Southeast Brook Falls
15 Stanleyville
16 Stuckless Pond
17 Tablelands
18 Trout River Pond
19 Western Brook Pond

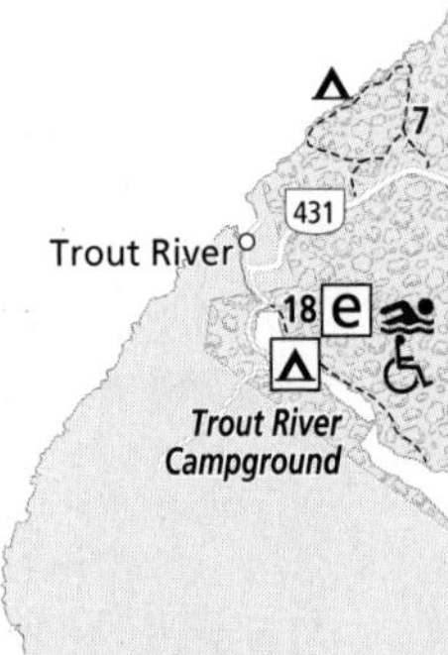

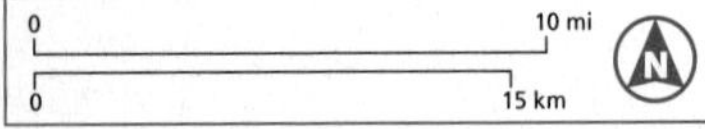

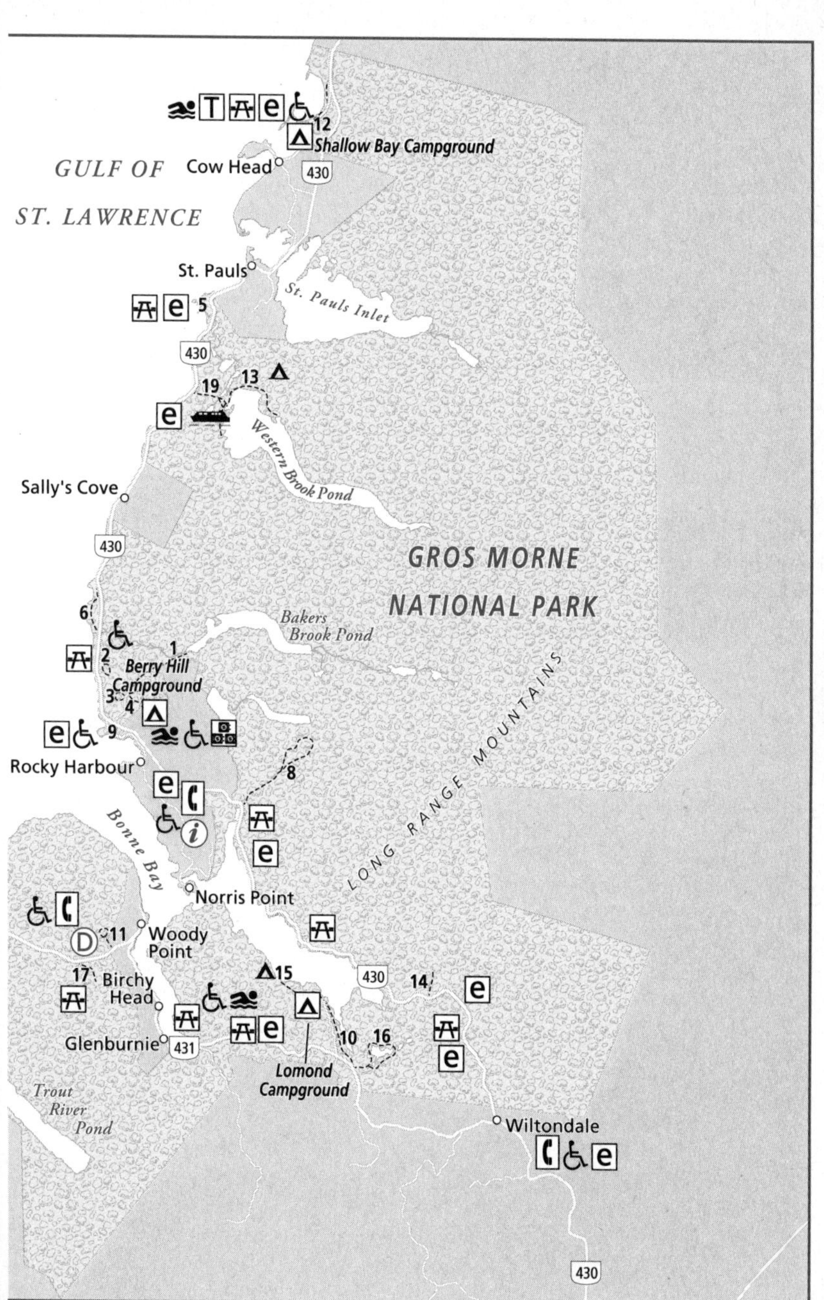

12
Shallow Bay Campground
GULF OF
ST. LAWRENCE
Cow Head
430
St. Pauls
St. Pauls Inlet
5
430
13
19
Western Brook Pond
Sally's Cove
430
GROS MORNE
NATIONAL PARK
6
Bakers
Brook Pond
2
1
Berry Hill
Campground
3
4
9
LONG RANGE MOUNTAINS
Rocky Harbour
8
Bonne Bay
Norris Point
11
Woody
Point
17
Birchy
Head
15
430
14
10
16
Glenburnie
431
Lomond
Campground
Trout
River
Pond
Wiltondale
430

You'll be pleased by the wealth of motel, inn, and B&B accommodations choices located in communities encircled by the park but outside park boundaries. If, however, you're hoping to stay in a luxury hotel, you're going to be disappointed—there aren't any, though there is always ample room at the best lodgings of all, where amenities include pine-needle carpets and starlight canopies.

During July and August, accommodations in Gros Morne—both campsites and motel rooms—can be difficult to come by. It's best to make your reservations as soon as you know you'll be coming.

There are several decent restaurants in the area, but not as many as you might think given the size of the park. It's the nature of the destination; most people aren't here for fine dining. They prefer to picnic or barbecue.

Entente Cordiale (Finds) Overlooking the ocean from beyond the park's northern boundary is Entente Cordiale, a delightfully welcoming bed-and-breakfast named for a 1904 agreement in which the French gave up their rights to Newfoundland's west coast. The trim, two-story wood-frame home is large by Newfoundland standards and is surrounded by an eye-catching driftwood fence. Inside are six comfortable guest rooms, two with unobstructed ocean views and the others with partial water views. A light breakfast is included in the rates, and dinner is available upon request.

The hosts will encourage you to spend time strolling along the sandy beach fronting Portland Creek or, for those looking for adventure, pepper you with suggestions that may include visiting Portland Creek Inner Pond and East Brook Gulch. They can also help with the logistics of hiking the 50km (31-mile) Four Ponds Traverse.

Main Rd., Portland Creek. ✆ **800/316-1899** or 709/898-2288. www.ententecordiale.com. 6 units. C$80–C$90 double. MC, V. Rates include breakfast. Closed Oct to mid-June. *In room:* No phone.

Frontier Cottages Located at the crossroads of Gros Morne National Park, thus convenient for day trips exploring both sides of Bonne Bay, this is a good choice for families. More than just a convenient exploration base, they're custom-made for outdoor fun. Stay at these fully winterized log cabins, and you'll be able to start skiing and snowmobiling from the minute you walk out the door. Want to try something a little more unconventional, like ice climbing? Talk to the owners—they'll customize an expedition you'll never forget. The two-bedroom cabins are adequately decorated with pine and other rustic furnishings. There is an on-site convenience store and gas bar, craft/souvenir shop, and restaurant.

Rte. 430, Wiltondale. ✆ **800/668-2520** or 709/453-7266. www.frontiercottages.com. 6 units. C$129–C$149 per unit, C$10 additional person. AE, DC, MC, V. Free parking. **Amenities:** Restaurant; playground. *In room:* TV, kitchen.

Gros Morne Cabins A short walk around the bay from downtown Rocky Harbour, these log cabins are separated from the water by nothing more than a strip of mown grass and have sweeping ocean views extending across the harbor to Lobster Cove Head Lighthouse. Each cabin has one or two bedrooms; a sitting area with TV; and a full kitchen with a stove, oven, microwave, and all the pots and pans you'd ever need.

Main St., Rocky Harbour. ✆ **888/603-2020** or 709/458-2020. www.grosmornecabins.com. 22 units. C$129–C$159 double. C$10 additional person. AE, DC, MC, V. Free parking. **Amenities:** Playground; barbeques; picnic tables. *In room:* TV, kitchen, Wi-Fi.

Java Jack's ★★ NEWFOUNDLAND Originally a cafe—as the name suggests—Java Jack's has grown into a great little restaurant within the confines of a restored heritage home brightened by a canary-yellow exterior. You could start with warm potato salad or fish cakes made with halibut, then move onto my favorite main, the Bubbly Bake, a richly flavored dish filled with local seafood. Still hungry? Try the Dark Tickle chocolates, made locally. Regardless of what you order, your meal will take full advantage of herbs and vegetables from the restaurant garden, which is also the source of flowers set on every table.

88 Main St., Rocky Harbour ✆ **709/458-3004.** Reservations not accepted. Main courses C$17–C$25. MC, V. Daily 9am–9pm.

Middle Brook Cottages & Chalets (Kids) Families love the quality and convenience of this full-service facility (especially the small playground and Laundromat). It's perfect for a day of on-site recreation or as a much-needed rest after hiking the nearby Tablelands. The cottages and the chalets get top marks for cleanliness and comfort, and their tidy landscaped exteriors. I especially like the chalets because of their bright decor, cathedral ceilings, and second-floor patio (a great place to enjoy your morning coffee and watch the sun come up).

There's a convenience store on-site, as well as a gift shop. There's also a picnic area with barbecues, and a fire pit for an evening marshmallow roast. When you're not enjoying the sights and sounds of Gros Morne, you can explore the waterfall and walking trails that are within walking distance of Middle Brook.

Rte. 431, Glenburnie–Birchy Head. ✆ **709/453-2332.** www.middlebrookcottages.com. 3 cottages, 2 chalets, 1 deluxe unit. C$115–C$135 double, C$10 additional person. Children 12 and under stay free in parent's room. AE, MC, V. Free parking. Closed Dec–Feb. **Amenities:** Playground.

Ocean View Motel For those who prefer the anonymity of a motel over the forced intimacy of a B&B, this is the largest facility in the largest town in Gros Morne. Guest rooms are standard motel style, although the bedding is of better quality than most. Access to upper-floor rooms is a funky old-style elevator. The ocean is across the road, so the gentle lullaby of the surf will help you sleep at night. You may even be drawn to have a closer look, a whim easily accommodated by simply crossing the road. Or, you can stay in the comfort of the Anchor Pub and dining room, enraptured by the fading sun as it sets over Lobster Cove Head Lighthouse. That's if you can draw your focus away from the superb dinner offerings. The pub gets busiest when local bands hit the stage.

Main St., Rocky Harbour. ✆ **800/563-9887** or 709/458-2730. www.theoceanview.ca. 52 units. C$95–C$145 double; C$7 additional person. MC, V. **Amenities:** Restaurant; lounge; pub. *In room:* TV.

Seaside Restaurant ★ SEAFOOD This casual restaurant is in a restored waterfront building along the boardwalk in Trout River, a picturesque fishing village at the end of Route 431. The decor is suitably nautical, with the most-sought-after tables on an upstairs balcony with sweeping ocean views. You can order light meals such as salads, but it is the simple presentations of local seafood, including chowders, crab, lobster, and cod, that get the most attention.

Rte. 431, Trout River. ✆ **709/451-3461.** Reservations not necessary. Main courses C$9–C$18. MC, V. Mid-May to mid-Oct daily noon–10pm.

Shallow Bay Motel & Cabins (Kids) Located 40km (25 miles) north of Rocky Harbour, there's something for everyone at Shallow Bay: natural wonder, peaceful solitude,

Gros Morne Theatre Festival

The Gros Morne Theatre Festival is an unforgettable experience of such rich cultural diversity that you won't be satisfied until you see it all. "All" in 2009 was seven different productions, three different venues, two shows a night, and more than 30 professional actors, musicians, technicians, writers, directors, and front-of-house staff. Focus on the word *professional*—that's your first indication of the superior quality of these dramatic events. That and the consistently sold-out shows.

A superb example of the intensely personal plays performed during the Gros Morne Theatre Festival is *Tempting Providence.* Written by Robert Chafe, it's the haunting story of Nurse Myra Bennett, Newfoundland's own Florence Nightingale. For more than 50 years, Bennett was the only medical person on the Great Northern Peninsula. During that time, she delivered more than 700 babies, extracted at least 5,000 teeth, and performed kitchen-table surgeries by lamplight. For information on the latest shows and to make a reservation, call ✆ **877/243-2899** or 709/639-7238, or go to **www.theatrenewfoundland.com/gmtf.html**.

and a sauna for adult enjoyment; and mini-golf, a small outdoor heated pool, and beachcombing for the younger set. One activity both young and old are guaranteed to appreciate is the Gros Morne Theatre Festival—a powerful production of Newfoundland drama, story, and song hosted here each summer.

The property offers a choice of standard motel unit or fully equipped cabin. Both are fairly modest, although enhanced by the ocean just 5m (16 ft.) away. This is a wheelchair-accessible facility. The on-site family restaurant serves a tasty assortment of pocketbook-friendly home-style meals. The specialty of the house is lobster, but you can get it only in season, from early May to early July.

Rte. 430, Cow Head. ✆ **800/563-1946** or 709/243-2471. www.shallowbaymotel.com. 72 units (55 motel units, 17 cottages). C$95–C$115 double; C$10 additional person. AE, DC, MC, V. **Amenities:** Restaurant; lounge; pool; sauna. *In room:* TV.

Sugar Hill Inn ★★★ **Finds** One of the more luxurious places to stay while in Gros Morne (and one of the only places that has air-conditioning) is Sugar Hill Inn. Most impressive is the King Suite. It features a king-size bed, private Jacuzzi for two, and gorgeous leather couch. This room is popular—especially with honeymooners—so be sure to book early. There is also a nice cottage with queen-size bed, Jacuzzi tub, and a private deck. Every room has a hardwood floor, and most have a private entrance.

The Sugar Hill Inn offers a set three-course menu nightly in a classy dining room. The specialty of the house is fresh local seafood, with choices dependent on availability—you may be invited to try halibut, cod, salmon, shrimp, or scallops. It's one of the very few restaurants in the province where *nothing* is deep-fried. One staple are the desserts made fresh daily (the baked custard with blueberry sauce is simply divine). Dining is by reservation only—primarily for guests of the inn—and is served from 6:30 to 8:30pm.

Norris Point Rd., Norris Point. ✆ **888/299-2147** or 709/458-2147. www.sugarhillinn.ca. 11 units. C$145–C$225 double. C$15 additional person. Off-season discounts. AE, MC, V. Free parking. Closed Oct–Jan. **Amenities:** Restaurant; lounge; sauna. *In room:* A/C, TV.

Victorian Manor Heritage Properties In Newfoundland and Labrador, it's a traditional measure of respect and affection to refer to older, unrelated acquaintances as "Aunt" or "Uncle," which is where the names of the four homes that comprise this complex originate. The largest of the four is **Aunt Jane's Place,** a 19th-century tourist home that evokes old-fashioned charm just as much as does its period furnishings and simple square construction. Only two of the five guest rooms have private bathrooms (with a tub only). If you aren't interested in watching TV in the common room, you can still mingle with your hosts and other guests in the upstairs sitting room while enjoying its view of Bonne Bay. Alternatively, walk down to the waterfront and explore the historic precinct that has changed little in generations.

Of the two holiday homes, my favorite is **Uncle Steve's Place,** a fully equipped three-bedroom traditional-style home, great for a small group or family. Those looking for a more modern setting should reserve one of the two-bedroom housekeeping units. Although the rooms are on the small side, you'll want to spend as much time as possible on your private deck looking out over the ocean.

1 Water St., Woody Point. ✆ **866/453-2485** or 709/453-2485. www.grosmorne.com/victorianmanor. 11 units, 2 homes. C$65–C$105 double; C$175–C$225 home for up to 6 people. MC, V. *In room:* Kitchen, no phone.

CAMPING IN GROS MORNE

A good number of visitors come to Gros Morne to camp and thus to fully appreciate the great outdoors. The campgrounds are justifiably popular, so reservations are wise. Contact the **Parks Canada Campground Reservation Service** (✆ **877/737-3783;** www.pccamping.ca). For general information on camping in Gros Morne, contact the **Park Visitor Centre** (✆ **709/458-2417;** www.pc.gc.ca/grosmorne).

Berry Hill Campground ★ With 146 wooded campsites, including four walk-in sites especially for tent campers, this is the park's largest campground. It also has the most facilities, as well as a hiking trail. It is close to Rocky Harbour, where grocery stores and restaurants can be found. If you want to combine culture with camping, you'll be pleased to know that the shuttle for the Gros Morne Theatre Festival makes a campground pickup.

Rte. 430, Rocky Harbour. 146 sites. C$26 per site; C$7 per firewood bundle. AE, MC, V. Closed mid-Sept to mid-June. **Amenities:** Shower and washroom facilities; water; kitchen shelter; dump station; picnic tables; fire pits; playground; hiking.

Lomond Campground Just down Route 431, 17km (11 miles) south from Wiltondale at Lomond, you'll find a full-service campground, the closest one to the main park entrance. This campground is ideal for people interested in fishing and boating, and it's popular with local residents. The area was once a logging community, and two easy walking trails follow old logging roads. The campsites have lots of open, grassy spaces and offer outstanding views of Bonne Bay, the Lomond River, and Long Range Mountains.

Rte. 431, Lomond. 29 sites. C$26 per site; C$7 per firewood bundle. AE, MC, V. Closed mid-Oct to mid-May. **Amenities:** Kitchen shelters; picnic tables; swimming; boat launching/docking facilities; fishing; hiking; playground; running water; dumping station; washrooms w/showers; fire pits.

Shallow Bay Campground Located near Cow Head (home of the Gros Morne Theatre Festival), this is the northernmost campground along Route 430, just before the northern entrance/exit to the park. The grassy campsites, sheltered from northwesterly winds by a protective stand of tuckamore, are a hop, skip, and jump from a 4km-long (2½-mile) white-sand beach—ideal for swimming and building sand castles. There is a trail that links the campground to the day-use area and a small outdoor theater for campfire programs.

Rte. 430 to Cow Head. 62 sites. C$26 unserviced site; C$7 per firewood bundle. AE, MC, V. Closed mid-Sept to mid-June. **Amenities:** Kitchen shelter; picnic tables; swimming; fishing; hiking; outdoor theater; playground; dumping station; running water; washrooms w/showers; fire pits.

Trout River Pond Campground ★ Campsites at Trout River are larger and more sheltered than in some other parts of the park and provide awesome views of the Tablelands and Trout River Pond. The drinking water is good, but it's still not a bad idea to filter it. This is a popular spot because of the nearby beach, boat tour, and boat launch. Although the most isolated auto-accessible campground in the park, it's also the best base for exploring the Tablelands, the Green Gardens area, and the community of Trout River.

Rte. 431, Trout River. 44 sites. C$26 unserviced site; C$7 per firewood bundle. AE, MC, V. Open mid-June to mid-Sept. **Amenities:** Kitchen shelter; picnic tables; swimming; fishing; hiking; playground; washrooms w/showers; water; fire pits.

EXPLORING GROS MORNE

While the town of Rocky Harbour is home to the main visitor center and a wide range of accommodations, as well as gateway to Western Brook Pond, plan on spending at least half a day exploring the southern section of the park, which is accessed from Route 431 west of Wiltondale. This narrow highway winds in and out of the park, passing a number of small fishing villages and ending at Trout River. The first official attraction along this route is the **Discovery Centre** (**✆ 709/458-2417**). Operated by Parks Canada, this modern interpretive facility is perched on the side of a hill above Woody Point and has huge windows that offer a spectacular view of Bonne Bay. You'll find interesting interpretive exhibits about Gros Morne's geology on the first floor and an art exhibit that changes regularly on the lower level. The Discovery Centre is open mid-May to June daily 9am to 5pm; in July and August daily 9am to 6pm (until 9pm Sunday and Wednesday); and from September to early October daily 9am to 5pm. Show your Parks Canada pass for entry.

The orange-yellow moonscape of the **Tablelands ★★** is an easily accessible geological wonder south of the Discovery Centre along Route 431. The Tablelands are an excellent example of plate tectonics (so much so that the park has been declared a UNESCO World Heritage Site) in which 470-million-year-old ultrabasic rock was brought to the Earth's surface as a result of faulting. In plain English, it means that this is what the world would look like if you turned it inside out (the Tablelands were once several km below an ancient ocean). Route 431 passes through the middle of the Tablelands, but to really appreciate the unique setting, plan on getting out of your vehicle and exploring on foot (see "Hiking," below). ***Note:*** All rocks, minerals, and fossils within national parks are protected and must be left as found. The collection of specimens for research or educational purposes requires a permit, which you must apply for well in advance.

Back on Route 430, **Lobster Cove Head Lighthouse** has marked the marine approach to Rocky Harbour since 1897. What's unique is the cast-iron structure of this lighthouse, one of the first of its kind to be built by Victoria Iron Works of St. John's. The setting of the lighthouse against a rocky backdrop has made it a photo favorite for visitors to the area. The Canadian Coast Guard now operates an automated light from the lighthouse. The former keeper's house is open to the public as an interpretive historical exhibit about the various peoples who have inhabited this coast over the past 4,000 years. It also explains the seasonal fishery's importance to the region. Guided tours leave on the half-hour from mid-May to mid-October daily between 10am and 5:30pm. As with the Discovery Centre, proof of park admission gets you into the interpretive exhibit and on the tour.

Regardless of how much time you have in Gros Morne, the one activity you simply must do is take a 2½-hour narrated cruise on **Western Brook Pond.** Western Brook Pond isn't what we traditionally think of as a pond. It's a 16km-long (10-mile), 165m-deep (541-ft.) inland fjord created during the Glacial Epoch. There's one point in the tour when the captain pauses 1m (3¼ ft.) from the base of a waterfall to declare that you are floating on water 91m deep (299 ft.). It's important you take note of instructions for reaching the tour boat dock, most notably the time you should allow from Rocky Harbour (where most tickets are sold). Access to the departure point is at the end of a 3km (1.9-mile) walking trail (allow at least 40 minutes, or an hour if you walk at a leisurely pace) beginning 27km (17 miles) north of Rocky Harbour. During June and September, there is only a 1pm sailing. In July and August, there are three daily sailings: 10am, and 1 and 4pm. The cost is C$48 adults, C$23 children 12 to 16, C$19 children 11 and under, and C$115 families. Tours are operated by **Bon Tours** (✆ **888/458-2016** or 709/458-2016; www.bontours.ca). There is a ticket office on the lobby level of the Ocean View Motel, Rocky Harbour. If you pay here, you can use major credit cards. If you pay at the boat dock, come prepared with cash. Departures are weather dependent. Bring rain gear.

After your boat tour, continue a short way north along Route 430 to **Broom Point.** Along the access road to the headland is a lookout, from where you can use the telescope to gaze back across the barren lands to the dramatic mountains rising on either side of Western Brook Pond.

Beyond the north end of the park, between Parsons Pond and Portland Creek, Route 430 passes an intriguing rock formation rising from a pebbly beach. The relentless power of the ocean has eroded softer rock and created an offshore rock stack that was once part of the mainland. Adding to the photogenic appeal is an arch through the stack. Protected within **Arches Provincial Park,** the natural attraction can be viewed from a roadside lookout, but it's hard to stop children wanting to get up close and personal by walking under the arch.

GROS MORNE OUTDOOR ACTIVITIES

Hiking

Whether it's an evening stroll along an interpretive trail or a trek to the summit of the park's namesake mountain, you should plan to hike at least one trail while visiting the park.

The trail to the 806m (2,644-ft.) summit of **Gros Morne Mountain,** second-highest peak in Newfoundland, is the premier day hike in all of Newfoundland and Labrador. But this 8km (5-mile) trail that starts just above sea level is very strenuous and only for fit and prepared hikers. The first 4km (2.5 miles) from the trail head along Route 430 7km (4¼ miles) east of Rocky Harbour are relatively easy. But then, through an area dotted with small ponds and covered in large boulders, the unrelenting climb begins. The summit is more of a plateau than a peak. Covered in tussock grasses and alpine plants, views are nothing short of stupendous, stretching across Bonne Bay to the ocean. You should allow at least 7 hours for the round-trip and be prepared with stout hiking boots, plenty of drinking water, snacks, and rain gear. It is also important you check the weather forecast and trail conditions at the visitor center before heading out. Along Route 431 in the south of the park are three interesting yet very different hiking trails. Starting from Discovery Centre, the 5km (3.1-mile) **Lookout Trail** is a moderately strenuous hike, but you will be rewarded with sweeping views of Bonne Bay and the Tablelands from a plateau atop Partridgeberry Hill. Allow 3 to 4 hours for the round-trip and bring drinking water.

Continuing toward the coast, the **Tablelands Trail** strikes off in a southeasterly direction from the signposted stopping area in the heart of the Tablelands. Many visitors don't step beyond the parking lot, but to really appreciate the unique setting, plan on walking at least a part of this easy trail, 2km (1.2 miles) each way. It takes about 40 minutes to reach the mouth of a canyon at the end of the trail.

Two hiking trails leading to **Green Gardens.** Both begin from Route 431 west of the Tablelands. The preferred option, beginning 4km (2.5 miles) west of the first trail head, is much shorter and therefore more popular. This 9km (5.6-mile) loop emerges at a lush green meadow high above the ocean, with offshore sea stacks adding to the photogenic appeal. Allow 3 hours.

One of the most popular overnight treks is the 35km (22-mile) **Long Range Traverse,** which usually takes 4 or 5 days. The trail head is reached by joining the boat tour on Western Brook Pond, which drops you off at the far end of the lake. From this point, it's a steep climb to the summit of the Long Range Plateau, where the unmarked trail heads south through total wilderness, before eventually joining the Gros Mountain Trail. The trail is open July to mid-October. Permits are required for all hikers attempting the Long Range Traverse. The cost is C$84 per person, plus a reservation fee of C$25per booking. For details, call © **709/458-2477.**

Cross-Country Skiing

There are some pretty amazing cross-country skiing opportunities in Gros Morne. If you're a beginner, the trails around Rocky Harbour and in the north of the park will be best suited to your abilities: The terrain is relatively gentle, with rolling hills and no steep inclines. Skiing on the Tablelands is comparable to skiing on glaciers with steep slopes better left for the advanced skier. The alpine terrain of the Long Range Mountains is also best suited to those with advanced skills.

Guided Packages

Whether you're looking to do some skiing, hiking, sea kayaking, backpacking, or snowshoeing, you should put yourself in the hands of an experienced outfitter—especially if this is your first visit to Gros Morne.

Gros Morne Adventures This company will customize a tour for you any time of the year. If your primary focus is on hiking, try the *Gros Morne Explorer,* a combination of coastal and mountain hiking that runs June through September. Over the course of 6 days, you'll hike a number of the park's most scenic trails. Plan to cover 10 to 16km (6.2 to 9.9 miles) per day and elevations of 700m (2,297 ft.) over uneven surfaces. The cost, including transfers from Deer Lake, lodging, and meals, is C$1,695.

Guided kayaking programs range from 2 hours to a full day. You can also rent single or double kayaks and go off on your own, if you're an experienced kayaker. Bonne Bay is a great place for sea kayaking because of the calm, sheltered waters. It's common to see whales, bald eagles, terns, mink, mergansers, and kingfishers throughout the summer. Winter programs include backcountry skiing and snowshoeing adventures. The scenery is awe-inspiring, the snow is plentiful, and moose and caribou are often spotted as you make your way along quiet trails.

For your overnight accommodations, Gros Morne Adventures chooses established properties to suit the individual client's preferences and pocketbook. All guides have at least 15 years' experience, and are CPR and wilderness trained and certified, in addition to having avalanche awareness and safety training. The company's website will provide you with a full range of prices and options.

9 Clarke's Lane, Norris Point. ✆ **800/685-4624** or 709/458-2722. www.grosmorneadventures.com.

5 NORTHERN PENINSULA

The Bonne Bay entrance to the northern peninsula is a dazzling panorama of surreal extremes: You'll scale near-perpendicular mountain heights through some of the tallest trees in the province, following a twining blacktop on what seems a perpetual climb, until a sudden final crest reverses your direction into a similarly stunning descent. All the while, your vehicle is regularly overtaken by tractor-trailers, logging trucks, and speeding grannies, who are obviously immune to the natural wonder.

It calms down considerably after that. As is typical elsewhere in the province, the highway follows traditional coastal settlement patterns. Virtually all settlement in the province is along the coast, a reflection of the importance of the fishery and ocean access to early settlers. From Cow Head north, the topography is mostly flat, with stands of tuckamore (trees whose growth has been stunted by wind and sea) to the right and the Atlantic Ocean to the left. Here and there, you'll encounter stretches of barrens and bog, much like the scenery along the Burin Peninsula.

PORT AU CHOIX

As the approximate halfway point between Deer Lake and St. Anthony, Port au Choix is a convenient stopover on the northern peninsula. With a population of 1,200, it's one of the larger communities en route and has a good number of services/facilities (for example, a bank, a post office, and restaurants). But the main reason to detour from the highway is to visit the site where archaeologists are uncovering evidence of ancient native cultures.

Essentials

Getting There

Port au Choix is 13km (8 miles) off of Route 430, and 230km (143 miles) north of Deer Lake. Both the main highway and the paved access road are in good condition, but you won't find a lot of services along the way—so be sure to tank up and have a few snacks with you before heading out. It's a 2½-hour drive from Port au Choix to St. Anthony.

Where to Stay & Dine

There is one motel in town, as well as a B&B, a small inn, and a couple of good restaurants—making it the best place to stay while in the area.

Anchor Café ★ SEAFOOD You won't have any problem recognizing the Anchor Café—the front of the building is shaped like the bow of a boat. It's a casual, fun (albeit kitschy) establishment decorated with lobster pots, fishing nets, and a sou'westered mannequin. With such an obvious fishing theme, it's no surprise this wheelchair-friendly restaurant specializes in local seafood. Of special note are any items that include coldwater

Moose Can Be Hazardous to Your Health

As you drive along the highway, you'll see moose silhouettes and bright-yellow signs depicting a crunched car and a moose. There's a good reason. However majestic these 450-kg (992-lb.) animals are to look at, they are a dangerous and mobile road hazard. Between 600 and 900 moose-versus-vehicle accidents occur every year in the province, causing more than C$1 million in vehicle damages, as well as serious injury and even death.

You'd think it would be easy to spot and avoid these massive animals, but they are masters of camouflage—especially in low light. Their mottled brown coats blends so well into the foliage that you may not see one standing in the brush to the side of the road until it walks into your path.

How to Avoid an Accident:

- Moose are nocturnal. Reduce your speed, or avoid driving altogether, in the early morning and at night.
- Be extra cautious when you see moose warning signs. They signal high-risk areas.
- Scan the highway as far ahead as possible, paying particular attention to areas where trees and shrubbery grow close to the road. Use high beams whenever possible.
- If you see a moose on the highway, pull over and turn off your lights. Like deer, moose are transfixed by light. They have also been known to charge at lights, rather than run away.

shrimp (those tasty little shrimp you see on shrimp rings), which are caught in local waters and processed in the waterfront factory across the road. The cod and shrimp chowder can be a meal in itself, or head straight for mains such as blackened halibut. The Anchor Café is on the main road through town and directly opposite the waterfront.

Main St., Port au Choix. ✆ **709/861-3665.** Reservations not necessary. Main courses C$6–C$18. MC, V. May–June and Sept–Oct daily 10am–10pm; July–Aug daily 9am–11pm.

Sea Echo Motel There's a wise manager in charge here: The hanging plastic seafood and lighthouse replica, while charming in the adjacent restaurant, are thankfully absent in the unremarkable decor of this motel's very spacious rooms. You'll be surprised at just how much space there is: besides the bed(s), there are nightstands, a bureau, a love seat, a table with two chairs, and still ample room to move around. It's not advertised as wheelchair accessible, but I don't think maneuvering around this single-story structure will be a problem for travelers with disabilities.

Fisher St., Port au Choix. ✆ **709/861-3777.** www.seaechomotel.ca. 33 units. C$92–C$115 double. AE, DC, MC, V. Free parking. **Amenities:** Restaurant; lounge; gift shop. *In room:* TV, hair dryer, Wi-Fi.

Exploring Port au Choix

Even if you're not a history buff, it's worth taking time to visit the Parks Canada Visitor Centre and explore the surrounding National Historic Site. Also plan on driving beyond the visitor center to **Point Richie Lighthouse** for sweeping ocean views.

Port au Choix National Historic Site ★★ Archaeological findings confirm that over the last 4,500 years, five cultures inhabited the barren peninsula extending into the Gulf of St. Lawrence, beyond the modern-day town of Port au Choix. Although these earliest residents didn't leave a written record, from 30 years of archaeological digs, we have a good idea of the way these ancient people lived and adapted to the harsh environment. The best place to learn about the site is the **Parks Canada Visitor Centre,** which is signposted through town, on the peninsula itself. Here, you can see a wonderful assortment of displays about the Maritime Archaic Indians, Groswater Paleoeskimos, Dorset Paleoeskimos, and more recent native cultures. Artifacts of note include stone axes, hunting tools, and bone carvings. Don't miss the life-size replica of a Dorset-Paleoeskimo dwelling from about 1,500 years ago. Whale bones were used to frame the structure, and animal skins insulated it from the region's harsh weather. The well-curated displays, such as the assortment of ancient stone and bone tools from the region's four prehistoric cultures, make for an enjoyably edifying experience.

Once you've seen the indoor displays, plan on exploring the rest of the historic site on foot. The two main walks are detailed below, or check at the visitor center for scheduled guided hikes, which generally depart daily through summer at 1:30pm.

Port au Choix National Historic Site. ✆ **709/861-3522.** www.pc.gc.ca/portauchoix. C$8 adults, C$7 seniors, C$4 children 6 to 16, free for children 5 and under; C$20 families. June–Sept daily 9am–6pm.

Museum of Whales & Things ★ It's not every day you see a 14m-long (46-ft.) skeleton of a sperm whale, but that's exactly what you'll find hanging from the roof of the appropriately named Museum of Whales & Things, at the entrance to Port au Choix. It's not a large building or a particularly well-organized exhibit, but every nook and cranny holds something with a story to tell.

The museum is the work of local entrepreneur Ben Ploughman, who is also a talented artist. If you're looking for a unique gift to bring home, visit the adjacent **Ben's Studio**

Walking Trails

Once you've had enough of the indoor displays at the Parks Canada Visitor Centre, head out on one of the two hiking trails through the peninsula.

Dorset Trail Beginning from the visitor center, this 8km (5-mile) trail cuts across the limestone barrens to the opposite of the peninsula and Phillip's Garden. Along the way, it passes Dorset burial caves and a lookout.

Phillip's Garden Coastal Trail **★★** Phillips Garden is an oceanfront meadow, where you can faintly discern the circular foundations of some 50 semi-subterranean houses. Every summer, teams of archaeologists can be seen working at the site—and they will be more than happy to answer your questions. On a clear day, you can see Quebec across the Gulf of St. Lawrence, some 96km (60 miles) away. This trail begins from Old Port au Choix (follow Main St. through town). It's around 1km (.6 mile) from the end of the road to Phillips Garden (watch for small rock cairns marking the trail across intriguing limestone outcrops). From this point, you can continue to the visitor center via the Dorset Trail or follow the shoreline for another 3km (1.9 miles) to Point Riche Lighthouse.

to see his "lath art," a type of 3D woodworking. His unique style depicts local life in colorful wooden squares patched together in a quilt-like fashion. The lath art is relatively expensive, at C$500 for a small piece and up to C$3,500 for a large piece.

24 Fisher St., Port au Choix. ✆ **709/861-3280.** www.bensstudio.ca. Admission by donation. June–Sept Mon–Sat 9am–5pm.

PORT AU CHOIX TO ST. BARBE

From Port au Choix, it's 104km (65 miles) north along Route 430 to the next town of note, St. Barbe. Along the way, the ocean is rarely out of view. You'll pass a smattering of seasonal fishing camps, but just one official attraction—an archaeological dig site at Bird Cove.

Bird Cove ★ At Plum Point, 18km (11 miles) before St. Barbe, a side road leads to the village of Bird Cove and a cluster of archaeological dig sites. Make your first stop **Big Droke Interpretation Centre,** where displays explain the history of the sites and the Beothuk, Dorset-Paleoeskimo, and Maritime Archaic Indians who lived here up to 4,500 years ago. Other displays include local rocks, fossils, and whale bones.

It wasn't until the 1990s that archaeologists even knew of these local sites, which puts the area's remoteness in perspective. What was uncovered were several completely undisturbed village sites, including two that are now encircled by a boardwalk. Ask at the interpretive center for directions. From the center, you will see a footbridge that leads across to the Dog Peninsula. More village sites were excavated here, but none are marked. Instead, a network of trails leads through the coastal forest to a pebbly beach and the broken-down buildings of a farm established in the 1880s.

84 Michael's Dr., Bird Cove. ✆ **866/247-2011** or 709/247-2011. www.bigdroke.ca. Admission to Interpretation Centre is C$3 adults, C$2.50 seniors, C$2 students 6–17. Additional C$4 per person for guided tour of the archaeological dig sites. Mid-May to late Sept daily 9am–9pm.

Creating New Money from Old Traditions

Economuseums use traditional manufacturing techniques or know-how in the production of goods and services. They provide income for skilled craftspeople while also instilling cultural pride and preserving a way of life that might otherwise be forgotten. Products available might include knitted goods, quilts, and handcrafted wooden furniture. In addition to being retail outlets, economuseums are frequently staffed by the artisans themselves—offering interested visitors the opportunity to learn about the history and process used to manufacture the products on display.

An economuseum of note on the long drive up the northern peninsula is **Borealis Crafts,** in Shoel Cove East, 78km (49 miles) north of Port au Choix (✆ **709/456-2123**), which presents a wonderful opportunity to purchase handicrafts made by local artisans. Specialties include whalebone carvings, which, aside from the aesthetic value, are affordable, small, and very lightweight, making them a fabulous gift idea that won't weigh you down. The gallery and workshop is open year-round Monday to Friday 9am to 5pm.

ST. BARBE

The most noteworthy aspect of St. Barbe is that it's the departure point for the ferry to Blanc Sablon on the Quebec–Labrador border. You probably won't stay here overnight unless you're catching an early-morning ferry, but if you are, you'll find a motel and dining room just up the road from the ferry terminal.

If you have time to kill while waiting for the ferry, take the short drive out to Black Duck Cove. Here, interpretive panels describe the region's history.

Essentials

Getting There

St. Barbe is on Route 430, 104km (65 miles) north of Port au Choix and a little less than 300km (186 miles) north of Deer Lake. St. Barbe is the departure point for ferries to Labrador. The MV *Apollo* sails once or twice daily from May to early January. The cost for the 2-hour trip is C$23 for vehicle and driver, additional adult C$7.50, and children C$6. Even with reservations, you need to check in upon arrival at St. Barbe at the office in the Dockside Motel, which opens 2 hours before official departure time. For ferry information, call ✆ **866/535-2567** or 709/535-0810, or visit **www.tw.gov.nl.ca/ferryservices**.

All vehicle sizes are permitted on the ferry, but if you don't want to take your RV, you can leave it at St Barbe in a secured parking lot across the road from the ferry office. The parking lot has electrical hookups, laundry facilities, and a common room; so, many RVers find themselves spending the night. Call ✆ **709/877-2272** for details.

Where to Stay & Dine

Dockside Motel & Cabins ★ The only accommodations in town is the Dockside Motel, on the road down to the ferry terminal. Though white-glove clean, the motel's sparsely decorated guest rooms are obviously intended for overnight stays, without long-term vacation ambience. Cabins offer a little more privacy and have basic kitchens. You may hear truck engines running outside your window around dawn, when large vehicles start to line up for the ferry. The motel's Docker's Diner is tastefully decorated with linen tablecloths—something you don't see much of in these parts. Dinner entrees offer generous portions and are reasonably priced at C$8.50 to C$17. The restaurant is open daily in summer from 6am to 9pm, and daily 8am to 8pm the rest of the year.

Main St., St. Barbe. ✆ **709/877-2444.** www.docksidemotel.nf.ca. 15 motel units; 10 cabins. C$75–C$95 double, C$95 cabin. AE, DC, MC, V. Free parking. **Amenities:** Restaurant; lounge. *In room:* TV.

ST. ANTHONY

Known as Newfoundland's northern capital, St. Anthony is at the mouth of horseshoe-shaped Hare Bay, near the tip of the northern peninsula. Isolated from the rest of the province by sheer distance, the community is worth visiting for its links to Sir Wilfred Thomason Grenfell, but it is also a base for those wishing to explore nearby L'Anse aux Meadows. You'll also find a hospital, a small shopping mall, a pharmacy, a bank, a few nice places to stay and eat, and vehicle servicing and rentals, as well as a nearby airport. A winter visit to St. Anthony allows for lots of outdoor fun—snowmobiling, cross-country skiing, and ice-fishing are popular activities.

Essentials

Getting There

St. Anthony is 443km (275 miles) north of Deer Lake along Route 430. If you're driving all the way from the east coast, plan on 15 hours driving time to cover the 1,090km (677

Roadside Peculiarities

While driving along the northern peninsula, you'll likely notice the garden plots alongside the highway. These are owned by private citizens who arbitrarily stake their claim and plant potatoes, beets, and other hardy crops for their own use. Occasionally a gardener will identify a plot with a flag or scarecrow, but on the whole, they're not afraid of anyone pilfering their harvest.

You may also wonder why you see wood piles (most often in the shape of a tepee) standing alongside the road. This is how the local residents dry their firewood. The trees are cut and cleaned of branches, and then propped together to let the sun and wind dry them out for winter burning in the woodstove.

miles) from St. John's. Time-wise, the town is a 2½-hour drive northeast of Port au Choix, 4 hours from Rocky Harbour (midway through Gros Morne National Park), and 5 hours from Deer Lake.

For those who wish to investigate the multi-lineal heritage and rugged landscape of the Northern Peninsula but want to avoid the long drive from St. John's, it's an hour's flight with Provincial Airlines from St. John's to St. Anthony. ***Note:*** St. Anthony Airport is not really *in* St. Anthony. It's 55km (34 miles) back down Route 430.

Visitor Information

For a complete list of services in St. Anthony, visit the **Town of St. Anthony tourism website** at **www.town.stanthony.nf.ca** or call ✆ **709/454-3454.** There is no official visitor center in St. Anthony, but information can be picked up at **Grenfell Historic Properties,** on West Street (✆ **709/454-4010**). The center is open mid-May to mid-June from 9am until 5pm, mid-June to September 9am to 8pm.

Getting Around

The only car rental company at St. Anthony Airport is **National** (✆ **800/227-7368** or 709/454-8522; www.nationalcar.com).

Note: Be aware that gasoline prices are higher on the northern peninsula than you'll find elsewhere in the province. Expect to pay about C10¢ per liter more for gas here than in St. John's.

Where to Stay

Personally, I prefer the lodging options in nearby L'Anse aux Meadows, but if you want the facilities of a regular motel, the following choices will suffice for a night or two—and I've included a good-value bed-and-breakfast as a bonus.

Haven Inn ★ Although soundproofing is almost nonexistent, the Haven Inn has good-quality standard rooms, as well as suites with a king-size bed, Jacuzzi, and fireplace.

The Haven Inn is home to the reliable **Cartier's Gallery Restaurant,** named in recognition of French explorer Jacques Cartier, who visited the peninsula in 1534 and named it "St. Anthony's Haven." Basic cooked breakfasts start at a reasonable C$6, while the rest of the day it's soup, salad, and seafood (and burgers). It's open daily in summer from 7am to 2 pm and 5 to 9 pm; the rest of the year, evening hours are only till 8pm.

14 Goose Cove Rd., St. Anthony. ✆ **877/428-3646** or 709/454-9100. www.haveninn.ca. 30 units. C$96–C$133 double. AE, MC, V. Free parking. **Amenities:** Restaurant; lounge. *In room:* TV.

Crows Nest Inn Bed & Breakfast Value The Crows Nest boasts exceptional prices for a professional B&B (it's not just a room in a private home). Even though all rooms are nonsmoking, some with en-suite and others with shared bathrooms, you won't be attracted to the Crows Nest for its amenities. Aside from the price, you'll enjoy the panoramic harbor view and waterfront proximity, as well as the large, comfortable sitting room—custom-made for mingling with other guests. A light continental breakfast (home-baked bread with partridgeberry and bakeapple jam) is included in the room rate, but if you'd like something more substantial, a full breakfast is available at a small additional charge.

1 Spruce Lane, St. Anthony. ✆ **877/454-3402** or 709/454-4401. 8 units. C$60–C$85 double; C$10 additional person. Rates include continental breakfast. MC, V. Free parking. Closed Dec to early May. *In room:* TV, no phone.

Triple Falls RV Park Located 8km (5 miles) from St. Anthony, this fully serviced tent and RV campground offers a freshwater beach, a playground, a games arcade, minigolf, great salmon fishing, and lots of hot water in the showers. Campsites are nicely wooded and located along a scenic river. Facilities are wheelchair accessible.

Rte. 430, north of St. Anthony. ✆ **709/454-2599.** 105 sites. C$18–C$24 per site. V. Closed mid-Sept to mid-May. **Amenities:** Convenience store; fully serviced sites; RV dumping station; shower and laundry facilities.

Vinland Motel Conveniently located in the heart of town, near shopping and other services, the Vinland Motel has the most extensive list of on-site amenities in St. Anthony but is an older property. The unremarkable double rooms have the bathtub and toilet separated from the sink and counter, which is convenient if you're traveling with a partner. There are some suites available, as well as two fully equipped cabins. The motel is accessible to travelers with disabilities, and there is an on-site restaurant, as well. The restaurant is open daily in summer from 7am to 10pm; the rest of the year, it's open 8am to 2pm and 5 to 9pm.

West St., St. Anthony. ✆ **800/563-7578** or 709/454-8843. 43 units. C$88–C$135 double. AE, DC, MC, V. **Amenities:** Restaurant; lounge; exercise room; sauna. *In room:* A/C, TV.

Where to Dine

Both the motels detailed above have dining rooms, or you can choose one of the following restaurants.

Great Viking Feast at Leifsburdir NEWFOUNDLAND If you'd like to become an honorary Viking, make a reservation at this Viking-themed dinner theater near the end of Fishing Point Road. The feast is served by costumed animators in a reconstructed sod hut overlooking the ocean. You'll sit on wooden benches at eight-person tables while "slaves" bring you an assortment of acquired-taste food (the menu includes roast capelin, cod tongues, moose stew, and squid fried rice). After dinner, you can participate in a mock trial at the "Althing" (Viking court). I guarantee your stomach will hurt the next day from the innumerable belly laughs caused by the raucous Viking high jinks.

Fishing Point Rd., St. Anthony. ✆ **877/454-4900** or 709/454-4900. www.fishingpoint.ca. Reservations required. C$42 per person. MC, V. July–Aug daily at 7pm for bar service, with dinner and ceremony commencing at 7:30pm.

Lightkeeper's Restaurant ★ SEAFOOD A combination of the best views and tastiest food in town make dining at this friendly cafe an easy choice. Once home to the local lighthouse keeper and his family, the building has been thoroughly renovated, with big windows added to make sure you don't miss the spectacle of an iceberg floating by. The traditional red-and-white lighthouse color scheme has been taken to extremes—even down to the salt and pepper shakers. Crab claws with melted garlic butter are a good choice to start, and then you'll want to get serious with mains such as the creamiest seafood linguini imaginable. Daily dessert specials and a well-priced wine list add to the appeal.

Fishing Point Rd., St. Anthony. ✆ **877/454-4900** or 709/454-4900. www.fishingpoint.ca. Reservations recommended for dinner. Main courses C$16–C$28. MC, V. Summer daily 11:30am–9pm; call ahead for winter hours.

Exploring St. Anthony

The historical highlight of a trip to St. Anthony is learning about **Sir Wilfred Thomason Grenfell,** a British physician who arrived here in 1892. Appalled by the desperate poverty and even more harrowing health problems (tuberculosis was rampant), Grenfell traveled the coast, healing the sick and feeding the needy.

The several Grenfell-related sites in St. Anthony come under the umbrella of Grenfell Historic Properties, of which the centerpiece is **Grenfell Interpretation Centre.** Another part of the Grenfell legacy is at the Charles S. Curtis Memorial Hospital, where you can view the thought-provoking **Jordi Bonet Murals** in its rotunda. Bonet is a Montreal artist who was commissioned in 1967 to create this tribute to Grenfell and life in northern Newfoundland and Labrador. There is no charge to see the stone murals and no specific hours of operation. Just stop in at the reception desk and pick up the brochure for your self-guided tour. The hospital is across the road from the **interpretation center** at 178–200 West St. (✆ **709/454-4010**).

Grenfell Historic Properties ★★ On the harbor front, the modern **Grenfell Interpretation Centre** displays informative panels that aptly explain Grenfell's life and his tremendous impact on Newfoundland and Labrador residents. It also houses a fascinating selection of his medical tools and equipment. Although there are interpreters on hand to answer questions, the center is to be explored by self-guided tour.

Beyond the reception desk is **Grenfell Handicrafts,** a large space filled with locally made clothing. It was Sir Wilfred Grenfell who originally established the business, encouraging outport residents to sell their homemade clothing, such as parkas and gloves, to outsiders. Traditions remain, and although the print work is done here, the actual clothing is put together by women who make their home in remote villages throughout the region. Also in the complex, on the lower level, a small cafe serves inexpensive snacks and afternoon tea.

Exiting the interpretation center through the cafe, you'll step into **Grenfell Park,** home to a playground and a statue of the man himself. Also here is the tiny **Dockhouse Museum.** Originally housing the winches that hauled Grenfell's hospital ships from the water for repairs, it's now home to a display of maritime tools and artifacts. This museum is open only July and August daily 10am to 4pm.

The final part of Grenfell Historic Properties is **Grenfell House Museum,** a 5-minute uphill walk from the waterfront. Built in 1910 as the Grenfell home, it has also been used as a mission. Exhibits here concentrate on the doctor's private life, with the vast majority of artifacts on display having been donated by the Grenfell family.

West St., St. Anthony. ✆ **709/454-4010.** www.grenfell-properties.com. C$7.50 adults, C$6.50 seniors, C$4 children; C$15 families. Mid-May to mid-June daily 9am–5pm; mid-June to Sept daily 9am–6pm.

Hero of the Northwest Labrador Coast

Sir Wilfred T. Grenfell: "The purpose of this world is not to have and hold, but to serve." By the time Grenfell retired in 1935, at 70 years of age, the following were in operation throughout Newfoundland and Labrador as a result of his efforts: five hospitals, seven nursing stations, two orphanages, 14 industrial centers, four summer schools, three agricultural stations, 12 clothing-distribution centers, four hospital ships, one supply schooner, 12 community centers, several cooperative stores, a cooperative lumber mill, and a haul-up slip for ship repairs.

Outdoor Pursuits

If you're looking for a scenic spot to just hang out and look for icebergs or whales, follow the main road through town to oceanfront **Fishing Point Park**, where you get the best view of St. Anthony Harbour. The peak iceberg viewing time is late May to early July, while whales are usually spotted in July and August, and as early as late June.

Northland Discovery Boat Tours ★★ This award-winning, family-run company is on a mission to provide an experience that will be the highlight of your vacation—and do they deliver! Owner Paul Alcock (a biologist and noted conservationist) will have you crossing paths with spouting humpbacks and racing dolphins as he navigates the natural wonders of Iceberg Alley. He'll explain why some icebergs are blue, and how you can tell when an iceberg is ready to roll. (***Hint:*** Watch the birds.) He'll even scoop a few bergy bits from the sea, giving you a taste of the purest water on Earth. Tours lasting 2½ hours operate rain or shine, from mid-May to late September, three times daily (9am, and 1 and 4pm).

Behind Grenfell Historic Properties, West St., St. Anthony. ✆ **877/632-3747** or 709/454-3092. www.discovernorthland.com. C$50 adults, C$25 children 13–17, C$8 children 12 and under.

L'ANSE AUX MEADOWS

At a barren outpost on a flat headland jutting bravely into the North Atlantic, you'll find several innocuous grassy mounds that are both a UNESCO World Heritage Site and a National Historic Site. These "mounds" are the footprints of the first European settlement in North America. Although the Viking Norsemen who first arrived on these shores more than 1,000 years ago didn't make a permanent home of what they called *Vinland,* they left evidence of their passage in the foundations of the original sod structures that once housed them.

The community of L'Anse aux Meadows and surrounding villages offer a limited number of services, including welcoming bed-and-breakfasts and one of Newfoundland's best restaurants.

Essentials

Getting There

L'Anse aux Meadows is 40km (25 miles) north of St. Anthony (turn off Rte. 430 onto Rte. 436).

Visitor Information

Visitor information is available at **L'Anse aux Meadows National Historic Site** (✆ **709/623-2608;** www.pc.gc.ca/eng/lhn-nhs/nl/meadows/index.aspx). The center is open June to early October daily 9am to 6pm.

Norseman Restaurant ★★★ SEAFOOD Without a doubt, the Norseman is one of the province's best restaurants in all regards—creative cooking, professional service, and faultless presentation. The setting alone is superb—a tastefully decorated room and adjacent deck, with water views from most tables. Seafood is the house specialty. For starters, the fish chowder is a delight, and the smoked char has a unique flavor. If you order lobster, your server will invite you across the road to visit the wharf and pick out your own lobster (in season). Other mains are as creative as cod baked in a Dijon mustard and garlic crust and as local as grilled caribou tenderloin brushed with red-wine glaze. At least one daily dessert is a pie crammed with local berries. The drinks menu is as notable as the food, with everything from bakeapple wine to martinis. Adding to the appeal on Tuesday and Friday evenings are local musicians performing traditional music.

Rte. 436, L'Anse aux Meadows. ✆ **877/623-2018** or 709/754-3105. www.valhalla-lodge.com/restaurant. Reservations recommended. Main courses C$16–C$38. MC, V. Late May to late Sept daily noon–9pm.

Valhalla Lodge (Finds) Look for these Viking-themed accommodations in a friendly B&B with understated appeal 8km (5 miles) before the L'Anse aux Meadows National Historic Site. The property is situated on a hill sloping down to the ocean. From the wide deck, you can watch icebergs, whales (up to a dozen have been seen here simultaneously), and seabirds. Guest rooms are warmly furnished in Scandinavian pine with cozy quilts on the beds and exquisite reproductions from local artists on the walls. Accommodations are fairly tight: Standing between the wall and the bed, chances are good that you'll bang into one or the other. But it's the memory of your gracious hostess Bella Hodge and her famously fluffy partridgeberry pancakes that will stay with you long after you've forgotten the minor discomfort of semi-cramped quarters.

Rte. 436 to Gunner's Cove, L'Anse aux Meadows. ✆ **877/623-2018** or 709/754-3105, or 709/689-4825 off-season. www.valhalla-lodge.com. 5 units. C$90–C$100 double, C$15 additional for cot. DC, MC, V. Free parking. Closed Nov–May. **Amenities:** Sauna. *In room:* No phone.

Viking Village Bed & Breakfast ★ (Value) A modern home within walking distance of L'Anse aux Meadows National Historic Site, this is as close as you can get to Viking habitation without actually sleeping in a sod hut. Its proximity to the Norsemen Restaurant is an added bonus. The Viking theme–named guest rooms all have patio doors and balconies, which is a lovely feature if you're visiting during summer.

A full breakfast and evening snack are included with the room rates, and the owners will cook you a Newfoundland-style dinner for an extra fee of C$20 per person. The owners will pick you up at St. Anthony airport or at the bus stop. The owners do not allow smoking. The same owners also run the more basic **Viking Nest B&B** with slightly lower rates, which can be reached via the same contact numbers.

Rte. 436 to Hay Cove. ✆ **877/858-2238** or 709/623-2238. www.vikingvillage.ca. 5 units. C$72–C$78 double. Rates include full breakfast and evening snack. AE, MC, V. Free parking. **Amenities:** Library; limited room service.

Exploring L'Anse aux Meadows

L'Anse aux Meadows National Historic Site and Norstead are complementary must-see attractions: One is a formal archaeological introduction to a 1,000-year-old Viking habitation, and the other brings the ancient Norse experience to life. ***Note:*** All Vikings were Norsemen, but only a small percentage of Norsemen were Vikings.

Escape to Quirpon Island

For splendid, majestic isolation, **Quirpon Lighthouse Inn** ★★ stands alone. The gateway to the island is the tiny fishing outpost of Quirpon (pronounced kar-*poon*), 8km (5 miles) from L'Anse aux Meadows. Now, look across the harbor. Here is Quirpon Island, a half-hour boat ride farther north than any other point on the island portion of the province. Both the dock and the helideck are a striking testament to the solitude of this sanctuary. Once ashore, you'll stay at one of two sturdy dwellings located near the base of an automated lighthouse: the 1922 lighthouse keeper's residence or the more modern adjacent house. Regardless of which building you stay in, you're guaranteed not to be bothered by cable television, clock radios, or in-room telephones. Instead, you'll spend hours contemplating the streaks and fissures of passing icebergs. Entertainment is provided by breaching and blowing humpback and minke—you may even be soaked by a spouting whale. All this, plus hearty home-cooked meals prepared by your hospitable hosts. Truly a rare gem of serenity in a world of sensory overload. Rates of C$250 for a single and C$325 to C$375 for a double include transportation, accommodations for 1 night, and all meals. For more information or to make reservations, call ✆ **877/254-6586** or 709/634-2285, or visit **www.linkumtours.com/site**.

L'Anse aux Meadows National Historic Site ★★★ Embark on your Viking journey at the visitor center, just off Route 436 and within site of the first European settlement in North America. The details of your adventure will be revealed in a 30-minute video (offered in the theater) that details the discovery of the site by Dr. Helge Ingstad and his wife, Dr. Anne Stine. As Norwegians, Ingstad and Stine had a strong interest in determining the exact location of *Vinland,* the legendary location referenced in the Norse sagas.

After watching the video, examine the many artifacts that confirm the Vikings' presence here as far back as A.D. 1000. You'll even see a model of how the settlement would have looked when it was inhabited. From there, it's on to the real thing. A short walk along a gravel path takes you to the excavated foundations of the Viking settlement, where the use of each structure is detailed. Beyond this point are reconstructions of the sod and timber buildings that the Vikings called home all those years ago. Costumed interpreters will educate and entertain you with demonstrations of their various crafts. "Gunnar" shares the secret of navigation and ship construction, "Harald" illustrates the power of forge and anvil, while "Thora" proves that Viking women are a force to be reckoned with (she plans to divorce her impractical dreamer of a husband—Bjorn, the "brains" behind the expedition—when they return to civilization).

Rte. 436, L'Anse aux Meadows. ✆ **709/623-2608.** www.pc.gc.ca/eng/lhn-nhs/nl/meadows/index.aspx. C$12 adults, C$10 seniors over 64, C$6 children 6–16, free for children 5 and under; C$28 families. Mid-June to early Oct daily 9am–6pm.

Norstead ★★ (Kids) If you want to walk like the Norse, talk like the Norse, eat like the Norse—in fact, become a Norseman or -woman—then you *must* come to Norstead.

Located 2km (1¼ miles) from the L'Anse aux Meadows National Historic Site, Norstead is a re-created Norse trading post. Enthusiastic and knowledgeable reenactors walk you through every aspect of early Norse life, including religion, weaponry, blacksmithing, activities in the "Trading House," the *scalley* (kitchen/cooking area), handicrafts such as pottery and the carding of wool, and the sleeping quarters. You'll also get a chance to climb aboard a replica of a Viking *knarr,* the type of boat Leif Eriksson used to sail across the North Atlantic back in A.D. 1000. Visitors are encouraged to participate hands-on in activities carried on in the settlement, including baking (and tasting) flatbread, carding wool, and watching the blacksmith forging tools from bog iron.

Rte. 436, L'Anse aux Meadows. ✆ **877/620-2828** or 709/623-2828. www.norstead.com. C$10 adults, C$8 seniors, C$6 children 6–15. Early June to late Sept daily 10am–6pm.

Beyond L'anse aux Meadows

Burnt Cape Ecological Reserve ★★ Finds Around 35km (22 miles) from L'Anse aux Meadows is Burnt Cape, so named for its barren expanse of limestone outcrops. While the site is renowned for rare flora, including the Burnt Cape cinquefoil, it is the starkly beautiful scenery that draws most visitors. You can drive onto the cape via a rough gravel road, but I recommend joining a guided tour. Not only will you save your vehicle from the rough road, the interpreter will be able to show you things that the casual visitor is prone to miss, such as sea caves and geological formations of stone rings created by heavy frosts. Guided tours depart June to September daily at 9:30am and 2pm.

Rte. 437, Raleigh. ✆ **709/454-7795.** Free admission. Guided tour C$5 adults, C$2.50 children; C$10 families. Tour check-in is at Pistolet Bay Provincial Park, along Rte. 437 just before Raleigh.

Shopping

Dark Tickle Company A delicious solution to the problem of wild-berry lovers everywhere: you can pick 'em, but you can't take 'em with you (they'd perish on the way home). The Dark Tickle Company uses only wild berries (bakeapple, partridgeberry, blueberry, crowberry, and squashberry) in their lip-smacking jams, preserves, and syrups. They even have something called Drinkable Berries: natural nectar in bakeapple and partridgeberry varieties. The result is just-picked freshness in a portable package. The Dark Tickle Company also sells products worldwide via its website.

Rte. 436, Griquet (between St. Anthony and L'Anse aux Meadows). ✆ **709/623-2354.** www.darktickle.com. Mid-May to Sept Mon–Fri 9am–6pm; Oct to mid-May Mon–Fri 9am–5pm.

Labrador

Labrador is Canada's last undiscovered frontier and North America's most pristine wilderness. In a word association game, it would likely be coupled with "cold," "vast," and "remote." The slightly more enlightened might add "fjords," "bakeapples," and "permafrost." All of which are true, but just barely hint at the complexity that is Labrador.

Its nickname is **The Big Land**—a moniker it well deserves. Physically, it dwarfs the island of Newfoundland by a ratio of two to one. It covers a distance of more than 1,080km (671 miles) from north to south and 839km (521 miles) from east to west, for a total landmass of 294,330 sq. km (113,641 sq. miles). Looking at it another way, it's almost identical in size to the U.S. state of Arizona but has a population of just 27,000 people (compared to Arizona's 6.1 million).

Within that epic terrain are natural and man-made wonders of immense proportion: the **highest mountain range** east of the Rockies, one of the **world's longest airport runways,** 7,800km (4,847 miles) of coastline, world-class nickel and iron-ore deposits, the **largest caribou herd** in the world, and the world's largest underground hydroelectric project at **Churchill Falls.**

It is simultaneously simple and mysterious, a place of ancient civilizations but few people, a land of glacial conditions and temperate breezes. Here, engineers have achieved numerous record-setting feats, but paved highways are few and far between.

Most visitors come to Labrador because they long for a back-to-nature experience untainted by excessive commercialism. No one comes here expecting a glitzy nightlife or Caribbean-style sun and sloth (if they do, they need to switch travel agents).

The twin towns of **Labrador City** and **Wabush** are in western Labrador, not far from the Quebec–Labrador border. They grew in response to mining operations by the Iron Ore Company of Canada. Between them, they have a combined population of 9,000 people. **Happy Valley–Goose Bay,** linked to Labrador City and Wabush by road and a major transportation hub, is home to 8,500 people.

The remaining 9,500 inhabitants live, for the most part, in scattered coastal communities. The largest of these are **L'Anse au Loup** (across the Strait of Belle Isle from the Northern Peninsula); **Port Hope Simpson** (200km/124 miles of gravel road north of L'Anse au Loup); **Cartwright** (close to Eagle River and world-class salmon fly-fishing); **North West River** (35km/22 miles from Goose Bay via a rare portion of paved highway); **Hopedale** (site of Moravian Mission Museum, accessible only by ferry and air transportation); and **Nain** (the largest Inuit community in Labrador, again accessible only by ferry and air transportation).

1 LABRADOR STRAITS ★★

In the southeastern corner of Labrador, an 80km (50-mile) paved highway extends northeast along the Strait of Belle Isle from Blanc Sablon, where ferries from St. Barbe, Newfoundland, dock. At Red Bay, the road turns to gravel and extends 238km (148

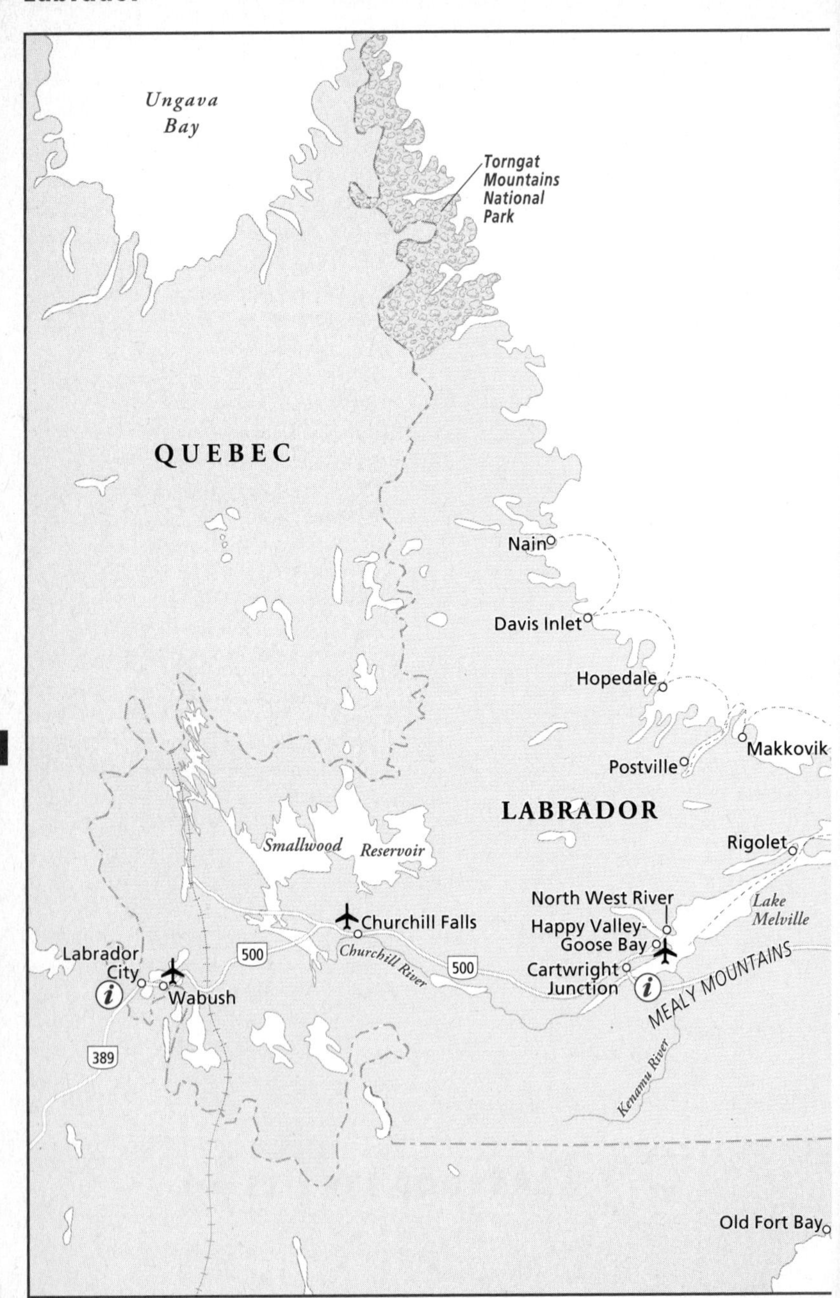
Ungava Bay
Torngat Mountains National Park
QUEBEC
Nain
Davis Inlet
Hopedale
Makkovik
Postville
LABRADOR
Rigolet
Smallwood Reservoir
North West River
Lake Melville
Churchill Falls
Happy Valley-Goose Bay
Churchill River
500
500
Cartwright Junction
MEALY MOUNTAINS
Labrador City
Wabush
389
Kenamu River
Old Fort Bay

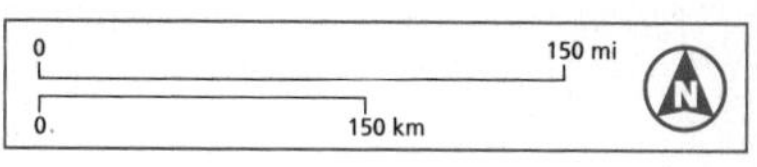

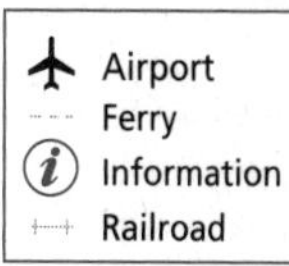

ATLANTIC
OCEAN

Hamilton Inlet
Cartwright
510
Charlottetown
514
Pinsent Arm
Mary's Harbour
Battle Harbour
Red Bay
510
Blanc Sablon
L'Anse-au-Clair
Strait of Belle Isle
St. Barbe

miles) north to Cartwright Junction. From this point, it's 87km (54 miles) northeast to the coastal community of Cartwright and 250km (155 miles) west to Happy Valley–Goose Bay along a remote stretch of the Trans-Labrador Highway. The route north to Cartwright is known as the Labrador Coastal Drive. Most attractions are concentrated along the paved road, where approximately 2,200 people inhabit nine small coastal communities. Each of the communities is so close to the next one, you really won't know when you're leaving one and entering another until you see a sign with a different town's name! This is the section of Labrador you'll be most likely to visit if you're planning a Newfoundland *and* Labrador vacation.

Be prepared for cold, damp weather along the Labrador Straits—whichever season you're traveling. Even in summer, the average temperature is a low 10°C (50°F) because of the cooling effect of the iceberg-carrying Labrador Current. It flows in a southerly direction past the east coast of Labrador and Newfoundland, except that Labrador, unlike southeastern Newfoundland, doesn't receive the warming benefits of the Gulf Stream. In sheltered areas that deflect the Labrador Current's onshore breeze, summer temperatures often rise to 25° to 29°C (77°–84°F).

ESSENTIALS

Getting There

You can take your car on a Labrador Marine ferry (✆ **866/535-2567** or 709/535-0810; www.labradormarine.com) from St. Barbe on Newfoundland's northern peninsula to Blanc Sablon, Quebec, at the south end of the Labrador Straits. There are one or two daily sailings between May and early January. The one-way fare for a vehicle and its driver is C$23. Additional adults ride for C$7.50 and the fare for children is C$6. Reservations are recommended for the 90-minute crossing. Even with reservations, you need to check in before joining the line of vehicles.

Alternatively, you can fly **Provincial Airlines** (✆ **800/563-2800;** www.provincialairlines.com) into Blanc Sablon, just a few kilometers southwest of L'Anse au Clair, from St. John's via St. Anthony. **Air Labrador** (✆ **800/563-3042;** www.airlabrador.com) connects Blanc Sablon with both St. Anthony and Happy Valley–Goose Bay. (If you fly into Blanc Sablon, take a few minutes to look at the arrowhead display, housed in a wall-mounted case. It's interesting to see the different shapes and sizes of arrowheads that have been found in the area).

Visitor Information

Information about the Labrador Straits can be obtained in L'Anse au Clair at the **Gateway to Labrador Visitor Centre** (✆ **709/931-2013**), located in a restored building formerly occupied by St. Andrew's Anglican Church. It's right on Route 510 and open

Fun Facts **What Time Is It?**

Labrador is home to two time zones. The Labrador Straits operate in the Newfoundland time zone, a half-hour ahead of the rest of Labrador in the Atlantic time zone. Quebec is in the eastern time zone, an hour behind the Atlantic time zone. So, if it's 4:30 in Red Bay, it's 4 in Happy Valley–Goose Bay and 3 in Blanc Sablon.

Understanding the Labrador Flag

The unique personality and heritage of Labrador is well depicted in the three horizontal bars of its flag. The top bar shows the twig of a spruce tree on a white background. This represents the three cultures that primarily make up the region's population—the Innu, the Inuit, and the settlers (or Europeans)—and how they have made a livelihood in harmony with the snow.

The middle bar of forest green represents the green and bountiful land, and the bottom blue bar represents the abundance of water in the region and how the many rivers, lakes, and seas have served as highways for the people and brought them a harvest of fish and wildlife.

mid-June through early October, daily 9:30am to 5:30pm. A helpful online resource for this region is the website for **Labrador Coastal Drive (www.labradorcoastaldrive.com)**.

Getting Around

It's only 80km (50 miles) of paved highway from the ferry terminal in Blanc Sablon to Red Bay, but there's so much to see that it'll take you a full day to travel the entire road. The official highway number is Route 510, but it is promoted as the Labrador Coastal Drive. The highlight north of Red Bay is Battle Harbour (once a regional commercial center, the former community has been opened as a heritage site). To get there, you drive to Mary's Harbour, 85km (53 miles) past Red Bay (where, unfortunately, the paved highway ends) along Route 510. From Mary's Harbour, it's a 1-hour boat ride to Battle Island, home to Battle Harbour.

The coastline north of Battle Harbour has been relatively inaccessible until recently. If you take the gravel road past Mary's Harbour, you'll come to **Cartwright,** the northernmost Labrador Straits community accessible by road. This section of road was completed in 2002, making exploration of Port Hope Simpson, Charlottetown, Paradise River, and Cartwright possible by vehicle. From Cartwright Junction, 87km (54 miles) southwest of Cartwright, Route 510—also known as the Trans-Labrador Highway—continues west through the foothills of the Mealy Mountains to Happy Valley–Goose Bay. This stretch of remote highway was completed in 2009.

Tip: Public transportation is nonexistent along the Labrador Straits. Those planning to arrive by ferry or air without a vehicle should make arrangements well in advance with **Eagle River Rent-a-Car** (✆ **709/931-2352**) in L'Anse au Clair.

L'ANSE AU CLAIR

Driving northeast along Route 510 from the ferry terminal at Blanc Sablon, the first community you'll come to will be L'Anse au Clair. This—like all other communities on the Labrador Straits—is small (less than 300 residents), but it has the largest hotel in the area.

Where to Stay & Dine

Beachside Hospitality Home You'll discover hospitality that's short on frills, long on warmth, in the welcoming home of Norm and Gloria Letto—walking distance from the L'Anse au Clair beach. The five guest rooms provide good value in terms of cleanliness and comfort, but the bathrooms are shared. For an additional C$15 to C$18 per person, Gloria will be pleased to cook you fish casserole or some other Labradorean dinner favorite with advance notice. And if you ask nicely, Norm may get out his accordion for an after-dinner sing-along. Guests have access to the telephone, the kitchen, and a private entrance.

L'Anse au Clair; turn at the Gateway to Labrador Visitor Centre. ✆ **709/931-2338.** www.labradorcoastaldrive.com/home/99. 5 units. C$48–C$58 double; C$10 additional person. Rates include continental breakfast. MC, V. Free parking. *In room:* No phone.

Northern Light Inn ★ With 49 standard hotel rooms, five suites, five housekeeping cottages, and 10 fully serviced RV sites, the Northern Light Inn is the largest accommodations option along the Labrador Straits. This clean, cozy, and cheerful place has facilities not found at local bed-and-breakfasts: wake-up service, in-room phone, coffee shop, licensed lounge, craft shop, and ATM. A nearby indoor swimming pool makes it a perfect location for water recreation. It has no elevator, however, so be prepared to struggle up stairs with your suitcase to the upper-floor rooms.

Even if you don't stay overnight at the Northern Light Inn, you may find yourself dining at the hotel's Basque Dining Room, which is open daily 7am to 10pm. Standard Canadian favorites are served, along with local specialties such as pan-fried cod tongues. No main meal is over C$24.

58 Main St., L'Anse au Clair. ✆ **800/563-3188** or 709/931-2332. www.northernlightinn.com. 59 units, 10 campsites. C$89–C$159 double; C$20 campsites. Weekly rates and seniors' discounts available. AE, MC, V. Free parking. **Amenities:** Restaurant; cafe; lounge; room service. *In room:* A/C, TV.

Exploring L'Anse au Clair

In addition to visiting the Gateway to Labrador Visitor Centre, plan on lacing up your hiking boots for the 1.6-km (1-mile) **Jersey Trail.** Officially designated in 2006, it leads along the coast back toward the ferry terminal from town. The rugged coastal scenery makes the walk worthwhile, but at the end of the trail is a bonus—the foundations and stone walkways remaining from an abandoned 200-year-old fishing village.

Gateway to Labrador Visitor Centre ★ Entering L'Anse au Clair on Route 510 from Blanc Sablon, you'll see the Gateway to Labrador Visitor Centre off to the right. This center will provide you with information on the entire region. Because you're so close to the Quebec border, you'll also find information here about the Lower North Shore of Quebec. The center, in a restored 1909 church, has an extensive selection of visitor information. There is a complete set of menus from local restaurants, literature on attractions and other services, helpful and friendly bilingual staff, assorted historical photos, quilts depicting local history, natural treasures from the sea (including a good selection of shells), and some very impressive fossils of 500-million-year-old *archaeocyatha* and 1-billion-year-old Precambrian granite found in the area of the Point Amour Lighthouse.

Rte. 510, L'Anse au Clair. ✆ **709/931-2013.** Free admission. Mid-June to early Oct daily 9:30am–5:30pm. Closed early Oct–mid-June.

FORTEAU

Just north of L'Anse au Clair is Forteau, a slightly larger community that offers a couple of interesting shopping opportunities and a good restaurant.

Where to Stay & Dine

Grenfell Louie A. Hall Bed & Breakfast (Kids) A Registered Heritage Structure 1 block from the harbor, this inn is in a former nursing station started by Dr. Grenfell and named after the Rochester, New York, woman who, in 1946, donated the funds to build it. Unlike some heritage sites (those with atmospheres as welcoming as a mausoleum), this is an enchantingly nostalgic building filled with curious antiques, old-fashioned radiators, and a resident dog. It's an ideal place for families because the upstairs attic has been converted into a guest unit with two double beds and lots of playroom for the kids. All guest rooms are comfortable (they're each named for a different nurse who once worked here) but share bathrooms. ***Hint:*** Be careful getting in and out of bed: The charmingly sloped bedroom ceilings can give you a nasty bump if you're not careful. Guests can order full breakfasts and other meals in the dining room for an additional charge.

3 Willow Lane, Forteau. ✆ **709/931-2916.** www.grenfellbandb.ca. 5 units. C$65 double. Rates include continental breakfast. MC, V. Free parking. Closed Nov–Apr. *In room:* No phone.

Sea View Restaurant ★ NEWFOUNDLAND Across the road from the water and with filtered ocean views, this friendly dining room offers home-style meals and local specialties that include bakeapple crepes, some incredibly hearty seafood chowder, and caribou roulade. Be sure to save room for unique desserts such as screech parfait and partridgeberry baked Alaska pie. Check the website www.preserves.nf.ca for information about delicious jams and preserves, which are made on-site by Pure Labrador (see below).

33 Main St., Forteau. ✆ **709/931-2840.** Lunch C$6–C$9; dinner C$14–C$24. AE, DC, MC, V. Daily 9am–9:30pm.

Exploring Forteau

While Forteau itself has little of interest, the **Overfall Brook Trail,** which is accessed from town, is one of the prettiest and most accessible walks along the Labrador Straits. Finding the trail head is easy: simply drive past the main wharf to the end of the road (it's within walking distance for guests of Grenfell Louie A. Hall Bed & Breakfast). From this point, the trail climbs gently to the headland, where you'll be rewarded with a great view of the Point Amour Lighthouse and a lovely waterfall. Allow a little over 1 hour to make the 4km (2.5-mile) round-trip.

Labrador Straits Museum Heading east from town, you'll arrive at a small museum and gift shop operated by the local Women's Institute. If you're interested in purchasing local handicrafts (primarily of the knitted or crocheted variety), or in finding out how women of the area lived before the modern world was opened up to them, you'll find this an informative stop. Other highlights are the collection of reproduction tools and weapons from L'Anse Amour Burial Mound and the replica of an early outport nursing station. The museum is wheelchair accessible, and items purchased in the craft shop are tax exempt.

Rte. 510 east of Forteau. ✆ **709/931-2067.** www.labradorstraitsmuseum.ca. C$3 adults, free for children 12 and under. Mid-June to Sept daily 9am–5:30pm.

Shopping

Pure Labrador ★ You can buy more than just lunch at Sea View Restaurant: You can also purchase a selection of jams, syrups, and preserves made from locally harvested bakeapples and partridgeberries. Under the name Pure Labrador, the products are made in the space right behind the main dining room, so you know you're getting them fresh and for prices lower than you may pay in gift shops throughout the area.

33 Main St., Forteau. ✆ **709/931-2743.** www.preserves.nf.ca. Daily 9am–9:30pm.

L'ANSE AMOUR

Your next stop along the Labrador Coastal Drive is L'Anse Amour (meaning "Cove of Love"). Through the village of just four homes is **Point Amour,** where you'll find Point Amour Lighthouse, the tallest lighthouse in Atlantic Canada and the second tallest in all of Canada. Between Route 510 and the lighthouse, a plaque marks the earliest known funeral monument in North America—a 7,500-year-old Maritime Archaic Burial Mound.

Where to Stay

Lighthouse Cove Bed & Breakfast ★ The ferry was delayed and the other guests had finished dinner by the time I knocked on the door. But welcoming owners Rita and Cecil Davis were more than happy to make sure I was well fed before turning in for the night at Lighthouse Cove—one of only four homes set around a picturesque cove. Cecil is a retired fisherman with simultaneously funny and poignant stories of how he made his living from the sea. His ancestors were granted this cove from the king of England back in 1922, so in effect, L'Anse Amour is a private cove—and very special to the Davis family that today inhabits all four homes.

Rita is the shining light of the home. From the moment you enter the door, you'll feel like your visit is the highlight of her day. With a little encouragement, she'll tell you about life in L'Anse Amour—including the story of how, in 1922, the family was able to retrieve six mahogany dining-room chairs and a piano from the HMS *Raleigh*—hung up on a sandbar just offshore—before it broke up and sank. A continental breakfast is included with your room rate. With advance notice, dinner is available at an additional charge (keep your fingers crossed that Rita makes you her delicious chocolate brownies). The three guest rooms are fairly compact, but completely spotless and very tidy. There are no private bathrooms.

L'Anse-Amour Rd., L'Anse-Amour. ✆ **709/927-5690.** http://lighthousecovebb.labradorstraits.net. 3 units. C$45 double. Rates include continental breakfast. MC, V. 1km (½ mile) from Point Amour Lighthouse; 3km (1¾ miles) off Rte. 510 on a gravel road. *In room:* No phone.

Exploring L'Anse Amour

Between Route 510 and the village of L'Anse Amour, watch for a small plaque and pile of stones on the side of the road. This is **L'Anse Amour Burial Mound,** a National Historic Site documented as the oldest native ritual burial site discovered in North America. An interpretive sign explains that archaeologists believe this is a 7,500-year-old Maritime Archaic Indian burial mound containing the remains of a 12-year-old child, who was wrapped in skins and birch bark before being placed in a shallow pit and covered in stones. Ritualistic artifacts found with the boy included a walrus tusk.

Point Amour Lighthouse ★ Walking the 127 steep steps to the top of the tallest lighthouse in Atlantic Canada is a worthwhile journey for anyone who doesn't have bad knees or a fear of heights.

It took 3 years (1854–57) to complete the 2m-thick (6½-ft.) walls of the lighthouse. The primary layer comprises locally quarried limestone covered first by brick and then wooden shingles to protect the mortar from disintegrating in the sea air. The lighthouse was first illuminated in 1858 and was manned until 1996, when it became automated. Today, the beam of light projects over 18km (11 miles).

Inside the old lighthouse keeper's house, informative panels explain the region's naval history and all aspects of early life here. There are also some fascinating maps from the National Archives of Canada. The costumed interpretive staff has a sense of humor:

Cove of Deaths

In times of heavy fog, even the strongest light can't help ships avoid the treacherous rocks at Point Amour. Eight shipwrecks have occurred here, including that of the HMS *Raleigh,* pieces of which can still be found along the nearby coastline. The original French name for this location was L'Anse aux Morts, meaning "Cove of the Dead."

they've set up "Fun Factoids" at each level of the lighthouse tower to divert your thoughts from the stress of the 33m (108-ft.) vertical climb. And a chair at every second level enables you to rest if you need to. This is one of only four Imperial Towers erected by the Government of Canada to protect ships traveling between Canada and England.

From the top of the lighthouse, you'll be rewarded with a magnificent view of Forteau Bay and a 500-million-year-old *archaeocyatha* fossil bed in the rock below. Give yourself 1 or 2 hours to explore the lighthouse exhibits and hike the adjacent trail leading across the barrens.

L'Anse-Amour Rd., L'Anse-Amour. ✆ **709/927-5825.** www.pointamourlighthouse.ca. Guided tours of the lighthouse C$3 for ages 13 and up. Mid-May to early Oct daily 10:30am–5:30pm.

Hiking

The **HMS *Raleigh* Trail** ★ begins at Point Amour Lighthouse and follows the shoreline past pieces of the HMS *Raleigh,* a 12,000-ton light cruiser that ran aground in 1922. Pieces of live ammunition and cordite can still be found washed ashore and in fishers' nets. The Royal Canadian Navy gets the job of safely detonating any ammo found. As you hike your way along the easy 1km (.6-mile) trail, you'll pass fossil beds, small but scenic waterfalls, crowberry patches, bakeapple plants (the berries ripen in August), and tuckamore—the wind- and sea-stunted spruce providing some greenery to this otherwise treeless land. Allow 20 minutes for the round-trip.

L'ANSE AU LOUP

Continuing north from L'Anse Amour is L'Anse au Loup, the largest community on the Straits. L'Anse au Loup offers a good range of services for local residents, including a credit union, library, public swimming pool, sports complex, and fish-processing plant. It's also home to the annual Bakeapple Folk Festival, the largest annual event on the Labrador Straits. You won't find many services in L'Anse au Loup for travelers and are better off overnighting in one of the neighboring communities.

PINWARE RIVER

From its source in the remote interior of Labrador, the Pinware River flows southward and drains into Labrador Straits between L'Anse au Loup and Red Bay.

Signposted from Route 510, **Pinware River Provincial Park** protects a spit of land at the river's mouth. Because of the shelter offered by the thick stands of spruce, fir, and birch, summer temperatures here climb considerably higher than in the more open coastal stretches. For river and ocean views, plan on taking the .6km (.4-mile) walking trail leading to the low summit of Pinware Hill; allow 20 minutes round-trip. The park also has unsupervised swimming, beachcombing, and a picnic area. Do bring your insect repellent or clothing with mosquito netting, as you'll find there are quite a few (many

Fun Facts Bakeapples

Bakeapples, also known as cloudberries, are similar in shape to raspberries and blackberries. They're red when they're unripe, turning a soft, cloudy orange when they ripen in mid-August. There are many bakeapple marshes alongside Route 510 and directions to them are freely given at information centers, gas stations, and local stores. Picking bakeapples is backbreaking labor: They grow close to the ground, as single berries on a short stalk. The tart but tangy flavor of these succulent northern beauties is unlike anything else you've ever tried. Then again, you're probably better off *not* developing a taste for them. There are only two places in the world where you can find bakeapples: Norway is one, Newfoundland and Labrador is the other.

Coinciding with the beginning of the picking season is the **Bakeapple Folk Festival,** hosted by various Labrador Straits communities the second weekend of August. This gathering has been running for over 25 years and offers 4 days and nights of traditional music, dancing, games, and displays, as well as great food. At other times of the year, head to **Pure Labrador,** at 33 Main St., Forteau (✆ **709/931-2743;** www.preserves.nf.ca) to purchase bakeapple jams and preserves.

more than you might expect!) airborne residents of the park anxiously awaiting your arrival.

Route 510 parallels and then crosses the river 9km (5½ miles) north of the village of Pinware River. Here, you'll enjoy spectacular views of the river cascading over swift rapids 21m (69 ft.) below. In the lower gorge area near the bridge are the best salmon-fishing holes. This is where several rustic angling camps are located. The Pinware River is a scheduled salmon river. Licenses can be purchased locally, and local residents are available as guides.

Note: It is mandatory for anglers from outside the province to be accompanied by a local fishing guide. For complete and current information on fishing regulations, licenses, fees, and outfitter information, contact the **Newfoundland & Labrador Department of Conservation** (✆ **709/927-5580;** www.env.gov.nl.ca).

Where to Stay

Pinware River Provincial Park This small campground comes equipped with vehicle parking, picnic tables, drinking water, bathroom facilities, and fire pits. A major plus is its proximity to a sandy beach, where you can enjoy unsupervised swimming (if you dare take a dip in these subarctic waters!).

Rte. 510 to Pinware. ✆ **800/563-6353** or 709/927-5516. www.env.gov.nl.ca/parks. 15 unserviced sites. C$15 per site. MC, V. Closed mid-Sept to May. **Amenities:** Picnic table; fire pits; pit toilets; drinking water; firewood (C$7per bundle).

RED BAY

Incredibly, it wasn't until 1977 that Red Bay was identified as a historic whaling port, and today, it is this history that is the major attraction. The first industry established on

Canadian soil was a seasonal whale-oil factory in Red Bay, and by the late 1600s, Red Bay was the largest whaling port in the world, with more than 2,500 men from the Basque region of Europe (along the Spanish/French border) calling the bay home during the summer whaling season. The bloodshed was so intense that the waters of the bay would be red with whales' blood. It is thought that this scene provided the origin for the name of the village. The whalers lived aboard Spanish galleons that were moored here for the season. Through the decades, four of these vessels sank in the bay, giving historians a unique opportunity to study these impressive ships in shallow water, where cold temperatures have helped in the preservation process.

Where to Stay

Basinview Bed & Breakfast The best place to stay in Red Bay, this modern home is the residence of Wade and Blanche Earle. It's an inviting waterfront property beside Route 510 on the south side of town. The home has a large sitting room with a great view where guests can enjoy satellite TV and have access to the telephone. Blanche will even cook you a real Labrador-style dinner, such as caribou stew or pan-fried cod, for an additional C$18. The three basement rooms share a bathroom but have the most privacy. The upstairs bedroom has a private bathroom and water views, but is directly off the living room.

145 Main Hwy. (Rte. 510), Red Bay. ✆ **866/920-2001** or 709/920-2002. 4 units. C$58–C$75 double. MC. Rates include continental breakfast (C$7 extra for a cooked breakfast). *In room:* No phone.

Where to Dine

Whaler's Restaurant ★ Value SEAFOOD A biggish restaurant with well-spaced tables, Whaler's serves some of the province's best fish and chips. The chalupa fish and chips is listed as a snack on the menu, but you'll get two generous filets of cod along with home fries and coleslaw. The fish is delicately coated with a light, spicy coating and is not greasy at all. The fries and coleslaw are also good, making this quite a meal for C$10. The seafood chowder costs C$5 and is also very good. Save room for ice cream topped with local berries. A small gift shop sells an assortment of souvenirs, including some lovely Labrador jackets. Whaler's is down on the waterfront, beside the Visitor Interpretation Centre, but unfortunately doesn't have water views.

Red Bay. ✆ **709/920-2156.** Lunch C$7–C$10; dinner C$11–C$20. MC, V. Daily 8am–10:30pm.

Exploring Red Bay

Like Basque whalers of old, you'll be immediately drawn to Red Bay Harbour—the present-day location of the Red Bay National Historic Site. While the essence and importance of the bygone whale fishery are eloquently explained here, don't limit your explorations to the formal site. The community itself has a story to tell through its location and topography. Picturesque rocks protrude peacefully out of the water in the harbor, and an eerie half-sunken ship lurks in the fog just offshore. Although there are no official trails, leave your vehicle behind and plan on spending at least an hour walking the hilly residential streets and exploring the waterfront.

Ask at the Visitor Orientation Centre about opportunities for harbor tours, including boat transfers to Saddle Island, where a walking trail winds through an area once inhabited by whalers.

Red Bay National Historic Site ★★ This important National Historic Site consists of two separate display areas. Start at the Visitor Orientation Centre at the top of the hill and watch the 30-minute video that explains the history of the Basque whalers who once populated this bay. This building also offers a remarkable display of a *chaloupe,* a 400-year-old preserved and reconstructed wooden whaling boat surrounded by the mandible of a 5.3m (17-ft.) bowhead whale. The bowhead is a member of the "right whale" family, so named because they were the *right* whales to slaughter for the best oil.

The Visitor Interpretation Centre, located down the hill at the waterfront, contains artifacts from the Basque whalers and one of their ships, the *San Juan,* which was loaded with about 1,000 barrels of whale oil when it sank in Red Bay during a storm in 1565. The wreck of the *San Juan* was discovered in 1978 and subsequently dismantled by underwater archaeologists. Part of its hull is on display at the Museum of Civilization in Ottawa, Ontario. Also here, you can view a replica of the *San Juan* (built to a scale of 1:10) and recovered artifacts such as pottery fragments and the broken remains of a sandglass.

If you step out the back of the Visitor Interpretation Centre, you can get a good look at the *Bernier,* a half-sunken French ship that ran aground in 1966 in the same spot as the *San Juan.* It provides an eerie reminder that other shipwrecks are well preserved in Red Bay due to the coldness of its water. Allow at least 2 hours at the historic site, plus another hour walking around town and to the harbor.

Red Bay. ✆ **709/920-2142.** www.pc.gc.ca/eng/lhn-nhs/nl/redbay/index.aspx. C$8 adults, C$7 seniors, C$4 children 6–16, free for children 5 and under; C$20 families. Early June to Sept 9am–6pm.

BATTLE HARBOUR ★★★

Red Bay is formally the end of the Labrador Straits, and it's where the paved road ends. But there is one point farther up the coast that, although it takes some effort to reach, will be a highlight of your trip—not just to Labrador Straits, but the entire province. Located on a rocky island accessible only by boat, Battle Harbour is the province's only intact salt-fishing village and is dutifully maintained by the Battle Harbour Historic Trust. You can come for just the day or stay overnight. Either way, visiting Battle Harbour is a poignant peek at history.

The mercantile salt-fish premises at Battle Harbour were originally established by the firm of John Slade & Company of Poole, England, in the early 1770s. Salt fish is cod that has been cleaned, split, salted, and dried; this is how fish was stored in the days before refrigeration. The population of Battle Harbour increased quickly after 1820, when fishing schooners adopted the community as their primary port of call and declared it the capital of the Labrador floater fishery. The term "floater fishery" refers to migratory Newfoundland fishermen who fished the bountiful Labrador waters each summer and returned to their permanent homes in Newfoundland each fall. A high point for the community occurred in 1892, when Dr. Wilfred Grenfell arrived in Battle Harbour. A year later, he built Labrador's first hospital here. (See more about Dr. Grenfell in chapter 9's section on the Northern Peninsula.)

Like so many other remote communities throughout Newfoundland and Labrador, the residents were encouraged by the provincial government to move closer to civilization beginning in the late 1960s, and by the 1970s, the permanent population of Battle Harbour had been resettled on the mainland, mostly at Mary's Harbour. The fully intact town of Battle Harbour was abandoned.

Getting There

Getting to Battle Harbour is half the fun. Ferries depart for the 1-hour trip from the Battle Harbour Ferry Terminal on Main Street in the small village of Mary's Harbour,

85km (53 miles) north of Red Bay along unpaved Route 510. Departures are mid-June through mid-Sept daily at 11am and 6pm. The return trip departs Battle Harbour at 9am and 4pm. Cost for the round-trip is C$55 adults, C$30 children. Guarantee a spot by making reservations at © **709/921-6216.**

Where to Stay

Battle Harbour Inn ★ It's possible to make Battle Harbour a day trip from points south, but for the full effect, plan on staying on the island overnight, at the Battle Harbour Inn or one of six associated restored buildings. Once the home of a merchant, the inn gives you a flavor of former glory in its antique furnishings and commanding hilltop location. Early in the season, you'll be happily distracted by the sight of passing icebergs as you contemplate the meaning of life from this historical property's wraparound porch. The other restored buildings each have one or more beds and kitchen facilities. The ferry (see above) is extra, as are walking tours (see below) and meals (except for guests staying at the Inn, for whom breakfast is included).

Everything is within walking distance of the inn, itself just a short stroll from the dock. At the Dining Hall, down hill from the inn, breakfast is C$10, a seafood-themed lunch C$15, and a three-course dinner C$20. Specialties of the house are crab, salmon, trout, char, and smoked fish products produced on-site. Day trippers are welcome to have lunch at the Dining Hall, while the downstairs grocery store sells snacks.

Battle Island. © **709/921-6325** or 709/921-6216. www.battleharbour.com. 5 rooms, 6 cottages. C$35 dorm bed, C$135–C$150 double (including breakfast), C$190–C$245 cottages. V. Closed late Sept to early June. **Amenities:** Restaurant. *In room:* No phone.

Exploring Battle Harbour

After arriving by boat at Battle Harbour, visitors are free to wander around the community. Around 20 buildings have been restored, including many along the harbor front, a narrow waterway facing the sheer rock cliff line of a neighboring island. Some are filled with interpretive boards telling the story of the history of the local fishery and how Battle Harbour was once the hub of Labrador. Others are simply historically important spaces, such as the low-roofed loft where, in 1909, Robert Peary held a press conference to tell the world of his successful expedition to the North Pole. Beyond the restored buildings, a boardwalk leads through the residential part of the village. While a small number of the homes are inhabited on a seasonal basis, the harsh northern weather has taken its toll on those that remain abandoned. The departure for many island residents was swift, and as a result, some homes remain furnished, complete with vases of now-wilted flowers left on windowsills.

An unmarked walking trail leads from the back of the homes through a rocky cleft to a cemetery, where the headstone engravings make for touching reading. If you're feeling spry, continue beyond the main cemetery to a smaller cemetery and then scramble up to the high point of the island, where a plaque marks the spot of a 1904 Marconi wireless telegraph station.

In addition to providing accommodations and transporting visitors to the island, the Battle Harbour Historic Trust leads 2-hour walking tours through the community. Costing C$9 per person, they depart from the dock when the morning boat shuttle arrives. No reservations are necessary.

2 HAPPY VALLEY–GOOSE BAY

Happy Valley–Goose Bay is Labrador's hub and its largest service center. The community is strategically located at the point where Labrador's coastline is naturally split by Hamilton Inlet and Lake Melville.

The town of Happy Valley–Goose Bay is a rather new entity, and was formally established only in 1973. The fur trade initially brought settlers to central Labrador and others were attracted to the region's abundance of fish, wildlife, and timber, as well as its rich soil and longer growing season. Slow growth continued until World War II. The turning point came in 1941, when the air base at Goose Bay was built as a landing and refueling stop for the Atlantic Ferry Command. During World War II, thousands of aircraft passed through Goose Bay. The airbase continues to provide support and coordination for NATO tactical flight-training activities. Military Base "5 Wing Goose Bay" provides support to Allied, NORAD, and Canadian Forces training and operations. Today, the foreign military component at 5 Wing Goose Bay has added a cosmopolitan flavor to the community and helped its population grow to 7,500.

ESSENTIALS

Getting There

Happy Valley–Goose Bay has an airport served by Air Canada, Air Labrador, and Provincial Airlines. If you decide to drive to Happy Valley–Goose Bay from Labrador West, you must travel Route 500, a gravel highway with few services other than what you'll find in Churchill Falls, the halfway mark between Labrador City and Wabush, and Happy Valley–Goose Bay.

A road between the communities of Labrador Straits and Happy Valley–Goose Bay was completed in late 2009. From the ferry dock at Blanc Sablon it's 568km (353 miles) of mostly unpaved road to Happy Valley–Goose Bay, with the final 250km (155 miles) through complete wilderness with no services.

Visitor Information

The **Labrador Lake Melville Tourism Association** operates a visitor center at 365 Hamilton River Rd. in Happy Valley–Goose Bay (✆ **866/441-1044** or 709/896-3489; www.tourismlabrador.com), open June to September daily from 8am to 8pm. They'll provide you with maps and brochures, as well as the most current information on services and events in the central Labrador region. They also provide visitors with free Internet access.

WHERE TO STAY & DINE

Davis Bed & Breakfast (Value) Set in a trim bungalow with well-tended gardens, Davis Bed & Breakfast is in a quiet residential area within easy driving distance of the airport, local attractions, and restaurants. Each of the four guest rooms has a private en-suite bathroom, and is appointed with basic, comfortable furnishings.

14 Cabot Cres. ✆ **866/996-5077** or 709/896-5077. www.bbcanada.com/davisbb. 4 units. C$70 double. Rates include full breakfast. MC, V. *In room:* TV, Wi-Fi.

Goose River Lodges (Kids) Just a 20-minute drive northeast from Happy Valley–Goose Bay, these two-bedroom cabins are clean and comfortable, with electric heat, air-conditioning, and solid (albeit mismatched) furnishings. Bedrooms and eating/sitting areas are spacious, but the diminutive bathrooms come with just a shower (no bathtub). A bonus is the barbecue and picnic table out front of each cabin. There is also a wheelchair-accessible unit. Other amenities include a playground, beach volleyball, and snowmobile rentals, all within walking distance of the namesake Goose River. There are also 10 RV sites that are well spaced and serviced with 30-amp electrical outlets.

North West River Rd. ✆ **877/496-2600** or 709/896-2600. www.gooseriverlodges.ca. 19 units (including 10 RV sites). C$95 double, C$24 campsites. V. Free parking. **Amenities:** Playground. *In room:* AC, kitchen.

Labrador Inn The Labrador Inn is as close as you'll find in town to a mid-priced chain hotel. Guest rooms and suites are simple but adequately furnished (although the bathrooms are on the small side). The in-house restaurant, Banniken's, features the usual Northern menu, with a wide range of familiar dishes interspersed with local specialties like caribou burgers. The inn is conveniently situated near the visitor center and is a 5-minute drive from the airport, seaport, seaplane dock, and Trans-Labrador Highway. One unit is specially designed to meet the needs of travelers with disabilities.

380 Hamilton River Rd. ✆ **800/563-2763** or 709/896-3351. 73 units. C$84–C$150 double. MC, V. Free parking. **Amenities:** Restaurant; lounge; business services; limited room service. *In room:* A/C, TV.

Mulligan's Pub BAR Because it's a pub that serves food (as opposed to a restaurant that serves alcohol), you must be at least 19 years of age to enter Mulligan's. The food is as good as it gets this far north—and inexpensive. The fish and chips are superb, and the Chicken Delight (grilled chicken served over a Caesar salad) is excellent. If you're looking for local flavor, Mulligan's also serves caribou burgers. On warm summer days, the patio remains full throughout the day. The pub is open until 2am, but the kitchen closes earlier (although you can still get light snacks after that).

368 Hamilton River Rd. ✆ **709/896-3038.** Reservations not accepted. C$8–C$19. MC, V. Mon–Sat 11am–6pm; Sun 11am–3pm.

Royal Inn & Suites ★ One block from the highway and in the main business district between Goose Bay and Happy Valley, the Royal Inn is my top pick for hotel accommodations in town. Facilities are limited (although it does have a pleasant picnic area, complete with gas barbeque), but this is more than made up for with smartly decorated rooms filled with modern amenities such as free high-speed Internet access. The least expensive guest rooms have a double bed, but for a few dollars more, you can get a larger bed and small kitchen. In a separate wing, the Royal Suites (starting at C$115) are newer and more spacious. Some have separate bedrooms, a sitting area, work desk, and two TVs.

3 Royal Ave. ✆ **888/440-2456** or 709/896-2456. www.royalinnandsuites.ca. 31 units. C$87–C$139 double. Rates include continental breakfast. AE, DC, MC, V. Free parking. *In room:* A/C, TV/DVD player.

EXPLORING HAPPY VALLEY–GOOSE BAY

A good place to get an idea of the lay of the land is from **Pine Tree Lookout,** signposted northeast of town off Route 510. The panorama from this lofty point includes the military base, the town, and Lake Melville. Although little remains, this site was once home to a radar station that was part of the North American defense system during the Cold War.

Aside from the two museums detailed below, other official attractions are limited to three **airplane monuments** that reflect the town's importance to the military. One of the monuments is along Hamilton River Road across the road from Town Hall, another is at the entrance to 5 Wing Goose Bay on Forbes Road, and a third is by the main airport.

Festivals & Special Events

The community hosts several fun cultural events, such as National Aboriginal Day (June 21).

The **Labrador Canoe Regatta,** a 3-day paddling event, features teams from all over Labrador who compete in six-person voyageur canoe races on Gosling Lake, a 20-minute drive from town. Male and female contestants paddle replicas of traditional two-person canoes in several age-specific category races. A variety of food booths will keep your tummy from growling, and bands provide traditional entertainment throughout the weekend. The regatta is held the first weekend in August; there is no entrance fee. For more information, visit **www.canoelabrador.ca**.

North West River Beach Festival (✆ **709/497-3339;** www.nwrbeachfestival.com), Labrador's largest outdoor music festival, takes place near Happy Valley–Goose Bay the 4th weekend of July. Free live entertainment can be enjoyed right on the lakefront at Lester Burry Memorial Park. Best of all, admission is free.

Happy Valley–Goose Bay hosts **Big Land Challenge** (✆ **709/896-3489;** www.biglandchallenge.com), a 20km (12-mile) dogsled race held on the second Saturday of every March. Unlike other similar races, the use of traditional sleds is mandatory.

SnoBreak, formerly known as the Happy Goose Winter Carnival, is a weeklong family-oriented winter event held the second to third weekend of March. SnoBreak is 8 days of continuous outdoor winter activities including snowmobile races, snowmobile rides to several surrounding communities, fireworks, geocaching, and more. Most activities are free—however, a small registration fee is required to participate in the races and trail rides. For more information, call ✆ **709/896-3489.**

Labrador Interpretation Centre This is Labrador's most important museum, which, although interesting, will require only an hour or less of your time. You'll see four galleries filled with life-size dioramas, exhibits, and archaeological artifacts that interpret Labrador's history, from the arrival of the first humans 9,000 years ago to today. The museum is off Portage Road in North West River, a neighborhood of Happy Valley–Goose Bay.

Hillview Dr., North West River. ✆ **709/497-8566.** C$2 adults, C$1 children. June–Aug Tues–Wed 1–4pm, Thurs–Fri 10am–4pm, Sat–Sun 1:30–4:30pm; Sept–May Wed–Fri 1–4pm, Sat–Sun 1:30–4:30pm.

Northern Lights Military Museum Check out this museum's interesting display of the region's military history, including a good collection of authentic World War II artifacts. The same building displays stuffed animals and a re-creation of a trapper's cabin, complete with the Northern Lights sparkling overhead.

170 Hamilton River Rd. ✆ 709/896-5939. Free admission. Mon–Wed 10am–5:30pm, Thurs–Fri 10am–9pm, Sat 10am–5:30pm.

3 CHURCHILL FALLS TO LABRADOR WEST

Labrador City and Wabush are the major centers of Labrador West, the resource-rich region that stretches along the Quebec–Labrador border. Churchill Falls is the halfway point between Labrador City/Wabush and Happy Valley–Goose Bay.

Labrador City was established as a community in 1958 and now offers a full range of services including visitor information, a hospital, lodging, camping, hiking, sport fishing, golf, skiing, and snowmobiling. The 9,000 residents of Labrador City and Wabush happily embrace their sometimes harsh—what some call a two-season—climate. Winter can seem never-ending when the snow is on the ground for up to 8 months! And summer temperatures in July and August are that perfect balmy warmth that more southerly residents dream of in the midst of their heat waves.

But what both Labrador City and Wabush are best known for are their open-pit iron-ore mines, the largest of their kind in North America. The community of Churchill Falls on the Churchill River is best known for having the world's largest underground hydroelectric generating station.

ESSENTIALS

Getting There

If you're coming from Baie Comeau, Quebec, on the Gulf of St. Lawrence, partially paved Route 389 will take you north to the twin communities of Labrador City and Wabush. Labrador City is less than 20km (12 miles) from the Quebec–Labrador border; Wabush is 3km (1¾ miles) farther along Route 500 and is home to the regional airport.

The 581km (361-mile) stretch of gravel highway from Labrador City to Happy Valley–Goose Bay is basically unserviced except for what you'll find in Churchill Falls—roughly halfway along your journey—and will take you about 8½ hours to complete. Churchill Falls is 238km (148 miles) from Labrador City and 288km (179 miles) from

Navigating the Trans-Labrador Highway

Many people are surprised to discover that the majority of the Trans-Labrador Highway is a two-lane gravel road. If it's wet, the road is slick and slippery; if it's dry, the dust is blinding; and if it's icy or snowy, driving can be lethal. Here are some tips to make the trip a bit easier:

- Try to drive on Sundays, when there are fewer tractor-trailers on the road. Even though the highway is supposedly two lanes, you don't want to be crowded onto the shoulders, which are not nearly as solid as they look.
- Never start out on the highway without a full tank of gas (an extra container in the trunk wouldn't hurt, either) and a spare tire.
- Be extra cautious in winter, especially with regard to traveling close to the outer edge of the highway. What looks like snow-covered highway may just be loose snow without a solid foundation.

 Happy Valley–Goose Bay, and it is pretty much the only service center you'll find along Route 500.

The towns along Route 500 have airports served by scheduled flights, so you can fly into Wabush, rent a car, drive as far as Happy Valley–Goose Bay, and then fly to St. John's or a limited number of other destinations without having to drive the return route.

Tshiuetin Rail Transportation (✆ **866/962-0988** or 418/962-5530; www.tshiuetin.net) operates a passenger rail service between Sept-Îles, Quebec, and Schefferville, 588km (365 miles) to the north. Around 7 hours north of Sept-Îles, a stop is made at Emeril Junction, 58km (36 miles) east of Labrador City. The train departs Sept-Îles on Mondays and Thursdays at 8am. The return trip departs Emeril Junction on Tuesdays and Fridays at noon. Call for information and reservations.

Visitor Information

Regional information for Labrador West is available through **Gateway Labrador** (✆ **709/944-5399;** www.gatewaylabrador.ca). This organization also operates an information center at 1365 Route 500, Labrador City. The information center gift shop is notable for its local jams and preserves, labradorite jewelry, and Innu art. From mid-June through August, the hours are daily 9am until 9pm. The center is open the remainder of the year from Monday to Friday, 9am to 5pm and from noon to 5pm on weekends. Another useful website is Labrador West (**www.labradorwest.com**), which represents both Labrador City and Wabush.

WHERE TO STAY & DINE

Carol Inn This is a good choice if you want to do your own cooking. The Carol Inn offers 20 motel rooms, each with a small kitchen. All units are spacious and are regularly refurbished. The inn is the only Labrador City lodging to have air-conditioning. There is an on-site gift shop. The inn features fine dining, a family restaurant, and pub-style food, as well as live entertainment.

215 Drake Ave., Labrador City. ✆ **888/799-7736** or 709/944-7736. www.carolinn.ca. 20 units. C$105–C$142 double. AE, DC, MC, V. **Amenities:** 2 restaurants; lounge. *In room:* A/C, TV, kitchenette, minibar.

Midway Travel Inn For those in town on government business, this property is conveniently located in the town complex. There's even an indoor swimming pool available for guest use, a real treat for this part of the world. Being in the town complex is a good thing if you're visiting during the winter, as you can get from one place to the next without having to go outdoors.

Ressigieu Dr., Churchill Falls. ✆ **800/229-3269** or 709/925-3211. 21 units. C$92–C$132 double. AE, MC, V. **Amenities:** Restaurant, lounge; pool; limited room service. *In room:* TV, Wi-Fi.

Northern Lights Fishing Lodge The vast majority of tourists traveling to Labrador West do so to fish for arctic char, land-locked salmon, brook trout, rainbow trout, and northern pike. Rather than stopping by for just one night, they come north and stay at a remote lodge as part of a week-long package. One such destination is Northern Lights Fishing Lodge, a self-contained resort with a main lodge for dining and socializing surrounded by two-bedroom A-frame cabins, each with a toilet and woodstove. Access to surrounding lakes and rivers is by road, boat, and floatplane, with packages offered inclusive of accommodations, meals, and guides. Some packages also include transportation from Labrador City.

3-hour drive north of Wabush. ✆ **709/944-7475.** www.labrador-frontier.com. 7 units. From C$1,750 per person for a 7-night package. **Amenities:** Restaurant.

Moments **Labrador: A Spiritual Experience**

It takes a big heart to appreciate the Big Land. You'll see "brown" ponds where the water is so clear the color comes from the sun reflecting off the rocks on the bottom. You'll see double and triple rainbows, their colorful clarity enhanced by the crisp, clean air. And you'll see the aurora borealis playing across the northern sky in flowing flames of golden-crimson-emerald light. Truly, a trip to Labrador is an unforgettable, life-altering journey.

PJ's Inn by the Lake ★ Perfectly located on the shoreline of Little Wabush Lake, this small B&B has sweeping water views (except in winter, when you're likely to see dog teams rushing across the frozen lake), with a deck taking full advantage of the view. Inside, you find five midsize rooms, four with en-suite bathrooms and one with a private bathroom across the hall. The ambience throughout is welcoming, with guests also having use of a book-filled living area and dining room.

606 Tamarack Dr., Labrador City. ✆ **888/944-6648** or 709/944-3438. www.pjsinnbythelake.com. 5 units. C$80 double. AE, MC, V. Rates include full breakfast. *In room:* TV, Wi-Fi.

Wabush Hotel A distinctive three-story chalet-style property built in the early 1960s, this hotel is the largest in the area, with spacious guest rooms, respectable customer service, and dependable food. The hotel features two dining rooms specializing in Chinese and Canadian cuisine—the Chinese food is good, something that is rare in Labrador. It is within walking distance of downtown and the recreation center. The hotel offers a complimentary shuttle service to and from the airport upon request, as well as a 24-hour reception desk.

9 Grenfell Dr., Wabush. ✆ **709/282-3221.** www.wabushhotel.com. 68 units. C$95–C$114 double. AE, MC, V. Free parking. **Amenities:** Restaurant; lounge; limited room service. *In room:* A/C, TV.

EXPLORING LABRADOR WEST

Labrador West is not a hotbed of tourist attractions. Even Churchill Falls, named for former British Prime Minister Sir Winston Churchill, ceased to exist when water from the Churchill River was diverted for the hydroelectric system. In addition to touring this megaproject, visitors can inquire at the **Gateway Labrador** office, at 1365 Route 500, Labrador City, about free bus tours of local mining operations.

Edmund Montague Exhibit Hall The distinctive log building that provides a home to Gateway Labrador, the local tourism organization, also contains a small museum, the Edmund Montague Exhibit Hall. In chorological order, displays tell the story of Labrador West from the arrival of the first human inhabitants 3,500 years ago through the establishment of a Hudson's Bay Company post in 1838 to the importance of mining and power generation industries today.

Gateway Labrador building, 1365 Route 500, Labrador City. ✆ **709/944-5399.** C$3 adults, C$2.50 seniors, C$2 children. June–Aug daily 9am–9pm; Sept–May Mon–Fri 9am–5pm and Sat–Sun noon–5pm.

Churchill Falls Generating Station Touring this facility, North America's second-largest hydroelectric system, is the highlight of a stop in Labrador West. On the tour, you'll hear some impressive facts and figures, but nothing will prepare you for the sheer size of the operation, especially the underground powerhouse holding 11 turbines, which is as high as a 15-story building and three football fields long. The tours are about 3 hours long and are indoors, so you don't have to worry about wearing special clothing. Hard hats are provided.

Churchill Falls. ✆ **709/925-3335.** www.nalcorenergy.com. Free admission. Tours daily 9am, and 1:30 and 7pm. Reservations required; call at least one day in advance. For safety reasons, children 8 and under are not permitted to participate in the tours.

OUTDOOR PURSUITS

Although the area boasts a limited number of hiking trails, those that do exist offer a good way to experience the local environment. One of the most popular is a 5km (3.1-mile) path encircling Jean Lake. It's a well-graded trail, with signage and rest areas. Access is from Grenfell Drive in Wabush. After the snow melts at the **Menihek Nordic Ski Club,** along Smokey Mountain Road, the Menihek Interpretive Trail comes alive with hikers. This 5km (3.1-mile) walk is lined with information boards describing local flora and fauna. Call ✆ **709/944-5842** or visit www.meniheknordicski.ca for information. In addition to cross-country skiing, winter brings downhill skiing to **Smokey Mountain Ski Club,** where lift tickets are C$30 adults, or pay C$38 including equipment rental. For information, call ✆ **709/944-2129.**

4 NUNATSIAVUT

North of Happy Valley–Goose Bay, Nunatsiavut, meaning "our beautiful land," is part of Newfoundland and Labrador, but is governed by the Inuit and Kablunangajuit people, who have called this large chunk of coastal Labrador home for centuries. The region comprises tiny outport fishing communities with a combined population of just 5,000. They are accessible only via ferry or plane. The farther north you go, the more icebergs you'll see (many break up or melt as they head south toward St. John's), making Cape Chidley, at Labrador's northern tip, the place where you're likely to see the most and largest icebergs.

ESSENTIALS

Getting There

The ferry trip to Nunatsiavut from Happy Valley–Goose Bay is an adventure in itself, and it's the main reason many visitors find themselves this far north. On the passengers-only **MV *Northern Ranger,*** you'll stop at several small villages and travel as far north as Nain. Operated by the provincial government, **Labrador** (✆ **866/535-2567** or 709/535-0810; www.labradormarine.com) charges C$142 per person one-way. Accommodations range from dorm beds (C$66) to en-suite cabins (C$573) for the 2-night trip. Ferries operate from early June to early November. As an alternative to the ferry, you can return to Goose Bay on an Air Labrador flight (✆ **800/563-3042;** www.airlabrador.com) from Nain.

NAIN

Established in 1771 as a mission, Nain today has a population of 1,100 and is the administrative capital of Nunatsiavut. The few visitors who do travel this far north arrive on the twice-weekly ferry, while only the adventurous few continue north by chartered boat or plane to the abandoned mission at Hebron or to the wilds of Torngat Mountains

The Inukshuk

The North Coast is inhabited by various native peoples, including the Inuit. As you travel this area, you may see unusual rock or stone figurines shaped in the rough outline of a person. They are *Inukshuk,* an Inuit word meaning "in the image of man." These lifelike figures originally served as signposts to mark the way across barren land and to offer guidance to those who followed. They are a symbol of friendship, caring, and the strong sense of community you find in the north.

National Park. While fishing is important to the local economy, a massive nickel and copper mine south of town at Voisey Bay draws the most outside business interests. Aside from simply soaking up life this far north, the only official attraction is Nain Piulimatsivik, a small museum displaying Inuit artifacts and telling the story of the Moravian settlers. It opens whenever the ferry is in town. For information on the museum or to make arrangements for charters into the Torngat Mountains, call the **Town Office** at ✆ **709/922-2842.**

Where to Stay

Atsanik Lodge The only place to stay in Nain, this 26-room property is a full-service hotel, with a dining room, lounge, laundry, room service, and airport shuttle.

Sand Banks Rd., Nain. ✆ **709/922-2910**. 25 units. C$115–C$125 double. MC, V. **Amenities:** Restaurant; lounge; room service. *In room:* TV.

11

Fast Facts

1 FAST FACTS: NEWFOUNDLAND & LABRADOR

AREA CODES All of Newfoundland and Labrador uses the **709** area code.

AUTOMOBILE ORGANIZATIONS The Canadian equivalent of the AAA is the CAA (Canadian Automobile Association), which does not have an office in Newfoundland and Labrador. If you are a CAA or AAA member, call ✆ **800/222-4357** for emergency road assistance. Call ✆ **800/947-0770** for emergency roadside service if you are a member of the Good Sam Club. (If you're not a member but would like to join, call ✆ **800/842-5351.**) Both clubs' operators will connect you with appropriate local service providers.

BUSINESS HOURS Most businesses are open weekdays from 10am to 5pm and on Saturday 10am to noon. In major cities, including St. John's and Corner Brook, mall shops have longer hours, with some open on Sundays.

DRINKING LAWS The legal drinking age is 19. Don't drink and drive, as Canadian laws are tough if you are caught impaired behind the wheel, and you will be charged under the Criminal Code.

DRIVING RULES See "Getting There and Getting Around," p. 44.

DRUGSTORES These are more commonly referred to as "pharmacies" in Canada. Many of the larger grocery chains fill prescriptions. Be sure to bring a copy of any prescriptions along with you in case you lose your medication and need to have the prescription refilled.

ELECTRICITY Electrical and phone outlets are the same as in the U.S.: 110 to 115 volts AC, 60 cycles. No special adapters are necessary unless you are traveling to Canada from outside North America.

EMBASSIES & CONSULATES All embassies within Canada are in Ottawa, Ontario, the national capital. Embassies include the **Australian High Commission,** 50 O'Connor St., Suite 710, Ottawa, Ont., K1P 6L2 (✆ **613/236-0841**); the **British High Commission,** 80 Elgin St., Ottawa, Ont., K1P 5K7 (✆ **613/237-1530**); the **Embassy of Ireland,** 130 Albert St., Ottawa, Ont., K1P 5G4 (✆ **613/233-6281**); the **New Zealand High Commission,** 727–99 Bank St., Ottawa, Ont., K1P 6G3 (✆ **613/238-5991**); the **South African High Commission,** 15 Sussex Dr., Ottawa, Ont., K1M 1M8 (✆ **613/744-0330**); and the **Embassy of the United States of America,** 490 Sussex Dr., Ottawa, Ont., K1N 1G8 (✆ **613/238-5335;** http://ottawa.usembassy.gov for general inquiries).

You can find a **U.S. consulate** in Halifax, Nova Scotia, at Suite 904, Purdy's Wharf Tower II, 1969 Upper Water St. (✆ **902/429-2480**). The closest **British consulate** is at 1 Canal St., Dartmouth, Nova Scotia (✆ **902/461-1381;** www.ukincanada.fco.gov.uk). The **Australian consulate** can be found at 50 O'Connor St., Ottawa, Ontario (✆ **613/236-4376**).

EMERGENCIES Call ✆ **911** for emergency services, including fire, police, or ambulance.

GASOLINE (PETROL) Gas stations are basically the same as in the U.S., but gasoline is sold by the liter, not by the gallon. (3.8L equals 1 U.S. gal.). Gas prices in Newfoundland & Labrador fluctuate, as they do everywhere else in the world; as of press time, 1 liter cost about C$1.05. Taxes are included in the printed price.

HOLIDAYS For a list of holidays in Canada, see "Newfoundland & Labrador Calendar of Events," in chapter 3.

HOSPITALS Hospitals are located in all major cities, including St. John's, where the **General Hospital** is at 300 Prince Philip Dr. (✆ **709/777-6300**).

INSURANCE Like all provinces in Canada, Newfoundland and Labrador has its own provincial medical plan. Wise travelers will obtain sufficient medical insurance before leaving home. Even though prices for health care in Canada are significantly lower than in the U.S., they are still costly for those not covered by the provincial plan.

Check your existing insurance policies and credit card coverage before you buy travel insurance. You may already be covered for lost luggage, canceled tickets, or medical expenses.

The cost of travel insurance varies widely, depending on the cost and length of your trip, your age and health, and the type of trip you're taking, but expect to pay between 5% and 8% of the vacation itself. You can get estimates from various providers through **InsureMyTrip.com**. Enter your trip cost and dates, your age, and other information, for prices from more than a dozen companies.

U.K. citizens and their families who make more than one trip abroad per year may find an annual travel insurance policy works out cheaper than buying insurance for each trip separately. Check **www.moneysupermarket.com**, which compares prices across a wide range of providers for single- and multi-trip policies.

Most big travel agencies offer their own insurance and will probably try to sell you their package when you book a holiday.

Trip-Cancellation Insurance Trip-cancellation insurance will help retrieve your money if you have to back out of a trip or depart early, or if your travel supplier goes bankrupt. Permissible reasons for trip cancellation can range from sickness to natural disasters to the Department of State declaring a destination unsafe for travel. In this unstable world, trip-cancellation insurance is a good buy if you're purchasing tickets well in advance. Insurance policy details vary, so read the fine print, and make sure that your airline or cruise line is on the list of carriers covered in case of bankruptcy.

For more information, contact one of the following recommended insurers: **Access America** (✆ **866/807-3982;** www.accessamerica.com), **Travel Guard International** (✆ **800/826-4919;** www.travelguard.com), **Travel Insured International** (✆ **800/243-3174;** www.travelinsured.com), and **Travelex Insurance Services** (✆ **800/228-9792;** www.travelex-insurance.com).

Medical Insurance **Blue Cross** is the most popular form of private medical insurance in Canada and widely accepted at most, if not all, hospitals. Find them on the Web at **www.bluecross.ca**.

Most U.S. health plans (including Medicare and Medicaid) do not provide coverage for travel to Canada, and the ones that do often require you to pay for services up front and reimburse you only after you return home. Even if your plan does cover overseas treatment, most out-of-country hospitals make you pay your bills up front and send you a refund only after you've returned home and filed the necessary paperwork with your insurance company. As a safety net, you may want to buy travel medical insurance, particularly if you're traveling to a remote area where emergency evacuation is a possible scenario. If you require additional medical insurance, try **MEDEX** (✆ **800/537-2029** or 410/453-6300; www.medexassist.com) or **Travel Assistance International** (✆ **800/821-2828;** www.travelassistance.com).

Canadians should check with their provincial health plan offices or call **Health Canada** (✆ **866/225-0709;** www.hc-sc.gc.ca) to find out the extent of their coverage and what documentation and receipts they must take home in case they seek medical treatment in Newfoundland & Labrador.

INTERNET ACCESS See "Staying Connected," p. 58.

MAIL It currently costs C54¢ to mail a letter or card (weighing 30g/1 oz. or less) within Canada. It costs C98¢ to mail that same letter or card to the U.S. and C$1.65 to all other international destinations. For more information, visit www.canadapost.ca.

NEWSPAPERS & MAGAZINES The major newspaper in St. John's is the Telegram (www.thetelegram.com). There are also many community newspapers throughout the province. See www.thepaperboy.com for a full listing. The province's major lifestyle/nostalgia magazine is Downhome (www.downhomelife.com).

PASSPORTS See www.frommers.com/planning for information on how to obtain a passport. See "Embassies & Consulates," above, for whom to contact if you lose yours while traveling in the U.S. and Canada. For other information, please contact the following agencies:

For Residents of Australia Contact the **Australian Passport Information Service** at ✆ **131-232** or visit the government website at www.passports.gov.au.

For Residents of Ireland Contact the **Passport Office,** Setanta Centre, Molesworth Street, Dublin 2 (✆ **01/671-1633;** www.irlgov.ie/iveagh).

For Residents of New Zealand Contact the **Passports Office** at ✆ **0800/225-050** in New Zealand or 04/474-8100, or log on to www.passports.govt.nz.

For Residents of the United Kingdom Visit your nearest passport office, major post office, or travel agency or contact the **United Kingdom Passport Service** at ✆ **0870/521-0410** or search its website at www.ukpa.gov.uk.

For Residents of the **United States** To find your regional passport office, either check the U.S. Department of State website at www.travel.state.gov, or call the **National Passport Information Center** toll-free number (✆ **877/487-2778**) for automated information.

SMOKING You must be at least 16 years of age to legally purchase cigarettes in Newfoundland and Labrador. Smoking is not allowed in public places, including restaurants and bars. Many of the smaller inns do not allow smoking at all. If you are a smoker, be sure to check with the establishment before making a reservation.

TAXES Newfoundland and Labrador has a harmonized sales tax (HST) of 13%, which represents a combined 8% provincial tax and 5% federal goods and services tax (GST). The HST applies to most goods and services. Note that in the city of St. John's, an additional 3% accommodation tax brings the tax on your hotel room to a total of 16%.

TIME Newfoundland has its own time zone, Newfoundland time zone, which runs a half-hour ahead of the rest of Atlantic Canada. Most of Labrador is in the Atlantic time zone, so be sure to check the time upon your arrival in Labradorian communities apart from the Labrador Straits, as they are most likely on Atlantic time. Daylight Saving Time is practiced throughout the province in summer.

TIPPING Tips of 15% are expected in larger cities such as St. John's, with 10% to 15% being more common in smaller centers.

TOILETS You won't find public toilets or "restrooms" on the streets in most Canadian cities, but they can be found in hotel lobbies, bars, restaurants, museums, department stores, railway and bus stations, service stations, parks, and visitor information centers. Large hotels and fast-food restaurants are often the best bet for clean facilities. Restaurants and bars in resorts or heavily visited areas may reserve their restrooms for patrons.

VISAS Citizens of the United States, Australia, New Zealand, Ireland, and the U.K. do not require a visa to enter Canada.

A complete list of those countries whose citizens do require a visa can be found at www.cic.gc.ca/english/visit/visas.asp.

VISITOR INFORMATION Contact **Newfoundland & Labrador Tourism** to request a free *Travel Guide, Hunting and Fishing Guide,* or *Highway Map.* Reach them by mail at P.O. Box 8700, St. John's, NL A1B 4J6; call ✆ **800/563-6353** or 709/729-2830; or visit **www.newfoundlandandlabrador.com**.

This Frommer's guidebook will give you a richly detailed, first-person perspective of travel throughout Newfoundland and Labrador. And because this guidebook follows the same regional divisions as the provincial *Travel Guide,* you can easily cross-reference the two. The **Newfoundland & Labrador Road Distance Database** (www.stats.gov.nl.ca/datatools/roaddb/distance) is a helpful online tool for computing driving distances and times between most cities and towns.

WATER Unless otherwise posted, tap water is safe to drink. For information on *giardia,* see p. 48.

2 AIRLINE, HOTEL & CAR RENTAL WEBSITES

MAJOR AIRLINES

Air Canada
www.aircanada.com

Air France
www.airfrance.com

Air India
www.airindia.com

American Airlines
www.aa.com

British Airways
www.british-airways.com

Continental Airlines
www.continental.com

Delta Air Lines
www.delta.com

Lufthansa
www.lufthansa.com

Northwest Airlines
www.nwa.com

United Airlines
www.united.com

US Airways
www.usairways.com

WestJet
www.westjet.com

MAJOR HOTEL & MOTEL CHAINS

Best Western International
www.bestwestern.com

Holiday Inn
www.holidayinn.com

Marriott
www.marriott.com

CAR RENTAL AGENCIES

Avis
www.avis.com

Budget
www.budget.com

Enterprise
www.enterprise.com

Hertz
www.hertz.com

National
www.nationalcar.com

Rent-A-Wreck
www.rentawreck.ca

INDEX

See also Accommodations and Restaurant indexes, below.

General Index

Accommodations

Restaurants

NOTES